Fires, Firemen and Other Mishaps
A Short History of Coggeshall Fire Brigade

Trevor Disley

Fire helmet worn by Stan Saunders, a Coggeshall fireman in World War II.

First Published in the United Kingdom by
Trevor Disley
13, Tilkey Road
Coggeshall, Colchester
Essex CO6 1PG
thdisleybooks@gmail.com

Copyright © Trevor Disley 2017

All rights reserved. No part of this publication may be reproduced, stored in a retrieval system, or transmitted in any form, or by any means, electronic, mechanical, photocopying, recording or otherwise, without the prior permission of the copyright holder.

Trevor Disley has asserted the moral right to be identified as the author of this work.

First Printed 2017
Layout & Design by Trevor Disley
Printed by 4edge Printers, Hockley, Essex
on paper from sustainable resources.

ISBN 978-1-5272-0629-8

British Library Cataloguing in Publication Data
A catalogue record for this book is available from the British Library

All profits from the sale of this book will go to The Firefighters Charity

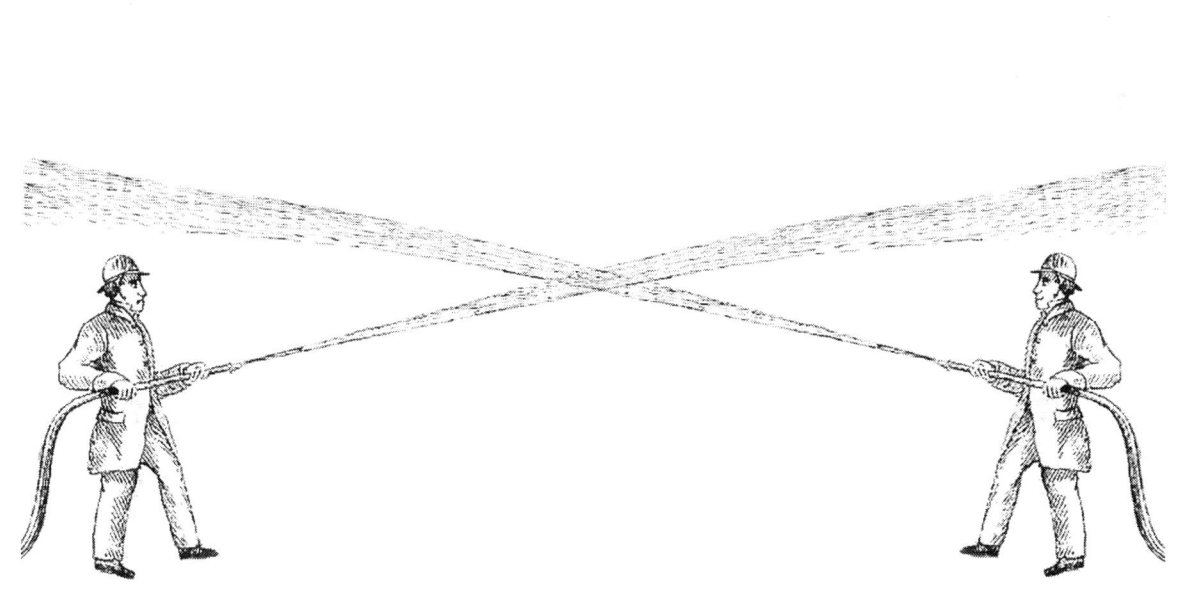

Dedicated to Firefighters and their Families

A basket strainer, used when drawing water from a pond or stream.

Contents

Chapter 1	First Fire Engines and the Essex Fire Office		1
	A Great Fire, Engines, Incendiarism and the Fire Office	*1764 – 1829*	
Chapter 2	Unrest and The Parish Vestry		14
	Fire, Riot, The Vestry, Agent Problems, a New Engine	*1829 – 1839*	
Chapter 3	The Essex & Suffolk Engine		28
	First Fire, Unprecedented Incendiarism, Arson, Beer	*1839 – 1849*	
Chapter 4	Daniel Leaper and the Essex & Suffolk		38
	Poverty, Fires, Lucifers, The Brigade at Work	*1849 – 1865*	
Chapter 5	A Time of Change		54
	Tooley Street Consequences, a Flawed System, Fires Galore	*1861 – 1886*	
Chapter 6	The Last Years of the Essex & Suffolk Brigade		84
	The Good and the Bad, Triumph, Farce and an Ultimatum	*1886 – 1903*	
Chapter 7	The Parish Council Fire Brigade		106
	New Brigade, Arson, Great Fire at Sach's, the Water Scheme	*1903 – 1914*	
Chapter 8	The First World War		140
	Air Raid, the Sad Case of Walter Brown, Captain Birkin	*1914 – 1918*	
Chapter 9	The End of an Era		152
	Biggest Fire, Eclipse, the RDC Brigades	*1918 – 1937*	
Chapter 10	The Second World War		178
	Rebirth, a New Station, Air Raids, ARP, AFS, & NFS	*1937 – 1948*	
Chapter 11	A New Start - Essex County Fire Brigade		218
	Post-war Developments to the Opening of the New Station	*1948 – 1981*	
	Bibliography		250
	Appendices		252
	Index		270

Coggeshall, the Town Clock on Market Hill and the view up Stoneham Street, 1900.

Preface

'Attempts were made from time to time to form a fire brigade..... but it was not until 1903 that it was possible to go ahead and form one.' [This Coggeshall 1959]

We organised a Centenary Party at Coggeshall Fire Station in 2003 and everyone with a connection to the station past and present, came along. As Officer in Charge at the time, I brought together a display of photographs, gave a short talk about the highlights of the past century and finally, to rousing cheers, the Chair of the Fire Authority and the Deputy Chief Fire Officer unveiled a commemorative plaque.

One of the photographs, scanned and enlarged for the first time, contained an intriguing clue that there was more to our history than we thought. This 1903 photo of the fire engine and crew also showed a brass plaque fixed to the side of the machine. Although partly covered by one of the firemen, we eventually worked out what was engraved on it. The fire engine had been, 'Presented to Great Coggeshall Parish Council by the Essex and Suffolk Fire Office on *the disbandment of their own brigade*' (my italics). So there had been an earlier brigade and our history did not start in 1903 as we thought! This set me off on what turned out to be many enjoyable years of research, which now, having hung up my fire gear for the last time, I have managed to assemble and present here.

This mostly chronological account begins in 1764 – when historical sources begin to provide a coherent story – and ends in 1981 with the move to the new fire station on the Colne Road and the start of my own service.

Coggeshall is very fortunate in still having a fire engine and the 'On Call' fire-fighters to keep it crewed. The station is always looking for new recruits and the Essex Fire & Rescue web site has details http://www.essex-fire.gov.uk. Having retired after more than 30 years' service, I would recommend it and feel privileged to have been part of such a rich, fascinating and continuing story.

Trevor Disley, Coggeshall, February 2017

This book is based on original research principally from newspaper reports, Coggeshall and Kelvedon Parish Council Minutes and Accounts, Coggeshall Parish Vestry records and the Minutes of the Essex & Suffolk Insurance Society. I carried out interviews with Mick Barnett, Sam Birkin, Peter Hale, David Honey, Roy Maddocks, Owen Martin, Bunty Moss, Jack Parry, Ken Speed, Tony Saunders and Janet Tansley.

The principal sources and the abbreviations used throughout the book are:

BWT	*Braintree & Witham Times*	BBA	*Braintree & Bocking Advertiser*
B&NP	*Bury & Norwich Post*	Cuttle	*Newspaper articles collection at the ERO*
CC	*Chelmsford Chronicle*	ERO	*Essex Record Office*
EH	*Essex Herald*	EN	*Essex Newsman*
ES	*Essex Standard*	EWN	*Essex Weekly News*
E&SE	*Essex & Suffolk Equitable Minute Books*	Haines	*Stan Haines transcript of newspaper reports**
KPMB	*Kelvedon Parish Council Minute Books*	LMA	*London Metropolitan Archive*
Log	*Coggeshall brigade Log 1939-41 authors possession*	MB1-4	*Coggeshall Parish Council Minute Books*
MDB	*Hadley Simkin & Lott Day Book*	SEFP	*Suffolk & Essex Free Press*
VCH	*Victoria County History*		

Coggeshall Parish Council Minute Books: ERO D/P 36/30/1-4   Bocking Parish Council Minute Books ERO D/J 138/2/5
Cuttle Newspaper Collection: ERO T/P 181/4/1 Several local newspapers are now online via The British Newspaper Archive
Essex & Suffolk Equitable Minute Books: LMA CLC/B/107/MS16206/001-008
Hadley Simkin & Lott Day Book: LMA/4516/01/001
Kelvedon Parish Council Minute Books are in the Kelvedon Parish Council Office and available by appointment.
Coggeshall Vestry Minutes, Memoranda, etc. 1812-1835: ERO D/P 36/8/7
* This derives in part from a collection of local newspaper articles belonging to Doug Judd and kept at the Coggeshall Museum.

Acknowledgements

I would like to record my grateful thanks for the many people who have assisted me in writing this book. In particular my wife Gill for her work in the archives and for her encouragement and patience, also to Stanley Haines whose knowledge and memory of Coggeshall's more recent history is unsurpassed, also to Robert Alston, Mick Barnett, Sam Birkin, Cecil Blackwell, Bryan Everitt, Peter Hale, David Honey, Roy Maddocks, Bunty Moss, Jack Parry, Ken Speed, John Lewis, Owen Martin, Jennifer Millin, Gail & Brian Mooney, Francis Nicholls, Andrew Rutkin, Bert Saunders, Tony Saunders, Janet Saunders, Janet & Len Tansley, David Tassel, Malcolm Taylor BEM, Andrew Webb, Denis Wood, Shirley Ratcliffe at Coggeshall Museum, Roger Pickett of the Essex Fire Museum, Annette Bayliss at the Feering & Kelvedon Local History Museum, the ladies at the Kelvedon Parish Council Office, Stephen Yates at the Colchester and Ipswich Museum, Claire Willets of the Braintree Museum, the staff of the Essex Record Office at Chelmsford, the Suffolk Record Office at Bury St Edmunds, the staff at the British Newspaper Library at Colindale, the staff of the London Metropolitan Archives and of the British Library at St Pancras, The Firefighters Memorial Trust and The Fire Brigade Society. Thanks are also due to Justin Knopp, letterpress printer of Typoretum, for printing and donating the launch party invitations. Lastly, a special thanks to Doug Judd who proof-read the manuscript, any remaining glitches are entirely the result of my own subsequent meddling.

An Essex & Suffolk Equitable Insurance Society Manual Fire Engine of c1830, with original signwriting. The engine was probably kept for display in the Equitable headquarters building but it is now lost.

About Coggeshall

View of Coggeshall from the south in 1832.

Forty miles north-east of London, Coggeshall is situated on the gentle south-facing slopes of the valley of the River Blackwater. Situated on a Roman road, Stane Street, it is nine miles from Colchester and seven from Braintree. Roman remains have been found, but the town developed after the founding of a Savignac Abbey in 1140, absorbed by the Cistercians in 1147. A barn built at this time is now one of the oldest timber framed buildings in Europe. A market, granted by charter in 1256, technically made Coggeshall a town and it has always been referred to as such. For most of its history the town was an important industrial centre. From the fifteenth to the mid eighteenth centuries it was famous and wealthy through the production of woollen cloth, especially the renowned Coggeshall Whites. The large parish church and Paycocke's House are a legacy of those prosperous times. As the wool trade declined, the town moved into silk, velvet, tambour lace and straw plaiting for hats. A silk factory powered by steam opened in 1839 and employed hundreds of people at its peak but the reduction and eventual removal of duty on imported silk saw the trade decline and eventually collapse. The 1851 census showed Coggeshall was still one of the most industrialised places in Essex but by 1900 the town's six hundred years as an industrial centre had come to an end. There was still a foundry, a tannery, a large Isinglass factory and several maltings and breweries. Coggeshall became famous for seed growing, the firms of E W King and John K King being the most notable, the latter holding the Royal Warrant for many years. There are two parishes, Great and Little Coggeshall, the two are contiguous but divided by the ancient course of the river. The population of the two parishes peaked at 4,500 in 1861 and then fell to 3,000 in 1891 and 2,700 in 1931. In recent years the population has steadily increased and reached 4,727 in 2011.

viii *Fires, Firemen & Other Mishaps*

Location

A map showing Coggeshall and the surrounding countryside c1870. The map spans about 3 miles side to side. Some of the places mentioned in the text are underlined. The map was not the most accurate made, Walcotts for example is shown as 'Wackets', probably due to an interpretation of the local dialect by the mapmaker.

A Short History of Coggeshall Fire Brigade   ix

Location

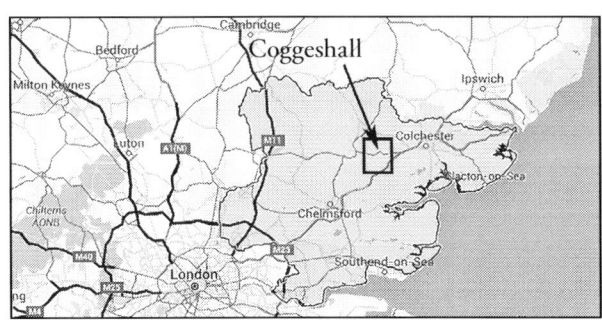

Within Essex: left
Within the local area: opposite page
Layout of the town and street map: below

Map of Coggeshall Centre c1875.
Running west to east on Stane Street are West Street, Market End, East Street and the Colchester Road. Market Hill, at the centre of the town, is just offset from this Roman road. Running north from Market Hill is Stoneham Street, Robinsbridge Road branching off to the west. From Market Hill, Church Street leads to the Church of St Peter ad Vincula before turning north and becoming the Colne Road, heading towards Earls Colne, three miles distant. Running almost parallel to Church Street is Back Lane latterly called Queen Street, also making its way to the church. Bridge Street runs south crossing the Back Ditch and the River Blackwater heading for Coggeshall Hamlet and Kelvedon, three miles distant. The Gravel links Bridge Street to West Street. Just out of the picture to the east, Dead Lane, now called St Peter's Road, joins Colchester Road with the Colne Road.

*Knowing one man, our foreman, I made my way to him.
I asked 'where was the fire-engine?' His reply*

**'It is sent for....
and if it don't come today, it may tomorrow.'**

1 FIRST FIRE ENGINES AND THE ESSEX FIRE OFFICE

Coggeshall was long famed for its 'traditional' Guy Fawkes' night celebrations, the relic of an earlier age that other towns had lost. Over the years people had been shot, blown up, burned and gaoled. Wagon loads of faggots were brought in for the bonfires on Market Hill which regularly blistered the paintwork of the shops and houses on both sides of the street. It was just such a bonfire that set a house on fire in 1764:

> 'Monday being the 5th of November, four bonfires were made at Coggeshall, when the wind being high, the sparks flew and set fire to the house of Mr. Whitaker, grazier and butcher: but by untiling the house and with the assistance of his friends, it was extinguished without doing any further damage.' *[CC 09/11/1764 Quoted in 05/11/1946]*

Coggeshall had no fire engine, people just did what they could with manpower and buckets of water but it was a risky strategy. Thirteen years after Whitaker's fire, in February 1777 a blaze broke out which could not be muddled through in the usual way.

Richard White was one of the last of the great Coggeshall weavers and had extensive premises in upper Church Street:

> 'Wednesday morning a dreadful fire broke out in the working rooms of Mr. Richard White, baymaker at Coggeshall, which in the space of three hours entirely consumed the same, all the stock and utensils in trade therein and a great part of the dwelling house adjoining: Mr. and Mrs. White, narrowly escaped with their lives, as well as their youngest child of about two years old, who was thrown out of a window into the arms of some persons standing by. A great part of the furniture was destroyed, as well as three tenements adjoining:

Left: Conversation during a fire at the West Street Tannery in 1878 [CC 15/03/1878]

An engraving of c1890 showing Richard White's house, a large part of which was involved in the 1777 fire. It stood at the corner of Vane Lane and Church Street in Coggeshall. It and its neighbours were demolished in 1902.

fortunately great quantities of wool which were lodged between the workshops and dwelling house, with the activity of the inhabitants and the timely assistance of the Bocking and Braintree engines, prevented the flames from communicating with some other buildings adjoining, or upwards of 20,000 pounds worth of property must have been consumed: some cash is lost and most of his writings destroyed. Yesterday 250 persons were rewarded for their assistance at the above fire. The loss sustained is considerable. This unfortunate accident is supposed to have been occasioned through the negligence of his servants.'
[CC 07/02/1777]

The scale and intensity of the fire had been shocking as was the town's inability to do anything to stop it. There is little evidence to say for certain what happened next but it is possible to speculate, based on similar cases and other occasions when the town was in turmoil and people needed to air their opinions.

The parish vestry was the forerunner of parish councils and consisted of a number of parishioners and elected officials. It was probably the vestry who called a meeting of parishioners to discuss the fire, where the overwhelming consensus was that the town should have its own fire engine and brigade. A committee would have been formed to organise a public subscription and to operate the engine. The vestry itself played no part in buying or running the engine at this time.

The subscription ended up over-subscribed to the extent that there was enough money to buy and equip two engines. The best fire engines were made by the firm of Richard Newsham and it would be reasonable to think that at least the main Coggeshall engine came from him. The engines were solidly made and if well looked after were very long lasting. One celebrated example was at Great Wishford in Wiltshire where the vestry bought a Newsham engine in 1728 for £33 and it successfully extinguished a fire nearly two hundred years later, in the mid 1920s.
[VCH Wiltshire Vol 15]

The secret of these engines was a 'pressure vessel' made of brass. Without getting too technical, the air trapped inside the vessel changed the pulsing effect of its two pumps into a continuous jet of water. Called 'manual' engines they were worked by two teams of men, standing on each side of the engine who alternately pulled down on a handle to work the pumps. These engines were usually dragged along by hand, on small solid wheels.

The Coggeshall engines were kept in rather rustic outbuildings at Crouch End, at the rear of Coggeshall workhouse on Stoneham Street. An association with a workhouse was not uncommon: the land was already in the hands of the parish and the occupants might be called on to pump the engines.

The Essex & Suffolk Equitable Insurance Society

Fire insurance companies had been established in London for many years, one of the oldest, the Sun Fire Office, founded in 1710, had insured Richard White's premises at the time of his fire. Unlike today, fire insurance offices not only insured properties but also, if they caught fire, paid the costs of putting them out. During a fire an account was kept of who was present and how long they worked and after scrutiny, the insurance office paid the bill.

It was a local rather than a London fire office that was to shape fire protection in Coggeshall and in many other Essex towns for many years. The proposal for a new fire insurance company was outlined to a packed public meeting in the Moot Hall, Colchester in November 1802. It was argued that London based fire insurance companies were charging London prices which took no account of the lower risks of rural Essex. A new Colchester based fire insurance company could not only charge lower premiums but by forming a 'mutual' society – one largely owned by its policy holders – offer the further advantage of returning any profits back to them. The argument was enthusiastically received and an agreement was reached to establish:

> 'A society in the County of Essex for insuring Houses and other buildings, Goods, Wares, Merchandise and Farming Stock from loss or damage by fire'.
> [LMA: CLC/B/107/MS16206/001- Minute Book 1]

The company, the 'Essex Equitable Insurance Society', was founded in November 1802 and renamed 'The Essex & Suffolk Equitable Insurance Society' in 1806 to give it a wider appeal in the two counties. With such a lengthy title, the name was inevitably shortened to the 'Equitable', the 'Essex & Suffolk' or 'The Fire Office'. To add some variety, all appear in this account and all refer to the same company.

The Essex & Suffolk had twenty-four

Directors, twelve from Colchester and twelve 'Country Directors' from outside the town among whom was Richard Meredith White of Coggeshall, a farmer and the son of the Baymaker whose premises had caught fire in 1777. It was either Richard or a sibling who had been thrown from a window during the fire. There was another Coggeshall connection, Robert Brightwen, a Colchester Director and one of the signatories to the foundation document, was in partnership with his brother, Isaac, in the Coggeshall Brewery on Stoneham Street, part of which is now the Village Hall. Outside of Colchester the Equitable did its business through agents, the first four appointed in 1802 were in Chelmsford, Witham, Ipswich and Coggeshall, evidence of the town's importance to the new company. The Coggeshall agent was Robert Matthews, an auctioneer who with his wife Bethia also ran a Drapers shop. The Essex & Suffolk preferred their agents to have a shop or other business premises, where customers could arrange and pay for their fire insurance. Applications for insurance were then sent to Colchester where the policies were drawn up and the premium calculated. The policy was countersigned by three Directors and returned via the agent to the customer. With no postal system a local carrier was used for the Coggeshall policies and he made the journey to Colchester and back twice a week on Wednesdays and Saturdays. An agent could offer immediate cover using a reference table which was later confirmed (or not) by the Colchester office. The rates charged for insurance were divided into classes,

A Newsham 'Bedposter' Manual Pump of about 1735 which would have been worth about £55 second hand in 1777.
The engine has solid wooden wheels, with no suspension and no steering, it would have been pulled along by hand.
The pressure vessel and the pumping cylinders are inside in the vertical part on the right and on early models like this, the long branch and nozzle was fixed to the top with a 'universal joint' to allow water to be directed onto a fire.
The pumping handles can be seen on each side and these were alternately pulled down by a body of men, the pumpers.

The Headquarters of the Essex & Suffolk Equitable Insurance Society in Colchester High Street. Purpose built by the Equitable in 1820 and later enlarged, it still stands.

depending on the likelihood of a fire: so for example, a brick built house with no trade carried on inside, cost 1s per £100 of insurance and barns or other agricultural buildings were charged at 6s per £100 insured.

As the agents might hold substantial amounts of cash from the premiums they received, the Essex & Suffolk were cautious in whom they appointed. After one agent defaulted, from 1805 they required every agent to find two sponsors willing to offer sureties of £200 each as a guarantee should anything go wrong. As a result, the agents were usually people of some substance and standing in the community. Some of the smaller agencies were granted exemption after several of them complained that the amount guaranteed was out of proportion to their income from policies.

The agents worked on a commission of 10% and it was claimed at one of the Annual Courts (as the Essex & Suffolk AGM was called), that no other fire office paid their agents a lower rate! As for agents' annual earnings, calculations based on figures first published in 1837, suggest that the Chelmsford agency with 1,300 policies on its books was worth about £120 a year to its agent and the Maldon agency with 677 policies, £63. The Coggeshall agent who had 310 policies in 1837 would have earned just over £30 a year. In contrast, the smallest agency with just twenty-one policies, brought in just over £2. As a measure of the value of these earnings, a live-in housemaid cost around £15 a year at that time.

Although the Essex & Suffolk claims were handled by head office in Colchester, the agents at first had a degree of autonomy in paying fire expenses. These would include payment for the use of a fire engine, the hire of horses, payments to the firemen, the pumpers and the helpers as well as the cost of refreshments. In 1808, following some excessive payments for large amounts of beer, the company limited the agents to paying a maximum of £5 for expenses, any larger amounts had to be referred to the Colchester office.

The company could be autocratic and agents were not expected to question decisions. When the Billericay agent, Mr Rolph, had the temerity to express an opinion, the response came back:

'He is to be informed that the Directors do not stand in need of his advice and observations and if

he feels himself dissatisfied, the sooner he pays his balance and quits the agency the better.'
[Drew 1952 p21]

The company could also be understanding of their agents' shortcomings:

'Do pray my good fellow be a little careful in the instructions you send for policies. You don't know what trouble you give me in sending wrong statements and names. It is impossible I can keep the office books at all fit to be seen, if I am in every day scraping out and altering them.' [Drew p28]

They could also be kindly. When their Romford agent Edward Graves died in 1815, owing the company a large sum in excess of £33, the Directors decided not to pursue the matter with his widow, 'On account of her peculiar distressed circumstances'. [E&SE MB1 04/09/1815]

The Directors of the Fire Office had no experience of fire insurance and seemed to learn the business by copying other fire offices and by picking it up as they went along. This seems to have been the case in one of the early claims to the Coggeshall Agency. In July 1803 there was a fire in a Brick Kiln in the nearby village of Bradwell. Having received a claim, the Essex & Suffolk asked Robert Matthews, the agent, to attend the office to discuss it. He did, but could offer no information as he had not visited the scene. He was requested to attend the brickworks and examine the damage done by the fire and 'to make a report thereon'. It was December before the claim, just over £7, was paid. It was to be another fourteen years, in 1817 before the Directors decided to employ a specialist to assess losses.

Other evidence of inexperience comes in 1807 when Mathius Gardner of Little Coggeshall applied to insure his premises (probably the Abbey Mill) where a steam engine was employed to drive cloth making machinery[1]. Matthews referred the matter to the Colchester office but this was outside their experience so they decided to ask other fire offices what they would charge,

---
1   It was a 2-3 horsepower engine made by Dixon of London

Nineteenth-century leather fire buckets.
The one on the left is stitched the other riveted and marked for the Essex & Suffolk Fire Office.
Reproduced by courtesy of Colchester & Ipswich Museums

'That the Directors may know how to charge Mr Gardner'. [E&SE MB1 06/07/1807]

The Essex & Suffolk would not fully insure any property. A letter of 1806 from the Secretary to one of their agents stated:

'It is not usual nor fair for any person to insure buildings to their full value - two thirds or three fourths is a fair value, the same of stock, household goods &c' [Drew p23]

The Directors thought that this degree of under-insurance would encourage policy holders to be more careful in avoiding fires! Even if a property was insured, the Directors might not pay out; witness this example:

'That the Directors present are of the opinion that Mr William Spooner's loss is so much the effect of downright carelessness, that it ought not to be paid.' [E&SE MB1 07/12/1812]

When a customer had been insuring with the company for a number of years, originally seven but later five, a proportion of the premium would be refunded at the end of each financial year. This dividend was announced at the annual court and varied year to year from 25% to 50% depending on the profitability or otherwise of the company.

Fighting Fires

The Essex & Suffolk was never just a fire insurance company. Right from the start it had a 'hands-on' approach to fire-fighting and the company eventually maintained, subsidised or provided engines and fire-fighting equipment in most towns where they held agencies[2]. This started in 1803, when the Directors wrote to the Colchester parishes who already had fire engines:

> 'The Directors would wait on the Churchwardens and Overseers of the several parishes in Colchester who have fire engines belonging to them, to permit the Directors to have use of the said engines in cases of fire upon condition that the said Directors keep the same in good condition' *[E&SE MB1 23/12/1803]*

In 1803, the Essex & Suffolk bought its first brand new fire engine. This was from Messrs Bristow & Sons, Fire Engine makers of London (formerly Newsham's). It cost £140 and was sent to Chelmsford. Three other fire offices, The Sun, The Royal Exchange and The Economic already had engines in the town so the move was as much about competition as it was about fire fighting.

In 1809, one of the Colchester parish engines was sent to Bristows for repair:

> 'We have ordered that the Parish Engine of St. Peter in this town be sent to you to be repaired. It will be put on board one of the Colchester Pacquets tomorrow morning which will sail tomorrow and probably be in London on Saturday....when repaired return it by the same conveyance...' *[Drew 1952 p39]*

In 1812, it was decided the company should have its own 'flagship' engine in Colchester and an order was placed again with Bristows :

> 'A capital good first size Carriage engine with Springs and apparatus complete, upon the most improved plan...it must go with springs and be capable of travelling on cross country roads if required where ruts are pretty deep... the town of Colchester is paved and if an engine is not on springs it shakes to pieces very soon.' *[Drew p40]*

This was still a manual engine, but it was a bigger machine, designed to be pulled at speed by a pair of horses. The 'improved plan' was a selling point and relates to the use of the latest improvements to the internal workings of the pump which increased its durability. When complete, the engine was delivered by being attached to the back of the Stage-Wagon on one of its usual runs from London

Some Essex & Suffolk agencies were provided with more basic fire fighting equipment – leather fire buckets. The first order was placed in 1804 for eighty, from Bristow & Sons. They were strongly made with riveted seams and at 10s each, they were not cheap, costing around what an agricultural labourer could earn in a week. *[Clarke p25]* It might seem odd that so many buckets were needed, the Maldon brigade for instance had seventy-five bought for them in 1814. A manual engine, might well pump over sixty gallons of water a minute, more than a gallon a second and if supplied by a hand to hand bucket chain, this needed a lot of buckets. Drew states that buckets often went missing after a fire when some of the helpers 'forgot' to return them. The practice of writing the company's name on the buckets might have been an attempt to discourage this activity.

An 1832 order for buckets for Mr Rolph the Essex & Suffolk agent at Billericay was placed with another firm, Hadley, Simkin and Lott of Greenwich;

> '1 Dozen new (2 gall) leather fire buckets with double stitched flat handles & writing Essex & Suffolk Equitable Fire Office on each in white lettering. Packing in a case and delivering & booking at the Bull Inn Aldersgate St.' *[MDB 02/02/1832 - See illustration]*

The 'Bull & Mouth' was a famous City of London coaching inn where the case of buckets would have been collected by the Essex carrier and taken on to Billericay. The buckets, including delivery, came in at just over 11s each. Fire hooks were also supplied. These were heavy iron hooks

---

2 Except for those like Woodbridge, with only a handful of policy holders.

A Newsham manual engine of c1800 of the 'Bedposter' design. This is a small engine designed to be moved by hand. Unlike the earlier design, the wheels are sprung and the body is cut away to enable the front wheels to be steered. This machine once had a nozzle fixed to the top but here (not visible in this photo) this has been modified to allow hose to be connected and run out to the fire, a much more practical arrangement. This might be the engine bought by the Equitable second-hand from Mr George Steel in 1807 for the sum of £36.
It was retired from Wivenhoe and is now in the collection of the Colchester and Ipswich Museums.
Reproduced by courtesy of Colchester & Ipswich Museums

fitted to long wooden poles, in three different sizes and lengths. They were used to pull down buildings and tear off thatch. Metal rings at the top of the poles allowed ropes to be attached to increase the pulling power. The first were ordered in 1804 from Bristow's but in 1805 they were being copied by a Colchester blacksmith.
[E&SE MB1 01/04/1805]

Co-Operation

Fire offices often worked together to provide equipment, for example, an Essex & Suffolk order in 1814 for twenty-five buckets for the Maldon engine was made on the understanding that the Sun and the Royal Exchange fire offices had each furnished the same number. When the Phoenix

Fire Office presented an engine to Sudbury in 1816, the Essex & Suffolk paid 'an equal part with the other offices in purchasing a carriage' to carry it. *[E&S MB1 06/05/1816]* In 1819 the company shared the cost of repairing the Billericay engine and supplying new hose with the Norwich Union and the Royal Exchange. A bit closer to hand, in 1820 the Essex & Suffolk agreed to maintain one of the Braintree engines 'the other being kept in repair by the Royal Exchange Office'. Such co-operation was the norm, at least in towns where the contributing offices had a comparable number of policy holders.

Water

The Essex & Suffolk also invested in water supplies. In 1813 they negotiated with the new Colchester Waterworks company to have the use of its water in case of fire - at the cost of £20 a year[3]. In 1819 they contributed toward the cost of sinking a well in Rochford and in 1820 they gave £20, 'towards improvements at Coggeshall in bringing water by means of pipes into the streets'. *[E&SE MB1 07/02/1820]* This was the 'main pipe'[4] laid from the St Peter's Well (near Vane Lane) and running down Church Street. In the days before fire hydrants, wooden stoppers called fire plugs were fitted into the mains at intervals, these could be removed to supply water in the case of a fire. There would have been no great water pressure. If a plug was removed, the water would form a pool in the ground into which buckets might be dipped. There is no record of water from this Coggeshall scheme ever being used for fire-fighting. The pipe did supply some of the better off with water for some years but as more people illicitly tapped in, it eventually ran dry but that is a whole other story. No doubt some remnants of the long abandoned pipe still remain below Church Street.

---

3   The waterworks had asked for £25
4   Still used to supply twenty-five houses in 1875
[CC 13/08/1875]

A copper Fire Mark of the 'Essex' and the 'Essex & Suffolk' Equitable Insurance Society used between 1803 and c1823
Reproduced by courtesy of Colchester & Ipswich Museums

Fire Marks

There was a tradition for Fire Offices to fix their own signs, called fire marks or fire plates, to the premises they insured, mainly for advertising purposes. The 'Essex Insurance Society' plates were 6 1/2" x 8 1/4" in size and designed by a Colchester pastor and artist, Isaac Taylor. The die was produced and the plates pressed in Birmingham and they were delivered to the agents by January 1803. The Deed of Settlement links policies and marks:

> 'The Badge or Mark of the Society shall accompany every policy which shall be issued by the Society with a view the more publicly to notify the insurance effected by the policy...'
> *[E&SE Deed of Settlement 1804 amended 1807]*

In practice, many more policies were issued than fire marks, in 1803 for example, eighteen policies were issued in Coggeshall but only six plates were provided and between 1805 and 1806, twenty-four policies were issued in Coggeshall but no plates were supplied. The Directors were never fully convinced as to the usefulness of fire plates which is why Essex Insurance Society plates continued to be issued even after the name was changed. No plates were made after 1818 and none seem to have survived in Coggeshall, although Kelvedon Museum has an example. (See Appendix XII)

A Short History of Coggeshall Fire Brigade

A Tilley manual engine, of the Braidwood pattern, 1823.
A rival of the Merryweather firm, they later became Shand-Mason.
Note that the pumping arms extend way out beyond the rear of the machine which allowed more pumpers but could be unwieldy when travelling or manoeuvring at a fire. Hadley & Simkin came up with the idea of hinging the arms so they could be folded up for transport but opened and locked when needed for pumping and it was this design which was used on Coggeshall's engine. On larger engines, the arms could also be folded out at the front of the machine, once the horses had been unhitched. The firemen travelled on top facing outwards and holding the handles so as not to be thrown off.

Part of a page from Hadley, Simkin & Lotts's (later Merryweather) Day Book dated London March 2nd 1832.
'Essex & Suffolk Equitable Insurance Comp.y. For Mr Rolph, Agent, Billericay. 1 doz new (2 gall) leather fire buckets with double stitched flat handles and writing Essex & Suffolk Equitable Fire Office on each in white lettering. Packing in a case & delivering & booking at the Bull Inn Aldersgate St. for Pearcly's [?] Van.'
Reproduced by courtesy the London Metropolitan Archive

Fire Protection in Coggeshall

Many Essex towns benefited from the Essex & Suffolk's policy on fire-fighting and Coggeshall was one of the first. On 26th May 1806 the Directors ordered:

> 'That £10 be allowed by the Society towards purchasing two leather pipes for the Coggeshall Engine in conjunction with the other offices.'
> *[E&SE MB1 26/05/1806]*

The Directors could afford to spend a little money protecting their Coggeshall policyholders. Among the Fire Office's many agencies across Essex and Suffolk (there were twenty-four by 1837), Coggeshall was the fifth most valuable in terms of property insured and premiums paid. Although Richard White and Robert Brightwen had resigned their Directorships, both remained members of the society and sometimes attended the weekly meetings at Colchester. In April 1807, Robert's brother Isaac became one of the Country Directors[5]. The Brightwen's not only ran the Coggeshall brewery but were also considerable property owners, their portfolio comprised numbers of inns and public houses across Essex and in Coggeshall. These included the White Hart, the Chapel, the Woolpack, the Bird in Hand, the Bull, the Black Horse and the White Horse.

In June 1812, the Essex & Suffolk made a further commitment to fire protection in the town, when the Directors ordered:

> 'That this Society pay their proportion with the other Offices in keeping the two engines at Coggeshall in repair and a man to look after them and keep them in order'
> *[E&SE MB1 01/06/1812]*

The other fire offices chose not to contribute so in December that year the Essex & Suffolk decided that they would keep the best machine in good order themselves and gave £10 a year 'towards defraying the expenses of repairing cleaning and working one of the engines at Coggeshall'.

The Coggeshall agent, Robert Matthews, died suddenly in September 1814 whilst in the middle of a bitter legal dispute concerning a valuation he had made in his auctioneering business, he was 66. His widow Bethia Matthews, was allowed to take over the agency and her late husband's two bondholders transferred their guarantees of £400 to her – one of them being Robert Brightwen.

Rick Burning and Riot

1816 was a year of great discontent among agricultural labourers, the result of poverty, the high price of corn and a shortage of work. Protest by rick burning had already become something of 'an Eastern speciality' *[Hobsbawn-p83]* and stacks and barns were fired across the region[6]. The first Essex incident was at Mile End in Colchester where a threshing machine was smashed and set alight. A barn was burned at Langham and there were farm fires at Henham and Tillingham. There were riots at Finchingfield, where another threshing machine was fired and at Great Bardfield and Sible Hedingham. At Halstead, the town was sealed off as a riot was suppressed by the military. Protests culminated in the 'Bread or Blood' riots at Ely and Littleport in Cambridgeshire, which were eventually put down by the military. This suppression, the trial and the harsh sentences handed out[7] effectively put a lid on open public protest. The Essex & Suffolk doubled the premiums for threshing machines and considered doing the same for farms and stock where the machines were at work.

---

5   Isaac may have taken the position of R M White, who ceased to be a Director at this time.

6   The word 'incendiarism' was used at the time for the deliberate burning of stacks, barns etc. An 'incendiary' was the person carrying out such an attack. An act of incendiarism was seen to have a social or political purpose – it was not just a personal act of retribution.

7   At Ely a large number of labourers were brought to court, twenty-three were condemned, five hung, the bodies displayed in a room and most of the rest transported for between seven years to life. *[Peacock p128]*

Fire Engines & Fires

In 1817, the Essex & Suffolk decided to buy new fire engines for Maldon and Chelmsford and asked two Directors, Mr Tabor and Mr Bawtree, 'to make enquiry of a good engine-maker in London'. *[E&SE MB1 01/09/1817]* Their recommendation was Hadley Simkin & Lott of Long Acre and this firm, from 1836 called Merryweather, became the supplier of choice. The Bristow's engines had been found wanting, the Chelmsford manual bought for £140 in 1803 was returned in 1813 for extensive repairs costing £56 and now in 1817 was to be sold rather than sent to another agency. Also in 1817, the Directors appointed Henry Hayward as surveyor to the company, on a daily rate of two guineas, 'to enquire into damage sustained at every fire where property is insured in this office and to report thereon.' *[E&SE MB1 20/06/1817]*

Coggeshall had a serious fire in November 1819, at the brewery premises of Isaac Brightwen of Stoneham Street:

> 'About one o'clock on Thursday morning, the 11th inst., the malt kiln of Mr Isaac Brightwen, of Coggeshall, was discovered to be on fire, which soon communicated to a range of thatched buildings adjoining the dwelling house, threatening destruction to the whole extensive warehouses and valuable stock therein: but from the early arrival of the engines and the most prompt and able assistance of the inhabitants, male and female which will ever be gratefully remembered by those interested in the property, the flames were got under about five o'clock, after doing considerable damage.' *[CC 19/11/1819]*

This is the first record of the Coggeshall engines at work at a fire. Hayward was dispatched to Coggeshall to assess the damage and in February 1820 the claim of £327 was paid in full. In the same year the Essex & Suffolk ordered that 'fire hooks and a ladder be allowed Mrs Matthews, the agent at Coggeshall'.

In September, the minutes record that:

'A new engine for the town of Colchester be

```
VIEW of the Relative Business of the various
      Offices for Fire Insurance in England, as shewn
by the Duties paid into the Stamp Office, in the
year 1823:—
  Sun .......................£112,163   3   9
  Phœnix ..................... 64,975   8   4
  NORWICH UNION .......... 64,407  18   4
  Royal Exchange ........... 50,018   1   9
  County ..................... 41,239   4  11
  Imperial ................... 32,392  14  10
  Globe ...................... 26,814  19   9
  Guardian ................... 21,042  11   9
  West of England .......... 17,365    6   0
  Atlas ...................... 16,075   5   1
  Union ...................... 15,507   3  11
  British .................... 15,126   3   9
  Eagle ...................... 14,888   0   7
  Albion ..................... 14,768   3   5
  Westminster ............... 14,223  10   7
  Hope....................... 14,124  17   3
  Hand-in-Hand .............. 12,637   6  11
  London ..................... 8,333  13   4
  Kent ....................... 7,767   9   2
☞ Essex and Suffolk .......... 6,469   1   3
  Suffolk (East) ............. 6,034   6   6
  Suffolk (West) ............. 5,778  16   4
  Birmingham ................. 5,116  15   0
  Newcastle-upon-Tyne........ 4,375   9   7
  Salamander ................. 4,664   6   4
  Bristol .................... 3,934   1   6
  Norwich Equitable ......... 3,008   0   4
  Hants, &c.................. 2,502  11   4
  Beacon ..................... 2,321   0   7
  Salop....................... 2,264   1   8
  Bristol Union .............. 2,170   5   1
  Bristol Crown .............. 1,746   6   0
  Sheffield .................. 1,652   0   6
  Old Bath ................... 1,644  18   4
  Bath Sun ................... 1,482   2   6
  British Commercial (2 Quars) 1,282   4   3
☞ Finchingfield .............    99    2   6
  Reading (1 Quarter) .......   12   10   5
                              ─────────────
  Total .........      £619,171   8   6
```

Relative Business of Fire Offices 1823.
This puts the Essex & Suffolk into the wider context. The local Offices include the Essex & Suffolk at £6,000 and the Finchingfield at £90. The Essex Economic started in 1824 and paid the equivalent of £1,600 in a full year.
[Advertisement in the Birmingham Gazette 24/05/1824]

ordered immediately and the present one be sent to the agent at Coggeshall as soon as the new one arrived'. *[E&SE MB1 04/09/1820]*

The engine in question must have been the sprung carriage engine ordered from Bristow's in 1812, but it was never transferred to Coggeshall, perhaps like the Chelmsford engine it was found to be unsatisfactory and sold off instead. Both of Coggeshall's engines were and remained old fashioned, unsprung and pulled by hand.

Threshing Machines Targeted

Since the ruthless suppression of the 'Bread or Blood' riots in 1816 nothing had happened to improve things and under-employment and unemployment haunted the lives of agricultural labourers. Threshing machines were taking away the work which had traditionally provided winter employment, they symbolised the changes that were taking place and increasingly became the focus of discontent. By 1820 so many threshing machines had been destroyed that the Essex & Suffolk decided: 'That no threshing machine be insured by this Society'. *[E&SE MB1 04/09/1820]* Incendiary attacks on stacks and barns were also on the rise and reached another peak in 1822 with fires at Great Clacton, Dovercourt, Goldhanger, Sible Hedingham, Henny, Pentlow and Tillingham.

The Coggeshall Agency

Although elderly and increasingly frail, with the occasional help of Isaac Brightwen, Bethia Matthews continued as agent. Brightwen's involvement is evident after a barn fire in Coggeshall in June 1824, the Fire Office minutes recorded:

> 'That if Mr Brightwen, the Director and the agent at Coggeshall are satisfied that Mr Brett's barn was worth £100 and the loss of stock amounted to £50, then the same to be paid.' *[E&SE MB2 07/06/1824]*

The Coggeshall engines were being regularly inspected and the Essex & Suffolk paid the bills for this in 1825. *E&SE MB2 03/01/1825]*. Bethia Matthews continued to decline and in 1827 the Directors came to the conclusion that she was no longer capable of running the agency as they would wish. Perhaps reluctantly, they decided to act:

> 'It was considered that Mrs Matthews, the Coggeshall agent, from her advanced age, was not competent to conduct the agency at Coggeshall and it was therefore directed that her sureties, Mr Brightwen and Mr F Hills should be informed that it is the intention of the office to appoint another agent in her place.' *[E&SE MB2 05/03/1827]*

Alarmed that her income was about to drop Bethia enlisted her son, John, to help and asked the company if she might continue as agent with his assistance. They had to wait almost a month but the Directors gave their assent on the understanding that John Matthews would: 'superintend Mrs Matthews accounts and the management of the agency at Coggeshall, it was ordered that Mrs Matthews be continued as agent.' *[E&SE MB2 02/04/1827]*

In 1827, as well as providing £10 for new hose ('the old hose to be returned to this office'), the Essex & Suffolk paid £20 for an engine-carriage:

> 'For the conveyance of the Coggeshall engines as per estimate delivered under the instructions of Mr Brightwen.' *[E&SE MB2 02/07/1827]*

The Coggeshall engines would be run into the carriage using a ramp and then, pulled by a pair of horses, could travel to more distant fires over rougher roads (see illustration). The purchase also provides confirmation that Coggeshall's engines were still of the small, old fashioned, hand drawn sort. It is also apparent that as well as supporting Bethia as agent, Isaac Brightwen was keeping an eye on the Coggeshall engines – but this was to be the last time. In 1828, came the extraordinary news that the Brightwen's had been declared bankrupt and their many properties in Coggeshall and elsewhere were to be put up for auction. As well as a personal tragedy for the Brightwen's, the bankruptcy was also a blow for Bethia and for Coggeshall's fire protection, which had probably become dependent on Isaac for its organisation and his brewery workers for crew.

Later that year, there was a fire at the Gravel Factory in Coggeshall, a large building 130 feet by 24 feet, on three floors which spanned Robin's Brook on the south side of Hare Bridge. The blaze was probably minor and

*An engine carriage with the ancient manual engine it carried.
The manual has pumping arms back and front and a long branch and nozzle fixed to the top.
A similar carriage was bought for the Coggeshall engines in 1827 for £20.*

the brigade was not called. In the aftermath, Bethia Matthews, finally lost the Essex & Suffolk agency. After the fire, she had paid out an amount of money to the occupiers of the factory, without reference to head office in contravention of the company's policy but also to people who it transpired, had no insurance policy with the company.

'The building now called the Gravel Factory at Coggeshall occupied by Messrs Sawyer and Hall, not having been insured by them, application for the amount of damage by the fire must be made by Mr White the landlord. Mrs Matthews be cautioned not to pay any loss in the future without the order of the Directors.'
[E&SE MB2 03/03/1828]

The owner of the factory was none other than Richard White, the ex-Director. In December when the Essex & Suffolk drew up their annual accounts, it was clear that Bethia's books were in a muddle. On 5th January the Directors decided that 'Application be made for a new agent in Coggeshall'.

In early February, her son John requested that he should take over the agency himself. That the Directors entertained this request is surprising as John surely bore some responsibility for the state of the accounts having promised to oversee them. Although the Directors agreed, John was not able to find two people as his guarantors. On 4th May, the Directors informed him:

'....as he has not found satisfactory sureties, he can no longer hold the situation of agent to this office at Coggeshall and that he must settle the balance of his account as soon as possible.'
[E&SE MB2 04/05/1828]

Although the Essex & Suffolk had helped maintain the Coggeshall fire engines, they neither owned nor had responsibility for them. In fact it seems at this time, no-one in Coggeshall did. Whatever arrangements had been made in the 1770s to operate and oversee the engines, by 1829 those arrangements had fallen out of use. The brigade had been kept going due to the efforts of the Essex & Suffolk in paying for maintenance and providing equipment and by the involvement of Isaac Brightwen. It was at this time, when the fire brigade was in some disarray, that rural unrest and incendiarism took a dramatic turn for the worse and the need for a brigade became more important than ever.

2 UNREST AND THE PARISH VESTRY

An unparalleled episode of violent unrest called 'Swing', affected much of southern England and East Anglia 1829-30. The name derives from threatening letters signed 'Captain Swing' which were sent to farmers using threshing machines or paying low wages[1]. When a Royal Commission was set up, Coggeshall was one of twenty-two Essex parishes to reply to their request for information and reported that three things: 'threshing machines, the rating of cottages and wages', lay at the heart of the protests. The 'Essex Standard' characterised an incendiary as 'an unemployed and half starved labourer.' *[ES 25/05/1849]* Incendiarism was not treated lightly by the law, under an Act of George IV, 'any person who unlawfully and maliciously set fire to a stack of corn, hay, straw or wood' would be guilty of a felony, which was punishable by death.

In January 1829, an incendiary started a fire in the neighbouring village of Blackwater[2], just to the west of Coggeshall. In the same month there were incendiary fires in Great Saling, Finchingfield and Great Yeldham. This wave of attacks provoked national concern, with both 'The Times' and the 'London Standard' carrying reports under the headline 'More Incendiaries', which described the fires at Great Yeldham and Blackwater:

'A haulm-stack[3] was set on fire at Blackwater near Coggeshall: the flames communicated to a stable, which was consumed and also part of the premises, formerly the Queen's Head public house.'
[London Times 21/01/1829]

The Queen's Head had been one of the properties in the Brightwen's portfolio, which at the time of the fire was closed and awaiting sale. The 'Essex Herald' commented:

---

1   This may derive from the Captain of the Harvest calling the beat of the flails during threshing with the cry of 'Swing!'

2   Blackwater is the old name for the part of Bradwell Parish where Stane Street crosses the river of that name.

3   Haulm is a generic name for the stems of peas, beans and potatoes which were used for animal bedding.

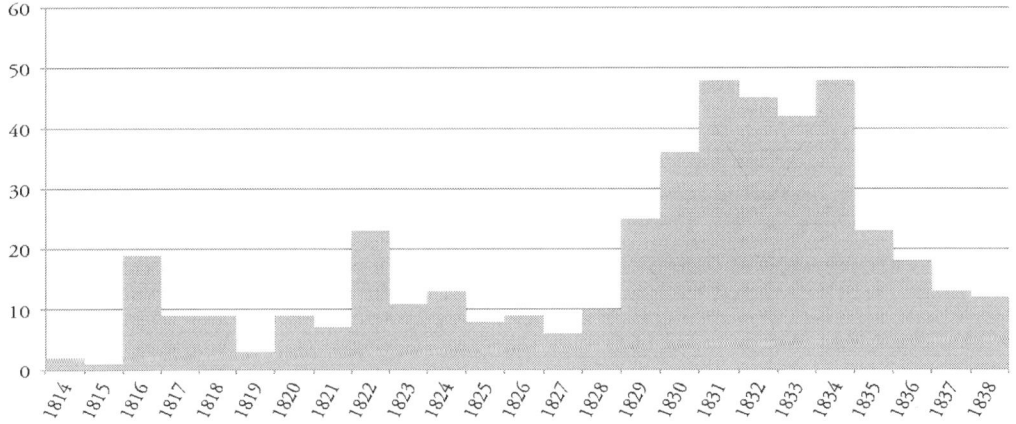

Incidence of the word 'incendiary' in the 'Bury & Norwich Post' 1814-1838.
Peaks of incendiarism can be seen in 1816, 1822 and 1829-1834.
Source: Search engine of the British Newspaper Archive

'The greatest consternation avails in that part of the country, scene of the late lamentable conflagrations: no one retires to rest without the dreadful apprehension of a similar affliction, many indeed employ a watch at night.' *[EH 13/01/1829]*

In March 1829, a second incendiary fire was set at Blackwater:

'Between the hours of 1 and 3 o'clock in the middle of the day, a fire was discovered at Blackwater near Coggeshall, which destroyed a barn with its contents and 40 quarters of beans, oats and straw.' *[Bury and Norwich Post 04/03/1929]*

In the same month there were a series of incendiary fires in Witham:

'The crime of arson nowise, we regret to state abates. The inhabitants... who have property of an inflammable description....take no rest until the hour arrives when such infernal deeds cannot be perpetrated in the dark.' *[EH 10/03/1829]*

A 16-year-old boy, James Cook, was arrested and accused of setting fire to the stacks at Olivers Farm in Witham where he worked. Despite very uncertain evidence and many appeals for mercy, he was found guilty and hanged in public at Chelmsford Gaol on 27th March 1829. The hanging provoked widespread condemnation and was one of the cases which eventually resulted in a change in the law. The hanging probably had a contrary effect to that expected. Instead of discouraging incendiaries it dissuaded witnesses from testifying and juries from convicting.

In the same month, the Essex & Suffolk sent for a Bow Street Officer – one of the celebrated London Policemen. The Officer, by the name of Ellis, consulted with the Essex & Suffolk Directors 'As to the discovery and apprehension of the perpetrators of the late incendiary fires in the neighbourhood'.[4] *[E&SE MB2 02/03/1929]*

Incendiary attacks in Essex continued throughout 1829 – at Layer de la Haye in April, Bradwell on Sea in August, Great Holland, Broxted and Stoneham Massey in September and at Beauchamp Roding, Rayleigh, Thaxted and Brightlingsea in November.

The attacks had a dramatic effect on the insurance companies and the 'Essex Herald' noted that they were 'doomed to be shaken to their very foundations by the excess of wickedness'. The provincial insurers including the Essex & Suffolk had been established boasting of the lower risks in rural areas, only to find themselves facing almost impossible odds and with the prospect of having to refuse insurance on farms. *[EH 24/02/1829]* Although premiums were increased, all the companies lost money and some were made bankrupt. One local insurance business, The 'Finchingfield', was so alarmed at the spate of incendiarism that in May 1829 after twenty-five years in business, it dissolved itself and returned its money to the shareholders. *[EH 09/06/1829]* Seeing an opportunity, the 'Phoenix' insurance company placed an advertisement listing nine fire offices that had failed and offered to take over their policies. The 'Sun' Fire Office did the same thing listing nineteen fire offices that had ceased trading as a result of incendiarism *[EH 24/03/1830 & 12/05/1830]*. These insurers were London based and less exposed to these emerging rural risks than the provincial fire offices. Responding to the crisis, the Essex & Suffolk suspended all insurance on farm buildings and stock in 1829, which amounted to around a quarter of their income. The policy was relaxed the next year but only for farms with no threshing machines. In an effort to bring incendiaries to justice, the 'Essex & Suffolk' had handbills printed offering rewards of £50 to £100 for information leading to conviction *[Drew p36]*. To the exasperation of the authorities, there was no rush to inform.

Incendiarism threatened those people in a position of power over the poor, the same people who were the ratepayers and voters who ran the parish vestry. As a result, many rural communities alarmed at the turn of events, set up or re-established brigades at this time.

---

4   It seems he returned to London without success. Convictions were uncommon.

In Coggeshall with Isaac Brightwen gone, the brigade had effectively ceased to exist, so that when the Blackwater fires broke out in early 1829, a messenger was sent to Braintree for an engine.

A New Coggeshall Agent

In May 1829, after John Matthews failed to find sureties, a local businessman, Lewis Allen was invited to take over the Essex & Suffolk Coggeshall Agency. His name was known to the Directors because he had written to them sometime before offering his services. Allen soon found two sureties of £200, one from the owner of Coggeshall Abbey, the other from a denizen of Lombard Street, the London Banking Centre. By early July his appointment was approved and notices to that effect were placed in the newspapers. Allen and his brother Charles were in partnership as tanners and timber merchants. Both were relatively well to do and were among the sixty or so Coggeshall residents then entitled to vote. They were closely related to one of England's most celebrated Quaker families. Their aunt was the eccentric Anne Knight, a social reformer, a leading campaigner for women's rights and a member of the Anti Slavery Society. The other famous relative was William Allen (FRS FLS FGS) scientist and philanthropist, a key player in the anti-slavery movement and friend of William Wilberforce. The Coggeshall Quakers would have been well aware of these illustrious connections, both Lewis and Charles being Elders at the Coggeshall Friends Meeting House. Lewis was himself politically active and played a role in the Essex Reform Committees which grew up in the wake of the Reform Act 1831. Lewis also accompanied his Aunt Anne on at least one of her campaigning European tours. With all these activities, it is perhaps no surprise that Allen was never fully engaged with the Coggeshall agency.

The Parish Vestry Steps In

Although incendiary attacks had increased during 1829, Coggeshall seemed unaffected by the troubles, at least until November when there was a riot in the town. A mob gathered outside the house of one of the Parish Overseers, angry at a decision to charge rates on some cottages inhabited by labourers.[5] The Overseer's windows were stoned and the crowd threatened to defenestrate him and 'tear him limb from limb'. Perhaps wisely, the Overseer did not put in an appearance and the mob moved on to a second Overseer's house and had his windows out before order was restored and seven men taken into custody[6]. *[Holland]* The incident showed that Coggeshall was not immune from trouble and the town's lack of a fire brigade increasingly became a focus for anxiety.

No doubt under pressure from the ratepayers in April 1830 the Churchwardens and Overseers of the Parish Vestry decided that they had no option other than to take over the fire engines themselves. A brief and ink-spattered entry in the Vestry Minutes dated 16th April 1830 records their decision:

> 'It was also proposed & unanimously agreed to that the Churchwardens and Overseers of Great Coggeshall for the time being have the care & management of the Fire Engines.' *[ERO D/P 36/8/7]*

The Engine House had fallen into disrepair and Mathias Gardner, a local builder, had already carried out extensive work to restore it. A payment of £15 for this refurbishment is minuted on the same page. No payments are recorded for any work on the engines themselves so it might be assumed that they were thought to be serviceable at least.

The takeover by the Vestry would not have been considered in normal times. The Parish

---

5   The owners would have paid the rate but made no secret that if they had to pay, they would increase rents to cover the charge.

6   A sympathetic magistrate later bound them over to keep the peace. [Holland p92].

The Coggeshall Vestry Minute Book, April 1830
The top entry relates to the Engine House:
It was proposed that Mathias Gardener [sic] be reimbursed the sum of fifteen pounds expended in the repair of the Parish Engine House which was unanimously agreed W Beckwith.
The entry below relates to the engines:
It was also proposed & unanimously agreed to that the Churchwardens and Overseers of Gt Coggeshall for the time being have the care and management of the Fire Engines.
Apl 16 1830   W Beckwith
[Courtesy of the Essex Record Office ERO D/P 36/8/7]

budget was already under stress from the cost of poor relief which had risen from £660 in 1776 to £2,600 in 1813 and continued to rise steadily until the New Poor Law of 1834. *[WEA 1951]* The Vestry must have recruited a crew to man the engines with parish officials taking charge as required.

The Lighting and Watching Act

'The Lighting and Watching Act' 1830[7] gave legal authority for parishes to provide fire protection. Section 32 of the Act stated:

> 'That it shall be lawful ….to provide and keep up fire engines ….for the use of the Parish …. and to provide a proper place or places for the keeping of the same and to place such engines under the care of some proper person or persons and to make him or them such allowances for his or their trouble as may be thought reasonable: and the expenses attending the providing and keeping such engines shall be paid out of the money authorized to be received by the inspectors under the provisions of the Act.'

Under this Act, parishes could buy and maintain engines, equipment, premises and a brigade and pay for them from the rates. The legislation was permissive, there was no obligation on parishes to provide fire protection.

When the Coggeshall Parish Vestry took over the engines in 1830, it was thought to be a temporary arrangement: 'for the time being'. The expectation must have been that the Essex & Suffolk, the key player in the fire brigade business in Essex, would soon take over the engines. This was not unrealistic as it was one of the Equitable's founding principles to establish brigades in the towns where they did business and they were doing quite a lot of business in Coggeshall. *[E&SE MB4 15/12/1848]*

---

7   An Act to make Provision for Lighting and Watching of Parishes in England and Wales.

The Vestry Engine at Work

It was more than three years before the Vestry engines were turned out. On a September night in 1833 they were called to a farm fire at Cows Hall in Wakes Colne. This was six miles distant so the fire had plenty of time to develop and was going well by the time the engines arrived. The brigade soon discovered that there was no water for fire-fighting, so as far as the engines were concerned that was that. A double barn, five stacks of corn, two wagons, livestock and other property to the considerable value of £1,000 were destroyed. A report of the fire concludes rather ungraciously:

> 'The engines at Coggeshall were speedily dispatched to the spot, but there being no water they were useless.' *[Bury & Norwich Post 02/10/1833]*

Despite this, the efforts of the Coggeshall Vestry had paid off and Coggeshall once again had a viable fire brigade; with a system in place for calling out a crew, the engines, the engine carriage and supplying horses to pull it and all done in good time.

By the end of 1833, just four years after he was appointed, the Directors of the Essex & Suffolk were well aware that Lewis Allen was spending very little of his time attending to their business in Coggeshall. In January 1834 the minutes recorded: 'The directors are dissatisfied at the long and continued absence of Mr Lewis Allen, the agent for Coggeshall, on the continent.' They requested that his brother Charles attend the next meeting, or Mr Lewis Allen, 'if he had returned by then'. *[E&SE MB2 17/01/1834]* In February 1834, the Essex & Suffolk asked all their agents to 'report on the state of their fire engines and the competence of their engineers'. Allen failed to respond.

Fifteen months later, the Directors wrote to Allen again and recorded the following in the minutes:

> 'Ordered that Mr Allen be requested to send in a report of the state of the Coggeshall engines,

pursuant to the circular sent to him in February last'

This did prompt Allen to report that the Coggeshall engines were old, in need of attention and of doubtful utility. After receiving this information, the Directors decided that the time had come to buy a big modern engine for the town. Hoping to share the cost of this, they asked Allen to send them a list of those fire offices with agents in Coggeshall and the amount of their respective insurance: 'The Secretary to then apply to those offices and enquire whether they will subscribe towards the purchase of a new engine.' [E&SE MB2 15/05/1835]

Before anything could be done, as is often the way of things, the engines were called out to a major fire.

The Curd Hall Farce

Curd Hall is on the far west of the parish on the edge of the Blackwater valley. On a Saturday evening in July 1835, the Looker[8] and his son had completed an inspection of the yard and found nothing amiss but twenty minutes later, a haystack 'whose condition had been giving concern for some days', suddenly burst into flames. The fire spread 'with astonishing rapidity' first to a hay barn, then to two sheds and to a double bayed barn a hundred and thirty feet long and thirty wide, to another stack, pigsties and a cart lodge. Other casualties included forty bags of caraway seed, a wagon loaded with straw and a dog which had been in the barn but was never seen again. In about 40 minutes, the whole lot was destroyed. Losses amounted to over £1,400 an enormous sum at the time. The fire had been seen in Coggeshall and drew a large crowd. Although the engines were called disorganisation and disrepair meant that they were useless:

'An attempt was made to convey the two engines, if so they may be called, to the spot, but no horses

> ### Launched into Eternity
> *Although very few incendiaries were ever caught, some of them were and 1835, the year of the Curd Hall fire, saw the final executions for arson before the law was changed. The last Essex man to be hung was James Passfield, who was convicted of burning Hill Farm in Toppesfield, sixteen miles from Coggeshall and the scene of many incendiary attacks. He was 'launched into eternity' at Springfield Gaol, Chelmsford on Friday 3rd April 1835, in front of 1,200 spectators. [Berkshire Chronicle 04/04/1835] The last person to be hung from hereabouts was George Cranfield who was from Suffolk and he was executed at Springfield Gaol on Friday 7th August 1835, after being convicted of setting fire to a barn at Bures, ten miles from Coggeshall on the Essex/Suffolk border. He mounted the scaffold with a firm step and till the end 'neither asserted his innocence or denied his guilt'* [ES 14/08/1835]

were to be had and, on enquiry it was ascertained that the person who has the care of one of the engine houses had gone to the fire with the key in his pocket![9] After a time they were set to motion, but they soon broke down and nearly an hour elapsed before they were got to the spot. When they arrived although there was plenty of water on hand, they were found to be so leaky as to be of no service.' [Surrey Advertiser 31/07/1835]

After the fire the Directors wanted to meet Allen and 'consider the Coggeshall engines' but once again he was away and the matter was deferred until his return. It was over two months later in October before he attended on the Directors and conveyed the unwelcome news that the other fire offices, had refused to contribute towards the cost of a new engine. As the minutes put it 'Further consideration was postponed'. [E&S MB3 16/10/1835]

---

8 Looker: One who looks after or has charge of anything – a child, a wood or a farm. Arthur Young noted the use of this word in 'Essex Agriculture' of 1813.

9 There was probably only one engine house. The key may have been to the building which housed the engine carriage but locked up or not it could not have been used without horses.

A New Engine

In November 1836, a year after the failed attempt to share the cost of a new engine, the Directors decided to buy the engine themselves:

> 'That this office will provide an engine to be stationed in Coggeshall, on condition that the inhabitants will erect a substantial and suitable house for it to be kept in and they referred to the engine committee to procure such an engine with the requisite hose, buckets &c. when they are satisfied that a suitable house is provided for its reception'. *[E&SE MB3 04/11/1836]*

It is possible that a new engine house was built in early 1837 on the site of the original building but there is no record of this in the Vestry Minutes. The existing building as we know, had been refurbished five years before and this may have been 'substantial and suitable' enough for the Directors.

Just a month later, the land and the Engine House were conveyed to the parish by its owners, the Society of Friends[10]. In the conveyance, dated 5th December 1836, it was described as:

> 'A piece or parcel of land used as a garden by the said Parish of Great Coggeshall with the building thereon at the east end whereof used as an Engine House and situate between the Poorhouse yard and a chase-way called Crouches.' *[ERO D/DU 609/14]*

The building, which survives today, is a simple rectangle in plan, fourteen feet wide and nineteen in length and built in local soft red bricks, its plain exterior relieved at the eaves by two decorative courses of brickwork. The roof is hipped and since 1902 at least, was slated. The interior had a brick floor, there were brackets on the wall for harnesses and a cast iron 'Tortoise' stove made by Portway of Halstead. When the Gas Works was opened at the end of the same year, a gas lamp was placed outside. Another parish building, the lock-up, stood against the west wall of the building. By late spring 1837, the new engine was installed.

---

10 This was in exchange for a nearby piece owned by the parish that the Quakers wanted.

Lewis Allen

A year earlier, in May 1836, Lewis Allen had been in the news when he was summoned to appear at Witham Petty Sessions: 'Lewis Allen and nine other persons, principally Quakers, appeared for non-payment of rates.' *[CC 06/05/1836]* The eventual outcome is not reported but this is just one episode in a long-standing national dispute about rates between the Quakers and the Vestry. As one of the Elders, Allen's name would have appeared as a representative of the church. In April 1837, Allen was in the news again:

> 'The working classes of Coggeshall, Essex, have made a most successful effort in making known their hostility to the new Poor Law Act by choosing Guardians in whom the numerous poor of this manufacturing town confide....A poll was demanded and ended with the complete success of the poor man's friends... Mr Stephen Unwin, Mr Lewis Allan and Mr William Appleford.' *[London Evening Standard 04/03/1837]*

The three defeated candidates were 'the nominees of the squire', Osgood Hanbury, the Lord of the Manor.

Allen's focus on these political activities took a toll not only on his agency work but also on his business concerns. The first sign that all was not well comes in May 1837, when the partnership with his brother Charles, 'Tanners and Timber Merchants of Great Coggeshall', was officially dissolved by mutual consent.

In July 1837, the Directors of the Essex & Suffolk, having invested a considerable sum in the new engine and its appliances, received a complaint:

> 'Of the state of the engine and buckets at Coggeshall and that the keys have not been provided as stated in the printed notice on the doors.' *[E&SE MB3 07/07/1837]*

The Secretary was directed to write to Mr Allen 'stating the disapprobation of the board of directors and the desire that Mr Allen will immediately give some explanation as to

Large manual engine by Hadley Simkin & Lott c1815-20.
They were the engine makers favoured by the Essex & Suffolk Equitable Insurance Society from 1817, when they ordered an engine for Maldon. Designed on the Braidwood pattern with firemen sitting on the top, the engine weighed just under a ton and was drawn by a pair of horses. Note in the foreground the single, short length of leather hose which by the absence of rivets, was probably of the earlier, pre 1819, stitched pattern. The hose is fitted with a long branch-pipe with a nozzle at its end. A hard suction pipe emerges from the rear of the engine and sits in a small pool of water, such as may be created from the opening of a hydrant plug.

the cause of this neglect.' Two weeks later, with no response from Allen, a further letter was sent 'expressing the surprise of the Directors that he has made no written reply' and 'requesting that he will send one'. *[E&SE MB3 07/07/1837]* In August a letter was received and although it seems his explanation 'appeared to be satisfactory', the episode cast further doubts as to his conduct and suitability and probably sealed his fate.

In October 1837 Lewis married, the ceremony taking place in the Friends Meeting House at Hertford and the bride, Rachael, was the only daughter of the late William Squire of Hertford, another old Quaker family. Quakers were obliged to marry within their faith. There must be some question as to whether they were fully acquainted with Allen's circumstances.

Some further incident must have come to the Directors' attention because in May the next year, they decided 'That the propriety of removing Mr Allen in consequence of his continuing neglect be taken into consideration at the next meeting'. That took place on the 18th May 1838 and the result recorded in the Minute Book:

'That Mr Allen be informed that the Directors have for a long time past been dissatisfied with the state of his accounts and the general management of the Coggeshall agency and have therefore come to the determination of appointing another agent and request that he will send in his resignation on the 1st June next'. *[E&SE MB3 18/05/1838]*

The Essex & Suffolk Secretary, was directed to 'make enquiries as to a proper person to succeed Mr Allen'. The decision, for once, brought a quick response from Allen. Realising his case was lost, he asked for a delay rather than a reconsideration. Financially on a knife edge, Allen had been making use of the company's money (and perhaps his wife's?). Some of it was spent on a new enterprise, 'The Tilkey Brickfield, six acres with a considerable depth of brickearth of the finest quality, with two new cottages, kiln

The Engine House at Crouches (on the left) built or rebuilt between 1830-37. It was in use as a fire station until the 1940s.

and shed' and described as being 'in full work' [ES 10/08/1838]. Given a little time, this may have saved him from ruin but the Directors would have none of it, they refused his request and as they put it:

> '..beg leave to call his attention to the state of his account, they desire that he will forward to the office as early as convenient an account of all dividends and other moneys paid by him for the office, together with the balance of his account.'

That was on 1st June 1838. On 23rd, 'Lewis Allen of Great Coggeshall, Tanner and Charles Allen of Isleworth, Middlesex, brickmaker', appeared on the list of Bankrupts in 'Perry's Bankrupt Gazette'.

Lewis Allen was not able to repay the considerable balance due to the Essex & Suffolk, which amounted to more than £375 (the equivalent of around £30,000 in 2016). Allen's sureties were called in. At some point, both of his original guarantors had withdrawn their support and Allen had found two new, perhaps less well informed, sureties. Neither would have expected Allen to default and one at least, a Taylor from Chelmsford, was of modest means. In February 1839 the Directors accepted £350 in full discharge of the debt.

Charles Allen was not in good health and retired to Boulogne hoping to benefit from the sea air. He died there on 11th April 1839 leaving a wife and four children. He was 47 years old. [ES 26/04/1839] Lewis Allen died eight years later in November 1847 at his sister's house in Stoke Newington. He was 55 years old. The newspaper announcement was made by his sister and made no mention of his wife, who survived him by twenty-nine years.

Two weeks after Allen had been forced to resign the Coggeshall agency, a local Solicitor, Anthony Peed, was appointed agent. He was a partner in Sadler & Peed, Attorneys and Solicitors of Coggeshall. His name first appears in the list of Essex & Suffolk agents in the 'Essex Standard' on 22nd June 1838. There was some urgency to encourage his quick appointment; policy holders paid their annual premiums on one of the quarter days and the next, Midsummer's Day, was on 24th June. With around seventy-five policies due for payment, the Directors needed someone and somewhere to receive the cash.

After Allen's neglect, the Directors also wanted to know that their new engine was properly looked after. Their first instruction to Mr Peed was that he should 'pay the expenses of keeping the engine in order and working it as the occasion demands.' [E&SE MB3 15/06/1838]

Fire Engine Development

One of the most significant figures in fire engine construction, Moses Merryweather, came to public prominence just as the Fire Office placed an order with him for the new Coggeshall engine. A Yorkshireman, Moses arrived in London in 1807 as an apprentice in the long established fire engine makers, Hadley Simkin and Lott of Long Acre, Greenwich. Merryweather remained in the firm after his apprenticeship had finished and supported Lott when he became the last surviving partner in the firm. Braidwood, the famous chief of the London Engine Establishment was a regular visitor to the works and it was said that the semi-aristocratic Lott could not stand him and left through the rear door whenever Braidwood came in at the front. Merryweather increasingly took on the burden of the business and when Lott retired, Merryweather took over. In 1836, he re-named the firm and married Lott's niece into the bargain!

By the late 1830s many of the major design improvements to manual fire engines had already been made. The basic shape of the engine with the firemen seated on each side of the hose-locker on top, owes much to James Braidwood and was described in his 1830 book on fire engine design, published when he was in charge of the Edinburgh fire brigade. This design became the standard for all large manual engines.

In 1792, Charles Simkin had patented a design of metal, rather than leather, non-return

---

Monsters in Human Form
November 1838
Ten desperate offenders none of them above 14 years of age, were put to the bar. The scene of the outrage was the Market-place of Coggeshall, the time 2 o'clock on the morning of Guy Vaux day.

It appears that these monsters in human form, having the fear of Popery more before their eyes than the fear of Constables, did, at 2 o'clock in the morning set fire to a certain quantity of straw and faggots in the Market-place with intent to annoy, frighten and alarm the friends and apologists of the late lamented Vaux. The prisoners were under the special care of Mr William Goodey, the constable of Coggeshall, who to our thinking (we might be mistaken) entertained no very great indignation against the culprits. The prisoners were each and all charged with the felony of stealing 91 faggots. Some of the ruffians pleaded guilty, some not guilty and others could not make up their minds whether they were guilty or not. The Reverend Chairman told them that on the faggot stealing charge they might be convicted of felony but seeing their contrition, the Bench was willing to deal with them mercifully and proceed only with the bonfiring account: of lighting a fire in the Market-place to the terror of her Majesties liege subjects, or of aiding, comforting or abetting those who did. The Chairman humanely hinted to them that the faggot stealing was a felony and that Pope burning was only a misdemeanour. They were each sentenced to pay a fine of 3s and 2s expenses or go to the treadmill for a fortnight.

It appeared that the whole ten of the delinquents had not as much money about them as would jingle on a tombstone. Four found persons who had faith and they were discharged. The four others were in doleful dumps at the thought of being obliged to go on the revolving ladder, but on advice from the good-natured constable, were given a fortnight for payment. The fate of the two hardened offenders was much more deplorable. They being the eldest and having added to their original guilt, that of pleading not guilty, the bench would not give them a fortnights grace, 5s on the nail, or their toes on the treadmill. They were led sorrowing away, but what became of them we have not heard. Extracted from ES 23/11/1838

A manual engine by W J Tilley c1825.
This was the engine favoured by Braidwood in his 1830 Book on Fire Engine construction. It proved to be a perfect combination of form and function and although there were improvements and minor variations, this basic design continued to be used by all fire engine manufacturers until the twentieth century. In about 1850 James Shand and Samuel Mason married two 'Tilley' sisters in a joint ceremony and carried on the firm as Shand-Mason.
The power of the engines depended on the size of the pump cylinders and on the number of pumpers who could be accommodated along the pumping arms on each side of the machine. On the engine illustrated, these arms extend some way beyond the rear of the machine about as far as was practicable. On later engines the arms were hinged to fold out front and back, allowing more pumpers but remaining within the length of the engine when housed.

valves, these were very robust and not easily fouled when pumping dirty water and easy to clear if they did become clogged. The cylinders and pistons, were also made of metal but used a leather washer to create a seal. Hadley & Simkin fitted pumping arms which could be extended to give space for more pumpers but remain within the length of the body when stowed for travel. The engines had a sprung chassis and a wide wheelbase allowing travel at speed on rough roads behind a pair of horses. The front wheels were on a turntable which was locked when the engine was worked, a device called a locking fore carriage. Merryweather had himself improved the design of the inside of the branch which reduced friction and gave the jet of water a longer reach. Escape ladders were carried on each side of the engine and although just six feet long, they were designed to be interlinked. In a competition in 1836, seven were joined to give a ladder of over

> ### A Victim of Her Own Imprudence
> *February 1834*
> *'On the 11th inst. about noon, as Mrs Howard, wife of Robert Howard, of Great Tey, a dealer in cows, was sitting by the fire asleep, a coal flew out and set her clothes on fire: so rapid were the flames that when she woke nothing but her stays and shoes remained. Her husband returned a few hours after the occurrence and every assistance was obtained, but the victim of her own imprudence survived the accident but a few hours. The deceased was a corpulent woman and fifty-eight years old.* [CC 10/01/1834]

forty feet in just twenty-one seconds.

A single day book of Hadley Simkin and Lott survives[11], one entry describes an 1834 manual engine:

> 'A new 1st Size patent Fire Engine, mounted on spoke wheels with a locking fore carriage, fitted with metallic pistons and valves... the whole in the best materials finished in the most substantial manner, painted in green and vermilion, including a copper branch pipe with brass nose pipes.'
> *[LMA/4516/01]*

Coggeshall's new manual engine ordered at the end of 1836, was one of the larger models, with a sprung chassis, a locking fore-carriage and designed to be fitted either with shafts or a pole so it could be drawn with one or a pair of horses. Although weighing around a ton the engine could be manhandled for short distances. The pumping arms could be extended allowing more pumpers to work and it was capable of pumping around a hundred gallons of water a minute through two lines of hose and throw it a hundred feet into the air. The engine would have been delivered from Merryweather's, painted and varnished in the Essex & Suffolk livery which was probably black with red detailing and sign-writing. The engine was beautifully made and ninety years later was still in use and working as well as ever.

Crisis at the Coggeshall Agency

In September 1838 and after just four months in the job, Anthony Peed informed the Directors of the Essex & Suffolk that he was leaving the district and would resign the agency. The move was unexpected, perhaps the result of a family crisis, as Peed returned to practice in Cambridge where his family had been solicitors for many years. He had already left Coggeshall by the time his business partnership with Thomas Sadler was officially dissolved in January 1839 and Sadler continued in practice on his own. Sadler probably suggested Peed's successor to the agency, Mr Daniel Leaper whom he knew and trusted, being ready to act as one of Leaper's sureties. Leaper was an upholsterer and cabinet maker of East Street and a native of the town. He came from a well-known and respected Coggeshall family, with a row of cottages and a lane named after them[12]. He was forty-two years old, married with four children; two boys, Daniel twelve, William six and a girl, Elizabeth, who was four. His eldest daughter Maria was married and lived away. Leaper played an active part in local affairs, serving as a Parish Constable, a Churchwarden and an Overseer for the Poor. He was not the Directors' ideal candidate, a working man, not the gentleman they would have preferred. The Directors' reluctance is clear in the minute recording his appointment;

> 'That in consequence of Mr Peed being about to leave Coggeshall and it being necessary to fill the vacancy without a delay, Mr Daniel Leaper of Coggeshall, cabinet maker be appointed agent in that place and he be required to give security by bond from him and two sureties of £400.'
> *[E&SE MB3 05/10/1838]*

In other words, Leaper was appointed because time was too short to find someone more suitable. Perhaps the Directors were concerned that a gentleman might not want to discuss

---

11　It was rescued from a skip outside the empty premises of the inheritor firm, Siebe Gorman in 1984, when they apparently did a 'moonlight flit'. *[LMA/4516]*

12　The cottages, 'Leaper's Row', now demolished, were off Robinsbridge Road and Leaper's Lane was probably what is now called Gas Lane

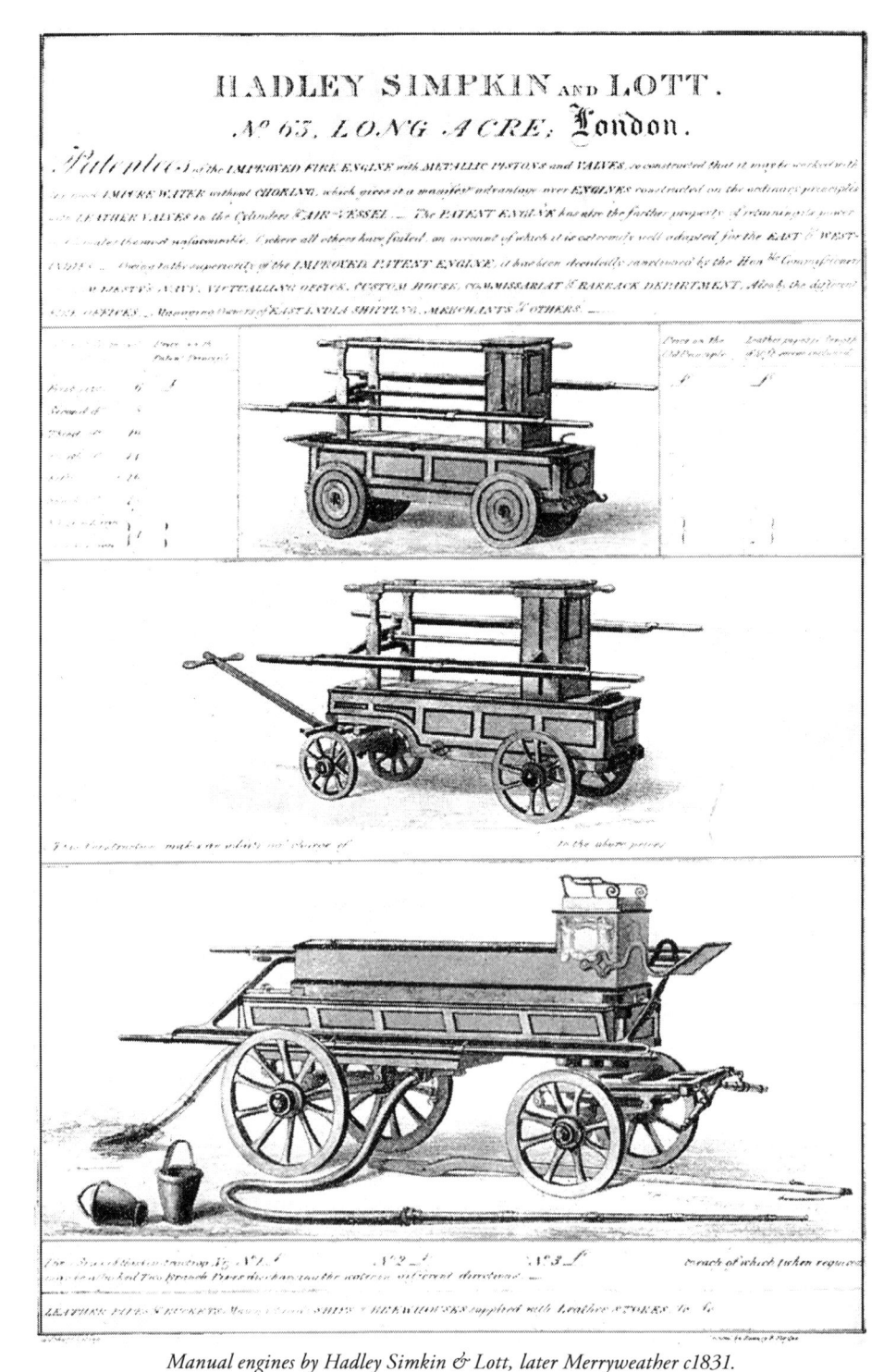

Manual engines by Hadley Simkin & Lott, later Merryweather c1831.
Although these might look like stages in the development of the manual fire engine, in fact all were available at the same time and each one was offered in a range of sizes and capacities to suit a customer's requirements and budget. The difference in scale between the two 'Bedposter' engines and the Carriage engine is very apparent here.

ESSEX AND SUFFOLK EQUITABLE
INSURANCE SOCIETY,
Established at Colchester in 1802.

PERSONS whose ANNUAL PREMIUMS fall due on the 24th Instant, are requested to apply for the Renewal of their Policies on or before the 9th day of July next, as the usual fifteen days allowed for payment beyond the Quarter Day will then expire.

Dividends of **£50** per cent. are now paying on Policies of FIVE Years standing instead of Seven as formerly.

F. P. KEELING, SECRETARY.
Colchester, 20th June, 1839.

AGENTS.

BILLERICAY............	Mr. WILLIAM ROLPH.
BURY ST. EDMOND'S.....	Mr. G. I. OLIVER.
BRAINTREE.............	Mr. THOMAS JOSLIN.
CHELMSFORD............	Mr. JAMES BUTLER
COGGESHALL............	Mr. DANIEL LEAPER.
CLACTON, GREAT........	Mr. WILLIAM WILSON.
DUNMOW, GREAT.........	Mr. JOSEPH SEWELL.
FRAMLINGHAM...........	Mr. WILLIAM EDWARDS.
HALSTED...............	Mr. JAMES JESUP.
HARLOW................	Mr. WILLIAM BARNARD.
HARWICH...............	Mr. EDW. CHAPMAN.
MALDON................	Mr. ALFRED MAY.
MANNINGTREE...........	Mr. THOMAS SCRIVENER
MENDLESHAM............	Mr. H. H. GISSING.
OAKLEY, GREAT.........	Mr. JOHN R. MOSS.
RAYLEIGH..............	Mrs. MARY BELCHAM.
ROMFORD...............	Mr. JOHN HIGGS.
SAFFRON WALDEN........	Mr. W. S. BARNES.
SIBLE HEDINGHAM.......	Mr. THOMAS SAVILL.
SUDBURY...............	Mr. RICHARD G. DUPONT.
THORP-LE-SOKEN........	Mr. EDWARD BLYTH.
WITHAM................	Mr. JAMES CATCHPOOL.
WOODBRIDGE............	Mr. JOHN LODER.
YARMOUTH, GREAT.......	Mr. W. T. TURNER.

Agents of the Essex & Suffolk 1839.

Nearest the camera is Daniel Leaper's Shop on East Street where he ran the Coggeshall Agency of the Essex & Suffolk for many years. The scene has barely changed to this day although the buildings are now residential.

the value of his house and possessions with a 'working man'. As for the urgency, the Quarter Day on which payments were due, Michaelmas, 29th September, had already passed and this left the policy holders with fifteen days to make their payments – just nine days away.

The wording of the appointment had a twist in its tail. Was it because of Leaper's 'ungentlemanly' status that the Directors required an additional personal bond as well as the usual two sureties? Whatever the views of the Directors, in Coggeshall at least, Leaper's standing, probity and good connections were in no doubt and this is borne out by the two people who were ready to stand as his guarantors, Osgood Hanbury Esq., the Lord of the Manor from Holfield Grange and the aforementioned Thomas Sadler, the Solicitor who had recommended him.

Leaper had a shop and premises at 19 East Street, next to the 'Bird in Hand' public house, for Coggeshall people this shop soon became known as the 'Fire Office'.

As time was short the Directors sent Mr Bland the chief clerk from the head office at Colchester to inform Leaper of his appointment, instruct him in the general business of the office and assist him in collecting the Michaelmas insurance renewals. So with a new agent and a new engine, the next chapter of the story begins.

3   THE ESSEX & SUFFOLK ENGINE

It was a few months before the Essex & Suffolk engine had its first call, to a farm in Earls Colne five miles to the north. A young lad had: 'very incautiously shot a sparrow on a thatched barn'. Some of the burning wadding from the gun set the thatch alight. A 'mounted messenger made all haste' to Coggeshall and the engine was quickly away with Daniel Leaper himself in charge. By the time it arrived the barn was beyond help and the heat had ignited a shed across the road. The farm house would have been next – but there was a good supply of water and plenty of willing helpers. The engine was soon set in and pumping two powerful jets of water, the progress of the flames was halted and the farmhouse saved. As the newspaper rather prosaically reported:

> 'The Coggeshall engine was very promptly on the spot and showered down a plentiful supply of water, or else the farmhouse must have been prey to the devouring element. ....Much praise is due to Mr Daniel Leaper, agent for the Equitable, for his exertions and management in working the engine.' [ES 14/06/1839]

Unusually the Minutes of the Essex & Suffolk have an account of the costs of this fire, so we know more about the fire-fighting effort than is usual. An astonishing total of twenty-four men travelled with the engine, a tribute to the efforts Leaper must have made in recruiting since his appointment. Once at the fire, plenty of assistance was on hand to provide labour and to pump the engine, amounting to a further forty-one men, one woman and four boys.

Payments reflect the status of each group: Leaper as Conductor was paid 10s 6d and the men who travelled with the engine 2s 6d each.

The usual rate for Essex & Suffolk firemen was 5s so the men may have been regarded as assistants. Although the amounts given to the pumpers and others are incomplete, they probably received half the men's rate. The horses were hired at a guinea for the pair. [E&SE MB4 21/06/1839]

Altogether, seventy people helped and were paid at the fire, a huge communal effort which was so normal at the time, that the newspaper report makes no mention of it.

It was a very successful first outing under the new regime, a solid endorsement of Leaper as the new agent and of the Essex & Suffolk for their investment in the town. In the light of this it is odd that it was ten years before Leaper took charge of the engine again. It may be that he wished to acquaint himself with the 'hot' end of the fire insurance business before continuing the more sedentary activities of selling policies, receiving premiums and getting on with his day-to-day work as a cabinet maker and upholsterer. There was another perhaps more compelling reason. In December that year and before the next fire call, his youngest daughter, five year old Elizabeth, became ill and died, the fifth of Daniel and Maria's children to die in childhood. Even in those times when the death of a child was not uncommon, to have lost so many was unusual. Perhaps Daniel decided that he needed to be at home to support his wife and not burden her with further anxiety occasioned by his attendance at fires[1].

---

1   The children were Sussanah who died in 1825 aged three, Suzzanah aged two and William, aged eighteen months who both died in 1830, Elizabeth died in 1831 aged twelve and the second Elizabeth as we have heard died in 1839 aged five.

Hall's Silk Mill showing the boiler house on the left and next to it in the centre, the building which probably contained the Reel Room. The factory is on the right. The Reel Room section survives.

Not Calling the Engine

Many fires took place without the engine being called. On 9th May 1840 just before midnight 'a great light' was seen in the upper apartments of a house in Bridge Street in Coggeshall. The alarm of 'fire!' was given and a great number of people and four police officers collected around the house and tried to break in. Perhaps because there was no tradition of having a brigade at readiness in the town, no one thought to call out the engine. Inside were 'Miss Corder and her mother, upwards of eighty years of age'. Eventually the light subsided, the upstairs window opened and Miss Corder called out: 'There is no reason for alarm!' A degree of understatement as the bed had caught fire, all the hangings and some of the bedding had been destroyed and the room much damaged by smoke:

> 'Had it not been for the extraordinary presence of mind of Miss Corder in keeping the doors and windows closed until she had extinguished the flames with her own hands, the building, with several others closely connected, must have become a prey to the devouring element.' *[ES 15/05/1840]*

Another fire that broke out in January 1842 was potentially catastrophic but again the engine was not called.

John Hall's silk mill was just off West Street in Coggeshall. It was Coggeshall's biggest employer and the factory its largest building, powered by a large steam engine. On the evening of Thursday 28th January, the overlooker locked up at eight o'clock. An hour later a youth who was passing through the garden of a nearby house saw the flicker of flames through one of the factory windows and raised the alarm. When the owners gained entry and climbed the stairs to the Reel Room, an alarming sight confronted them:

> '... the casing over the steam pipe which connects the boilers to the cylinder was in a blaze, the flooring and railway [balustrade] round the engine

Makers plates from Merryweather and its precursors. Lott joined in 1791 & it became Merryweather in 1836. The Merryweather plate adorned the Coggeshall engine. Photograph copyright The Firefighters Memorial Trust with acknowledgement to The Fire Brigade Society.

had just ignited and the heat was so intense as to break the glass in the windows above the steam pipe.
Great numbers of the inhabitants of all classes hastened to the spot to render assistance. To the vigilance and strenuous exertions of the persons present, who nearly to a man provided themselves with a bucket and formed lines instanter communicating from the fountain of water to the fire, can alone be attributed, says our correspondent, to the little progress of the flames and had they not been so fortunately discovered there is too much reason to fear that they would have rapidly communicated to the mill and oil rooms, which from their combustible nature would have rendered the whole manufactory and dwelling house a prey to the devouring element.'
[ES 04/02/1842]

Later Mr Hall 'liberally rewarded those who proffered their assistance'.

Incendiarism

After the intense protests of 'Swing' in 1829–32, the number of incendiary attacks declined and by 1841 the situation had eased enough for the County Fire Office to state:

> 'Due to the diminution of incendiary practices on the property of farmers during the last few years, the Directors of the County Fire Office feel enabled to reduce their premium for the insurance of farming stock.' [EH 21/06/1841]

The Essex Economic and several other Fire Offices also advertised reduced rates at this time. In this they were premature, as the number of incendiary fires began to increase and by 1844 were at levels never known before. Lexden Hundred (the ancient administrative district which included Coggeshall) was particularly affected and nearby West Bergholt was the worst hit parish of all, with 15 fires in 1844 alone. Even closer at hand, Braintree and Bocking were also regularly hit. The incendiaries again targeted landowners and farmers who seemed to be taking advantage of the competition for work whilst profiting from the increases in agricultural production and prices. Some of the farmers who were attacked were known to be kind and decent employers suggesting that for some the discontent was political as well as economic. Arthur Brown, that wonderful historian of Essex life, took the view that 'a general class resentment' was intrinsic in the protests. [Brown] The Poor Law Amendment Act of 1834 had added further grievance and focus to the discontent. This closed local Poorhouses and replaced them with Union Workhouses built in the larger towns where the regime was made deliberately harsh. Only the very desperate applied to them. The Coggeshall Poorhouse on Stoneham Street closed in March 1839 and those in need were sent to the Union Workhouse at Witham.

The incendiaries may have been few in number, but there was complicity among the agricultural labourers. This is evident in the

A cart-lodge and haywain on fire after an arson attack near Coggeshall in modern times.

difficulty in finding witnesses to incendiary attacks, despite considerable rewards being routinely offered. There was a real fear of social revolution, so the actions of the labouring classes during a fire came under particular scrutiny for evidence of their loyalties.

> 'At the incendiary fire at High Roothing [High Roding] on the 22nd December last [1843] our engine attended and worked for some hours and received considerable damage (some miscreant having cut the hose in several places).'
>
> *[Letter from the Dunmow brigade to the EH 02/04/1844]*

There were fires where onlookers refused to help, greeted falling barns with cheers, obstructed fire-fighting, damaged hoses and feasted on burnt animals. Such actions were not always reported. The 'Essex Herald' gave an account of an incendiary fire in February 1844:

> 'It is with extreme regret that we have to record the most extensive daring instance of the diabolical act of incendiarism that has occurred in the county. On Monday night between ten and eleven pm no less than three fires burst out almost at the same instant, in the parish of Ardleigh about five miles from Colchester, which so illuminated the atmosphere that objects could be discerned a mile distant. The fire engines from Colchester, Dedham and Manningtree hastened to the spot.'
> *[EH 06/02/1844]*

The 'Herald' and the 'Chelmsford Chronicle' went on to claim that the firemen were 'assisted by a numerous body of persons'. *[CC 02/02/1844]* However, reports in the 'Essex Standard', the 'Ipswich Journal' and the 'Suffolk Chronicle', paint a different picture:

> 'A considerable crowd of labourers witnessed the fires but...their conduct was most heartless and disgraceful: many of them instead of rendering assistance, frequently endeavoured to obstruct the firemen and openly exalted in the progress of the flames.' *[Suffolk Chronicle 03/02/1844]*

There was of course an incentive for the labourers to assist at a fire, those who did would expect to be paid for their work. The

A Merryweather manual engine 1850, much like the Coggeshall engine.
This has two deliveries with a length of the riveted hose attached to each. The pumping arms have extensions which can be hinged out front and back to allow more pumpers to work on this more powerful machine. A Merryweather's improved ladder is attached to each side. The hard suction at the back of the engine (not visible here) is placed into the large square container, called a 'suction tub' which would have been filled with water by means of a bucket chain. Some suction tubs had an opening at the bottom and were placed over an open fire plug to capture the water as it flowed out.

fires continued:

'Colchester: this town was thrown into great alarm, in consequence of two fires being visible within a few miles, one in an eastern and one in a southern direction. The engines of the fire office were immediately dispatched. One of the fires had taken place in the farm yard at Martell's Hall in Ardleigh and the other proved to be at Peet-Hall, West Mersey.' *[EH 06 & 13/02/1844]*

The 'Herald' reported on one of several fires in the Braintree area:

'The inhabitants of Braintree and Bocking were again thrown into a state of alarm by the general cry of fire! There is too much reason to fear that the origin of the fire was the work of an incendiary, although the diabolical perpetrator has not yet been detected.' *[EH 26/03/1844]*

In March there were incendiary fires at Tendring, Rayne and again at Braintree. These were all reported in the 'London Times', under the headline 'Incendiarism in Suffolk and Essex' where the 'abominable spirit of incendiarism has in no way been subdued'. *[Times 20/03/1844]* The fire at Rayne (just west of Braintree) destroyed nine corn stacks, several haystacks and all the farm buildings, the damage amounting to between £2,000 and £3,000.

The incendiary attack at Braintree in March 1844 was one of the most destructive that has ever taken place in the town and destroyed nineteen cottages, a barn and other buildings, the ruins extending for one hundred yards. In addition to the Braintree and Bocking brigades, the Coggeshall and Witham engines were also called in to help. The account in the 'Essex

> ### Samuel Hersom, Parish Constable & Sometime brigade Superintendent October 1834
>
> *Henry Cotton, 15, labourer, pleaded guilty to an indictment for stealing a rabbit, belonging to Isaac Beard, Coggeshall. The prosecutor recommended the prisoner to mercy on account of his being a friendless lad.*
>
> *Samuel Hersom, constable of Coggeshall said he could relate a few facts about this boy. He was an orphan: his father left a sum of money to apprentice him, but his mother marrying a second time, her husband had spent the money, turned him out of doors and the youth was quite destitute. Hersom stated that he understood that the boy having no home, had been accustomed to lie upon the steps of people's doors and had said that he had nothing to eat. He had been sent once to his own parish which he believed had been Cheltenham, but had returned. There was another indictment against him for stealing a donkey. Mr Disney [the Chairman] thought the most merciful course would be to transport him for life, when employment would be secured for him. Mr Neale the Governor of the Convict Gaol, having communicated with Mr Disney, the Learned Chairman said he was glad to find that a middle course could be taken which would give the boy a chance of education. He understood that if he were transported for seven years, he would be sent to the Penitentiary, where he would be taught a business and upon proper representation, his sentence could be commuted. He was then sentenced to seven years transportation and told that if he ever left the Penitentiary, or again appeared at the bar, he would be sent out of the country for the rest of his life.* [CC 17/10/1834]

Herald' gives a vivid picture of the fire and of the techniques and difficulties involved – and of course, the Coggeshall engine was there:

'The scene of the conflagration ... consisted of about twenty cottages all weather-boarded with thatched roofs ... principally occupied by weavers and in the majority of houses, looms were fixed. At about eight o'clock a body of smoke was observed and a few minutes afterwards flames burst forth which almost instantaneously communicated with the barn and other buildings in the yard. The alarm of 'fire!' was spread throughout the town and hundreds of people flocked to the spot. The Braintree and Bocking engines were upon the spot as quickly as possible and were got into play: but the supply of water was extremely scanty, it being obtained principally from the neighbouring pumps which were zealously worked and the water passed in buckets to the engines. It was soon apparent that any attempt to save any portion of the property to which the flames had extended would be futile: the exertions were therefore directed towards checking their further progress by pulling down the two cottages nearest the Coggeshall lane. At ten o'clock the engines from Witham and Coggeshall arrived: by them a stream of water was poured on the roofs of the houses adjacent, which several times caught fire and were considered in imminent danger of destruction but the spreading of wet blankets upon the roofs and the pulling off the thatch and the upper story of two cottages, the fire was happily confined to the nineteen houses where it fearfully raged until by twelve o'clock the work of destruction was complete....There is too much reason to fear that the origin of the fire was the work of an incendiary, although the diabolical perpetrator has not yet been detected. The chimneys alone are standing and the ruins which extend for nearly 100 yards were still burning in some parts.' [EH 26/03/1844]

Two incendiary fires at Tollesbury broke out just a few days apart, attended by the Essex & Suffolk engine from Maldon. Afterwards the 'clergy, owners and occupiers' asked for police protection and offered a reward of £50 for each fire on the conviction of the incendiary.

Even a small manual engine, if well maintained, could make an enormous difference at a fire. On a windy night in late May 1844, a stack was fired at Assington Hall about twelve miles north of Coggeshall, the flames quickly spread to the farm buildings but as people rushed to help they discovered to their horror that burning brands blown by the wind, had started fires back in the village itself. The diminutive, unsprung and solid wheeled Boxford Parish engine travelled an epic four and a half miles, eventually arriving an hour and a quarter after the fire broke out. The engine had a dramatic effect on the seemingly inexorable progress of the flames and by common consent it saved the village. Four houses, a barn, cowhouse, sheds and stacks were destroyed and £5,000 of damage was caused. *[CC 31/05/1844 Bury & Norwich Post 29/05/1844]*

Closer to home, on 28th June, a barn and other buildings at Jenkins Farm in Stisted were destroyed, 'the ninth incendiary fire that has occurred in the neighbourhood of Braintree in the last 10 weeks'. *ES 28/06/1844]*

The Coggeshall engine was called to a stack fire at Pattiswick Hall in July, superintended by Samuel Hersom who, like Daniel Leaper, was a Coggeshall parish official, a Constable. Hersom was a local character, in business as a builder and plumber who employed a number of men. Against everyone's expectations this was not an incendiary fire, the stack, twenty tons of hay, had been: 'got up in a bad condition which caused it to reek much for several days.' Eventually on a warm Sunday evening, fearful that the stack was about to burst into flames, a man was dispatched to fetch the Coggeshall engine:

> '..which was promptly brought to the spot. The men then set to work removing the hay and as soon as the air gained admission to the seat of the fire the flames burst forth to a considerable height and then instantly disappeared: a powerful stream was then poured upon the smoking embers by the engine which quickly removed all apprehension of further danger.'*[ES 02/08/1844]*

In April 1844, Daniel and Maria Leaper suffered yet another personal tragedy, when their eldest son, Daniel, died 'after an affliction of 13 months'. He was nineteen years old and had worked closely with his father as an apprentice cabinet maker. Their other son, William, showed no interest in the business. Daniel was the sixth of their children to have died.

Samuel Hersom*, Parish Constable At the Insolvent Debtor's Court March 1837

Samuel Hearsum, plumber & glazier of Coggeshall, was unopposed. His debts amounted to £537 and his credits to £385. The insolvent attributed his insolvency to the loss of his wife, nine years ago.
COMMISSIONER - Then you attribute your loss to not having her service in your business?
INSOLVENT - Yes, but I had the good fortune to get another good one, five years back. (Laughter)
COMMISSIONER - Indeed! It is said to be difficult for one man to find two good ones. Then your misfortune was counterbalanced, for you have got a young and more active woman. (Laughter)
INSOLVENT sorrowfully - Yes but she is likely to bring me a large family. (Laughter)
In the course of the insolvent's examination, he stated that he had lost £100 by a person at Southend, who afterwards took the benefit of the act: he appeared as a debtor in the insolvent's schedule for £117. 2s. 7d.
COMMISSIONER - What was he?
INSOLVENT - Why I don't know what he was: he was a Presbyterian sort of fellow. (Laughter)
COMMISSIONER - I mean what business?
INSOLVENT - I know he was a great rogue. He had been apprentice to a mast builder.
COMMISSIONER - But why call him a Presbyterian sort of fellow?
INSOLVENT - Because he used to go to meetings a great deal and tell a good many lies. (Laughter)
COMMISSIONER - Other people went to meetings as well as him.
INSOLVENT - Yes they are not all alike
COMMISSIONER - But he used to go to meetings and cheat his creditors?
INSOLVENT- Yes but he always said he would not cheat me.
COMMISSIONER - So he said : Rogue I have been to others, I will be honest to you?
INSOLVENT - Exactly so, leaving the word 'rogue' out: he always said he would see me righted.
The Commissioner, upon the insolvent handing over some gas shares, ordered him to be discharged. *Spelt 'Hersom' & Hearsum in the same report. *[ES 17/03/1837]*

Mount Park c1890 looking along what had been until 1888 the Turnpike Road to Colchester. The brick walls are the only feature remaining from the original house. The present house was built for Mr T C Swinborne on the site of the mansion burnt down in 1844.

Robbery, Arson and an Eccentric

In November 1844, the Coggeshall engine was called to a spectacular fire in one of Coggeshall's biggest mansions (now known as The Mount), the property of Charles Skingley. A wealthy and eccentric man, he had on several occasions refused to pay either rates or taxes and some of his effects had been seized under distraint in consequence. To avoid any further depredations by the authorities, he had left his house in Coggeshall and boarded up the windows. With most of the contents still inside, it was an obvious target for criminals and the house had been targeted at least three times before the fateful night of 21st November 1844. Argent Osborne later recalled the night and paints a vivid picture of the scene that confronted him:

> 'I heard a cry of fire at Mr Skingley's between three and four o'clock and was the first person there: the flames were bursting through the cupola in the roof. I went for assistance and returned in ten minutes, when we broke open the gates and went into the yard, the house being then in flames in every part of it: we burst open the door and went into the kitchen: there was a hole on the outside of the house leading to the counting house, through which any person might easily get into the house, a large iron chest in the counting house was red hot - the lid was open'. *[CC 02/02/1849]*

The 'Essex Herald' also ran a report:

> 'Between two and three o'clock on Thursday morning last, the respectable residence of the late Henry Skingley Esq., near the turnpike in Great Coggeshall, now the property of Mr Charles Skingley, his son and which for some time has been unoccupied, was discovered to be on fire. This occurrence caused considerable alarm amongst the inhabitants, a similar calamity not having visited the town for nearly 70 years [The Richard White fire of November 1777]. The parish engine was quickly on the spot but notwithstanding the exertions of the firemen, aided by the police and the inhabitants generally, the house was entirely destroyed, the walls only being left standing.

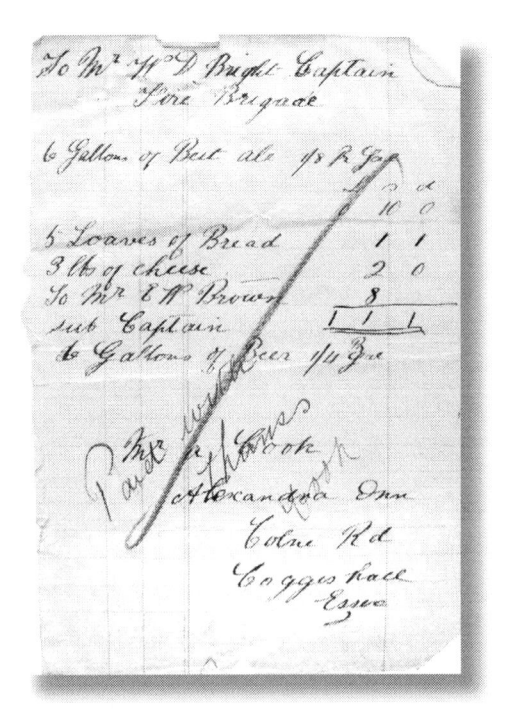

Coggeshall Fire Brigade Refreshments Bill at a fire in 1911 includes twelve gallons of beer, Best Ale at 1s 8d a gallon and Ordinary Beer at 1s 4d, also five loaves and 3lbs cheese. Ordered by Capt W D Bright & Sub Capt E W Brown. Reproduced by courtesy of the Essex Record Office [ERO D/P 36/30/19]

The flames communicated to the outbuildings and stables, which were also burnt down. An investigation is going on and we believe a clue is discovered to a party who has been heard to threaten Mr Skingley' *[EH 26/11/1844]*

The 'Essex Standard' reported:

'The house, which has been for a long time unoccupied, has lately been the resort of a number of lawless characters, who having plundered it of most of its contents, are supposed to have set fire to it to conceal their depredations.'

It was some years before it became apparent that the Skingley burglary and arson attack were part of a string of increasingly vicious offences perpetrated by the notorious Coggeshall Gang who were eventually brought to trial five years later in 1849.

It seems likely that the fire had been started by John Brand, sometime bailiff or looker for Charles Skingley who was meant to be guarding the house. He had been stealing wine from the cellars and it was said, fired the house to cover this up. A witness overheard him say:

'The best way was to pour turpentine on the bed and floor'. *[Morning Post 03/02/1849]*

Brand was charged with burglary in 1849, but after summing up the case, the judge ordered an acquittal on the strange grounds that with no-one living in the house, the premises were not a dwelling house, so the charge of burglary must be abandoned! The more active and vicious members of the gang were transported for life. *[ES 16/03/1849]*

As for Charles Skingley, it was said that his mental condition had begun to deteriorate following a fall from his horse in Copford in 1841, when he suffered a concussion. Whatever the cause, his eccentricity grew eventually into madness. In 1851 he was declared a lunatic 'and to have been so since May 1843'. *[ES 22/08/1851]*

A Commonplace Toll

The most appalling fires were those where people, usually children or the elderly, were involved – an event almost commonplace at the time and usually meriting just a couple of lines in the local papers. In the Coggeshall area alone, during the decade 1839 – 1849, there were five deaths involving domestic fires – one death in every two years[2]. In April 1839, the three-year-old girl of 'a poor cottager' from Coggeshall died of her injuries after her clothes caught fire: in December 1841 a child from Feering died in the same circumstances: in January 1844 an old Coggeshall woman 'fell on the fire in a fit' and in May 1847 a two-year-old Coggeshall child called Jemima Storehold, also died from burns. Another child, the four-year-old son of Mr Pudsey a Coggeshall shopkeeper, died in July 1849 a week after being scalded by boiling water from an overturned kettle.

---

[2] For a full list of such fires, see Index under 'Fire Injuries & Deaths'.

A Dray from Gardner's Brewery, Little Coggeshall, ready for the next blaze? Coggeshall was blessed with several breweries and far more inns and alehouses than was strictly necessary. The Wagoner is sitting on a cask, for the others 'O' is for Ordinary Beer, there are two barrels of 'M' for Mild and two of 'PA' for Pale Ale. Wine and Ginger Beer fetches up in a basket behind.

An Allowable Expense

Fire-fighting and pumping often carried out for long periods was hot and thirsty work and the men (and sometimes women) were usually refreshed with beer and occasionally food. Providing beer during a fire was common practice even in Braidwood's tightly organised London Fire Engine Establishment:

> 'While at work at a fire, a moderate allowance of beer or spirits is served to the men at the expense of the office, the foreman of the district regulating the quantity according to the length and nature of the service.'

Presumably the old boys got the most! The Essex & Suffolk also paid for beer for those working at a fire, although sometimes the sheer amount consumed was questioned. After a fire in Harlow in May 1832:

> 'It appears that the beer consumed by the assistants amounted to upwards of 150 gallons and no order for it was given.'

The Essex & Suffolk thought 'that the quantity was so enormous' they refused to pay the agent more than £5: 'the rest to be the agent's loss'. He appealed but the company would not be moved. *[E&SE MB2 07/05/1832]*

After one fire in 1849, the beer bill cost more than the fire damage:

> 'That Mr Smith be allowed 15s. for his loss and 20s. be allowed for beer for the men assisting' *[E&SE MB4 021/07/1849]*

A written order, hastily scribbled down on a scrap of paper and signed by the officer in charge, was usually enough for an alehouse to send supplies to the scene of a fire. Remarkably, a couple of these notes have survived from Coggeshall fires. These date from 1911 when ordinary beer was 2d a pint. Coggeshall had something of a proud tradition for sociability and beer drinking over the years and may have recorded a 'first', when the quantity of beer consumed at a fire was extraordinary enough to be reported in the national papers. This happened in 1920, when a remarkable twenty-three gallons of beer was consumed during the 'Kings Seeds' factory fire and reported in 'The Times' of London. It is only recently that the close working relationship between a Coggeshall fireman and a pint of beer has been consigned to history.

4   DANIEL LEAPER AND THE ESSEX & SUFFOLK

After ten years as agent, in 1849 Daniel Leaper also took on the job of Superintendent of the Coggeshall fire engine. Quite why he decided to do this will probably remain a mystery. He was fifty-four years old and for the next twenty years, *every* time the engine went out, Daniel Leaper went with it as superintendent[1]. He was in robust good health, described in newspaper reports as 'energetic' and 'active' and he brought a new sense of dispatch, professionalism and organisation to the Coggeshall brigade. The engine was just ten years old and under Leaper's meticulous care it was in perfect order and looked it. The first fire under the new regime was at Aldham, a parish four miles east of Coggeshall:

> 'On Monday se'nnight[2], about 9 o'clock, a fire which at one time threatened serious consequences broke out on a farm called Chickley's, in the Parish of Aldham, in the occupation of Mr. Pettit. A mounted express was immediately dispatched to Coggeshall for the engine belonging to the Essex & Suffolk Fire Office which .... was forthwith dispatched under the superintendence of Mr. Daniel Leaper. Owing to the exertions of Mr. Pettit and the praiseworthy assistance of neighbours and the surrounding peasantry the fire was kept at bay until the arrival of the engine, which being in admirable working order and with a plentiful supply of water at hand soon succeeded in putting a stop to further conflagration and all fears for the surrounding property. Had it not been for the speedy arrival of the engine the destruction of property would have been much more extensive and though .... several outbuildings became prey to the devouring element we are glad to say that beyond this there was no loss either of stock or corn. It is satisfactory to know that the fire was not caused by an incendiary as there is every reason to believe it arose from the extremely reprehensible practise of discharging a squib from a gun. We understand the premises are fully insured in one of the County offices.'[3] *[EH 13/11/1849]*

The Rural Idyll

Although 1844 proved to have been the worst year, with forty-six incendiary attacks reported in the county, between 1847 and 1853 three hundred and four incendiary fires were reported in Essex and these were 'probably less than half those committed'. *[Brown 1990]* Incendiarism and the social conditions at its root, were a continuing preoccupation. Some of the wealthier landowners tried to promote a sense of responsibility toward the labourers. At a meeting of the Coggeshall Agricultural Society at the White Hart in December 1848 its chairman T P Honywood of Markshall, hoped:

> '....now that winter was coming on the farmers would try to employ all the poor they could...and not turn them off, but put them to cutting down useless fences and other useful work' *[ES 22/12/1848]*

The problem of winter work continued to preoccupy him:

---

1   As officer-in-charge of the engine his official rank would have been 'Conductor' but I shall follow the newspapers' convention at the time which would typically report: 'the engine was Superintended by...'.

2   A word then in common use now archaic and meaning a week - a seven-night. The related word for a fourteen-night, a fortnight, has survived.

3   A squib was a home-made firework which probably jumped around and produced one or more loud 'bangs'. Home-made Coggeshall squibs enjoyed a wide reputation for liveliness and loudness.

'The farmers of the district should employ the poor as much as possible during the winter season. For three years past they had been getting capital prices for their corn and it behove them to alleviate in every possible way the privations and sufferings which the poor too often endured during the winter months from the inclemency of the weather and the want of employment.' [ES 12/12/1856]

This was probably not the prevailing view among farmers, for whom the abundance of labour had brought real economic benefit.

The Coggeshall brigade attended a stack fire in August 1851 at Pattiswick. At first this was thought to be another incendiary fire but the report, with almost palpable relief, instead describes a romantic rural idyll:

'Some harvestmen had been drinking and smoking under the stack in question, there seems little doubt that some ashes from a pipe were the cause of the conflagration'. [CC 22/08/1851]

Incendiarism was such a 'hot' topic (no pun intended) that newspapers trod a fine line between reporting and stoking up a frisson of outrage and appalled fascination. Any unexplained fire might be attributed to an incendiary. A severe and extensive farm fire at Copford[4] in the summer of 1849 was reported in the 'London Daily News':

'To make the event still more lamentable (as there was no other mode of accounting for its origin) the conclusion seems almost unavoidable that it must have been the work of an incendiary.'
[London Daily News 06/08/1849]

This prompted a letter from the owner of the farm, a Coggeshall resident, the baroquely named Fisher Unwin Pattisson and introduces us to Inspector Brown, the 'Sherlock Holmes' of the Essex Constabulary:

'Sir, ..I perceive I have the satisfaction of being able to state that there is no ground whatever for this conclusion. Inspector Brown of the Essex Constabulary, noticing that the hair of my bailiff's child, about six years old, was partially burnt, questioned the boy, who confessed that he had been playing with lucifer matches in a shed on the premises containing straw and that he thus became the undesigning cause of the calamity.'
[London Daily News 09/08/1949]

On a Sunday afternoon, 9th November 1851 at 3.30pm the cry of 'fire' was given in the parish church at Inworth[5]. The alarm was raised by a domestic at the vicarage who had seen flames emerging from a shed at the adjacent farm. As people rushed to the spot, they found that a wagon and a tumbrel loaded with straw, were well alight. Someone rode off for the Witham engine and then the Coggeshall brigade were remembered and sent for. The Witham engine suffered a dramatic 'breakdown' on the way to the fire, when one of the horses fell at Gore Pit on the Inworth Road 'and instantly expired'. The horse had been hired from Mrs Coke at the Witham White Hart, who described it for insurance purposes as 'a valuable mare.'[6]
[CC 14/11/1851]

'The engine, which was hurried to the spot and ...brought into play, but the shortness of the supply of water materially increased the labours of the brigade. The engine attended by Mr D Leaper, the agent of the Essex Economic Office [sic] at Coggeshall, was also quickly on the spot and it is much to be regretted (says a correspondent) that information was not sent to Coggeshall in the first instance, it being much nearer the station. Mr Leaper exerted himself very much for about 7 hours, but owing to the bad supply of water, but one engine could work. They were however, most readily assisted by the labourers and others present, but we lament to state that before any effectual check could be given to the ravages of the flames, the shed in which they originated and its contents, a large barn containing about ten loads of wheat, some dressed in sacks, the rest unthreshed, stables, a cow-house and other out buildings, several wagons and other implements, a stack of oats, another of beans and a large quantity of straw, were totally consumed. ....The fire was not completely

---

4   About five miles east of Coggeshall.

5   Just under five miles south of Coggeshall.
6   The E&S shared the loss of the horse with the 'Globe' Fire Office. The E&S allowed £10 so the horse was probably worth £20. [E&SE MB4 06/12/1851]

East Street with Daniel Leaper's shop on the right. He had his business, ran the insurance agency and brought up his family there before moving further along East Street. Daniel took over the licence of the Bird in Hand in 1864.
Photo by courtesy of Coggeshall Museum.

got under, nor did the engine leave the premises until yesterday morning.' *[CC 14/11/1851]*

The fire was thought to be deliberate: 'All these lamentable consequences were the result of the fiendish act of an incendiary' as the Chronicle put it. This 'tabloid-like' characterisation was probably incorrect. The fire may have been deliberately started, but not as a social protest, rather a cry for help by an unhappy sixteen-year-old domestic servant called Eliza Cornwall. She had not long been in service, had 'cried to go home' and run away, only to be returned by her mother. *[CC 14/11/1851]* She was arrested immediately after the fire and we will hear more of her later.

Poverty, Fire and the Engine

With a private company responsible for the fire engine, it might be assumed that either an insurance policy or ready cash would be needed before the fire engine would turn a wheel. In fact, this did not happen. In 1856 for example the Coggeshall brigade attended a fire which destroyed two uninsured cottages owned and occupied by an old man and his son-in-law who were left destitute. Leaper submitted a bill to the Essex & Suffolk for the expenses – the hire of horses, payment for the firemen, helpers and refreshments and the account was paid without demur. *[E&SE MB5 02/08/1856]* The Essex & Suffolk had minuted their policy over thirty years earlier:

'All public Insurance Offices are bound to give assistance at fires and that this Office has always acted upon that principal, without being insured or paid for their exertions.' *[E&SE MB2 06/01/1823]*

This sense of working for the public good was to be an abiding attribute of the Essex & Suffolk and if it was at times compromised, it was usually the actions of other fire offices that challenged it. Throughout the time that the Essex & Suffolk maintained a brigade in Coggeshall no instance has come to light of the engine ever being refused or of those in poverty being pursued for payment.

It is possible that the poor were less likely to call out the brigade; of the fifty-nine reported fires during Leaper's twenty year tenure, there were perhaps ten where the engine did not attend[7] and about half of these were to uninsured cottages occupied by labourers. Consider this fire in Kelvedon in May 1847:

'On Wednesday afternoon, shortly before six o'clock, flames were seen issuing from a cottage in the occupation of a labourer named Elliot and situated in the middle of the village, behind the line of houses forming the street. In an incredibly short space of time the whole was in a blaze, the materials being old and the roof thatched. The neighbours rendered most effective service in removing furniture and tools of the unfortunate tenant, but the cottage was burnt to the ground.' *[ES 28/05/1847]*

The thatched cottages of the poor were particularly susceptible to fire and as difficult to extinguish then as they are today. The secret was to cut a fire-break through the thatch ahead of the fire, this was inevitably downwind which usually meant working in dense smoke:

'On Monday last, about noon, a fire broke out in a thatched cottage, occupied by a labourer named Diceter, in the Parish of Coggeshall. The wife of a neighbour had been baking and a spark from the oven is supposed to have been the cause of the fire.

The houses adjoining were in great danger, but by the aid of the fire-engine the flames were confined to the house where they broke out, which was completely consumed.' *[ES 06/07/1849]*

Leaper must have known what he was doing but it did not always work. An almost identical fire at cottages at Cockerill's Farm, Feering in 1852, was again caused by sparks from an overheated oven lighting the thatch. The brigade was defeated by a strong wind and two cottages were completely destroyed. As was usual, a lot of people assisted at this fire, Leaper wanted to pay them 3s a head which the Directors of the Essex & Suffolk thought 'excessive' but allowed Leaper £5 to distribute at his discretion. With the usual forty to fifty people helping, this represents something like 2s each, not a trivial amount at the time. *[ES 30/04/1852 & E&SE MB4]*

Whilst the fire at Feering was at its height another fire broke out in Robinsbridge Road in Coggeshall. The newspaper report of this incident gives a glimpse into the living conditions of the occupant, a man called James Horsley, who it seems had only a single room with straw on the floor:

'...some lighted soot falling down the chimney ignited some straw by the fire-place and that, with the bedding and other furniture in the room, was entirely consumed.' *[ES 30/04/1852]*

Such fires were devastating to the poor who, like Horsley, may have lost everything they owned. Reports are usually very sympathetic in such cases and the community often offered practical support by raising a subscription for the unfortunates. Such was the case after a fire at Tey Road in Feering in May 1866:

'Two cottages occupied by Blackwell and Lanham were burnt to the ground. The fire originated from overheating the oven. The poor people had nearly all their little furniture[8] destroyed and a subscription has been set up to meet their loss.' *[ES 30/05/1866]*

---

7   It is difficult to be certain as sometimes the engine is not mentioned in reports although other evidence shows that it was in attendance. Newspaper reports of such fires are sometimes very brief with little or no additional detail.

8   'All their little furniture' sounds very condescending but is perhaps better understood in today's language as, 'what little furniture they had'.

Lucifers & Rushlights

A Lucifer was originally a patented friction match but the name soon came to be used for all friction matches. Lucifers were pricey when they first appeared in 1827 but soon became cheap and readily available, by 1851 matches were sold door to door by distressed labourers to bring in a few pence. A policeman pretending to be a match seller used this means to gain entrance to a suspect's house in Coggeshall (see box). Compared to using a tinder box, flint and steel, the lucifer made fire-starting reliable, quick and easy. This caused much disquiet – a Kelvedon man recalling the 1850s exactly describes the problem:

> 'The farmers were strongly opposed to the use of lucifers, they said their stacks and barns would be set on fire and they would be ruined and burned out of house and home by mischievous boys and dissatisfied men.'
> [An Octogenarian's Recollections CC 06/04/1917]

Lucifers were responsible for many serious fires, accidental and deliberate and they were of such benefit to incendiaries that the possession of lucifers at the scene of an unexplained fire might in itself invite suspicion. After a stack fire at Colne Engaine in 1859 for example, the suspected incendiary was found to have matches 'three in his right hand trouser pocket and two in his waistcoat'. [CC 18/11/1859] Found guilty in December 1859, the incendiary and his companion were sentenced to ten years' penal servitude. [CC 11/03/1859]

Investigating the 1851 Inworth fire, where the servant Eliza Cornwall was suspected, Superintendent Cook searched the wash-house and found 'A Lucifer box, containing two matches'. He went up to the suspect and said:

> 'It is my duty to take you into custody on suspicion of setting fire to this property.'
>
> Eliza replied: '...I didn't do it: I can swear I did not. I never touched any lucifer matches'.
>
> 'I had not', said Cook 'then, nor had any one in my presence, said a word about Lucifer matches.'

It was enough for Mr Cook, the prisoner was committed on the charge. [ES 14/11/1851] The case came up at the Lent Assizes in March 1852. However, the evidence was circumstantial and there was no confession so the case was dismissed. [CC 12/03/1852]

Lucifers were a continuing source of fascination to children, a correspondent in the 'Chelmsford Chronicle' in 1849 summarises:

> 'We have frequently had to reprehend the careless way in which the children of the labouring classes are suffered to have these matches in their possession.' [CC 29/06/1849]

The 'Standard' reported on a fire in two cottages in Little Baddow, which is striking in its description and the light it casts on the contemporary social mores:

> 'It appears a child, living in one of the houses, had possessed itself of some lucifer matches with which it repaired to a hovel and was amusing itself by striking them upon the wood, when the straw and rubbish in the place ignited and the child narrowly escaped with its life. Both houses were quickly in flames and the poor cottagers had barely time to remove their furniture. There was but little water in the place and the engines were not called into requisition.' [ES 29/06/1849]

Coggeshall had its fair share of such incidents. In June 1853 a labourer called Raven, who lived on Grange Hill, lost all his furniture in a fire started by his children playing with lucifers. The brigade under Daniel Leaper confined the fire to one room. [ES 17/06/1853] In 1856 children playing with lucifers, started a fire in the premises of Arthur Sadler, a Coggeshall seedsman. He almost lost his house in the blaze, which destroyed a large shed and killed his donkey. [CC04/07/1856] A stack on the Colchester Road was destroyed 'by a little boy named Cask, striking a lucifer match and throwing it upon the stack'.[ES 21/09/1864] In April 1866, children playing with lucifers started a fire in a Stoneham Street outhouse which threatened to spread to the neighbouring houses and a granary. Luckily there was a good water supply and plenty of help and 'indefatigable exertions' saved the day. *[CC 27/04/1866]* In 1876 four-year-old Ernest Blackwell was 'playing with a lucifer' and started a fire in his father's shed in Kelvedon. His mother was 'much burnt about the arms in trying to save the child and property'. *[CC 25/08/1876]* There were many other examples some of which will crop up as the story continues.

Smokers also had their moments. Two stacks were destroyed at Highfields farm in August 1857 when sixteen-year-old Arthur Plumstead, leaning against a stack, aware that two young ladies were watching, nonchalantly lit his pipe and flung down the lucifer. As he sauntered away, the girls' shouts alerted him that the stack was alight but his frantic efforts to put out the flames failed and fearing the outcry, he made off and hid. Eventually, cold and hungry he turned himself in but does not seem to have been prosecuted. As the 'Essex Standard' rather unnecessarily put it: 'This ought to be a caution for those who are in the habit of lighting their pipes near stacks and farm yards'. *[ES 28/08/1857]*

The rushlight was for centuries a cheap source of light for the poor. Made by soaking the dried pith of a rush in fat or grease, it was held in a specially made stand[9]. In 1853, one was used as a nursery night-light by Coggeshall's Vicar, the Reverend Dampier at the Vicarage in West Street and almost cost the lives of his children:

> 'Between eight and nine o'clock one of the servants incautiously left a rushlight upon a book in the nursery, close to the window and when she returned, found the table on fire, the window curtains in a blaze and the room filled with smoke. The servant having rescued two young children, who were asleep, from the impending danger, gave an alarm, when the inmates were soon on the spot and speedily extinguished the flames. The fire, it is supposed, originated with the candle, which, breaking, fell upon the book and ignited it.' *[CC 28/10/1853]*

---

9   The stands were apparently never mass produced and are now collectors' items, see overleaf.

Lucifers

> **Matchless**
> November 1851
> *The police stationed at Great Coggeshall have held a warrant since September last for the apprehension of Thomas Beckwith of Rivenhall, charged with having obtained two watches under false pretences from Mr James Bennett, watchmaker of Coggeshall, belonging to Challice and Burton, two labourers living in Kelvedon. Although the police have exerted themselves to the utmost they were unsuccessful, until Wednesday last when the following novel mode fully succeeded:- Policemen Smith and Oakley, stationed at Great Coggeshall, disguised themselves in the habit of labourers, having the appearance of being in great distress and selling lucifer matches. Thus equipped they went in search of the delinquent and after scouring the wood and visiting many houses where they disposed of sundry boxes of lucifers, P.c. Smith went to a cottage to solicit a purchase of his matches, when he discovered Beckwith, who had so long eluded the vigilance of other members of the force. Having communicated to him his real occupation and that he was his prisoner, Beckwith appeared quite astounded to find himself caught. Too much praise cannot be given to the police engaged in the capture of this daring character who for some time past has been the terror of the neighbourhood.*
> *[CC 14/11/1851]*

It was a candle that started a blaze in the parlour of William Spurge a tambour master of East Street, in 1854. He was packing lace for London, when a sudden gust of wind blew the curtains into the flame of a candle and 'in a moment they were in a blaze'. *[ES 04/08/1854]* Astonishingly, forty-six years later, William's grandson, James was in the same house and still making tambour lace when he also had a fire. This started in a timber beam running through the chimney. *[CC 07/12/1900]* In both cases, neighbours rushed to help and no major damage was caused.

Suspect Farm Fires in the Teys

The Coggeshall brigade attended a suspected incendiary fire at Bucklers Farm, Great Tey in January 1853:

> 'On Saturday evening at about half-past seven, a fire broke out at Buckles Farm[sic], Great Tey. Immediately on receiving intelligence of the outbreak, Mr Daniel Leaper, the Coggeshall agent of the Essex & Suffolk Fire Office, proceeded with an engine to the scene of the conflagration and with a good supply of water to hand (the wind also being in a favourable direction) was able to preserve the dwelling house, stabling, cow-house, granary, gig-house and piggeries from destruction. The property consumed consisted of a barn (at the back part of which the fire originated), two cattle sheds, stacks of wheat, barley, oats, beans, peas and hay. Six loads of threshed and unthreshed wheat and barn utensils including a threshing and dressing machine, were also destroyed. Every assistance was rendered by labourers and others of the neighbourhood in extinguishing the flames, there being 30 at a time working upon the engine for 10 hours and as many as 300 persons were present at the fire. Suspicions attaching to two young labourers, named George Breed and Alfred Carey, from Coggeshall, they were at once apprehended by Inspector Smith and policeman Sparrow. On Monday they were brought up at the County Magistrates Office and were remanded till Monday. The only motive that can be assigned for the act is the fact of Mr Kemp having had a threshing machine at work on the farm.' *[ES 07/01/1853]*

Rushlight holders.
The holder is in the form of a pair of pliers on a heavy base. The curved arm is a weight to keep the jaws closed.

Note that the report makes particular mention that the labourers were assisting, not hindering the fire-fighting efforts and that the presence of the threshing machine was thought significant. Also evident once again is the number of people helping at the fire, thirty pumpers working the engine for ten hours and three hundred at the fire.

Carey and Breed were occasional labourers at the farm and had been employed for two days on the threshing machine (which like all the early machines was powered by a pair of horses). On the Saturday evening, they were seen in the lane outside the farm gate. A groom who passed by asked them 'What's up?' Breed replied that they were waiting for 'our old man' to come home from Colchester Market so they could collect the wages. Breed asked for a match and the groom gave him two lucifers.

No lucifers were found on the pair when arrested. They said that they had seen the farmer go out to the barn with a 'lanthorn'[10] and they thought that this must have been the cause of the fire.

William Kemp, the farmer, said that when he returned home he paid Breed but was surprised to see Carey as he had 'already settled with him in the morning'. They then asked for a little beer.

> 'I gave Breed a pint which they drank between them. Breed thanked me but Carey seemed very angry and said nothing.'

Carey was later heard to say,

> 'The old beggar hasn't paid me all my money for threshing… I saw the old devil about the yard with a lantern and I said I think he will set fire to something one of these days.'

The two labourers were brought to trial two months later but acquitted by the order of the judge for procedural errors and lack of evidence. Not for the first time, an incident with all the attributes of an incendiary fire was more likely to have been a personal act of retribution or a simple accident. *[ES 04/03/1853]*

Another suspected incendiary fire, this time at Marks Tey[11] shows how quickly the Coggeshall engine turned out under Leaper's superintendence and the perennial problem of fire-fighting in those days with a limited supply of water:

> 'The inhabitants of Marks Tey were thrown into great excitement, in consequence of a fire breaking out in a barn called Hammer Barn. A labourer named Keeble, who with others, had permission to thresh their corn in the barn, left his son to sweep up the corn whilst he went to breakfast. The latter states that while so engaged he heard a crackling noise and saw fire coming out of the barley bay. An alarm having been given, a messenger was dispatched to Coggeshall for a fire-engine and that belonging to the Essex and Suffolk Equitable Society with Mr Leaper, the active agent, was brought to the spot in the short space of 20 minutes: considerable difficulty however

---

10 A now archaic term for a lantern.
11 Just over four miles from Coggeshall on the Colchester Road.

Well Found
On Wednesday morning David Cheek, 4 years of age, son of Charles Cheek, labourer, residing on the Kelvedon-road near Coggeshall, by some means fell down a well, which is used to supply the cottages in that locality with water. A neighbour soon after went for a pail of water and while in the act of winding it up she thought it unusually heavy, when, on looking into the well, to her astonishment, she saw the little fellow clinging to the pail, his face covered with blood. The poor child looked up very pitifully into the face of the woman and said "Don't let me down again:" before, however, he reached the top he became so exhausted that he was obliged to loosen his hold. And he again fell to the bottom, the fall rendering him insensible. The woman gave an alarm which brought to her assistance a labourer named Rootkin, who at once descended the well and rescued the little fellow from a watery grave, there happily being but little water in the well at the time. [CC 08/09/1854]

Woodward's Wayward Assistant
Between 9 and 10 o'clock an assistant of Mr Woodward, ironmonger of this town, very improperly went into the street to try a pistol which he had been repairing, when it exploding, the stock broke in his hand and the barrel was carried a considerable distance, shattering Mr Mounts shop window. No injury was sustained. [CC 10/11/1854]

The Wanderer's Return
A girl named Brown, living about two miles from the town and aged between seven and eight years, was sent by her mother to fetch some yeast from one of the breweries in this place and she had procured it, when she was allured by the sound of a band parading the street: in following the players she mistook the road and reached Marks Tey, instead of the Colne Road. The anxious parents finding she did not return at night, were in great anguish the mother and grandmother coming and giving information to the police here and authorizing the crier to cry her and the distracted father walking the streets with the police in the hope of finding some sign, but in vain. On Thursday morning however due to the indefatigable efforts of the police and the child's friends, it was restored in joy to its parents by a person at Marks Tey, who had kindly fed and sheltered the poor little wanderer. [CC 27/03/1860]

*Bert 'Boxer' Nichols,
a Coggeshall Quoits Champion.*

was experienced in working the engine from the scarcity of water, which had to be conveyed by hand a distance of thirty rods [150m], consequently very little could be done: and the building (with its contents) was entirely consumed.' *[ES 04/10/1854]*

An eight-year-old boy, Charles Pettitt, first denied that he had been anywhere near the barn, then told police constable Heigho that he set fire to it with some lucifers he had from his grandmother. The lad was brought before the magistrates at Colchester Castle where his mother claimed the child had never left the house and was bullied into the admission. This led to the magistrates censuring the woman for hindering police enquiries and pronouncing: 'If lucifer matches were placed out of the reach of children many calamities of this sort might be averted'.
[ES 20/10/1854]

The Water Problem

Daniel Leaper was felled in June 1854 when he put his head into the way of a quoit. He had been enjoying a pint and a game at 'The Greyhound' on Church Street. The quoit was thrown by the correspondent of the 'Essex Standard'. Leaper recovered.

A couple of months later there was a minor blaze at 'The Padlock' just down the road on Church Street. It was started when a servant lit a fire in a bedroom not realising that a chimney board had been fitted to stop draughts:

> 'Mr Leaper, the active agent for the Essex and Suffolk Equitable Office, was promptly on the spot: but the fire was extinguished without having recourse to the engine.' *[ES 18/08/1854]*.

The fire was the first where the question of the town's water supply for fire-fighting was brought up. The quoit throwing 'Essex Standard' correspondent wrote:

> 'There formerly existed a capital reservoir of water, called Church Pond, situated at the top of the street, admirably adapted for use in case of fire and cleansing the streets, but recently, the pond has been filled up and the inhabitants deprived of this important and useful supply. Within the last twelve months, four fires have occurred in this very street, happily attended with little damage: but had they broken out in the night and obtained a hold before they were discovered, the sacrifice must have been great, with little chance of subduing the flames. Few towns in England have the facility of obtaining a good supply of water as that of Coggeshall but for the want of proper arrangement, few places get so badly supplied.' *[ES 18/08/1854]*.

Although the pond had gone, the same underground spring supplied the nearby St Peter's Well, and this was used to good effect in later fires. The problem of water in Coggeshall, both for fire-fighting and for drinking, was to be a continuing and controversial subject that generated nothing but hot air for the next seventy years.

Considerably Surprised

May 1855 saw one of Coggeshall's most destructive fires which broke out in Back Lane behind the Woolpack Inn. At that time, a stable and a row of cottages stood at the top of Back Lane, opposite the alms houses which survive to this day. At 10.45 on that Saturday night, 'The alarm of fire resounded through the streets' and 'several hundreds of people' turned out to see what was going on. The fire had started in the stable at the rear of the inn, this was timber built with tarred weatherboarding and contained a store of straw and wood: 'The whole of the stabling was quickly one mass of flame'. Next to the stable the first cottage was occupied by John Goodson and his family. They were asleep in bed and unaware of the fire until the flames burst through their bedroom wall which, it was reported, left them 'considerably surprised', they escaped still in their night-clothes. Their lath and plaster cottage rapidly went up in flames. In the meantime, the fire engine had arrived with Daniel Leaper. He made his way through the crowds to the fire and left the engineer to set into the water supply, possibly St Peter's well. At this point 'helpers' tried to move the heavy engine into position by pulling the 'hard suction' hose which was fatal because the hose split. With the suction out of action, water had to be poured directly into the engine's cistern using buckets and it did not work well as the pumpers had to work very slowly so as not to outrun the water supply. The fire was some distance away and only a thin jet of water emerged from the branch, quite lost in the inferno of the fire. With this 'very scanty' water supply the next two cottages occupied by Haywood and Humphreys were threatened and Leaper had the roofs pulled off to 'check the raging element'. This and the continuing work of the crowd throwing buckets of water on the buildings eventually proved successful and in the early hours of the morning, the fire was finally subdued. Of the three cottages, one was destroyed and the others severely damaged by fire, water and demolition.

The 'Woolpack' fire. View of the top of Back Lane with the church beyond c1910. The stable and cottages would have been to the right of the horse and cart. The 'rescued' furniture was thrown into the church yard.

> 'A few articles of furniture were got out and thrown into the churchyard but most of them were more or less broken in the hurry of the occasion. We understand that a subscription is to be raised to help these poor creatures and we have no doubt it will meet with general support.' *[ES & CC 11/05/1855]*

All the properties were insured but the meagre possessions of the tenants were not, as the 'Standard' put it 'They will be the great losers in the unfortunate occurrence.'

The engine was examined by Mr Bland, chief clerk of the Essex & Suffolk on his annual inspection a few days later. He found it to be in excellent working order, its paint and brass-works highly polished, a testament to Daniel Leaper's care and attention. The Fire Office immediately ordered two fire hooks and three hatchets for the Coggeshall brigade, items which may have been on Leaper's 'most wanted' list after his experience at the Woolpack fire. A reward perhaps for his good work. *[E&SE MB5 19/05/1855]*

*The Long Bridge with the ford running alongside. The Short Bridge, which crosses the Back Ditch, can just be seen to the right of the tree and marks the boundary between Great and Little Coggeshall.
The ford is where the engine would be placed for testing, especially it seems on warm summer nights.*

Warm Friends

In the 1850s the Coggeshall Society of Friends met in an old house, on the same plot of land as the present building (now the library). One cold Sunday in November 1854 the iron stove which stood at its centre was stoked up and the flue set the roof alight to the 'considerable excitement' of those gathered inside. A ladder was pitched and work started to strip the roof of its slate to expose the burning timbers beneath, the flames threatening to spread to the adjoining brewery which was partly thatched. The engine turned out under Daniel Leaper, 'prepared for any emergency' *[ES 01/11/1854]* but could not be worked as there was no suitable water supply. So a bucket chain was set up involving forty to fifty people drawing water from the brewery supply and to the great relief of all, the fire was finally defeated.

A newspaper report of the account concludes:

'Had it not been for the prompt assistance thus rendered by the mechanics and labourers, the building must have been entirely consumed, if not the whole street.' *[ES 01 & 03/11/1854]*

In identifying the 'mechanics and labourers' (the labouring classes) the report discloses the same anxiety as to their loyalties here, as was evident in the attention given to their behaviour at incendiary fires.

The roof had only just been expensively repaired when on another Sunday morning just four months later the iron chimney set the roof alight again. In a marvellously ecumenical gesture, people walking to both Church and Chapel joined forces to defeat a common foe. Some twenty-three years later in 1878, the old house was demolished and the present building put up by Mathias Gardner.

A Labourer's Life

The engine was called to a fire involving two cottages near Chalkney Wood in August 1856. The fire had reached the upper part of the buildings by the time the brigade arrived and with little water available the fire spread inexorably. Leaper decided that his only course was to demolish part of the burning building to establish a fire break and this undoubtedly saved a second row of cottages. The owner of the burnt out cottages was an old man called Humphrey Willis. He had occupied one of them, his son-in-law and family, the other. The report gives a tantalising glimpse of a life being lived:

> 'The greater part of the furniture was saved but among the things burnt were a quantity of livestock including two pigs some rabbits and guinea pigs. It is stated that a short time before the fire, Willis, who is very old and feeble, was seen smoking his pipe in an out building and it is conjectured that some of the ashes may have fallen from his pipe and ignited the straw. The poor old man has sustained a most severe loss, the premises not being insured.' [ES 01/08/1856]

As noted earlier, although the property was uninsured the Essex & Suffolk paid the costs of fighting the fire.

Practice at the River

A letter from the Essex & Suffolk to one of their agents, allows that their engine might be set into water twice a year to 'test its operation' and that half the usual number of pumpers, 'will be enough to work it for amusement, half an hour or an hour at a time', at a payment of 2s each man. [Drew p45] Leaper tested the Coggeshall engine in this way in the river at the Long Bridge where a ford allowed it to be safely run into the water.

> 'On Wednesday evening a little girl was knocked down by the horse of John Cleveland, whilst trying to avoid the water from the fire engine practising at the river. Happily her injuries are confined to a few bruises.' [ES 04/08/1854]

Not for the Squeamish

Sawing

A severe accident occurred on Friday last to a youth named William Crosby working at the silk factory belonging to J P Hall Esq. While he was in the act of pushing some timber through a large circular saw, worked by steam, for the purpose of its being cut, his hand coming into contact with the saw, was nearly severed in two. [CC 30/11/1854]

Thrashing

On Wednesday last, George Boor, a labourer employed with a thrashing machine at Oldfield Grange, the residence of Osgood Hanbury Esq., was in the act of oiling one of the pivots whilst the machine was in motion, when the sleeve of his frock coat caught in the spindle and drew his arm between the wheels, by which it was most fearfully crushed and the hand was nearly severed from the wrist. Mr Giles, the surgeon, was promptly in attendance and finding the operation indispensable, skilfully amputated the arm just below the elbow. We are glad to state that the poor man is going on favourably. [CC 08/12/1854]

Screaming

On Tuesday, a serious accident occurred to Emma Cook, a girl in the employ of Mr. J. Hall & Son, Orchard Silk Mills, Coggeshall. By some means her frock became caught in the cogs of the machinery and her arm being drawn in, it was fearfully crushed. She was attended by Messrs Giles & Hart, surgeons, who extracted a number of pieces of bone and she is at present in a critical state, as should amputation be superseded a stiff arm for the rest of her life must be the consequence. By an admirable arrangement, a bell is rung immediately any scream is heard and the machinery stopped or the consequences would have been even more serious. [EH 05/10/1858]

Pulping

A boy named Webb, 14 years old, in the employ of Walter Dennis, Maltbeggars Farm, got his hand crushed in a root pulping machine. Two fingers of the right hand were smashed: one has been amputated by Mr Simpson, the other it is hoped, may be saved. [EN 16/02/1878]

> ### Riding on the Shafts
>
> *John Rootkin, in the employ of Mr John Halls, of Coggeshall was returning from Colchester with a wain load of coals and when he arrived at Broad Green, in the parish of Great Tey, he by some means slipped off the shafts and fell under the wheels, which passed over his body, crushing his ribs in a frightful manner. Several persons saw the accident and were quickly on the spot, but the poor fellow instantly expired.*
> [ES 11/12/1847]
>
> *William Amos, horseman to Osgood Hanbury Esq, Holfield Grange, was riding on the shafts of his masters wagon, when, in attempting to get down in West Street, he fell and two wheels of the wagon passed over his back. It is feared that his back is broken and the issue is deemed by his medical attendant very doubtful.* [CC 03/08/1855]
>
> *A man named Wade, in the employ of Mr. Joseph Unwin, of Bourchier's Grange, met with severe accident. The harvestmen were returning with an empty wagon and Wade was attempting to ride on the shaft and caught hold of the front ladder to raise himself, but this giving way fell the ground, the fore wheel of the wagon passing over the back of his head, inflicting a terrible wound. He was conveyed home in a tumbrel ....but as he is 65 years of age, it is feared his recovery will be slow. It should be stated that Wade was quite sober at the time of the accident.*
> [EH 27/08/1876]
>
> *Riding on the shafts was a regular cause of accidents and death. Although the practice was illegal, it was commonly done, so that many of those who had charge of wagons had a conviction for the offence. The Haverhill agricultural show included a prize for Horsekeepers - 'For having served the longest period in that capacity, with the same employer and upon the same farm, not having been convicted of riding on the shafts.'*

It was a warm August evening and no doubt the test degenerated into horseplay but the incident shows Leaper's professional management of the engine. The time would come when this day to day care would be noticed but only by its absence.

A Fine Body of Men

In 1857 Daniel Leaper's son William took over the 'Greyhound Inn' on Church Street. Like his father, William Leaper seems to have been an active, likeable and hard working man. Daniel Leaper had become Coggeshall's principal funeral director, an occupation which probably developed from coffin making for which his woodworking and upholstery skills were well suited[12]. William was solicitous of his father who in 1857, was sixty-one years old and although he had no ambitions as a fireman himself, began to accompany him to fires. When a call came, William's customers in the Greyhound may have translated into firemen and encouraged to make their way to the Engine House and to glory. For the drinkers the enterprise might be seen more as a change of venue than a career choice and unlike the pub, the beer at a fire was free!

Hamlet Brewery Saved

In May 1857 Leaper and his firemen were called to a fire threatening a brewery in the Hamlet. The premises probably adjoined Hamlet House and both were owned by Samuel Skingley. The fire started in a stack of straw in the next door field;

> 'A messenger was despatched to inform Mr. Leaper, ...who at once proceeded with the engine. By the time he arrived, the fire was making great progress and eventually spread to two other straw stacks standing near by, which were consumed; but by the strenuous exertions of the firemen a large stack of wheat and the brewery, which is built of timber and thatch, and stands but a few yards from where the fire raged, were saved from destruction'.
> [CC 15/05/1857]

The brigade had a good amount of hose as they set into the river, two hundred yards from the stacks. It was ten hours before the fires were extinguished and the pumpers could stop work.

---

12   Daniel Leaper arranged the funerals of Osgood Hanbury of Holfield Grange in 1852 & William Honywood of Markshall in 1859

Stoneham Street from Market Hill.

Leaper Doubly Confounded

In March 1859, a range of outbuildings caught fire at Hungry Hall, situated in a remote location on the boundary with the neighbouring parish of Earls Colne. A messenger was sent the three miles to Coggeshall for the engine and Daniel Leaper with his son 'and a body of men' were quickly on their way. They found that the barns and other outbuildings were already one mass of flames. The newspaper report continues:

> 'Mr Leaper, on his arrival, with praiseworthy exertion, rendered every assistance and soon brought the engine to play upon the buildings. The wind fortunately lay in a contrary direction to the house and other sheds and much property was consequently saved. Before he left the still smouldering remains, Leaper left strict injunctions that they should be kept constantly doused with water.'

The farmer ignored this advice with the result that the fire broke out again. Too embarrassed to face Leaper, he called out the Courtauld's factory engine from Halstead instead. *[CC 11/03/1859]*

The Leapers, both father and son, appeared in a curious newspaper report in June 1858 which discloses something of their character and relationship as well as the pride Daniel had in the fire engine:

> 'A very respectfully dressed young man called on Mr. Leaper jnr., who keeps The Greyhound Inn, Church-street and in course of conversation stated that.... he had been in the employ of Messrs Merryweather and Co for ten or eleven years and foreman over forty or fifty men the last two or three. While chatting, Mr Leaper senior called on his son who was introduced. The stranger being a young man of good address and from his conversation appearing to understand machinery,

Mr Leaper took him to see the town engine, manufactured by the above named firm. ...and then to see his house and garden where he was joined by Mr. Leaper junior and plentifully regaled with strawberries after which he again visited the Greyhound and called for some brandy and water which he just tasted and bade the landlord a hasty farewell ....The abrupt manner in which the young engineer left the house after the kind treatment he had received, induced Mr. Leaper to follow him to the door and watch him. Instead of going in the direction of the Chapel Inn ..., he went towards the house of Mr. Leaper Senior where .... he was invited to partake of some refreshment and re-entering the parlour, drank a glass of wine, after which he took his leave. He, however, no sooner had reached the front door, accompanied by Mr. Leaper, when he turned back with the exclamation, 'I have left my handkerchief'. At that time a sovereign and seven five shilling pieces were lying on the mantelpiece but were missed when Mr. Leaper was about to retire to rest. It being suspected that the very amiable stranger had borrowed them, Inspector Scott was informed of the affair.' *[EH 29/06/1858]*

The amiable stranger, Thomas Ritchie, was tracked down that night in Braintree and was eventually brought to trial but after twenty minutes' consideration, the jury found him not guilty and he was discharged. *[ES 02/07/1858]*

Explosion at Walter Good's

Mr Walter Good, a tailor and hatter of Stoneham Street had been working late one January night in 1864 and it was midnight when he put out the gas and went to have supper with his wife and niece. A strong smell of gas became apparent and they all went to the shop to investigate. Walter climbed onto the counter to examine a large gas burner which had never worked well. Mrs Good had just placed her hand on the gas meter 'when there was a terrible explosion', which brought the ceiling of the shop down and set fire to the paper in which the hats were wrapped. One of the shop windows was blown out and glass, coats and hats were thrown to the other

Availed Himself of the Delay
On Saturday afternoon, two boys named Ager and Kellick, were playing together in Stock Street in this town when the former took up a gun and threatened to shoot the latter, but finding no cap on, the latter availed himself of the delay by taking to his heels, which, there is little doubt, saved his life, as Ager on capping the gun, fired after him, lodging some shot in his neck and head, but happily not deep enough to prove of serious consequences. [EH 04/05/1858]

Bird Scaring Powder
On Friday evening, the eldest daughter of Francis Hunwick, blacksmith, of Coggeshall, after having supplied a boy who was scaring birds for her father with gunpowder from a drawer in the house, was incautiously carrying a quantity of the explosive compound loose in a paper in one hand and a lighted candle in the other, when a spark is supposed to have fallen upon the powder and the young woman, being clad in a light dress, was at once enveloped in flames. Her hands, arms and face were dreadfully burned, but Mr Giles, surgeon, was immediately summoned and we are happy to add that under his care she is doing well. [CC 04/09/1863]

To Shoot a Guinea Fowl
It appears that a guinea fowl belonging to Mr Rowland of the Yorkshire Grey had escaped from his yard and lighted on the top of a house opposite. After a fruitless attempt to get it off, Joseph Ardley of this town took a gun to shoot at it when the gun burst and blew his thumb and two fingers off. The other part of his hand is so shattered that fears are entertained by his medical attendant that it will be amputated.
[Suffolk and Essex Free Press 16/12/1858]

Maidservant 1 Burglars 0
Abbey Farm House...The maid-servant states that on hearing a noise at about eleven o'clock in the evening she looked out of the chamber window when she saw a man in the act of entering the parlour window with a second standing at a little distance as if on watch. She immediately procured her master's gun which she fortunately found loaded, opened the window and fired at one of the fellows but though her courage was good her aim was defective, the burglars making off.
[EH 02/10/1855]

side of the street. Mr Bright, the brewery owner, had just passed the shop and was uninjured but considerably surprised.

> 'The blast passed along a passage past Mrs Good at the meter, to the third in a row of windows in the kitchen, which it smashed completely out...and from thence, like electricity found its way upstairs to a room where a son of Mr Good was sleeping, passing harmlessly by him and forcing a third window out to a great distance with terrific force.'

Walter's eyebrows and whiskers were burnt off and his face 'otherwise disfigured': he was so traumatised that it was some time before he recovered. Mrs Good was uninjured but the niece, although standing at some distance, 'had her hair net much burnt.'
[EWN 14/01/1864 & EC 15/01/1864]

In trying to discover the source of the leak, Mr Good had opened the doors to ventilate the shop, and then and this was his big mistake, 'incautiously procured a lighted candle and with it proceeded to examine the hydraulic burner'.
[ES 13/01/1864]

Crime and Punishment

On the afternoon of 27th May 1863, a labourer attending to his horses at Godbolts Farm, Little Tey, saw that a stack of straw in a nearby field was on fire. He raised the alarm and the fire was confined to two stacks. Suspicion fell on a tramp who was soon detained. John Witham, described as a labourer, was brought to trial in July 1863 and pleaded guilty. Also in court at the same time were four others also found guilty of the same offence at various farms in Essex:

> 'The learned Judge in sentencing the prisoners said he was not altogether without some sort of pity for them, but it was really a most abominable crime they had been guilty of. He could satisfy them that if they thought of living an easy life, being well fed and having little to do, they would be miserably disappointed. They would be made slaves of and punished with the utmost severity that humanity would allow. They were all sentenced to 10 years penal servitude.' [ES 05/06/1863 & CC 17/07/1863]

The Great Fire at Great Tey

Late September 1864 saw a dramatic fire at Great Tey. It started in a stable behind The Street when a lantern was tipped over and the candle fell out onto some straw. There were two horses, pigs and ducks in the stable but the fire spread so quickly that only one of the horses escaped. The fire spread to a barn and outbuildings and Mr Golden Gooday rode 'with all speed' the four miles to Coggeshall where Leaper with his usual dispatch had the engine horsed, crewed and underway in minutes. Alongside Daniel Leaper and his son, 'about a dozen firemen were immediately got ready'. On arrival the engine was quickly brought into full play 'working admirably' but once again, water was a problem. The locals did what they could to keep the engine supplied via a bucket chain but despite their efforts, burning brands aided by a strong wind, were blown over two tiled houses to catch the thatch of the cottages beyond. Even as the roof was burning above, the occupiers and neighbours were running in and out to rescue furniture and effects but 'within minutes' the cottages were a heap of smoking ruins. 'The street was a scene of great confusion being filled with the goods and chattels of the sufferers and their neighbours'. [CC 30/09/1864 & ES 5/10/1864]

The village suffered a further loss just four months later. Great Tey windmill was at work on a stormy afternoon in January 1865 but as it grew dark the wind strengthened and the sails 'got away'. Under enormous pressure, friction from the brake started a fire and before long the whole mill was ablaze, the fiery sails turning in the dark sky providing an awesome spectacle. The Coggeshall brigade arrived but could do nothing except damp down the debris when the fire had burnt itself out. [ES 13/01/1865, B&NP 24/01, E&SE MB5]

Whilst it was business as usual for Daniel Leaper and the Coggeshall brigade, a huge fire in 1861 was bringing dramatic developments to the London Fire Insurance Offices.

5   A TIME OF CHANGE

The Great Fire at Tooley Street 1861

In 1833, ten of the London Fire Offices had combined their resources to set up and fund 'The London Fire Engine Establishment'. Usually called 'the Establishment'. It was an efficient and well run organisation, largely due to its famous and charismatic chief, James Braidwood.

On Saturday 22nd June 1861, a fire broke out in stored hemp at Scovell's Warehouse in Tooley Street. Developing rapidly, it spread to other warehouses alongside the Thames and became the biggest fire in London since 1666. The Thames itself seemed to be alight as melted tallow flowed out of one of the warehouses and burned on the surface of the river. People watching from small boats were drawn into these flames by the tide and engulfed, to the horror of those watching on London Bridge. Nearly every engine in London was called in and messages for assistance were sent into the country for yet more machines. It was estimated some 30,000 people came to watch the spectacle.

Tragically, Braidwood was killed during the fire when a warehouse wall collapsed on him. His body was not recovered for two days and it was fourteen days before the fire was finally extinguished. The whole country went into mourning for Braidwood, huge crowds lined the streets to watch his funeral procession which was a mile and a half in length.

The fire and Braidwood's death marked a turning point for the insurance brigades. They had been providing London with universal fire cover, yet it was estimated that only a third of properties were insured. The number of fires

James Braidwood, Chief of the London Fire Engine Establishment for 38 years.

had increased dramatically and reached 1,400 in 1864. It was said that there were more fires in London than in Paris, St Petersburg, Berlin, Vienna and Philadelphia combined. *[CC 02/06/1865]* The Tooley Street fire alone had cost the insurance companies the enormous sum of two million pounds and in the aftermath of the fire, they served notice that they were going to pull out of the fire brigade business. They saw their future in insurance, not fire fighting. They made that determination quite clear to the Government who set up a Select Committee to investigate.

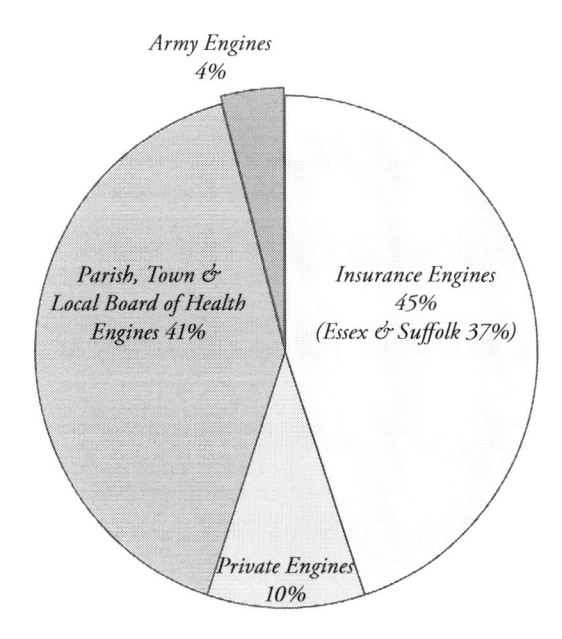

Ownership of Engines Attending Essex Fires in 1868
Source: Essex fires reported in the 'Essex Chronicle'.
For full details see Appendix V

- Army Engines 4%
- Parish, Town & Local Board of Health Engines 41%
- Insurance Engines 45% (Essex & Suffolk 37%)
- Private Engines 10%

One of the witnesses, Mr Newmarch of 'The Globe' Insurance company said:

'There was not the smallest moral obligation on the Offices .... to continue the Establishment, the public should be much obliged to them for having born the expense so long without grumbling... It was no more part of the business of the fire offices to maintain a fire brigade than of the life offices to maintain physicians...'

New legislation was brought forward to set up the 'Metropolitan Fire Brigade', largely funded from the public purse, but with a significant contribution from the fire offices, although this amounted to less than half of what they previously paid for the Establishment. Another remarkable man, Sir Eyre Massey Shaw was the first Chief Officer of the new brigade. He thought that, 'the Committee took the advice of all who were in a position to offer any and many who were not'. *[Quoted in Blackstone p165]* The Bill, whose provisions only covered London, was enacted in 1865.

The Different Situation in Essex
...Other brigades

In Essex, the Fire Offices were not the only providers of fire protection. Although they attended the most fires, around 45% of the total, the various public bodies such as parish and town councils and local board engines attended almost as many, at around 41%. Private and army brigades account for the rest.

Of the fires attended by the Fire Offices, The Essex & Suffolk Equitable was by far the biggest provider, the other offices with engines in Essex at this time, The Manchester, The Sun and The Phoenix attended just a few fires a year. (See chart)

...The Cost of Engines

So how much did the Essex & Suffolk pay to provide the county with fire engines? In terms of money spent, the average annual cost was £206 in the 1850s and slowly increased to £212 in the 1870s and £274 in the 1890s[1]. These amounts are small compared to what the company paid out in fire insurance claims. In 1856 fire claims were almost £5,000 and the cost of the engines was £202 (4%), in 1870 fires losses exceeded £11,000 the engines cost £160 (1.4%), in 1882 the fire losses were over £17,000 the engines cost £251 (1.5%). (Outgoings over two very different years are shown in more detail overleaf.)

The real cost of the Essex & Suffolk brigades is probably best understood when compared to the Essex & Suffolk's income and this proportion declines between 1850 and 1900. In the 1850s the engines on average cost 1.8% of income in the 1870s, 1% and in the 1890s, 0.9%.[2] If the Essex & Suffolk had followed the lead of the London Offices and pulled out of the fire brigade business, the savings would have been minimal.

---
1   The increase may have been partly due to inflation.
2   Taken from the Essex & Suffolk annual accounts.

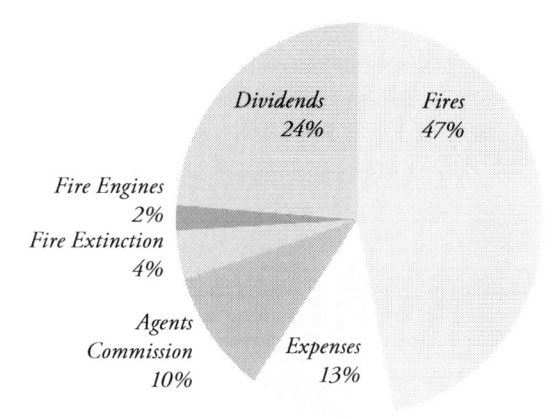

Essex & Suffolk Outgoings 1856
Total Outgoings £10,000, Extinction £400, Engines £202
Source: E&S Annual Accounts [LMA CLC/B/107/MS16206/01-08]

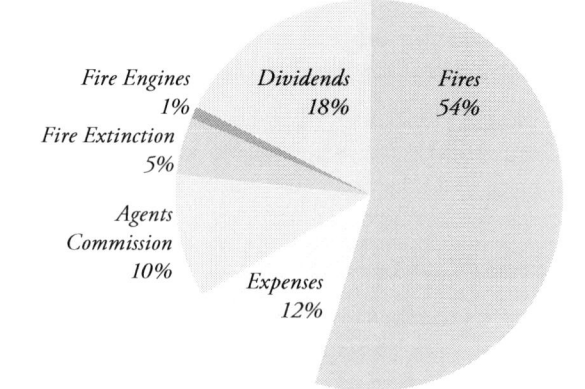

Essex & Suffolk Outgoings 1873
Total Outgoings £17,000, Extinction £800, Engines £170
Source: E&S Annual Accounts [LMA CLC/B/107/MS16206/01-08]

...The Cost of Fire Extinction

The major expense of fire extinction however was not the cost of the engines but the people; paying the firemen, pumpers and helpers. In London the fire offices had been funding an expensive round the clock, full time fire service. By contrast, the provincial insurers like the Essex & Suffolk had a low cost service, only paying out when there was a fire.

So what were the costs? Smaller fires were relatively expensive, the second fire at Coggeshall's Meeting House in 1854 resulted in a claim of £1 12s to repair the building but almost as much, £1 10s, was paid to the people who put it out. A clamp of mangel-worzels in Little Coggeshall which was destroyed by fire in 1855 was valued at £2 and cost 14s to put out. For the larger fires, the proportion reduces, that at Harlow in 1832, where so much beer was drunk, had an insurance payout of £150 and extinction expenses of £13. Leaper's first fire in 1839 had an insurance claim of £125 and cost less than £7 to extinguish, the Inworth fire of 1851 with two brigades, was expensive to put out at £28 and £200 of property destroyed. Using the limited information in the Essex & Suffolk minutes suggests that the average extinction cost was around 8% of the total insurance claim. This was a relatively minor part of the total outgoings of the company: fire losses, the annual dividend, general expenses and agents' commission all take a greater proportion of the total (see charts).

Extinction costs may have been minor but they were still significant, so why did the fire offices continue to pay? For the majority of fires there was no question that paying to extinguish a fire was well worth it. The extinguishing costs at the Coggeshall Meeting House fire may have doubled the bill to around £3 but this is a fraction of the claim that would have resulted had the place burned down. Even at a farm fire, the value of saving just one stack[3] would outweigh the relatively minor cost of having a brigade in attendance for hours at a stretch. Labour was cheap, the seventy people who worked at Leaper's first fire in 1839 were paid £6 13s and saved a farmhouse. The 'expensive' Inworth fire may have cost £28 to put out but several valuable stacks were saved. Although the fire offices discussed the principle of pulling out of the fire brigade business, self interest meant that they remained content to pay the costs of fire extinction and continued to do so well into the twentieth century.

---

3   Two stacks of corn destroyed by fire in Dagenham, Essex in 1839 were valued at £200 *[CC 27/09/1839]*

An Imperfect System

The system of insurance brigades was not without tensions and these were as much about 'fair play' as they were about money. Problems were first reported in 1843 when the Essex & Suffolk had used its engines and men to extinguish fires in premises insured by another company, who then refused to reimburse them. *[E&SE MB3 25/08/1843]* Most fire insurance companies accepted the responsibility for extinguishing expenses and paid up but others refused and ignored all correspondence on the matter, leaving the Essex & Suffolk out of pocket. It was especially galling of course, because by putting out a fire, the Essex & Suffolk had reduced the amount of the subsequent claim, to the benefit of the other insurance company:

> 'Even so respectable a Corporation as the Royal Exchange had refused to pay expenses'.
> *[ES 05/05/1867]*

Drew asserts that this is because the London insurers had a haughty and disdainful view of the provincial offices – they would not, as it were, give the Essex & Suffolk 'the time of day'. *[Drew]* Whatever the reason, it made no commercial sense for the Essex & Suffolk to go to the expense of putting out fires in premises insured by such a company, so unless arrangements had been made, they decided not to do so. In 1855, a fire broke out in the warehouse of Mr Horatio Bunting, an old-established seed company in Lexden Road, Colchester:

> 'The engine of the Essex and Suffolk was speedily got out and the firemen were mustered and four horses from the Cups Hotel were in readiness awaiting the order to start when a messenger arrived from the office and informed them that they must not proceed..... This order arose, we are informed, from the fact that no written or special application had been made to the office requiring the engine; a regulation which... has been adopted by the office, it having previously sustained considerable loss in dispatching engines to fires at premises not insured therein and the subsequent denial by the occupiers or owners of the property that they sent for their assistance, with a refusal to pay the expenses.' *[CC 23/02/1855]*

The building was left to burn – the premises had been insured but with the 'Sun' Fire Office.

In 1858 children playing with lucifers, started a fire at Langham and the Essex & Suffolk engine at Colchester was called:

> 'But the premises not being insured in that office and there being no guarantee that expenses would be paid, the engine was not sent.' *[EC 14/05/1858]*

In October 1866, the Fire Office took out an advert in the 'Chelmsford Chronicle' to explain themselves:

> 'On frequent occasions in which their engines have been employed in extinguishing fires where the property has been insured in other offices, the Directors have been unable to recover the expenses unavoidably incurred, they are under the necessity of announcing that in future whenever the property is insured in any office other than their own, the parties engaging the engine will be required to pay the expenses or give a guarantee for the payment before its departure and also £2. 2s. for the use of the same.' *[CC 26/10/1866]*

Alongside this more robust stance toward those who *would not* pay, is evidence of a change in providing engines to those who *could not* pay. In 1846 the Essex & Suffolk restated their position, 'in all cases of alarm of fire, when the spot is ascertained, an engine be sent'. *[E&SE MB4 03/04/1846]* In contrast is the situation described by the 'Chelmsford Chronicle' in 1865:

> 'The position assumed by the fire-offices must be taken into consideration. They are very chary of sending out their engines except for the protection of their own risks and this was a cause of some delay on the present occasion, so that if a fire breaks out in a cottage uninsured and occupied by a person of insufficient responsibility to order an engine, the use of the engine might be denied.' *[CC 17/03/1865]*

The 'person of insufficient responsibility' is of course, code for someone who did not have the wherewithal to pay - the poor. Even if the key phrase is, '*might* be denied' not '*would* be denied', this is quite a change.

The problem received a very public airing in May 1867. There had been a major fire in Colchester High Street, but difficulties arose the day afterwards. Debris in one of the buildings re-ignited and the Police hurried to the Engine House to call out the brigade, but were referred to the Essex & Suffolk office in the High Street. According to the Police account, when they arrived there, Mr Bland the Clerk, 'Refused to have the engine brought out until he knew who would be responsible for the expense', an account later disputed by Mr Bland. The circumstances became such an issue that the Borough Council decided to formally investigate the matter and Mr Bland, the police and the owners of the properties were brought before them.

In the event, the Council accepted Bland's account, that there was no question, on this occasion, of the engine not attending but only because the property involved was insured with the Essex & Suffolk. Bland took the opportunity to explain the continuing problem of other Fire Offices refusing to reimburse expenses. Answering a question from the distinguished Councillor, Mr Tabor, Bland reiterated what had become company policy. Tabor asked, 'What would be done if a private individual went for the engine?' Bland answered, 'If a Gentleman says he will pay the working expenses, I will always send it.' Bland was making it quite clear that the Essex & Suffolk provided a commercial service – not a public one. Colchester Borough Council, on the other hand of course did have a public responsibility and Bland made sure they understood the point:

> 'It was a very serious matter for a town like Colchester to be dependent upon an Insurance Office for fire engines.' *[ES 05/05/1867]*

There was probably some satisfaction at the 'Essex & Suffolk' that this central point had been made clearly and publicly – that the council should take responsibility for fire protection in

---

Less Than Perfect

The parish engine at Walthamstow produced so little water it was nicknamed 'The Squirt': one at Ongar was 'of the first class', but when called to a fire at Kelvedon Hall in 1863, it would not pump water. [CC 17/04/1863] Called to a fire at Dunmow Workhouse 'the engines ....were found to be useless' [CC03/02/1843]. The Epping parish engine was called out in February 1868 'but was of little avail'. [CC 21/02/1868] A new Superintendent at Stratford in 1856 had repaired the engine at his own expense but not been paid, so when a fire broke out, he 'positively refused to allow it to go until he knew what remuneration was to obtain', no assurances were given so the engine stayed in the station. [CC 07/11/1856]. At a fire in Chadwell Heath in 1868 messages were sent for assistance to the West Ham parish engine but the Superintendent refused to go, being on instruction not to take the engine outside the parish. A request to Bow parish brigade met with the same response but the private engine of the Ind Coope Brewery of Romford did attend. [CC 10/04/1868]. In 1856, Witham had engines but no Superintendent or regular firemen. When called to a fire at Rivenhall: 'Some parties took possession of the branch and occasionally amused themselves by turning water on some unfortunate person instead of endeavouring to quench the flames and when spoken to, refused to give up the charge to parties who were better able to direct the same.' [CC 05/09/1856]. In 1887 the whole of the Dengie Hundred had just one fire engine at Southminster 'a totally useless machine that looks as if it came out of the ark'. When a fire broke out at Tillingham, no one bothered to send for it. The nearest engine was at Maldon, fourteen miles away and they would not attend as they were prohibited to go more than seven miles from the town.[EN 20/09/1887]. Tollesbury had no engine and did not know about the rule, so when a major farm fire broke out: 'visible for many miles around', a telegram was sent to Maldon, nine miles away. There was no reply and the engine, expected by the minute never arrived. All efforts at salvage were abandoned and the huge crowd looked on as the buildings burnt to the ground, the embers damped down by heavy rain. [ES 03/09/1887]

Firemen running out leather hose during a fire brigade competition, Westcliff on Sea, Essex c1865.

their town. However, for the Directors of the Essex & Suffolk, the episode, in hindsight, had an unsavoury air of overt commercialism about it, not really in keeping with its patrician roots. Conversations must have taken place among the Board members and the policy was reconsidered. The revision was explained by the Chairman at the Annual General Court of the Essex & Suffolk, in April 1869.

> 'He was sorry that occasionally they received such conduct from other offices as greatly astonished them and almost made them decide that their engines should be reserved for their own insurers: but such a reflection would be cast upon humanity by their withholding the use of their engines when life might be in jeopardy, that they had decided, with certain restrictions …they should be at the service of the public (hear hear!) and that the office was entitled to some recognition on that point (hear hear!).' *[ES 07/05/1869]*

The episode demonstrates that the factors that brought about change in London, are also being felt in Essex. For the first time, questions are being raised publicly about the role of fire offices and public bodies in providing fire protection. For the time being, the Essex & Suffolk maintained their network of engines and brigades, the fact that there was no-one else to do the job made it difficult for them to withdraw and leave people unprotected. Even after the High Street fire inquiry Colchester Borough Council took no action, the cost probably discouraged them and as long as the Essex & Suffolk provided the service free of charge, there was no pressing need. Underlying all this was the fact that the government had not seen fit to legislate, which left the Borough free of any legal obligation.

Other fire offices worked under different constraints. The first of the 'local' insurance companies to extricate itself from the business of fire protection was the Manchester Fire Office[4]. They had no interest in continuing with their Chelmsford brigade, so in 1869 they wrote to a newly created public body, the Chelmsford Local Board of Health, offering their engine and appliances free of charge. The Board accepted the offer and engaged two of the firemen.
[CC 03/09/1869]

Other Essex Brigades

With no legislation, monitoring or control, the provision of fire engines and brigades in the mid nineteenth century was a tribute to free enterprise. As we have mentioned, there were still many parish engines of various sizes and conditions and in the larger towns, some of these were being taken over by the newly established Local Boards of Health[5]. As well as Chelmsford, both Braintree and Halstead had 'Board of Health' engines by the 1860s. In addition there were several volunteer brigades, usually with engines bought by public subscription and included those at Bardfield, Leytonstone, Brentwood and Southend and eventually at Colchester. Several large businesses had engines and brigades of their own, including Courtaulds at Halstead and Bocking, Hoffmans and the

---

4 They were 'local' because they took over the business and engine of the Chelmsford based 'Essex Economic', when that Office was dissolved in 1857.

5 These were set up as a result of the Local Government Acts 1848-1858.

Robert Anderson, Secretary of the Essex & Suffolk Equitable Insurance Co. 1868–1902.

Writtle Brewery at Chelmsford and the Ind Coope Brewery at Romford. There were some private engines belonging to landed gentry; Octavius Mashiter Esq. had an engine in 1852 which was kept at his farm in Hornchurch, Audley End House had its own machine, as did Stisted Hall, near Coggeshall. Felsted School had an engine and brigade with the pupils acting as firemen. The military at both Colchester and Warley Barracks had engines and would turn out with a body of soldiers to fight 'civilian' fires. The connection with beer drinking seems to have developed beyond that at Coggeshall and brought to its ultimate conclusion at Leaden Roding (then called Roothing), where the 'King William IV' Inn had its own engine and brigade and successfully attended a thatch fire at 'Aythorpe Roothing' in January 1854.

Although many of these brigades were well organised and run, at least as many were not. The absence of any legal requirements or standards and the lack of regulation and inspection of these disparate brigades meant that fire protection remained a lottery.

New Broom at the Essex & Suffolk

The day-to-day business of the 'Essex & Suffolk' had been the responsibility of its Secretary of sixteen years, George Bawtree. Although well liked and respected, he had been dogged by poor health for the whole of his service. When he retired there was a short interregnum, then in 1868 Robert Anderson was appointed Secretary. He was a man of great ability and strength of character, methodical, good at assessing risks and clear in his advice, he slowly brought about a change in the finances of the company. He saw the opening of new agencies and overhauled policy conditions and premium rates.

Coggeshall: The End of an Era

Daniel Leaper had enjoyed years of success as superintendent of the Essex & Suffolk brigade but at seventy-three, he must have been thinking of retirement. On 16th December 1868, his wife Marie died in her 74th year, 'after a long affliction'. She was buried two days before Christmas. In March the next year, Leaper attended two serious fires, just days apart, that would have been physically challenging even for a younger man and these probably sealed his conviction to retire.

The first of these fires, on Monday 1st March 1869, was caused by an exploding steam engine at Walcotts, Great Tey. The fire that resulted threatened the destruction of both the hall and the extensive farm buildings adjoining it. A messenger was dispatched to Coggeshall for the 'Essex & Suffolk' engine which was soon at the scene along with the fire brigade, superintended as ever, by Daniel Leaper. Leaper found that two barns and three stacks of corn were well alight. The fire had a good hold and 'raged with such fury' that it was thought the Hall was going to be lost and frantic efforts were made to move the furniture and contents to a place of safety. Importantly, there was a good and plentiful

Church Street c1916
The entrance to Beard's Maltings and Brewery was beyond the tall building on the right, now the Conservative Club. The dropped kerb allowed wagons to pass under the arch and into a yard and premises behind.

supply of water from a pond. The blazing barns were linked to the Hall by a stable and coach-house and these became the focus of the brigade's attention. Every time the brigade knocked down the flames, they re-ignited in the intense heat but eventually the firemen gained the upper hand. The stable and coach house suffered superficial damage and the Hall was untouched – the result, it was reported, of 'the praiseworthy efforts of the brigade'. *[CC 05/03/1869]* Damage was in the region of £1,300 and the buildings were insured through the Manchester Fire Office – exactly the sort of fire that the Essex & Suffolk had regularly vowed not to attend! Away from head office in Colchester, different rules seemed to apply.

Just three days later, another fire broke out, this time in the centre of Coggeshall and the emergency showed how well the community could work together in a crisis.

John Beard was a maltster, brewer and corn merchant with extensive premises in a yard off Church Street, behind what is now the Conservative Club and accessed via a narrow covered carriageway through the frontage. It was Thursday 4th March 1869 and the man in charge had left the premises earlier in the evening, when all seemed well. It was approaching midnight when flames were seen issuing from outbuildings in the yard, the fire apparently started in a stable lit by gas. The cry of 'fire!' echoed around the streets and the inhabitants 'roused from their peaceful slumbers'. The alarm brought a considerable number of people to the scene. The 'Chelmsford Chronicle' reported:

> 'Almost every trade and profession in the town were represented by some member or members, Messrs D Leaper and Son with the engine of the Essex and Suffolk Equitable Insurance Society and the police under the direction of Sergeant Bacon all discharged their duties with efficiency.'
> *[CC 12/03/1869]*

The fire developed rapidly and at one time seemed to imperil the buildings on Church Street itself. There were 'one or two decided acts of bravery', especially in the rescue of the horses which was only managed with the greatest difficulty. Efforts to subdue the fire were aided because that night, (unlike those before and after) was windless, but it was two or three hours before the fire was brought under control. The fire consumed a range of stabling with lofts over, a counting house with a corn-bin over, 'containing a very large quantity of very heavy small horse beans', a coach house and a grinding house with wood work, malt and bean mills and a chaff engine. The combined efforts of the brigade, police and helpers meant that the principal buildings were saved and a grateful John Beard placed an advert in the next edition of the 'Chelmsford Chronicle', thanking everyone for their help 'and through whose exertions much valuable property was saved'. *[CC 12/03/1869]*

Beard's premises were insured with the 'Royal', the Office particularly identified by the Essex & Suffolk as problematic with regard to paying expenses. Once again though, country rules applied and there was never a question as to whether or not the Coggeshall engine would attend. Afterwards, Leaper drew up a statement of all the expenses and the Essex & Suffolk paid the bill apparently without demur.

And that was it, after a tenure of thirty years, Daniel Leaper, had attended his last fire. He remained as the Coggeshall agent of the Essex & Suffolk and continued his occupation as cabinet maker and undertaker. His son, William, also retired from the fire brigade and in truth had probably only joined to assist his father. William continued in his occupation as brewer and wine and spirit merchant based at the Bird in Hand Brewery next to his father's shop on East Street. There is no record that Daniel Leaper received any thanks or recognition from the Essex & Suffolk for his years of work with the Coggeshall engine.

The Inheritance

Three years after he retired as Superintendent, Leaper was finding the agency more than he could manage, he came to an understanding with Alfred Gardner in expectation that he would take over in due course. Mathias Alfred Gardner had a brick and pipe making business just beyond the ford in Robinsbridge Road and was always called Alfred to distinguish him from Mathias his father. Gardner was exactly the 'right sort' for the Essex & Suffolk and the arrangement would ensure a smooth takeover when Leaper eventually retired. Leaper wrote to the Directors about the arrangement and his hopes for the succession, eliciting this response:

> 'That Mr Leaper be informed that he may make what arrangements he wishes with Mr Gardner, but the Board cannot pledge themselves to give Mr Gardner the Agency after his retirement.'
> *[E&SE MB6 16/03/1872]*

Despite this cool response, Gardner increasingly took over the work of the Agency and responsibility for the care of the engine.

In financial terms, the Coggeshall agency during Leaper's tenure seems to have underperformed. When he became agent in 1837, the company had 310 insurance policies in the town, by 1840 there were 270, a drop of almost 13%, in the same period the number of policies with the company as a whole increased by almost 8%. In 1837, the Coggeshall agency was the sixth most valuable, by 1843 it was the tenth and it remained eighth or ninth until 1857 when detailed figures were no longer published. Perhaps the Directors were right to doubt Leaper's suitability - or might the figures record Coggeshall's own economic decline? Whatever the reason, there is no evidence here that the Essex & Suffolk derived any benefit in providing Coggeshall with a fire engine. In effect they offered a public service which apparently brought no business advantage and which they never sought to exploit.

On the right is the white weather-boarded house of Mr & Mrs Gepp and beyond it Mr Brazier's premises where Mrs Gepp first noticed an unusual smell of smoke. Beyond Mr Brazier's is the Cricketers Public House. Only the Cricketers remains today but as a private house. The tall brick building with dormer windows was demolished in the early twentieth century to widen the road. On the left are the premises of J K King & Son with the royal warrants on display.

After Leaper

In July 1872 there was a 'most terrific tempest which reigned over Coggeshall and the neighbourhood'.

> 'At about half past eleven on Saturday morning when the tempest was at its height, the lightning struck the house of Police Sergeant Savill splitting the kitchen chimney, loosening the slated roof and then playing around the stack of chimneys in the front of the house, knocking the centre chimney pot quite down, considerably frightening the inmates. About 12 am a messenger drove rapidly into the town with the news that a barn of an off-hand farm[6] at Ivy Brook, a distance of about 4 miles was on fire. A pair of horses from an Hotel were quickly harnessed to the engine belonging to the Equitable Fire Insurance company (being the only engine which is stationed in the town), which under the command of Mr Thomas Potter, with several gentlemen, was soon on the spot and by the prompt assistance prevented the fire from extending beyond the barn.' *[CC 19/07/1872]*

Thomas Potter was the foreman of Mathias Gardner's building business and had been the station key-holder for some years, as well as a regular member of Daniel Leaper's crew. Although he took charge on this occasion and continued to be involved with the engine, it seems that he had no desire to become Superintendent. Perhaps this first fire in charge of the engine was enough to convince him that he did not want the responsibility. The description of the crew as 'Gentlemen' although no doubt accurate for every man who hailed from Coggeshall, was probably used in the honorific sense

In 1874 there was a serious fire in a cottage near the Cricketers Inn, which 'threw the inhabitants of this usually quiet town into

---

6   A farm managed by someone living elsewhere.

a state of excitement'. Mrs Gepp was in her neighbour's house when 'she noticed an unusual smell of smoke and on sending to her house found the kitchen was on fire'. The alarm brought plenty of help and the 'strenuous exertions' of blacksmith James Pudney and baker Henry Chaplin, prevented a more destructive result. No candlestick maker put in an appearance. £50 worth of damage was caused to house and furniture, the unfortunate Mrs Gepp was only insured for £5. The fire engine was not troubled. [ES & CC 14/08/1874]

The same year saw a major fire at Hill House Farm (also known as Fabians Farm, which was on the Colne Road just south of the modern junction with Gurton Road). A horseman who lived in the farmhouse spotted flames in the farm buildings around ten in the evening. In the yard were two horses and 250 sheep which were penned overnight on their way from Colchester market to Pattiswick Hall. The horseman raised the alarm and with help, the animals were safely driven out of harm's way. Within fifteen minutes:

> 'The entire farm buildings in which were about 20 acres of wheat, were one mass of flame and a wheat stack the produce of 10 acres, the produce of 12 acres of beans, fifty fowls, two waggons, a tumbril, seed cart....fell prey to the devouring element.'
> [ES 25/09/1874]

The glow of the fire was visible from Kelvedon to the south and Earls Colne to the north. The house itself looked doomed and all the furniture was removed, but was saved by the direction and strength of the wind. It was said that the engine was not called because there was no water at the farm. [ES 25/09/1874] After an investigation, the 'Essex & Suffolk', concluded that the fire had been the work of an incendiary and issued posters offering a £50 reward:

> 'For information leading to the conviction of the incendiary who fired the premises of Mr Unwin at Coggeshall.' [ES 02/10/1874]

Joseph Unwin who owned Hill Farm, also farmed at Bouchiers Grange where he

---

A Kind and Ever Ready Friend
August 1872
Considerable excitement was caused in this town on Monday evening by a report that Mrs Matthius Gardner, had been thrown out of her chaise and killed in the neighbourhood of Stisted. Mr Gardner jnr. accompanied by Dr Lett, instantly started in a fly and found the news indeed to be true. The deceased lady had gone for a ride with her husband, who is a builder of this town and he, having gone to look at some workmen, left the deceased alone in the chaise, in the road: the horse, whilst grazing, slipped his bridle and started off along the road and the poor lady was thrown out and killed on the spot. Mr Bridge, of Stisted, endeavoured to stop its rapid progress and in doing so both wheels grazed his trousers. Failing in this attempt he followed the chaise and after running about two miles found Mrs Gardner lying quite dead. After procuring assistance he had her conveyed into a cottage nearby to await the arrival of her friends. She was brought home in Hunwick's van about eight o'clock the same evening.

The event has cast gloom over the whole town, as the deceased lady was well known and much respected: in her the poor of the parish will lose a kind and ever ready friend. [CC 02/08/1872]

[Mrs Gardner's son Matthius Jnr, known as Alfred, supported Daniel Leaper as the Coggeshall agent for the Essex & Suffolk Equitable Insurance Company.]

---

lived, just half a mile away. Unwin should have been expecting trouble after an earlier and controversial incident. He had received a notice from the Agricultural Labourers Union 'requiring' him to increase the wages of his men and his response to this impertinence was to sack twelve of them. Jobless and unemployable, the men had left Coggeshall with the union's assistance to seek employment in the north. [CC 09/05/1873] The fire was not isolated however, just a couple of weeks earlier there had been an incendiary attack at nearby Messing causing an enormous fire with two barns and fifteen stacks destroyed. A correspondent linked both these attacks to the fact that 'farmers were contemplating lowering wages..and labourers were smarting under the failure of the Labourers Union.' *[Bury and Norwich Post & Suffolk Herald 06/10/1874]*

Whether or not these incidents were linked, incendiarism was again on the increase, incidents reported in the 'Chelmsford Chronicle' show a steady rise, from just two in 1860 to thirty-six incendiary attacks in both 1882 and 1883. Unwin may have been the victim of another incendiary in 1879 when a stack at Bouchiers Grange was destroyed by fire and no explanation found as to how it started. *[ES 09/08/1879]*

Interlude: Guy Fawkes Fun

It might be recalled that a bonfire-night fire in 1764 began this history. Incidents were a regular feature of the Coggeshall Guy Fawkes celebrations which continued to liven up the town. Indeed the town was famous as one of the last to have a 'traditional' night. In 1841 much amusement resulted from the young, 'throwing about pieces of sacking soaked in gas tar and lighted'. A Constable detained one of the celebrants, 'this caused a great tumult', the constable was punched in the eye and pelted with stones and squibs. A mob gathered and the constable drew out his pistol and holding it high in one hand and the prisoner in the other shouted 'Do you see this!?' In court, it was claimed that it was a normal 5th of November, with bonfires lighted in the town, 'everyone was alike and it was never cried down and there was never any accident.' This explanation cut no ice and the man was given six months with hard labour. *[ES 03/12/1841]*

In 1853 the voice of authority was broadcast by the town crier who tried to dissuade those of a joyful inclination by threatening that anyone throwing 'squibs, crackers or any other kind of fireworks would be prosecuted according to the law'. This was greeted with a continuous volley of cannons, pistols and firearms as well as squibs,

> ### Gunpowder Allowance
> **1875**
> *If more than 28 llbs [12.7 kg] of gunpowder be deposited on the premises insured, no benefit or advantage shall be derived from such insurance by the party insured unless he is a dealer therein, in which case he shall be allowed to keep any quantity not exceeding one hundredweight. [50.8 kg]*
> In other words, policy holders could keep up to 28lbs of gunpowder in their house under the standard policy and still be fully insured.
> One of a list of policy clauses on an Essex & Suffolk Equitable Insurance Society Policy dated 1875
>
> ### The Dangers of Smoking
> **November 1874**
> *Two boys named Johnson and Prior were making fireworks at the house of the former's parents in East Street, having half a pound of gunpowder on the table for that purpose, when one of them in lighting a pipe accidentally dropped a lighted paper upon the powder which caused an immediate explosion, injuring Prior very seriously in the face, Johnson escaped uninjured. The room and furniture were also damaged.* [CC 23/10/1874]

crackers and other fireworks from first thing in the morning and continuing throughout the day, into the evening. A man called Spurgeon was severely injured in the thigh that year when an overloaded cannon burst. *[CC 11/11/1853]* A similar accident happened in 1854 when another cannon burst and a piece of barrel, weighing nearly one pound, blasted through the shutters and smashed six panes of glass in Mr Mount's confectioners shop. *[CC 10/11/1854]* Just a week earlier some boys were letting off serpents in Bridge Street when one of the fireworks dashed through a bedroom window, alighted on a bed and set fire to the bed curtains, much to the alarm of Mrs Heather, who had retired for the night. *[CC 03/11/1854]* On 5th November 1859 a man called Sharp, walking down Stoneham Street, was shot in the face, the

*A load of faggots at the bottom of Grange Hill c1910.
On the left is the track down to the ford with the Long Bridge behind the wagon.
The tall chimney was part of Hall's silk factory owned at the time by J K King.*

bullet went through his cheek and knocked out one of his teeth. 'If apprehended' the 'Chelmsford Chronicle' reported 'the offender might consider himself fortunate if he escaped with a severe reprimand'! The town, it was reported, was 'a scene of uproar and confusion.' *[CC 11/11/1859]* Such events refreshingly demonstrate how moderation and caution were not quick to catch on in Coggeshall. The meek and the miserable regularly complained about the situation, so in October 1874, when it was reported that the, 'inhabitants of the town have been greatly annoyed by boys letting off fireworks', an order was issued by the magistrate threatening any further offenders with prosecution. This order was again announced around the streets by the town crier and may have been successful because on the 5th of that year, the usual fireworks and bonfire on Market Hill passed without incident. *[CC 23/10/1874, EN 20/11/1874]* The status quo was somewhat restored the next year. There was a four hour firework display, a large fire balloon and several wagon loads of faggots thrown onto the Market Hill bonfire. 'Some windows were of course broken' but this was, 'taken joyfully as a tribute to a spirit of old English Protestantism'. The 'few people' that were injured were hurt entirely as result of 'their own imprudence'. *[EN 13/11/1875]* In 1879 the 'Essex Standard' commented:

> 'Coggeshall is one of the few places where, for some unaccountable reason, this day is allowed to be celebrated in the old style. Early in the morning inhabitants were aroused by the reports of innumerable small cannon fired off by youngsters. In the evening thousands of fireworks were discharged on the Market Hill and a tremendous bonfire kindled.' *[ES 08/11/1879]*

Fire at the Gas Works

It was six years before the effects of Leaper's retirement became apparent. People were so used to the engine turning out and working efficiently, that it was something of a shock when this did not happen. Coggeshall gasworks was built between East Street and the Back Ditch. On Wednesday 2nd June 1875, workers were using an 'open furnace' to burn tar off one of the gas-holders, when a sudden gust of wind blew sparks onto the thatched roof of a range of cattle sheds which began to burn. The workers climbed onto the blazing roof and tried to stifle the flames, but one of the men slipped and fell, badly injuring himself. The cows and pigs from the sheds were freed but there was great alarm about the closest gas-holder, as the burning thatch was so hot that the tar covering the gas-holder began to bubble and boil off. The holder was full of gas and an explosion seemed almost certain. Just in the nick of time it seemed, the engine arrived but could not be quickly got to work 'owing to the scarcity of water'. It is true that there was very little water in the nearby back ditch, but there were also problems with the equipment. Efforts to use the engine were eventually abandoned and the considerable crowd of people did the best they could, using pails of water, pulling off the burning straw and removing the timber and thatch not yet alight. Eventually the efforts and perseverance started to tell, the fire was brought under and nearby premises and a slaughter house, once under threat, were saved. Most importantly the gas-holder did not explode. *[ES 04/06/1875]* The buildings destroyed belonged to Messrs F and J Sach. *[ES 04/06/1875]*

The fire brought considerable anger in its wake as people realised how close things had come to a disaster and how unprotected they had become from fire.

> ### Cure for an Irritable Hound
> The following is an extract from a letter quoted in court and written by the Rector of Marks Tey, Rev Donald M Owen, to Mrs Honywood of Marks Hall after her dog bit him.
> *'I enclose perfectly reliable prescription for calming an irritable hound, such as yours. The quantities may be reduced by your own medical man, to suit the case of smaller dog :— Pulv Nitrati fortissi, Dr.111 ; Plomb No. IV, oz 1¾ ; Capsula (arida), una ; Fiat mixta in fistula jerreci communi ad pass; duo applicanoa instanter. Mr. Beaumont: I have a translation which I had better perhaps read, "Gunpowder, three drachms; shot No. 4, 1¾oz ; one dry cartridge; make mixture; to be applied at two paces, by means of a common gun.'* [CC 26/05/1876]

Barney Beard and the Tea Meeting

The fire was informally discussed at a parochial 'Tea Meeting' at the White Hart Hotel on 7th June 1875. After a presentation to a retiring parish officer, a well liked Coggeshall patriarch, Mr Barney Beard, brought up the subject of the recent fire and as he saw it:

> 'The necessity of forming a fire brigade in this town and of having an engine in good repair upon any emergency.' *[CC 11/06/1875]*

After some discussion it was thought that perhaps the question of the water supply should be addressed before any steps were taken regarding a brigade. A parish meeting was then called: 'to consider the question of forming a fire brigade and the sufficiency of water supply in many parts of the town in case of fire'. *[ES 18/06/1875]*. A Parish Meeting was the usual way at the time to allow people to have their say, whenever an issue was exercising public attention. It was held in the Assembly Room at the White Hart Hotel on Thursday 10th June 1875. It was well attended, but although fire protection was on the agenda, the debate soon moved on to the provision of water. The churchwardens were then asked to convene a meeting of

> ### The Owen Mixture Applied
> 'A labourer named Frost was proceeding to his work, [when] he was savagely attacked by a white bulldog belonging to Mr Leatherdale, which attempted to fasten on to him. Seeing the man's danger, Mr Joseph Nunn*, blacksmith, came to the rescue, but the dog instantly turned furiously upon him, and inflicted a severe bite on the hinder part of the right leg.... Messrs Giles and Simpson are attending him. In the after part of the day of the occurrence, Mr Nunn, seeing the dog at large in the street, took up a gun, and administered the Owen mixture, recently prescribed by the Rev D M Owen, in the Marks Hall case'. The mixture proved very effective.
> [CC 13/10/1876]
> *Joseph was the father of the famous 'Dick' Nunn.

ratepayers to consider the matter and this led to further meetings but the focus was always on water supply. In fact the whole thing seems to have been hi-jacked by those concerned about Coggeshall's sanitation and water supply, who used the opportunity to promote a public health agenda. The Rural Sanitary Authority became involved and the original concerns about the lack of a fire brigade, the state of the engine and the appliances were sidelined.

As for the water question, the majority of ratepayers (who would have to pay for any scheme), were against it. Most if not all, already had good supplies of drinking water from their own private wells. Their persuasive spokesman was a local solicitor, Joseph Beaumont[7], who argued that major works and expense were unnecessary. The matter was dropped: questions about the fire brigade remained unanswered and those about the water supply were unresolved.

Daniel Leaper, now ailing, attended only one of the meetings and it must have been disheartening for him to see the state things had reached after all his years of work. It was Alfred Gardner, now carrying out the duties as agent, who was responsible for the engine.

---

[7] He was the father of George F Beaumont author of 'The History of Coggeshall'.

The Coggeshall Shrimpman

James Bearman sold fish from the back of a cart and had premises in Robinsbridge Road. These included a stable and a 'drying house', built of timber and having (as the Essex & Suffolk would have put it), 'fire heat therein', would have attracted a high insurance premium, which is probably why it remained uninsured. The place caught fire in March 1876, his horse was killed and the buildings and their contents, 'Herrings, sprats, harness and other articles, were destroyed'. Bearman, 'the Coggeshall Shrimpman', started again, he bought a mule and continued to sell fish until he was 96 years old. He died aged 97, in 1911, a testament to the benefits of a fishy diet. *[EH 19/05/1896]* His wife, Sophia, was something of a character. She once represented her husband in court (he was fined 5s for allowing his mule to stray) and in her eighties was found 'Drunk and Incapable' on Market Hill and fined 2s 6d.
[CC 25/07/1879 & 09/12/1893]

After the problems at the Gasworks fire in 1875, the engine was sorted out and was in good order at the next fire, in August 1876. This was at Coggeshall Hall, an ancient Manor House and farm south of Coggeshall. The fire that broke out there proved to be serious, eventually involving eight stacks, a barn and outbuildings. The engine was quickly on the spot 'under the vigilant and active management of Mr Walter Gardner and others'. Walter Gardner was the youngest son of Walter Gardner Snr. owner of Gardner's Brewery in Little Coggeshall and cousin of Mathias 'Alfred' Gardner, the acting Essex & Suffolk agent. In his one outing as superintendent of the engine, he seems to have done an excellent job and with plenty of water available, the engine proved effective. A neighbouring farmer sent his workmen to assist and the combined efforts of men and engine saved a hundred foot barn and further stacks. There is no record that Walter ever took the engine out again. *[CC 25/08/1876]*

Fire at Frith's 1877. On the left, the Chemist shop and dwelling on three floors, owned by Mr Frith. Next door are the premises once occupied by Mr Perkin's Drapers shop (the International Stores at the time of this photo of 1907).

Fire at Frith's, Market End

The next fire broke out six months later at Mr Frith's Chemist shop and home on three floors at Market End. Frith was about to go to bed one Sunday night in March 1877, when suddenly aware of the smell of burning, he rushed upstairs to find that his child and two servants were deeply asleep in a room dense with smoke. He roused them, and raised the alarm. The fire developed quickly and before long had burst through the roof. Frith and many ready helpers began to remove furniture and stock but the fire was soon 'raging so furiously' that it seemed only a matter of time until it spread around the corner into Market Hill. The engine arrived and was set into the flooded cellar of a neighbouring house, where the water lay three feet deep. This was briefly effective but soon ran out. Showing some degree of organisation, the engine was then moved down through the Gashouse yard and set into the back ditch, which this time did have water and a long line of hose was run out towards the fire. The parish water carts were also called in and filled up at the river, bringing a valuable supply for the buckets that were brought into use and some 'hundreds of persons were on the spot' and lending their aid. The fire spread into the next door shop, a drapers, owned by Mr Perkins. Efforts were made to move his stock in trade and household furniture which were threatened both by fire and by the large amount of water pouring in. Those fighting the fire began to get the upper hand and it was eventually stopped 'by dint of great exertion'. The older part of Frith's house was completely gutted and in Mr Perkins shop, the upper part suffered fire damage but nearly all was damaged by water. The delays in getting water to the fire were critical and again highlighted the lack of a ready supply for fire-fighting:

'An impressive sermon has (by this calamitous

The water cart being filled at the river on a less troubled occasion. It was used to spray the roads with water to keep down the dust. It was formerly used to supply drinking water to parts of the town, the water drawn from St Peter's Well.

occurrence) been preached upon the necessity of a better water supply.' *[CC & ES 16/03/1877]*

Although an engineer probably supervised the engine, newspaper reports make no mention of a superintendent, although a number of people were praised, including (and unusually), the pumpers:

> 'Particular praise is due to the men who worked the engine with such desperate perseverance and ultimate success.' *[EN 17/03/1877]*

Not everyone at the fire had been there to help and some items went missing from Frith's. Sergeant Savill reported:

> 'I saw Tansley working at the fire and on Sunday, from information received, I went to his house and found him in bed….while I was talking with him I saw his wife taking something from a box and endeavour to put it in her pocket. I told her to put it down, she did so, I found it to be part of the [missing] toilet set. The prisoner asked me to forgive him, he was sorry he took it.'

Tansley was later convicted of stealing part of a toilet set and half a pound of tea value 4s 3d. He claimed he had, '…in a careless way put them in his pocket' and that he had a wife and five children. He was sentenced to six weeks' imprisonment with hard labour. *[CC 30/03/1877]* Tansley was a violent man and probably a career criminal. In August 1888 he was sentenced to three months' hard labour 'For attempting to make a meal off a police officer'- having twice bitten a policeman attempting to arrest him. Another man, George Rayner, alias 'Han'som Burton' was also found guilty of theft of articles from the shop during the fire, to the value of £5 10s. He was sentenced to three months hard labour. *[ES 06/04/1877]* It should be mentioned that there were other 'Tansley' families in Coggeshall who were decent and upright citizens, one of them will appear later in this account.

Calling out the Brigade, 1878

A fire broke out in March 1878 at the tan-yard[8] adjoining the gelatin factory on West Street. The first report seems straightforward:

'On Tuesday morning about 6 o'clock a fire broke out in some buildings in the tan-yard, the property of Mr G P Swinborne. Mr Pfander, Mr Foster and several others were soon on the spot and the men from the adjoining factory rendered prompt assistance. The fire-engine was quickly brought to the scene and there being a plentiful supply of water, the fire was prevented from spreading and at great trouble put out, but not before the sheds were destroyed.' [CC 15/03/1878]

Following this, a correspondent, calling himself 'one heavily insured' sent his observations to the Editor of the 'Chelmsford Chronicle' and his critical account gives a unique insight into the organisation of the brigade at this time.

When the fire was discovered, a man called Mr Cant ran with all speed to fetch the engine, all the while calling out 'fire!' He later reported:

'I asked several people where I was to go to. They told me to the old Fire Office in East-street [Daniel Leaper's shop and Office]. On calling up the gentleman there I was told I must go to the office in Church-street [Where the acting agent, Alfred Gardner had his office]. On arriving there I was again told that I must go and call up another gentleman, as he had the keys of the engine-house. Having got to the engine, the next step was to go some distance and call up the chief engineer. By this time the engine was drawn down the street. At last a horse was attached and away went the engine to the fire. But not so quick as I have seen some funeral processions.'

In the meantime, 'Heavily Insured' was at the fire:

'I saw two men belonging to our fire-brigade on the roofs of the gelatine factory. All honour to them for manfully keeping off the fire from the gelatine factory by the use of cloths and a continuous supply of water by pails from the men of the factory. Knowing one man (our foreman) living close to the engine-house, I made my way to him. I politely asked him "where was the fire-engine?", His answer was, "It is sent for and if it don't come today, it may tomorrow." It would be well if some printed boards were placed in some conspicuous parts of the town. We have had many narrow escapes, I hope we may receive a lesson. Your report of the fire states that the engine was quickly brought to the scene. The fire broke out at 5.40 a.m. and it was 6.35 when the engine arrived. Not so very quick Mr Editor. I hope after this we may have some alteration for the better in case of fire.' [Both CC 15/03/1878]

The letter brought a riposte from Alfred Gardner, the acting agent. Gardner pointed out that the engine did not belong to the parish but was privately owned and kept for the protection of property insured with the Essex & Suffolk Fire Office:

'That when a fire occurs to property not insured in this office, as was the case in the fire under discussion, I am authorised to let the engine out on hire and to charge for such hire....It is also very well known in the town that the key of the engine-house has been for years and is now, kept at Mr Thomas Potter's, Upper Stoneham-street and is always obtainable at a few minutes notice night or day.'

This was the same Thomas Potter, who took out the engine in 1872. Gardner also disputed the turn-out time:

'Your correspondent says the fire broke out at 5.40. Probably so but the alarm was necessarily later than this. The Tanyard is half a mile distant from the engine-house and I was informed by a gentleman who was on the spot at 6.15 that the engine was ready for work at 6.20 and not 6.35 as stated by your correspondent, was worked directly and all danger of the fire spreading to the gelatine works was over by 7.00.' [CC 22/03/1878]

Alfred Gardner must have been confident that he was representing the views of the Essex & Suffolk, yet he apparently goes further than they did in claiming a simple business-driven

---

8   Where the tanning of leather took place. As to the factory next door, glue and size-making is a closely related industry. Gelatin was the finest grade of glue size.

model for fire protection. In doing so he again brought to public notice the Directors' increasing conviction that they were ill-used by public bodies who should themselves be providing a public fire service.

A Year to Remember

1879 turned out to be the busiest in the brigade's history to date. There was an early start to the year with a fire at Prested Hall on 28th January. This old house is a couple of miles or so from Coggeshall just off the London road in Feering. Smoke had been seen emerging from a large double barn, which quickly turned into flames and within minutes the whole barn was alight and the fire began to spread, a carpenter's workshop and various other sheds were soon involved and eventually destroyed. The Coggeshall engine was called but it seems there was some difficulty in assembling a crew and a call went out for men to volunteer. As a result an hour had elapsed before the brigade arrived and it was under the management of a new man on the scene, James Tansley. The engine was set into a large pond and got to work almost at once. Many of the buildings were already lost but under Tansley's orders the firemen were working well:

> 'The water was pumped onto a large tarpaulin sheet which was placed on the end of a large wheat stack, the first in a row of from six to eight and by this means this range of stacks were saved.'
> *[CC 01/02/1879]*

James Tansley was a formidable character, a keen fisherman, a trustee and the oldest member of the Coggeshall Good Samaritan Lodge of Oddfellows. When he took charge of the fire at Prested Hall in 1879 he was 58 years old, a millwright and head of the family engineering business 'James Tansley and Son', employing two men and a boy. He lived next to Hare Bridge on West Street with a workshop nearby at Gravel End. He had nine children, including four boys, all of whom became engineers or fitters.

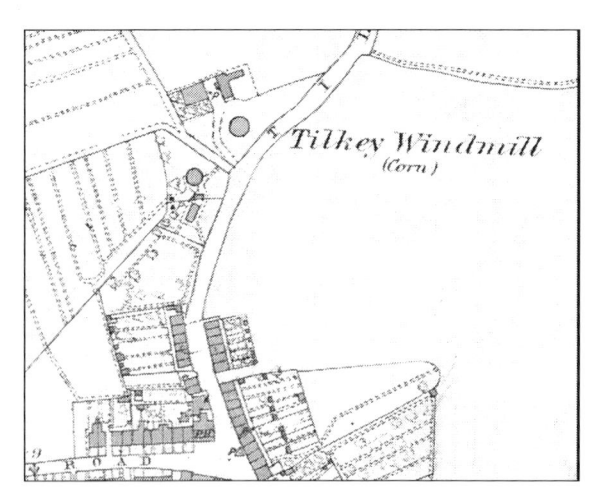

Tilkey Windmill from a map of 1875. The hedge and track, top right, is where Jaggards Road now runs.
Reproduced by courtesy of the Essex Record Office

Daniel Leaper

On 23rd February 1879, The Essex & Suffolk's long-serving agent and ex-superintendent of the engine, Daniel Leaper, died aged 83.

> 'A native of this town, he had spent his whole life here and during a long course of business transactions and parochial work, he commanded the respect of all….He had outlived most of his friends, but still has many who keenly regret their loss.' *[CC 28/02/1879]*

On 1st March, Alfred Gardner was officially appointed the Essex & Suffolk agent. The family were well known, and respected both in the town and beyond. Perhaps for this and because of their social status, the normal sureties were waived and Alfred's father Mathias was accepted as the only guarantor for £100, a quarter of the usual amount.

In October that year, following the death of his father, William Leaper sold the Bird in Hand brewery, along with the various public houses and licensed beer-houses that went with it. 'Mr Wm Leaper who has successfully carried on the business for many years, retires into private life'. He remained in Coggeshall but his days as a fireman, publican and brewer were over.
[EH 07/10/1879]

Coggeshall's Last Windmill

The next fire saw the end of Coggeshall's last and biggest windmill, the Tilkey corn mill. Its roundhouse was thirty feet in diameter and contained a small steam engine, the mill above measured some twelve feet wide by twenty-four feet deep. It was one of the largest mills in Essex and was being worked by Mr Scower, a recent new-comer to the town. The fire was discovered after midnight on Tuesday 4th March 1879 and seems to have started in the upper part of the mill but because of the late hour, the fire had a good hold before anyone noticed. James Tansley's name crops up again as he and Police Constable Barber 'did what they could', but it was obvious that with no water nearby, the mill could not be saved and the fire engine not even sent for. The adjacent mill house survived because the wind was in the west and blew the flames and sparks away. The image of the mill alight in the middle of the night formed a tragic and awe-inspiring spectacle, described in the 'Essex Herald' a few days later:

> 'A fire broke out in the upper part of Coggeshall Windmill in the Tilkey-road and the whole structure (which was one of the largest in the county) was speedily in flames….The timbers of the mill were very massive, the oak cross-beam being about three feet in diameter and the mill, one red-hot mass, appeared to be floating in mid air. The sails as they burnt formed a brilliant display but were dangerous as the fragments fell. There was a small steam engine in the basement and it was feared there might be an explosion, as about 30lbs of steam had been left in the boiler over night. It is supposed that the machinery oil may have got over-heated and thus caused the fire. The fabric of the mill is the property of Mr F Smith and Mr Scower the occupier, losses a quantity of corn as well as mill moveables and machinery. The iron shaft, large timbers and millstones came to the ground with a heavy crash and some amusement was caused by the dislodgement of a colony of rats, some of which were running about with singed backs.' *[EH 08/03/1879]*

The mill was never rebuilt but the Mill

A Serpent through the Fanlight
November 1871
About nine o'clock a fiery serpent went through the fanlight of Mr Munder, Grocer, into the hall and burning the matting and very much frightened the ladies of the household. [EN 11/11/1871]

Saucy and Rude Boys
November 1878
Alfred Tansley stated that the three boys let off the cannon close to Mr Fricker's door at about five o'clock on the morning of the fifth. Mr Fricker said he heard the report of the cannon several times but did not think it was at his door: but when he came downstairs he found the door completely riddled with stones, numbers of which were embedded in the wall opposite and paper was burning in the passage, the door was about two inches thickness. Police sergeant Raven gave the defendants a character for being saucy and rude boys who stood about in the streets in the evening and annoyed passers by. Each fined 15s or seven days. [EN 23/11/1878]

A Silly Lad
November 1882
Two lads, C Howe and Varley Kirkham, were making squibs for fifth November at Mr Judges house, Stoneham-street, when Howe in testing a squib, accidentally set light to half a pound of gunpowder. One side of the kitchen and the sink were blown away. Both lads escaped unhurt. [EN 7/10/1888]

Curse of Temperance
November 1882
It had been intended to burn several effigies of the clergy who had recently been zealously advocating temperance, but many of the tradesmen and others were naturally indignant and on the first appearance of 'Guy Parson', it was attacked and after a sharp fight, carried off and destroyed by Messrs G and R Browning, W Tansley and others. [CC 11/11/1882]

To be Expected
November 1883
Sydney Green, assistant to Mr Frith, Chemist of Market-hill, was mixing some ingredients used in the manufacture of fireworks when the compound in the mortar exploded and he was severely burned about the face and arms. Little damage was done to the laboratory though a customer had a narrow escape. [CC 02/11/1883]

Bradwell Hall, an early photo of this ancient building which from the outside seems to give few clues as to its great age.

House and store still stand (this is where I was brought up). The roundhouse of another, smaller mill next door had been converted into a dwelling but this was demolished in the late 1940s.

Bradwell Hall

The third big fire, even more than the Tilkey Corn Mill, was an irreplaceable historic loss. Bradwell Hall was described in the 'Essex Chronicle' as:

> 'One of the most ancient seats in the county... in an out of the way spot, little known to any except for those whose business called them there'.

The old house was close to Bradwell Church, about a mile from the village now called Bradwell, along a winding lane that leaves Stane Street, near the Blackwater Bridge. The house it was said, formed a portion of a once more extensive mansion. Living in the house was the unmarried Henry Brunwin, brother of the Rev T M Brunwin of Glazenwood, who owned it.

It was 4.30 in the morning of Friday 21st March 1879, when Henry Brunwin, was woken by an unusual sound. Looking out of the window he saw light cast out from the kitchen below. Thinking he was being burgled he picked up a life-preserver and made his way downstairs to confront the thieves and a glow beneath the kitchen door reinforced his conviction. His fears would have been compounded because the notorious Coggeshall Gang had broken into a house in Bradwell some years before and tortured the occupants to disclose the secret hiding place of their cash. Perhaps understandably, Brunwin approached carefully and when he opened the door, instead of thieves he found the whole kitchen on fire. Brunwin shared the house with his two servants, a 'looker' also described as the groom, his wife and two children. With 'great presence of mind', he closed the door and dashed upstairs to alert them:

> '..and it was well that he did so for the flames spread with such rapidity – there being a great deal of old varnished timber and wainscoting – that there was but little time to lose to save the lives of the inmates.'

Henry Brunwin's concern for his much loved dogs sent him to the kennels before he thought to send a message for the brigade. The Coggeshall engine was quickly dispatched but the convoluted journey and the spread and intensity of the blaze meant that by the time it arrived, nothing could be done to save the house:

> 'The old fashioned mansion with its fine carvings are destroyed, while of the furniture, papers and other valuables, scarcely a vestige was saved.'

Close by was a farm house and a range of buildings including a barn and this twice caught fire and was extinguished. The spring just below the farm flows into a large body of water[9] so this time the firemen had the advantage of a good water supply. Both barn and farm were saved and according to the report: 'but for the service rendered by the Coggeshall fire engine, both would probably have been destroyed.'

The house was never rebuilt and all that remains today are the cellars, although parts of its woodwork were incorporated into the porch of the church. Henry Brunwin's effects were only partly insured but those of his groom – 'a quantity of new furniture' together with everything else he owned, was completely destroyed and uninsured. It was thought that a large beam in the kitchen, which ran into the chimney, was the cause of the fire. *[CC 28/03/1879]*

Brewery Fire

The last fire of 1879 was in November. It was 11.30 on a Wednesday morning when James Page, walking in his garden next to Beard & Bright's Brewery, on Stoneham Street[10], saw that its thatched roof was on fire, started it was thought by a 'spark from the engine shaft'. The proprietor, Mr Frank Beard was alerted and immediately set his men to work with buckets:

> '..in the meantime he procured the fire engine, which, however, when it arrived, failed to do its work for some time and it was not until the fire was all but extinguished that it could render any assistance.'

A large number of men were soon assembled and they quickly began to pull off the burning straw and throw it down to those below who doused it with pails of water. A strong wind was blowing at the time and this hampered the operations. The fire was eventually stopped and this 'was much to the credit of the vigorous way the men set to work'. The thatched roof and a few of the rafters in the malting were destroyed. Several men were named as 'having rendered material aid', among these was the engineer James Tansley and his youngest son, nineteen-year-old William. *[EC 4/11/1879 & EH 18/11/1879 & ES 15/11/1879]*

His father Mathias having retired, Alfred Gardner took charge of the family building business and in 1878 secured the contract to build the new Friend's Meeting House on Stoneham Street for £700. He was in poor health and these additional responsibilities did nothing to help. Five years earlier while giving evidence during a court appearance, his obvious frailty caused the judge to order a chair for him in the witness box[11]. He was then just thirty-five years old.

In 1882 the engine was called to a chimney

---

9   The 'Broad Well' after which the village takes its name.

10   Now the village hall.
11   He was prosecuted for employing children under 13 at his brickworks. He said that he had employed the boys on the prompting of their fathers, who told him they were over 13. He was fined nonetheless. *[CC 07/08/1874]*

fire at the Bull public house at Bradwell. The fire spread and soon had a good hold on the building which was eventually burnt to the ground. The Coggeshall engine was quickly in attendance and prevented the fire spreading to the adjoining premises having plenty of water from the nearby river Blackwater. Four Policemen were in attendance and helped to remove property.
[CC 27/10/1882 & EN 28/10/1882]

1883 was another busy year for the brigade and despite some real successes, it ended with a very public demonstration that fire protection in the town was again in a sorry condition.

One of Coggeshall's many public houses was The Bull Inn on Church Street almost opposite Albert Place. A serious fire broke out at 11.30 at night on Monday 5th February 1883, on premises at the back of the inn. A lack of water hampered efforts and allowed the fire to spread to some cottages in the yard, one of which was destroyed and the other badly damaged but Gardner's extensive workshops and timber yards which adjoined were saved by the actions of the brigade. [EH 10/02/1883] The next fire was a suspected incendiary attack which started in a stack at Chalkney Mill, Earls Colne. The fire spread to further stacks and then to a barn, sheds, stables and a cow-house. The Coggeshall brigade put in some excellent work, assisted by the constabulary, but there was a problem with the engine:

> 'The Coggeshall Fire Brigade were in attendance and the engine was not in good working order, it is largely due to their efforts that the fire was prevented from reaching the coach house which adjoins the house and mill.' [CC 03/08/1883]

Alfred Gardner's health continued to decline and his limited energies were focussed on his business. It is possible that the problems with the engine were not reported to him but more likely that he simply did not get round to dealing with them. Nothing had been done when the next fire broke out four months later.

East Street. Mr Buck's shop on the corner of Gas Lane. The buckets are for the daily delivery of drinking water.

Indignation at Buck's Workshop

This fire started at 6.20 on a windy Saturday evening in December 1883. William Buck was a cabinet maker who had a house and shop in East Street, with workshops behind on Gas Lane. The fire started from a workshop stove but developed rapidly because inside were highly inflammable materials including varnishes, paints and solvents and the outside was weather-boarded and tarred. Being right in the middle of town and fanned by the wind, it was not just the house that was threatened but also several cottages close by. The engine was soon on the spot but to great dismay once again there was little water in the Back Ditch and the hoses were in such poor condition that barely any water reached the nozzle. In a panic, a telegraph was sent to the Witham brigade for help – the first recorded use of the telegraph in the town to summon a fire brigade.[12]

A room used as a kitchen linked the blazing workshop to the house and it was decided to try and demolish this in order to stop the fire. With 'scores of people' to help, many hands set to break open and pull down the structure, already being scorched by the heat. At the same time, others began to remove furniture and effects from the cottages. This was done with such haste that a lot of damage resulted both to the cottages and furniture. At this point providence leant a hand, for the wind suddenly dropped and the fire lost some of its intensity. This and the timely demolition, the application of buckets of water and the thin spray from the hose, all prevented the fire from spreading further and it became evident that the blaze was diminishing. A second telegraph was sent to the Witham brigade, cancelling the first. Two hours after it started, the fire was all but extinguished. The newspaper names several individuals who distinguished themselves at the fire including James Tansley's son, William now 23 years old whose good work had also been recognised at the Stoneham Street Brewery fire, four years before.

The 'Essex Newsman' reported:

> 'Much indignation is felt that there is so little protection from fire in the town. The local fire engine, it is said, has been proved to be nearly useless when required.' *[ES & EN 08/12/1883]*

We know more about what happened, because the Coggeshall Curate, the Rev Evans, addressed the Witham Young Men's Friendly Society just a couple of weeks later:

> 'He supposed they may have noticed in the papers that they had lately had a fire at Coggeshall, which at one time threatened to become a very serious conflagration. In their extremity they telegraphed to Witham for help, but another telegram soon afterwards stopped them from undertaking the journey (A voice: "We were all ready, sir"), he

---

12   Coggeshall Post Office had been wired up for the Telegraph in 1871.

wished to thank them for their readiness to assist. The Coggeshall engine wanted looking to. It was supplied with four lengths of hose, two of which were canvas. While at work the smallest possible stream of water appeared to go in the direction of the fire and plenty went in other directions. [Laughter].' *[EN 22/12/1883]*

Both leather and canvas hose needed to be cleaned and dried after use. Both were susceptible to rot which caused damage only evident when the hose was charged with water. This lack of maintenance suggests that the brigade was not functioning as it should and probably lacked leadership. A problem compounded by the agent's ill health. The young men of Witham may have found the episode amusing but in Coggeshall, people were not quite so sanguine. It was decided that a public meeting should be held to discuss the problem.

A Town Defenceless against Fire

Eight years after the previous public meeting following the Gasworks fire, another was held, again at the White Hart, on Friday 21st December 1883: 'To consider the defenceless state of the town against fire'. The Reverend Green taking the chair thought everyone would agree that the town 'ought to be more carefully guarded against the ravages of fire'. Whatever they did, 'it could not but improve on what might .. be considered the worst state of things in England'.

> 'Referring to the recent conflagration, he said that nothing but the providential change of wind which was blowing most fiercely at the time, saved at least an entire block of houses from complete destruction. There were scores of willing helpers but the engine was found wanting and the hose apparently rotten.'

Mr Thomas Simpson continued the theme. He was a surgeon, a Vestry inspector and a member of several town committees:

> 'They were blessed with an engine which he understood was powerful enough to throw water over the highest building in the town and which

> **Decaying Coggeshall**
>
> September 1885
>
> *'Having occasion recently to take a hasty survey of the town of Coggeshall and remembering its once large corn market and its flourishing factories of woollen and silk &c., I was painfully impressed with its present retrograde position as evidenced in the wholesale destruction of cottages and other dilapidated property...'*
>
> *'....Twenty years ago upwards of 300 men and women were employed in velvet weaving earning from 20s to 40s per week, while at the present time not a dozen looms are at work. Twenty years ago a large silk factory employing 200 to 300 hands was in full swing. It has now been closed nine years. During that time nothing has been introduced into the town to give employment to those who have thus been thrown out of work and they have therefore been compelled to move elsewhere.'*
>
> [Letters to the editor CC 04 & 14/ 09/1885]

if kept in repair would be most useful – but it was the private property of the Essex and Suffolk Fire Office and they might at any time remove it.'

A committee was appointed to consider several matters: the supply of water and its use in case of fire, to discuss the custody and use of the engine, to solicit subscriptions from all local fire insurance companies to form a fire brigade[13] and to enrol the names of volunteers. It seems that the Committee did not report back in January 1884 as promised, probably because they were unsuccessful. The problem over water supply was intractable and would continue to haunt the town for another thirty years. The problem of the engine and the lack of leadership in the brigade was much more straightforward. Once they were aware of the situation, the Essex & Suffolk Engine Committee sorted out the hose and serviced the engine. Perhaps even more importantly, for the time being, the engineer James Tansley agreed to take charge of the engine and reorganise the brigade.

---

13   The same appeal in Braintree was declined by all insurance offices who responded. *[EN 11/10/1887]*.

The Dramas of 1884

1884 was to be extraordinarily dramatic. It started with another close scrape at the gasworks. It was at about 3.00am on a Saturday morning in March and the night-man at the gasworks, George Humphreys was 'clinkering', an arduous process where a long straight fire iron called a 'dart' was used to break up the layer of clinker in the retorts before raking out. Whilst engaged in this, George became aware of the crackling sound of burning wood and looking up he found to his alarm that the rafters on the south side of the gas house were in flames. The previous afternoon, irons had been used for drawing coke and these must have been put away hot onto the rafters eventually setting them alight. Humphreys immediately ran to wake up Thomas Sawkins who lived nearby and had been until recently the manager of the works. A ladder was pitched and Sawkins, armed with a crowbar, climbed up and set about breaking through the roof then using buckets of water to douse the fire, which he eventually put out. Fearing that they might have been blown up in their beds, there was considerable consternation in the town next day as the news circulated. *[ES 22/03/1884]*

Exactly a month later the gasworks suffered a real shock:

> 'About 9.20 am. a rumbling noise, resembling several steam traction engines, accompanied by a wavy up-heaving of the ground, setting all the bells ringing and stopping the clocks. At the gas works a large chimney reeled about 18 inches out of the upright and then went back to its proper position without damage. Mr Wynn, the manager, had to clutch hold of the column of the gas holder to save himself from falling. The whole of the works seemed to be in motion. One of the five inch main pipes was completely severed, but being observed, was quickly repaired without an explosion.'
> *[EH 28/04/1884]*

This was the famous Colchester Earthquake which rocked the town in April 1884.

The Brigade Reinvigorated

James Tansley's efforts had reinvigorated the brigade but the first fire of 1884 left them with little opportunity to shine. The fire started in the stables at Bouchiers Grange, a farm belonging to Mrs Honywood, part of her Marks Hall estate. Most of the men were out hay-making so the fire was going well before anyone noticed and then all worked to release the livestock before finally calling the brigade:

> 'The engine of the Essex and Suffolk Fire Office was speedily on the spot, but owing to the buildings being principally of wood and well tarred, a large block of stabling, horse and cart sheds, coach houses and granaries 96 by 70 feet, were entirely destroyed, as well as the produce of 24 acres of clover, grass and tares, a large quantity of mixed grain and a number of farming implements.'
> *[EN 12/07/1884]*

The next call showed the 'new' brigade at their best. Called to a stack at Hay House farm, Earls Colne, the 'Essex Newsman' reported that the Fire Office engine 'proved to be of great service in preventing the fire spreading to the surrounding stacks' and the 'Essex Standard' praised the 'smart and energetic way in which the engine was worked, giving great satisfaction.'
[EN&ES 16/08/1884]

There was more praise for the firemen at the next fire. Alfred White was a basket maker with a workshop in West Street. It was there in January 1885 that a benzoline lamp[14] was accidentally overturned and started a fire which spread to the dry stock of osiers and canes which were stored on two floors. Before any assistance could be summoned the whole workshop was ablaze and the eaves of the neighbouring house were catching fire:

> 'Owing to the admirable manner in which the Essex and Suffolk engine was manned and to a good supply of water being available, the flames were soon extinguished.' *[EN 24/01/1885]*

---

14 Benzoline, also called Naphtha, is a highly inflammable petroleum product. The lamps gave a good light.

The Earthquake in Coggeshall

22nd April 1884 at 9.18 a.m.
'At Mr Ely's bakehouse at the corner of Bridge-street, a large chimney was shaken over doing considerable damage to the house and alarming the inmates. Another chimney was shaken down in a house occupied by Mr. Moss, Church-street. This fell onto the roof of Mr Anthony's adjoining house, crushing through and occasioning great damage and loss. At the National Schools the shock was so severe as to shake one of the supporting beams about two inches out of its socket in the wall and dislodge part of the partition in the boys school. In the girls schools a frantic rush was made for the staircase and about fifty of the girls fell from top to bottom of the stairs, many of them receiving severe bruises. Two of the girls – viz., Alice Eley, who is very badly bruised from head to foot and Eliza Lawrence, who has received a severe shock to the nervous system - were much trampled upon and who are under surgical treatment. At the British Schools, the presence of mind of the teachers, who at once locked the door of the exit, fortunately saved a serious calamity, the staircase being very steep and dangerous. At Feering the schoolmaster heard a rumbling sound and soon after heard mortar rolling down the slates and found himself moving forwards. The children were panic stricken and one boy fainted. At Feeringbury farm all the bells were set ringing and some chimney pots were set at liberty. At Church Farm Feering, a great noise was heard, the floor of the house heaved, the pictures slapped against the wall and the chimney ornaments were overturned.' [EH 28/04/1884]

July 1885
'On Monday last the festival of St Peter was kept with the greatest rejoicing by the Church workers and others at Coggeshall, the occasion being well chosen for the re-opening of the tower (which had been injured by the earthquake, the bells having been necessarily silent since that calamity), the celebrating of the dedication festival, the Sunday School scholars treat and the annual tea of the Mothers Meeting. The pealing of the bells by members of the Kelvedon, Braintree, Feering and Coggeshall Ringers' companies during the day elicited great praise from those skilled in the science of campanology.'
[CC 03/07/1885]

Kelvedon

The fire that broke out at the Roman Catholic College on the Angel Corner in Kelvedon, was one of the most serious that the Coggeshall brigade attended. The events of 20th December 1886 had a profound effect on the people of Kelvedon, with no fire engine of their own and a long delay before help arrived, they were powerless to do anything whilst one of their proudest buildings was consumed by fire in front of their eyes.

The College formerly known as Wiseman's Collegiate School, was bought for charitable use by Mr Rann of Messing Hall and used as a Catholic school for the education of poor London girls. It was Christmas and most of the girls had gone home for the holidays but twelve remained as well as four 'Sisters of Mercy', the resident priest Fr. Kelly and the domestics. The girls had their boxes packed ready for departure. It was said that after Felix Hall the building was the largest in the area. Some 400 years old it had a commanding position looking down the length of Kelvedon High Street.

Monday 20th December was bitterly cold. At the school, breakfast had been prepared and at about 6.30 am Sister Mary heard a crackling sound in the dining room and opening the door to investigate, found that the end of the room was in flames. The dining room had only recently been built, it had stud walls, weather-boarded on the outside, canvassed and papered inside and with a boarded and freshly tarred felt roof. It could almost have been designed as a fire hazard. A small heated greenhouse lay against the building on the north west side and this is where the fire started, probably from an overheated flue.

The fire was spreading very rapidly. The occupiers of the neighbouring houses were warned of the danger:

'Mr Cornwall the Tailor, Mr Palmer the Grocer, Mr Last the Baker and Mr Ashwell the Miller could all see how quickly the flames were spreading and "deemed it advisable to remove their furniture to the houses of their friends".' *[CC 24/12/1886]*

One of the first to arrive at the scene was constable Mills and he ordered a telegraph to be sent for fire engines from Witham, Coggeshall and Colchester. He had arrived 'before seven o'clock and with commendable promptitude' sent off the telegraphs, but for some reason, the messages were not immediately sent. In the meantime the children with their boxes and the Sisters of Mercy were removed to what must have been to them, the racy surroundings of the Angel Inn. Furniture was rescued from the flames and much of it left to stand forlornly on the pavement. A painter named Girdlestone was helping to remove furniture when he slipped and fell onto the spiked railings outside the building and was impaled through his thigh. Two local builders, Messrs Braddy and Siggers with a body of workmen cut through the roof of the Chapel and, aided by a brick party wall, miraculously, it was said, stopped the spread of the fire at that end. Much of the interior of the church was dismantled and its valuable fittings and appointments rescued.

A growing crowd had gathered, wondering when the engines were coming and many worked desperately in the intense heat, throwing buckets of water at the blaze. The town pump, a ten foot high tribute to abstinence, 'The oldest teetotaller in Kelvedon', was just over the road. All these efforts had little effect on the progress of the flames and before long the fire 'had obtained a complete mastery of the school-room, dining-hall and conservatory'. The range of buildings constructed mostly from wood, old and dry, was soon a mass of flames.

The call for assistance requested at about 07.00 arrived at Colchester police station at 08.30 – an hour and a half after it was supposed to have been sent. Superintendent Beaumont and the Colchester Essex & Suffolk brigade, were quickly assembled:

'Well horsed by Mr Pearce, of the Cups Hotel Yard

*Angel Corner, Kelvedon: Wisemans Collegiate School, later a Roman Catholic College.
Caught fire on 20th December 1886. Also visible is the large obelisk-like water pump on the right.*
Reproduced by courtesy of the Kelvedon Museum

and was taken to Kelvedon in fine style by George Wells, arriving at the scene of the fire at 9.30am., just an hour after the call came in.'

In Coggeshall, the telegraph was received at 08.35 and the engine, horsed by the White Hart, was manned by three men: James and William Tansley and Mr Rustell who was the landlord of 'The Cricketers Inn', just a few steps away from William's house. They lost no time in getting the engine to the fire and drew up at just after 9.00am – the first brigade to arrive. The Witham brigade turned up some ten minutes later.

Coggeshall did not have enough hose to run the 300 yards from the water, a moat, to the fire, so the Witham engine set into the moat and supplied water via its hose to the Coggeshall machine which ran out its hose to play on the fire. The arrangement worked admirably and with plenty of people on hand to provide the pumping power, Coggeshall had a good jet working at the rear of the building. When the Colchester engine arrived they also set into the moat and ran their hose up the London Road to fight the fire from the High Street side and at this point the three brigades were using a total of 1,100 feet of hose. For half an hour, the jets of water seemed to have no effect on the progress of the flames which were:

'Leaping and raging, constantly increasing in power as they fed upon the dry woodwork. But the firemen persevered in their endeavours and as the supply of water increased a distinct impression was made. By this time the whole of the front of the noble building was a mass of powerful red-tongued flames but gradually and slowly the volume of water told on them, reducing their power and confining them to those parts of the building which could not be saved.'

The fire was contained and by midday was

brought under control. The spectators had been increasing all morning and some five hundred were present to see the last of the flames put out at about 12.30pm. The 'Essex Chronicle' reported 'The gutted school presented a most deplorable picture, only the walls of the burnt parts being left standing.' People stood in groups for most of the day whilst the firemen doused the remaining hot spots, 'wondering at the destruction of what was once the pride of the town'.

The recently widowed Mrs Dowcra and some of her five daughters freely supplied the beverages, tea and coffee, as all were fierce workers in the temperance movement. The Coggeshall, Colchester and Witham firemen:

> 'worked together hard and heartily.. and left the town amid the hearty congratulations of the inhabitants who were unanimous in their praise for their gallant conduct'.

Mr Rann, the owner, visited the site two days later. Large volumes of smoke continued to rise from the ruins and every now and again flames erupted from the heaps of glowing embers. *[CC 24/12/1886 EN & ES 25/12/1886]*

The hour and a half delay between the time the telegraph was supposed to have been sent and its arrival, was a matter of much local discussion and suspicion centred on the Kelvedon Postmaster, Mr Meade who, it was said, refused to open the telegraph office until its usual time of 8 o'clock. A claim he described as 'untruthful' in a letter to the 'Chronicle'. *[CC 24/12/1886]*

In circumstances like those after the Richard White's fire at Coggeshall more than a hundred years earlier, there was a growing clamour that Kelvedon should have its own brigade and engine. The subject was the talk of the town over Christmas and before the year's end, a poster was produced announcing a public meeting 'To consider the question of purchasing a fire engine'.

At the meeting on 30th December, Mr Joseph Polley said: 'the disastrous fire about a week ago proved to us our utter helplessness....'

The Poster issued in December 1886.
Reproduced by courtesy of the Kelvedon Museum

A representative from the engine-makers Shand Mason was present and he had offered one of their 16-manual engines, used 'a few times' by the Metropolitan Fire Brigade. This would have cost £120 new but was offered for £50. Support was wholehearted and a subscription raised. The Kelvedonians were ready to dip their hands deep and before long had collected a remarkable £116 18s 6d. The engine was bought and fully equipped with hose and appliances and the brigade kitted out, all for £91. The year 1887 was Queen Victoria's 50th year as Queen, so the engine was christened 'The Jubilee Fire Engine'

The founding Captain, George Braddy, was the same builder who had helped save the school chapel. The engineer, Will Moore, was a carrier and haulier, whose business was later to become Moore's Buses. The engine was probably kept at Will Moore's premises but given the feeling in the town toward their brigade, when the time came

The newly formed Kelvedon Fire Brigade with their Shand-Mason manual engine 1887.
Photo by courtesy of Bryan Everitt

a few years later to build a fire station, nothing ordinary would do. The design was like no other fire station, designed in the Italian style complete with a campanile from whence, amidst the drying hoses a bugler would sound the alert, summoning the manly crew to the shy and admiring glances of the local girls.

The Coggeshall and Kelvedon brigades would prove to have a close if uneasy relationship over the coming years and a future where first one and then the other, was in the ascendant. This had unexpected and significant consequences, as we shall discover.

The contrast between the two brigades is telling. Coggeshall had long had the benefit of an engine for which there was no sense of ownership and no civic pride. When problems came to public attention, there were demands that 'something should be done', but the outrage was brief and the discussion, as we have seen, diverse and inconclusive. The town had never taken the engine or the brigade into their hearts. When the long serving Daniel Leaper retired, for example, there was no ceremony or public thanks for his years of effort and service to the town. In fact, his brief newspaper obituary did not even mention his work as superintendent of the engine. The Kelvedon experience was quite different. After the disastrous fire, the discussion was focused, a decision made, funds raised, the engine bought and a brigade signed up all with apparent ease. The achievement was communal and it continued to be celebrated.

6 THE LAST YEARS OF THE ESSEX & SUFFOLK BRIGADE

In the three years since the débâcle of the East Street fire James Tansley had effected a real improvement in the Coggeshall brigade. Every fire had brought favourable comments as to their smartness and efficiency and there had been no problems with the engine or the equipment. The Kelvedon fire was to be James Tansley's last. At sixty-seven he had decided to retire and devote himself to fishing. His son William would take over the business.

Alfred Gardner the Essex & Suffolk agent died in November 1886, he was just forty-seven years old. He had been suffering from the degenerative disease, 'chronic rheumatism' (now called rheumatoid arthritis) and had been blind for the last three years of his life. The new Essex & Suffolk agent, William Bright, was appointed on 6th December 1886. He was sixty-four, the head of another well connected and prosperous Coggeshall family and part owner of the 'Beard & Bright' brewery business in Stoneham Street[1]. A member of the parish Council, he also represented the parish on the Braintree Board of Guardians. He lived near the brewery at Cromwell House but would have conducted the business of the agency from the brewery office.

Bright would have understood the importance of having someone in regular charge of the engine and probably encouraged James Tansley's son William to take on the job. Although only twenty-six years old, William knew the ropes having ridden to fires with his father and his ability had been recognised. These experiences, his practical ability as an engineer and fitter and perhaps the exciting circumstances of the Kelvedon fire, no doubt all played a part and soon after Christmas 1886 he decided to take on the job.

James Tansley was straightforward, practical and confident, his son William was a more complex character, sensitive and artistic. He was an accomplished musician and took a leading part in many of the events that ordered Coggeshall's social calendar. William sang sentimental songs, was a banjo player[2] and a violinist who conducted his own string band. He regularly gave concerts both in the town and around the district. His wife five years his senior, Margaret Cameron Tansley, was a Scot and also very musical. They had five children and lived at Factory House on West Street next door to James. William could be a kind man. In July 1891 Mrs George Laud died after childbirth leaving a husband and twelve children. William organised a subscription for the bereaved family and raised £24. He did the same thing in 1895 when Mrs John Hills died leaving five children and a distraught husband. He was also quick to take offence and not ready to forgive a perceived slight. Appointed Bandmaster to the Coggeshall Brass Band in November 1888, he resigned in April the next year – 'because of the misconduct of some members of the Brass band'. The band was a social institution in the town and always played at public events but when they asked William to reconsider, he declined and the band broke up 'until a bandmaster could be obtained' *[ES 10/04/1889]*

---

1   In 1899 William bought the brewery outright and it became 'William Bright & Sons Ltd.' The purchase price of £49,250 included the Chapel Malting and thirty hotels, public and beer houses in various places in Essex which produced annual sales of £12,000 in 1899. *[London Evening Standard 06/11/1899]*

2   In February 1887 it was reported that his 'banjo solo "business", evoked roars of laughter'. *[EN 14/02/1887]*

Market Hill showing the Chapel Commercial Hotel.

Pub and Cottage Destroyed

A destructive fire broke out in August 1887 near the Bird in Hand Public House half-way between Coggeshall and Earls Colne. The fire was seen: 'at about 11 o'clock in the forenoon' in a haystack close to a thatched cottage where children had been seen playing. The flames spread from the stack to the cottage which was soon well alight and this set fire to the weather-boarded public house. Most of the people were at work in the fields so there was no-one to help fight the fire or fetch the brigade. The stack, the cottage and the public house were all completely destroyed, only a few items of furniture survived. *[ES 13/08/1887]*

Also in August, William Tansley suffered a serious accident whilst working on some machinery at the Kelvedon Brewery:

> '..his hand became entangled in the wheels: Although the hand is much disfigured it is hoped that amputation of any of the fingers will not be necessary.'

The Coggeshall surgeon, Mr T Simpson attended and must have done an extraordinary job because Tansley was able to resume his violin and banjo playing later the same year.
[CC 05/08/1887 & ES 06/08/1887]

Near Tragedy in the Chapel

On a dark November night in 1888 almost a hundred men packed into the Large Room at the Chapel Hotel in Coggeshall for a meeting of the Working Men's Conservative Association. The room, on the first floor, was reached by a narrow, unlit stairway and the first meeting of the season was underway when 'with a great crash', a large oil lamp fell onto the table in front of the chairman. The oil burst into flames and formed a spreading pool of fire on the floor prompting a rush for the stairs, the only means of escape, a scenario that has sealed the fate of many. Fortunately, 'thanks to the coolness of several present in advising steadiness and care in passing down', evacuation progressed in a hurried but orderly way and this undoubtedly prevented a disaster. The room steadily cleared of people but the last twenty or thirty suffered rapidly in the worsening conditions. The flames by this time, were leaping up to the ceiling and thick choking smoke gathered in a layer which drew ever closer to the floor. Still waiting their turn, several men got down to the floor in an effort to avoid the heat and smoke, whilst others bent down with handkerchiefs over their mouths. The last few

> **Dismantling the Great Silk Factory**
> July 1886
>
> 'This building which was closed in 1861, owing to the decline of the English Silk trade, is about to be sold and the splendid machinery with the ponderous engines, erected at enormous cost, is being broken up by Messrs Tansley and Sons, engineers, to be sold as old metal. Messrs Durant, the proprietors of the factory, had 400 persons in their employ and the looms kept upwards of 1,000 persons employed in the various mills in the surrounding towns and villages, finishing the work commenced here.' [CC 30/07/1886]

> **ORCHARD SILK MILLS, GREAT COGGESHALL.**
>
> *Messrs. Abrey and Gardner*
> Are favoured with instructions to SELL BY AUCTION on Tuesday, August 31st, 1886, at Eleven for Twelve o'clock,
> 12 H.P. HORIZONTAL ENGINE, 10 H.P. Vertical BOILER, by Davey and Paxman, Egg-ended Boiler, 100 Tons of Cast and Wrought Iron, 16 Cwt. Brass, 8¼ Cwt. Lead, Lathes, vices, hot water pipes, lots of useful boards, mahogany-top tables, two large bills, 80-light gas meter, and other miscellaneous lots arising from the pulling out of the entire machinery and fittings at the above mills.
> Catalogues and further Particulars may be obtained of Mr. Jas. Tansley, Coggeshall; or of the Auctioneers, Witham and Braintree.

got down the stairs to the 'deliciously cool air outside', moments before they would have been overcome. Everyone, 'who so narrowly escaped death' the report concludes, was thankful 'for such a providential escape'. There is no record of how the fire was extinguished. *[ES 10/11/1888]*

Hay House farm at Earls Colne was occupied by Thomas Sampson Bell a farmer and brewer and was the scene of several fires. A stack fire in 1884 was thought to have been caused by spontaneous combustion and another in 1887 was started by the children of some pea pickers playing with matches. Having set a stack alight the frightened children ran away leaving a child in a perambulator who, 'before it could be rescued was much burnt'. *[ES 10/11/1888]* A fire which broke out on the night of 7th April 1889 was almost certainly the work of an incendiary who set fire to a wheat stack which stood close to farm buildings and just a few yards from a road. A mounted messenger was sent to Coggeshall for the engine and William Tansley described as the 'foreman of the Essex and Suffolk Equitable Fire Engine' was soon at the scene, his first recorded appearance in charge of the brigade. There was a good supply of water and the fire was confined to the stack.

Edward Sach

In 1889, in an extraordinary gesture of generosity, Matthias Gardner whose only son Alfred had died three years before, decided to hand the carpentry side of his business to Edmund Sach[3], a man he had employed for thirty-six years, eight as foreman. In a cruel turn of fate, no sooner was the handover signed and sealed than Edmund suddenly died, aged fifty-two, his death, 'brought on by the mental excitement' of taking over the business. *[CC 11/10/1889]* Edmund's son, twenty-nine year old Edward, found himself in charge. Someone may not have been happy at the turn of events because one night in March 1892 flames were seen issuing from the top floor of the firm's workshops in Back Lane. The fire, which had started outside the building, burnt through the wall and 'had got hold of a lot of made up work in the shop'. Two neighbours with axes made a breach on each side of the burning boards and Edward and others brought up buckets of water. When William Tansley arrived with the engine it was not needed. Whoever started the fire was not satisfied and Edward Sach's premises on Back Lane were to become the most fire-prone in the town. *[EN 12/03/18892]*

---

3   Pronounced 'saych'

Prospect Place, date unknown.

Walcotts

In August 1892, Mrs Crocker of Walcotts, Great Tey, invited 120 children from the Coggeshall Day and Sunday Schools for tea at her house. The tea 'was much enjoyed as were afterwards, the sports in the beautiful meadow opposite the house where the Messrs Crocker provided amusements.' *[ES 20/08/1892]* Providence did not reward this kindly gesture because three weeks later to the day, a fire broke out in the stackyard there. A messenger went to Coggeshall for the engine and William Tansley quickly mustered his crew and arrived at Walcotts, two miles from Coggeshall just thirty minutes later. The owner of Walcotts, Mr Lay, was alerted and remembering the 1869 fire, he decided to call out the Colchester brigade as well, so for the only recorded time both the Coggeshall and Colchester Essex & Suffolk Equitable Insurance Brigades worked together at a fire. The buildings threatened by the fire were saved but two stacks of wheat and two of hay were destroyed.
[EN 10/09/1892]

Bravery at Prospect Place

Prospect Place was a terrace of four houses in the area of the modern day road called 'Windmill Fields'. It stood on its own and faced West and had a splendid prospect across the valley of Robin's Brook. One Sunday in November 1892, George Godden who lived there, set off with his daughter to attend Choral Evensong at the parish church, its tower visible across the fields a half-mile away. His other two children, aged ten and seven were left asleep in bed. On her way to church, the daughter briefly returned home to collect her gloves. Striking a match to see her way, she found the gloves in the bedroom and continued on to church. The match, had not been properly put out.

At about seven o'clock, the next door neighbour, Mrs Perry, was putting her own children to bed when she heard muffled cries from the house next door. Very alarmed, she rushed outside and opening her neighbour's door, found the place full of smoke and the children upstairs, screaming for help. Her calls brought

> ### The Condition of Agriculture in Essex
> Joseph Beaumont of Coggeshall 1892
> *Responding to a newspaper report of remarks by Mr Justice Field concerning the prosperity he claimed to have seen in Surrey and Kent, Beaumont suggests he visits Essex, its 'very antithesis';*
> *'...although fifty prisoners were tried at sessions last week, a calendar of dark crime and a large number of prisoners await him......Should he care to inquire he will learn that the agricultural aspect of the county of Essex has never been so dark as it is at the present moment; landlords cannot find tenants, that tenants cannot find money and that labourers cannot find employment; ... where forty and fifty pounds per acre could 15 years ago be obtained for Essex farms, some of these same lands have changed hands at five pounds and ten pounds per acre and that others are absolutely unsaleable.' [ES 29/10/1892]*

The Guy Fawkes Arsonist

The Bonfire Night celebrations of 1892 went relatively quietly. An overloaded cannon was blown off its trunions and 'flew some distance before striking the plate glass window of Mr A Nunn's shop' but it was claimed that 'no wanton damage was recorded'. The evening culminated in a parade of Masqueraders around the streets, led by the combined Coggeshall and Earls Colne bands and ending up on Market Hill with the usual bonfire and fireworks.

> 'The home-made squibs for which Coggeshall is famous seemed extra fierce and plentiful and were most erratic in their movements. Several windows were broken in the vicinity of Market Hill. Whilst the bonfire was burning, a large glare was noticed in the direction of Stoneham Street. A rush was made to the spot where a warehouse was found to be enveloped in flames.' *[CC 11/11/1892]*

This was the first of a series of arson attacks that was to strike Coggeshall on or about Guy Fawkes night for years to come. At the time, however, it was assumed that a particularly lively squib was to blame. The weather-boarded warehouse occupied by Harry Saunders was filled with his stock in trade including more than 100 chairs. The engine was quickly on the spot with a Mr Rolph in charge and the ruins were quickly damped down. Tansley was probably somewhere in the district music-making. As far as the records show, this was the only fire that he ever missed.

Alfred Godfrey and his son Harry to the scene. Alfred forced his way upstairs and in thick smoke he felt his way to the bedroom, where he found and rescued the children. Harry, went in with a bucket of water and doused what proved to be a smouldering fire in the bedroom.

> 'Had it not been for the timely assistance rendered by Messrs. Godfrey, the children would doubtless have lost their lives and probably the whole row of houses have been destroyed.'

Alfred and Harry Godfrey's bravery was recognised by the 'Royal Society for the Protection of Life from Fire'. In February 1893, the Vicar presented the pair with a sum of money and a framed certificate.
[EN 12/11/1892 & ES 18/02/1893]

The autumn of 1892 brought torrential rain and flooding to much of low-lying Essex. After a storm at the end of October, a huge volume of water poured down Robin's Brook which flooded West Street, Gravel End and Bridge Street leaving many houses knee deep in water, including James Tansley's near Hare Bridge. *[EH 05/11/1892]*

The medal of the Royal Society for the Protection of Life from Fire.

Heatwave

1893 was a year of record-breaking heat. On 19th August, the temperature had exceeded 80°F for eleven days in a row. Several fires were reported to have been started by the extreme heat. A parade and collection at Colchester in June had a very disappointing result and it was suggested rather imaginatively perhaps, that 'the weather was too hot for people to put their hands in their pockets.' [ES 24/06/1893]

On the 8th July the Coggeshall engine was called out to a fire at Herons Farm, near Bradwell. The 'Essex Standard' reported:

> 'It is presumed that the fire was caused by the extreme heat of the sun playing on some glass that had somehow found its way into the stack.'

With everything tinder dry and only a limited supply of water, the brigade worked hard to save the buildings not already alight and did 'excellent service'. The fire destroyed:

> '....two large barns, cattle sheds, two horse sheds, stables, bullock shed and piggeries and damaging other buildings and also destroying two wheat stacks, an oat straw stack, a barley straw stack, a stack of old pea-rice, a stack of trefoil and pea-rice, a stack of clover hay, a stack of clover and grass hay, a quantity of mangel, a clamp of manure, 70 quarters of red wheat in the barn, a lot of chaff, rick frames, six cattle cribs, dressing machines, oil cake breaker, turnip cutter, nearly a dozen fat hogs, a lot of poultry, cattle food &c. The damage is estimated to exceed £1,000' [EN 08/07/1893 CC 14/07/1893]

A severe thunder storm later in August caused havoc across Essex with several lightning strikes in Coggeshall, including one to the church tower which threw down a pinnacle. Hot weather conditions with severe storms and lightning meant that the two years 1892-93 saw enormous insurance claims for farming losses covered by the Essex & Suffolk, amounting to £39,000. This was more than double the average loss over a thirty year period and resulted in an unprecedented trading loss. Drawing on its substantial reserves, the Essex & Suffolk was never in any danger and even managed to offer what had become the usual annual dividend, a 50% refund on premiums.

Father and Son

Humphrey Willsher, the bailiff of Mrs Honywood's Marks Hall estate, lived at Crowlands, a remote farm on the north-west edge of Coggeshall. On a July evening in 1893 he was 'burning some wasps nests' accompanied by his five year old son. The next day the boy used some matches to light some straw and soon a stack and then the farm buildings became involved. The engine was called and set in to a good supply of water from one of the farm ponds. A barn, bullock shed and stacks of straw and clover were destroyed but under William Tansley's direction, the house, another barn and other buildings were saved. Although all are now gone, the overgrown site and its two ponds, are still there, next to the footpath along the edge of Little Monks Wood and well worth a visit. [ES 05/08/1893]

The last fire of 1893 was at the Bird-in-Hand, on the Earls Colne road, a pub rebuilt on the same site as the one which had been destroyed in a fire just six years earlier. Hearing a noise, wonderfully described as 'of a tumbril approaching the house and drawing into the shed', the landlord went outside and seeing fire, went straight to the stable and broke open the door: 'the flames met him and beat him back and his mare which had been kicking furiously, fell dead before his eyes'. A messenger was sent for the brigade, who 'quickly attended and did splendid service'. By then, the fire had spread to a cart-shed but the brigade soon had things under control, saving the house and other outbuildings. It was claimed that four barrels of beer and all the spirits and wine were destroyed. There is no evidence as to William Tansley's relationship with alcohol but there must be some suspicion on this occasion as to the brigade's. [EN 07/10/1893 SEFP 11/10/1893]

A Question of Payment

It was 1.30 in the morning when a fire broke out in the harness-room at Hall Farm, Stisted. Arthur Harrington, the local postman, went off on his horse to Braintree Fire Station for the brigade[4]. The firemen, under Captain Dunlop, quickly assembled but would not turn out because Arthur 'did not know the name of the insurers' of the farm. Braintree was a Local Board brigade – run under the auspices of the council. Their responsibility only extended to the residents and ratepayers of Braintree so as the fire was outside the town, they wanted to know who was going to pay for their services. Although the farm was part of the Stisted Hall estate, the brigade knew from experience that they could have no legal claim on the owner, James Paxman, as he had not personally called for their services. The impasse was resolved by the intervention of the local Essex & Suffolk agent, Mr Prykes who apparently happened to turn up at the fire station and knew that the contents of Hall Farm were insured with his office and instructed the brigade to attend.
[EN 12/05/1894]

The incident shows the legal and moral void at the heart of fire protection at the end of the nineteenth and into the early twentieth century. A situation where a publicly funded brigade like Braintree might refuse to attend a fire but a so called 'commercial' brigade like the Essex & Suffolk at Coggeshall would have turned out without question. In this case, the difference between a house being destroyed or saved was decided by the chance involvement of an insurance agent. Other places were not so lucky.

---

4   Tragically, Arthur Harrington's sister was to be killed in a fire just a few months later. Mary Harrington was 62 years old and lived in a cottage on The Street, Stisted. As she was going to bed about 10 o'clock one night, carrying a paraffin lamp in her hand, she suffered a fainting fit. Dropping the lamp she fell into the flames and was terribly burnt. She died in the infirmary of the Union Workhouse in Braintree four days later.

Before the fire: On the left is the door to the Red Lion and next to it, the bay window below and sash window above that feature in the story.

The Great Fire at The Red Lion Inn

The Red Lion Inn occupied the corner site at Market End where Market Hill meets Stane Street. It was owned by Beard & Bright, the brewers of Stoneham Street and occupied in 1894 by Mr Daniel Walne, his 16-year-old son Randell and an 11-year-old daughter. On the night of 7th April, his wife and youngest daughter were away.

At about 11.30pm that night Daniel Walne, had locked up and was making his way upstairs to bed. In one hand he carried the cashbox and in the other, an oil lamp. A hammer left on the stairs by one of the children made him stumble and he dropped the lamp. The glass reservoir, full of paraffin, smashed as it hit the stairs, flames flared up then seemed to go out. Walne said that he examined the stairs and 'thoroughly satisfied that there was no sign of fire', he went to bed, thinking to deal with the mess in the morning.

At about ten minutes past one he became conscious of a 'stifling sensation' and waking up, found his bedroom full of smoke. He got up and

*The Red Lion fire, April 1894 – the Doubleday photo sent to the fire crews.
The doorway can be seen centre right but nothing remains of the bay next to it or the sash window above.*

opened the door to the staircase and was hit by a wall of heat and flames roaring up the stairs like a chimney. He managed to close the door on the inferno. 'Had I not done so' he said later, 'it would have been another Colchester job.'[5]

Walne roused his son and pulled on a few clothes. The bedroom window was the only means of escape and it was lucky that the roof of a bay window was immediately underneath and reduced the drop. Showing some presence of mind, he pulled off the bedding and pushed the mattress out of the window onto the pavement below, then helped his son onto the roof of the bay window. The lad jumped down onto the mattress and ran up the street calling 'Fire! Fire!' as he went for the brigade. Daniel then made good his own escape, but his daughter was still in her bedroom at the rear of the building. Walne fetched a ladder and used it to smash the window

and get into her bedroom. Inside his daughter was still asleep unaware of the unfolding drama. He shook her awake and helped her escape down the ladder. His next call was to the stable where he released two colts. Returning to the house, he went back inside to try to save some furniture but only succeeded in rescuing 'a small quantity of linen and a box or two'. He made a snatch for a watch (an old family relic) hanging on a bedstead, but missed it, the heat being more than he could bear.

People were now gathering and the brigade under William Tansley was soon at the scene. It was now about half past one and a lot of people had gathered and 'rendered such assistance as was in their power'. The brigade found a good supply of water at the Short Bridge, some hundred yards away and ran the hose up Bridge Street towards the fire. Despite the excellent water supply the firemen were hard pressed; as soon as they knocked back one part of the fire,

---

[5] In December the previous year, 1893, the charred remains of Mr Welch a Colchester Outfitter had been found after a fire at his shop.

Red Lion fire, Market End. A wide view of the site of the fire.

another grew in strength. After a sudden loss in pressure, the hose was found to have been deliberately damaged, with a cut about 8 inches long, 'evidently done by some evil-disposed person unknown'. Shortly afterwards as William Tansley was carrying a hose up a ladder he was hit by a falling roof tile which knocked him to the ground, ten feet below. Friendly hands pulled him to safety and the Chemist, Mr Frith, patched him up, so he could get back to the fire.

Meanwhile, the fire was spreading with great rapidity and huge clouds of smoke rose into the sky. Mr E W King (the Sweet Pea King) set off on his bicycle for the Kelvedon brigade, and the engine, with seven firemen was quickly horsed over to Coggeshall, the Messrs Moore winning particular praise for the manner in which it was done[6] – this was to be their first major fire. The brigade, under the superintendence of Mr George Braddy were in attendance by three o'clock and they also set in at the back ditch on Bridge Street and brought their hoses to play on the burning buildings. The Coggeshall firemen had been working well to try to subdue the flames and the night was windless, but even so, the Red Lion stood right in the centre of the town with other buildings on both sides, so 'great fears were entertained that the fire might assume huge dimensions'. All the buildings were of timber and lath construction and burned easily. At immediate risk to the north was the lock-up butchers shop of Mr Joyce, which was under the same roof as the Inn and beyond it, Mr Studd's grocers shop. On the other side were the extensive premises of E & T P Doubleday – shop, warehouse and dwelling house. Mr Joyce transferred his stock of meat to his own house just in time because his shop was soon well alight. At the other end, the Messrs Doubleday and their assistants had been woken up by the hubbub to find their rooms full of smoke. They and several helpers started to remove the contents of their premises to safety. The combined efforts of the brigades seemed to be having an effect and the intensity of the fire somewhat stayed, when the flames having gutted Joyce's shop, suddenly broke through the roof of Studd's shop next door. Water was poured in through the hole in the roof, finally extinguishing the flames but also causing much damage to the bedroom and the shop beneath. The corner had been turned and by 6 o'clock in the morning all danger was over. The Kelvedon brigade was able to leave the scene at 7 o'clock leaving the Coggeshall brigade to turn over and damp down and by nightfall there was no possibility of a further outbreak. *[EN 07/04/1894: Bury and Norwich Post 10/04/1894: ES 07/04/1894]*

---

6   The fire engine was only fitted with shafts so the horses were harnessed one in front of the other with one of the men astride the leading horse. They could travel at great speed and it must have been a wonderful sight to see them flying along the 'Serpentine' with the firemen in their brass helmets, in what was a great display of horsemanship. *[CC 10/08/1894]*

During the fire a drunk called Walter Payne and nicknamed 'Payne the Pest' had continually accosted the firemen. A couple of days later he was brought to court charged with being drunk and disorderly. Pc Mills said that he had to carry Payne up the street to his cottage on the night of the fire and the next day had to see him home twice more, eventually placing a constable at the door to keep him in. Payne had six previous convictions and was fined 10s with 9s costs.

The Doubledays had spent a very fraught night expecting the fire to spread to their shop. The next day they had a photograph taken which shows how close the fire came and in grateful thanks they sent the framed photo to every crew member of both fire brigades (see illustration). William Tansley, was also given £5:

> 'To distribute among the deserving men who worked so energetically to save their premises. Had the men not worked as they did, the large warehouses and shop adjoining the Inn must have been destroyed'. [EN 14/04/1894]

Daniel Wade 'who worked so exceptionally hard' received a letter and a new suit of clothes to replace those ruined during his work at the fire[7]. [Coggeshall Almanac 1895 CHC]

Walne had made free with his own beer during the fire to refresh the firemen and pumpers but when he presented the bill to the Essex & Suffolk they refused to pay it. Walne was incensed and sent them a letter in June, threatening legal action. This was recorded in the minutes without comment and nothing came of it. The fire presented an opportunity to widen the approach to Market Hill which had been restricted by the old buildings. When this was done seven and a half feet were added to the width of the roadway. Beard and Bright submitted applications to keep the licence of the Red Lion, even though it had not been rebuilt. On the second occasion, the chairman commented:

> 'The bench wished Mr. Bright to understand that they were not by any means anxious for the house to be re-built. Indeed, on looking over the list of Public Houses in Coggeshall, they considered there were more than enough to supply the needs of the people, unless the latter were very well off. [Laughter].[8] They could not however keep issuing a fresh licence when there was no house for it. The licence would be granted this year, but next year, unless the house was re-built, or the licence sold, it would have to lapse.' [EN 31/08/1895]

The inn was never rebuilt, the Doubledays

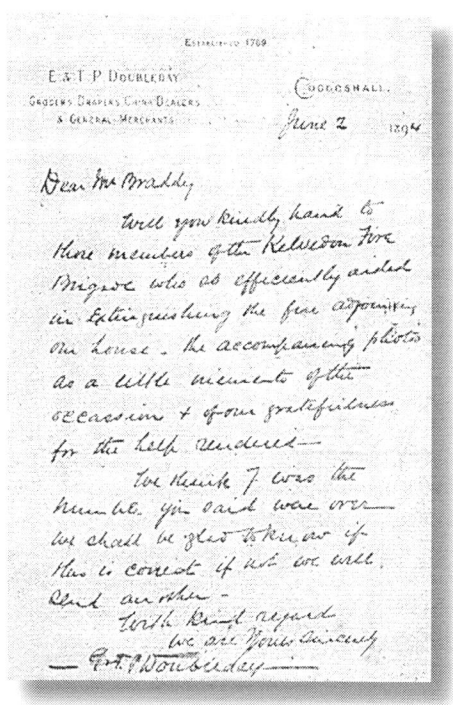

Letter to George Braddy, 2nd June 1894.
'Dear Mr Braddy, Will you kindly hand to those members of the Kelvedon Fire Brigade who so efficiently aided in extinguishing the fire adjoining our house - the accompanying photos as a little memento of the occasion & our gratification for the help received. I think 7 was the number you said were over – we shall be glad to know if this is correct if not we will send another. With kind regards, We are yours sincerely, G&TP Doubleday'
Reproduced by courtesy of the Kelvedon Museum

---

7   Daniel Wade was an agricultural labourer with eleven children who lived on West Street near the Fleece. A building that was itself to burn down some years later. His Great Grandaughter, Shirley Ratcliffe, thinks the Doubleday suit may have been the only one he ever owned.

8   There were 26 public houses and beer shops in 1885 and 17 in 1910. [CC 04/09/1885 & EN 05/03/1910]

View of the top of Bridge Street from the Short Bridge over the Back Ditch. On the left side of the bridge, there is usually a good depth of water and this is where the engine stood during the Red Lion fire and at the Gravel House fire before the hose burst. George Baker, the Blacksmith, stands on Eley's Corner. The Gravel runs to the left behind him.

bought the site and built themselves a house. Both this house and the other old buildings along the road were demolished in the 1960s and a monstrosity erected on the site. Daniel Walne left Coggeshall after the fire and took over the 'Lion Hotel' in Lavenham. Intriguingly, the police opposed the application to transfer the licence:

> 'Based upon a police report from the Superintendent at Witham, who did not appear to be satisfied with Mr Walne's explanation of the origin of the fire in one of the public houses he had owned.'

The application was adjourned and next time Walne was armed with a Solicitor and a letter from the Essex & Suffolk Fire Office. He said that he had been 'unlucky enough to have had one or two fires'[9], but had never had any difficulty in recovering insurance money. The transfer was granted. *[Bury & Norwich Press 08/09/1894]*

---
9 The only other fire reported had broken out in December 1893 when rooms at the Inn and at the Doubleday's premises were smoke-filled in the middle of the night. Walne claimed that he had discovered a mat on fire in an outbuilding, which he had extinguished with a bucket of water. *[CC 15/12/1893]*

The New Parish Council

Parish Councils were created under the Local Government Act of 1894. They had no statutory responsibility to provide fire protection but the permissive facility under the Lighting and Watching Acts still applied. Coggeshall's new Parish Council met in December 1894 and the brigade was not on the agenda. The Directors of the Essex & Suffolk however, saw that the new parish councils could provide them with a way of withdrawing from the fire-brigade business. In Colchester, there were no two ways about it, in an open letter in February 1895, they stated:

> 'For more than 70 years this Office had borne the responsibility of the extinction of fires within the borough. They have for some time considered that such responsibility should rest with the Corporation....As no steps have hitherto resulted, the Directors of the Fire Office feel bound to give notice that their fire brigade can no longer take responsibility for the extinction of fires within the borough.' *[28/02/1895, Quoted in Drew]*

For the time being, the Essex & Suffolk's rural brigades were not directly threatened.

Beard and Bright's Brewery

The fire of May 1894 was the most serious to hit the Stoneham Street Brewery. The main building was constructed of brick, timber and weatherboarding on two floors with an extensive cellar full of stock beneath. The roof was partly tiled but most was thatched with straw. One of Frank Beard's maidservants saw the fire start, when sparks from the engine-room chimney fell onto the malt-house thatch. She raised the alarm and the brewery workers together with a number of painters and other workers at the site quickly got to work. Apart from the many helpers, a large crowd of people assembled to watch the spectacle as the fire developed. Ladders were pitched and buckets of water passed up to be poured on the thatch using water from a large tank in the roof. The fire engine was called and 'in a very short time' William Tansley had the engine out and set into a good supply at Robin's Brook. The hose was run out some eight hundred feet, across Crouches meadow, through the back entrance of the brewery and across Mr Beard's garden (of which he was very proud) and on to the burning building. A very strong north-westerly wind was blowing flames and burning straw towards Mr Beard's house and Stoneham Street and great efforts were made to prevent the fire from spreading.

> 'The smoke rose in clouds from the building and was beaten down by the wind filling the whole street. The men had to work right in the face of this and the charred straw which filled the air was almost blinding.'

On one side, the men cut through the thatch ahead of the fire, stripped it off and threw it down to the ground. At one point, the straw lying in piles on the ground ignited and caused further anxiety until it was finally smothered. Meanwhile the fire in the roof was slowly being brought under control and the remaining thatch thoroughly saturated, further slowing down any spread.

> **All over a Ferret**
> Witham Court June 1893
> *Frederick Hunwick said he met Edward Rowland in Tilkey Road and asked him if he knew anything about a ferret which he had lost. Rowland said he knew nothing about the f*****g ferret and followed Hunwick home and assaulted him.*
> *Fine 5s and costs 9s were imposed, in default fourteen days hard labour.* [CC 09/06/1893]

The enormous quantity of straw stripped from the roof was piled up on Mr Beard's lawn and garden which was 'very much marred' during the emergency. By seven in the evening there was no sign of fire but because of the gusty wind and the risk of a hotspot re-igniting, the firemen stood by at the scene overnight. A successful job for all concerned. [CC 11/05/1894 EN & ES 12/05/1894]

Tilkey

A stack fire 'situate in a pasture in Tilkey' on 30th August 1894 was put down to 'some lads returning from the circus'. The brigade attended but was unable to prevent a total loss. [EN 08/09/1894]

The 5th November 1894 saw another Guy Fawkes arson attack, this one at Tilkey. Mrs Matravers heard a cracking noise and went out to discover that their large thatched shed full of teazels and teazel poles was on fire. It stood just twelve feet from the house and close by was the house of Mr Prail. The shed was lost but the brigade managed to stop the fire from spreading to the houses. [EN 10/11/1894]

William Tansley's father, James, died peacefully in April 1895 at his house near Hare Bridge in West Street. William was now in sole charge of the engineering business.

In September that year, the Parish Council hired the engine to help clean out the Back Ditch, the original course of the river before it was diverted by the monks of Coggeshall Abbey in the twelfth century. The Ditch had become an open sewer and a long standing source of foul smells. Two dams were formed to stop the inflow from the river, the engine used to pump out the water, and the sewage dug out by hand, more than 1,400 yards of it. Working round the clock, the men were paid 6d an hour. *[MB1 & ES 21/09/1895]* The effect was disappointingly short lived and the great stink soon returned. The venture cost a hefty £245. Little Coggeshall Parish Council refused to pay any part of it and claimed it was entirely Great Coggeshall's problem. An appeal was made to Braintree District Council who unhelpfully suggested that the matter should have been discussed first. The obdurate little parish eventually paid just £20. *[EN 03/11/1895]* The sewage laden river water was used downstream at Kelvedon to 'refresh' watercress before it was dispatched by train for the London markets.

Guy Fawkes Arsonist

There was another Guy Fawkes arson attack at 7 o'clock in the evening of 5th November 1895. A stack of wheat straw and a stack of runner beans were destroyed and a clamp of mangels damaged. They were in a field behind the Tollhouse on Colchester Road:

> 'A barn standing close by was at one time thought to be in danger, but fortunately the wind was blowing in the opposite direction. There was also a cottage standing within a few yards of the spot, the inmates of which were at one time alarmed as to their safety.'

The stack eventually burned itself out. The police were called and carried out enquiries and for the first time, a newspaper report noted:

> 'It is a strange thing that during the last four years, three fires have taken place on the day of the anniversary of the Gunpowder plot, but in no case has the cause been ascertained.' *[EN 09/11/1895]*

In 1896 celebrations 'passed off very quietly', in the evening a number of home made squibs were discharged on Market Hill 'some of which were exceedingly fierce' and the whole day

Accidental Assault by Battery
July 1888
On Wednesday the Hanwyn Battery, Royal Artillery, consisting of 95 men and officers, 74 horse and six guns, on their road from Ipswich to Okehampton, stayed at the White Hart Hotel for refreshments. The men had just remounted, when one of the horses backed on to the fire with a cauldron of molten lead, in use for relaying the gas mains of the town. The boiling metal, falling onto the damp pavement flew about in all directions, several of the bystanders and shop windows being bespatted with it. The Rev. A. D. Phillips and Messrs Gervans, Mount and Potter came in for a plentiful shower of metal, which fortunately did no harm beyond frightening the children and injuring the clothes of the recipients. [EN 14/07/1888]

Schoolboy, Cart and Cow
October 1897
A man named Osborn in the employment of Fred Mayes, of Stisted, was returning from Colchester with a horse and cart. When coming down the hill near the Toll House, the horse was frightened by a schoolboy and made a jolt forward, breaking the harness. The animal then dashed down the hill at a furious speed. When opposite the Mount the cart collided violently with a cow belonging to Mrs Warren. The cart was turned completely over, the horse fell and the man was thrown heavily onto the ground, sustaining fearful injuries to his head and face. The poor fellow was picked up in an unconscious condition and was taken into the Mount, the residence of Mrs Surridge, where every possible attention was given him. Dr Caudwell was sent for and he attended to the man's injuries. Osborn was conveyed home in Mr Brown's 'bus' still in an unconscious state and he is now lying in a critical condition. The cow was slightly injured and the cart and harness, much damaged. [CC 29/10/1897]

Cow in a China Shop
September 1897
On Monday a cow belonging to Mr Stebbing was being driven up Church Street and when near Mr Gowers China and Earthenware establishment it made a dash up the flight of four stone steps leading from the street into the shop, which it entered. It 'walked the counter' and caused some consternation to those inside the house. Mr Mike Dalton, who was near suggested that the door leading to the private house should be opened, as there was not room for the cow to turn in the shop. This was done and the animal then ran through the house and out of the private door. Only about £2 worth of damage was done.
[Cuttle 04/09/1897]

Gravel House fire, October 1897.

resulted in only three serious injuries 'requiring surgical aid', and they were to one young man and two children. No unexplained fires were reported. *[CC 13/11/1896]*

The Essex & Suffolk brigade under Tansley's stewardship had enjoyed fourteen years of success, the reservations and questions that had once exercised the townspeople were no longer a topic of public concern. However by 1897 things were not going well for William Tansley. His father's death seems to mark a turning point, the family engineering business was probably in decline and once financially secure, he was struggling to keep up appearances. The brigade had dwindled away, perhaps everyone knew it was a sinking ship and its days were numbered. Tansley's pressing business problems did not help and his own personal failings in the way he dealt with people probably made its own contribution. He was left to run the engine on his own and in hindsight the consequences seem inevitable and the denouement was not long in coming.

The Great Fire of 1897

At about a quarter to nine in the evening of 26th October 1897, Mr Lawrence put his pony in the stable on the Gravel and left for home. His lad Perceval followed ten minutes later, after putting out the light in the lantern. An hour later two friends, Walter Brown and James Melville were walking along the Gravel and saw that the stable was on fire and raised the alarm. Hearing a horse inside, they found a crowbar, broke open the door and saw that the pony had fallen to the ground. They tried to get in but were forced back by the heat. Mr E W King arrived and with some difficulty managed to get his pony out of an adjoining stable and once free, it galloped away up the street. The fire engine was sent for and arrived either 'shortly afterwards', or 'almost an hour later' (the accounts vary) superintended by William Tansley but it is not clear if he had any men with him. The engine was first taken to the nearest water, Robin's Brook at Hare Bridge on West Street, where the water proved too shallow for the engine to work properly but in the attempt, stones and rubbish were drawn in which partially blocked the hard suction hose. The engine was then moved past the fire to the Back Ditch at Short Bridge but the hose was still attached and was damaged as it was dragged along the ground – there were just too many excited people anxious to assist. It will be recalled that a similar thing happened to Daniel Leaper at the 'Woolpack fire' but this time the result was disastrous:

> 'Very little water had been got on the burning buildings when the hose burst. Meanwhile Messrs E W King & Co removed their cart and a quantity of oats from their store house, which adjoined Mr Lawrence's stable and the flames leapt up from there to the house belonging to Captain Townsend, occupied by Miss Popham, tambour lace manufacturer. Upwards of 1,000 people had by this time arrived upon the scene of the conflagration, but hardly a person among them thought for a moment that the fine three-storied house adjoining, which had been substantially built, would be burned to the ground. Nor would it have been, had there been an organised brigade of men present with proper equipment, who knew their work. Mr Tansley did all in his power with the fire engine but with the faulty appliances and no brigade but volunteers, who like the well-known Coggeshall volunteers of old, all appeared to be officers in command[10], efforts to combat the fire proved futile and no practical good was done. The flames gradually found their way under the eaves and into the house adjoining and the crowd stood looking on, helpless to do anything. Miss Popham, Mrs Cook, the servant and two assistants living in the house were appraised of the danger and with the assistance of willing helpers they removed some of the articles of value from the house which were not covered by insurance, including a dozen sewing machines and a quantity of lace. Tongues of fire crept through the roof and quickly worked their way from one room to another and from floor to floor until the whole building from top to bottom was enveloped. Within the space of about two hours the place was razed to the ground. Some of the chimneys and walls fell with a terrific crash and many of the spectators had a narrow escape from being injured from the falling debris.......Mr Lawrence had two carts ....a cob, harness and a quantity of stock and fodder destroyed and he estimates his damage at about £150. Messrs E W King & Co's loss included nasturtiums, oats, three sets of harness, chaffcutter &c., estimated to be worth £200. Nearly the whole of Miss Popham's furniture and effects were destroyed, including a quantity of antique furniture and stock-in-trade. The total damage is estimated at about £1,600. Most of the people cleared off about one o'clock.
> *[Cuttle October 1897]*

At the Red Lion fire three years earlier, the Kelvedon brigade had been called to assist, this time, when there was even more reason to do so, they were not. It seems impossible that no-one thought of it because the man who called them then, E W King, was not only in attendance but this time his own property was involved in the fire. Had there been a disagreement at the Red Lion fire which meant that this time it was impossible to ask the Kelvedon brigade for help? Given William Tansley's sometimes prickly personality, could he have been at the root of it?

Aftermath

The 'Chelmsford Chronicle' included the headline: 'A Fire brigade Wanted' and some people were quick to air their views on the fire.

> 'With reference to the fire at Coggeshall on October 26th, the miserable way in which the Fire brigade managed or mismanaged the whole affair was a complete farce. A woman with a garden hose would have effected more real service. It must have been nearly an hour from the time of the first alarm to the arrival of the manual engine, which was placed near Hare Bridge, where I should think there was not more than nine inches depth of water, the suction pipe drawing up grit into the valves of the engine and hose, rendering them unworkable. Realising their failure they decided to move the engine to another part of the ditch. To

---

10 A reference to a farcical comedy 'The Coggeshall Volunteers' written c1820.

West Street at Hare Bridge. The water of Robin's Brook can be seen as it exits the bridge and enters a culvert, lower right. The Gravel factory once stood on the right.

expedite matters (time and distance being of no consideration) they ran the engine around Eley's corner, a considerable distance further, dragging the hose across the sharp gravel. During this delay the fire had gained very considerably, reaching to Miss Popham's house. On recommencing pumping the hose burst, rendering the whole thing absolutely useless. The Fire brigade were then compelled to abandon further effort and had to watch the building burn to the ground. I don't understand this ditch being selected for the water supply, when they had two wells on the premises, one across at King's Brewery almost inexhaustible, within 50 yards and the main river within 200 yards. With such resources at command they ought at least to have saved Miss Popham's house easily. Had the fire occurred in Church-street, with the present bad supply of water in that locality, the town would have been wrecked. I should like to suggest to the Parish Council that they can no longer pooh-pooh the idea of providing an ample supply of water. Were the town thus provided (as it sadly needs to be) with hydrants at various points such a catastrophe as occurred on Tuesday would be easily averted. I would also suggest that the Council should have an engine of their own and form a volunteer fire brigade under responsible management. Under existing circumstances the lives and property of residents in Coggeshall are not safe. An Onlooker.' *[Cuttle 05/11/1897]*

The 'Chronicle', as well as reporting the fire, also had an editorial on the state of affairs:

'Coggeshall is sadly in need of a fire engine and a fire brigade with proper equipments. This was sadly evidenced on Tuesday night. With half a dozen good firemen properly equipped, the house might have been saved. At present the town relies upon the services of a manual engine belonging to the Essex and Suffolk Fire Office and of which W H Tansley has charge. It is seldom given a trial, except when a fire occurs and then its weak points are detected. Under the circumstances one would think the Parish Council would make some arrangement with the Essex and Suffolk for the use of their engine and get a proper fire brigade appointed. *[CC 29/10/1897]*

Despite these dramatic events, the Guy Fawkes arsonist attacked again, just two weeks later on 5th November. This time the target was a thatched barn on the Old Road near Surrex to the east of Coggeshall. The barn with thirty-three quarters of barley was burnt to the ground, as was a stack of mangel seeds nearby. *[CC 12/11/1897]*.

A Parish Meeting

At the next meeting of the Parish Council the Chairman said that he had received a requisition from a large number of ratepayers asking him to call a Parish Meeting to discuss the situation. A Parish Meeting was just like those previously organised by the Vestry and allowed people to have their say before any decisions were taken. In a break with tradition, the meeting on 11th November 1897 was held at the Lecture Hall in Queen Street[11] rather than at the meeting Room at the White Hart. Mr Dodds (Stationer and Post-Master) seemed to speak for the town:

> 'He did not think there would be two opinions as to whether a fire brigade was wanted or not, especially after the deplorable manner in which things were managed at the recent fire. It was a disgrace to them and one could not think of it without a feeling of dread. Had the fire occurred in Church-street or in one of the other principal streets the result must have been disastrous. At present the appliances in the town were utterly useless to cope with a fire. They ought to have an engine of their own and a proper brigade and they would then know who was responsible.'

This went down well with those present, but when the matter of paying for the new brigade was raised, an undercurrent of parsimony surfaced and damped down any enthusiasm that threatened to break out. A brigade supported voluntarily was one thing, one paid for through

---

11   Opened in 1890 and built by Gardner & Son. Queen Street was previously Back Lane.

The Gasworks March 1898

The gas company are renewing the retort benches and while a young man named James Meredith [sic] was assisting in taking out one of the old retorts, the arch over suddenly collapsed. George Johnson, one of the workmen, observed the brickwork slipping and called out to Meredith, but before the unfortunate man could get out a large quantity of bricks, sand and mortar fell and buried him. The retort next to the one that was being removed, was in use and so the debris which fell on Meredith was much heated. Mr W P Hotchkin and his son and Johnson quickly set to work to remove the bricks and material from Meredith who could be heard groaning and within three minutes they had extricated him from his perilous position. He was found to be badly burned about his hands, arms and neck and one of his feet. His face and hands were also cut and his body was much bruised, but on examination no bones were found to be broken. First aid was rendered and Meredith was afterwards conveyed home in a van. Messrs Cauldwell and Clowes are attending the patient and we are pleased to state that he is progressing favourably. Owing to the collapse of the arch over the retorts, the gas supply to the town is somewhat curtailed. [CC 25/03/1898]

Joseph Mereday, 23, died just over a week later.

Undomesticated Bullock   October 1898

A bullock entered the open door of the shop of Mr Marchant, pork butcher and greengrocer, it proceeded down the passage and pushed open the door to the living room where the family numbering seven persons, were seated at tea. The bullock dashed into the room, frightening the occupants and went for a picture frame smashing it to pieces, cutting itself and bespattering the wall with blood. It knocked over Maud Harper, a niece and lifted a child two years of age over the table, jumped over the girl, upset the table and a paraffin lamp setting fire to the table cloth. Mr Marchant picked up the lamp and threw it outside. The bullock 'ramped' around the room with a lady's blouse on its horns and smashed up five mahogany chairs, most of the ornaments, a sewing machine, a chiffonier and another table and then left. Mrs Marchant has been confined to her bed, much upset by the screams and commotion. [CC 28/10/1898]

the rates was quite another: 'It would be like paying a second fire insurance premium' claimed the frugal E E Surridge, Chairman of the Parish Council. The example of Kelvedon's brigade was cited, not just as model but to fire up the latent competitiveness between the two communities. Mike Dalton the parish clerk cried to some applause, 'If they could do it in Kelvedon, we can do it in Coggeshall!' Then someone suggested that perhaps the people who requested the meeting should form themselves into a fire brigade and practice occasionally, so that at the next fire under the direction of Mr Tansley:

> 'They would then be able to render assistance, instead of looking on and saying what ought to be done.'

This shocking idea was received in silence. Eventually a form of words was agreed, 'It is necessary we form a brigade.' The matter was referred back to the Parish Council requesting an estimate of the cost to establish and run a brigade and to find out if the Essex & Suffolk Fire Office 'would agree to an arrangement with regard to their engine.' *[CC 19/11/1897]* Just over a month later on 15th December 1897 a second public meeting was convened to hear the results. Merryweather's had offered a steam fire engine for £230 and a choice of manuals at £140 and £100: Shand Mason & Co had an engine for £285. Two of the Parish Councillors had visited Robert Anderson, the Secretary of the Essex & Suffolk who, 'Did not think that the Directors, if asked, would object to the Parish Council taking over their engine'. Mr J Surridge, who chaired the meeting, had taken advice about the engine already based in Coggeshall and 'understood that the Essex & Suffolk fire engine was a good one although somewhat old-fashioned'. Given the option of paying at least £100 for an engine against having one for nothing, the Council predictably decided to make an official request for the Essex & Suffolk engine and then try and find some volunteers to form a fire brigade.
[CC 17/12/1897]

From a Disgrace to a Farce

In February 1898 the Essex & Suffolk agreed to give their engine to the Parish Council. This offer was provisionally accepted and the call went out for men to form a brigade. By May just one man had put his name down. By September the situation had become a joke. The Parish Clerk, Jacob Dalton, proprietor of The Locomotive Inn on Stoneham Street:

> 'Called attention to the subject of the fire brigade [laughter]. They had a fire the other day at Pattiswick. A man came racing over to the town on horseback, but could not get the engine as the man who superintended it was away [A voice "he was out for a holiday" Laughter]. It was a shame on the young men of the town that no one would come forward and volunteer. There was the engine and no one to look after it. He was surprised they were not made a laughing stock of. There was no public spirit in the town. If he were 20 years younger, he would volunteer at once [laughter].'
> *[MB 1 19/09/1898 & Cuttle 23/09/1898]*

The official Guy Fawkes celebrations of 1898 went off rather quietly with few cannons discharged and no bonfire on Market Hill. People were anxious about another arson attack and the farmers concerned for their stacks and barns. Sure enough, at 10.30 that evening, two straw stacks were fired near Windmill house on Tilkey Road (where the Tilkey corn mill once stood). The horses were taken out of their stable close by, but the wind blew the flames away and the fire did not spread. Mr Rose of Magnolia Villa wrote to the local newspaper:

> 'Once again the cry of "Fire" has been heard in Coggeshall and once again the inhabitants have had to stand idly by and talk of the need for a volunteer Fire brigade. Fortunately it was not a dwelling house this time so that no life was in immediate danger. But Sir, how long is this state of things to continue? Surely the Parish Council can do something in the matter....For the sake of the town we cannot remain any longer in this dangerous situation.' *[Cuttle 07/11/98]*

On 5th November the next year, 1899, William Tansley undertook a lonely vigil at the fire station but the night passed quietly and there was no fire. At a Parish Council meeting the next evening, Jacob Dalton commented:

> 'He understood that there was a light in the fire engine house all ready for the call, but they had no brigade. There was only one man to look after the engine and if a fire occurred, he had to pick up what men he could. It was a shame that the matter had been brought forward at the parish meetings and then allowed to drop.' [ES 11/11/1899]

Earlier that year and with the agreement of the Directors of the Essex & Suffolk, William Bright passed the Coggeshall agency on to his son Richard. William died three years later, in 1902 aged eighty. [E&SE MB8 22/02/1899]

The Colchester Question

In 1900, five years after the Essex & Suffolk's public announcement that they were no longer going to attend fires in Colchester, the Council there formed their own fire brigade and took over responsibility for fighting fires within the borough. The Essex & Suffolk received a letter from the Colchester Town Clerk, telling them:

> 'In future, no private brigade will be allowed to interfere in extinguishing fires within the Borough except by the direct request of the Borough.' [E&SE MB8 06/01/1900]

This started a chain of events that would see the Essex & Suffolk finally withdraw from the fire brigade business. The first move was by one of the Essex & Suffolk Directors, Mr Marriage, who suggested that their Colchester engines, now redundant, should be given up. The Engine Committee was instructed to consider the matter and reported back a year later:

> 'Your Committee would suggest that this opens up a very large question and must be considered and acted on with great care We find that we have two engines at Colchester and one each at the following places: The Hythe, Wyvenhoe, Thorpe, Manningtree, Maldon, Chelmsford, Billericay and Rayleigh and consider that whatever is done, is done in a comprehensive way.' [E&SE MB8 05/01/1901]

The 'very large question' was whether the company should give up all their engines but such a momentous decision needed further consideration. The Committee had either forgotten that they had an engine in Coggeshall or were under the impression it had already been given away.

> **Pink Cheeks**
> Five young ladies walking by the river in Coggeshall were attacked by nesting swans.. *'Two ran behind a haystack and three got up a willow tree. Two left the tree and joined their friends but when Miss Dalton tried get down her petticoats became entangled in the tree, and she was suspended head downwards.'* She was rescued by a passing Curate, the blushing Rev H Anson. [EN 22/04/1899]

Saved and Lost

John Poulton had two jobs, a Veterinary Surgeon and the proprietor of Coggeshall's White Hart Hotel, practising both for thirty-two years. His son Charles also practised in the town, having qualified as a Veterinary Surgeon in 1878 and being possessed it was said, of exceptional skill. In 1890 he had narrowly escaped death when his house on Church Street caught fire whilst he was asleep. He was saved by the 'furious barking' of his dog which woke him up. Charles became a heavy drinker and it killed him, he died suddenly aged just 40 in 1898. At the inquest held at the 'Greyhound', his wife said that on 'this occasion' he had been drinking 'for about a week' before his death. On the day of his funeral, shutters were put up and blinds drawn throughout the town whilst a large concourse of people attended. [CC 24/06/1898] Just a year later in 1899 his grieving father John died at home in the White Hart. Crucially, this brought Frederick Baylis to Coggeshall as the new proprietor of the Hotel. He was to play a key role in our story.

The Straightened Serpentine

In May 1901 the engine was called out to a house on fire in Coggeshall Hamlet belonging to Mr Cleeland a retired Naval Officer. The fire started just before six in the morning in the scullery, probably from an oil stove and was discovered by the maid. The fire spread so quickly that Cleeland, his wife and their three young children escaped only partially dressed. The engine with William Tansley in charge was soon on the spot and set into the river at Pointwell Mill, giving a 'splendid supply of water' but it was soon evident that the old timber house was doomed and efforts were concentrated on the stables just twelve feet away. These were saved but of the house only the blackened chimneys remained. Among the helpers at the fire was Frederick Baylis of the White Hart, who had horsed the engine.

The winding road to Kelvedon that passed the house was known locally as 'The Serpentine' and the fire provided an opportunity to build a new road across the site of the house, making a short cut which avoided some of the bends. An enterprising George Beaumont raised a public subscription[12] which allowed him to buy the land, fence it and demolish a barn which stood in the way. He offered it to the county but it was Braintree District Council who took up the idea and they built the new road which saved 'several sharp bends, two inclines and 345 yards' before rejoining the old road at the foot of the Halfway hill. It cost a thousand pounds and was opened three years after the fire in October 1904. *[EN 08/10/1904]* Because 'certain persons' had been very vocally opposed to the scheme, a Local Board of Inquiry was held in Kelvedon in 1906 to find out if there were still misgivings. Not a single person turned up but as the inquiry closed, an official from Braintree arrived claiming that his lateness was, 'owing to the strange behaviour of a Coggeshall horse who had insisted on laying down flat in the middle of the road.' *[EN 06/10/1906]*

---

12   This brought in just over £210.

Last Embers

In September 1902, the Essex & Suffolk Engine Committee, reported their findings:

> 'No adequate saving appears to have been affected by the Society's brigades in attending fires, to warrant continuance of the present expense involved.'

A resolution followed:

> 'That the principle of abandoning the maintenance of the engines be adopted and the Committee be empowered to carry out the details and report back to the board.' *[E&S MB8 20/09/1902]*

After almost a hundred years, the days of the Essex & Suffolk Insurance Brigades were numbered.

1902 saw two unexplained farm fires. The first, at Crowlands Farm, broke out at about midnight on 26th September:

> 'The Essex and Suffolk Fire brigade were soon in attendance from Coggeshall under W H Tansley. Two barley stacks and an oat stack were destroyed. There was a plentiful supply of water from a pond and a stack of peas were successfully saved.' *[Cuttle 26/09/1902]*

The next on 3rd November was at the nearby Nunty's Farm and elicited an almost poetic report:

> 'Two sheds, containing a large quantity of teazel, a tumbrel and a double tom plough were destroyed. The fire engine attended.' *[Cuttle 07/11/1902]*

The next year, 1903, was to prove significant in our story and had a fitting and dramatic start:

> 'The storm raged with great violence in Coggeshall and the surrounding district. The lightning was very vivid and the thunder deafening, while snow, hail and sleet poured down. Such a storm in January has not been experienced in the district for upwards of 20 years. Many trees were shattered and birds fell dead from the trees. A wheat stack, the produce of 12 acres was fired by the lightning at Edward's otherwise Goslins Farm Bradwell. The

Essex and Suffolk fire engine from Coggeshall was dispatched to the scene under the superintendence of Mr. W H Tansley and Mr. F Baylis and did good work in preventing two other stacks, one on either side from catching.' *[EN 10/01/1903]*

Some two years after his first appearance at a fire, Frederick Baylis has returned to share command with William Tansley. There was a social connection between them through Mrs Baylis who was very musical. Tansley had virtually disappeared from the music scene by then and it may have been Mrs Baylis who encouraged him to take part in a 'Smoking Concert' at the White Hart in November 1902. She accompanied him on the piano in what was to be his last musical performance in the town.

Frederick Baylis was 35 years old and came originally from Banbury. Previously a publican at the 'Goat and Boot' in Colchester, he moved to Coggeshall first to take up the tenancy of the White Hart Hotel and then in March 1901 when it came up for sale, he bought it. He soon became involved in local affairs and had pronounced on a tricky Coggeshall problem, that of the water supply. At first he was in favour of the scheme to bring in piped water, but had a sudden change of heart when he realised that all his best customers were very opposed to it (they were the ones who would end up paying). This switch of allegiance was well known, so when he intervened at a public meeting called to discuss the matter, the chairman's dry comment, 'Everyone has a right to change his mind' was greeted with merriment among the assembled crowd. Undaunted, when Mr Dodds of Market End said that his water had a strange taste, Baylis replied that his supply came from the same well:

'I had noticed no objectionable taste about it... a voice from the back "You have Whisky in yours!" (Loud laughter)'. *[EN 11/10/1902]*

Frederick Baylis was a character and very sociable, he had excellent and wide-ranging local contacts via the White Hart and when the time came, that would prove to be useful.

An Ultimatum

The Annual General Court of the Essex & Suffolk met in February 1903. It had been finally decided that their fire brigades were to be disbanded:

'The Directors do not propose to continue the maintenance of the Society's Fire brigades and engines, the Legislature having delegated to local authorities the responsibility of dealing with fires'. *[E&SE MB8 21/02/1903]*

In May they sent a letter to their Coggeshall agent, Richard Bright, with an offer to make a 'free gift of their fire engine and appliances now stationed in the parish'.

The Parish Council realised that this was an ultimatum as much as an offer. It was unthinkable for the town to be without an engine so the council agreed, but their response was less than confident:

'That we accept the offer of the engine &c. and will do our best to ensure that it is efficiently used in the case of emergency'.

The clerk was instructed to make enquiries about the cost of running a brigade.

The very next day, 26th May, saw what was to be the last call for Coggeshall's Essex & Suffolk engine. A Stisted lad had returned home from school and lit some paper in the hearth which was drawn up the chimney and fell onto the thatched roof. In just a few minutes the whole roof was burning fiercely. The Coggeshall engine was quickly horsed by Fred Baylis and directed for the last time by William Tansley. They were too late, although there was a good supply of water, the cottage was completely destroyed. A 'willing band of helpers' did manage to save the furniture. Not much of a swansong. *[CC 29/05/1903]*

On 6th June 1903, the Directors of the Essex & Suffolk formally agreed:

'That the Coggeshall Fire Engine be presented to the Parish Council of that place as a free gift together with the equipment belonging thereto.'

William Tansley

William Tansley's story, both professional and personal, was a sad one. His years of commitment with the Essex & Suffolk engine were eclipsed by the disaster at the Gravel, where the absence of a drilled brigade and a crowd of excited and well-meaning helpers made proper management of the engine close to impossible. Despite that William continued to man the engine to the very last call.

For years William Tansley had been at the centre of Coggeshall's musical scene but at about the time of the Gravel fire, his appearances fell away and by 1900, his name only rarely crops up. His wife may have been showing the early signs of the illness that would eventually kill her and these circumstances took away much of his enjoyment in performance. He must also have been very concerned about his engineering business and this may have affected his public confidence but whether or not this was due to any personal failings or from the town's general economic decline it is difficult to say. The fact is that when the business did close, Tansley was not able to sell it as a going concern and his tools and machinery were disposed of by public auction. In October 1903 an advert was placed in the 'Chelmsford Chronicle':

> 'Messrs Surridge and Son are instructed by Mr William H Tansley, who is relinquishing business, to sell by Public Auction on Thursday next October 29th 1903, The whole of the engineering machinery and tools at the well known Engineers works, The Gravel, Coggeshall...' *[CC 23/10/1903]*

He was 43 years old with a wife and five children. He left Coggeshall and moved to Kingston-by-Sea near Brighton, perhaps in the hope that the sea air would benefit his wife's health. Margaret Tansley died seven years later in 1910 aged just 55. In 1911 he was living alone in a boarding house and employed as a fitter. His youngest son, a flight sergeant in the Royal Flying Corps, was killed in action in the Balkans in 1917 aged 23.

Lighten our Darkness
January 1903
During the services at Church and other places of worship on Sunday evening in Coggeshall, the gas nearly went out. At the Parish Church, almost directly after more pressure had been put on, the Vicar gave out the Epiphany hymn, "The people which sat in darkness saw a great light."
[CC 17/01/1903]

The Essex & Suffolk

The Essex & Suffolk Equitable Insurance company had grown cautiously – after the first 25 years, income had only reached £6,400 and after 50 years it had crept up to £9,000. Following the appointment of the very able Secretary, Robert Anderson, in 1868, growth became a little more vigorous: £20,000 in 1877 (75 years) and almost £34,000 in the centenary year of 1902. Slow and sure was probably no bad thing in a period when many other fire offices fell by the wayside.

Although the Essex & Suffolk may have been the biggest provider of fire insurance in Coggeshall[13] it never achieved a dominant position in Essex. Even in Colchester, the value of premiums in 1868 were less than those of the 'Sun' Fire Office, which had no engine in the town. Evidence of the Equitable's caution lies in a clause which limited individual policies to a maximum of £3,000. Although designed to limit risk, this and the inability to re-insure amounts surplus to this, undoubtedly restricted growth. Within the limits it had set however, it was very successful, it withstood hard times and always provided a return for its policy holders. In 1887, a trade paper, the 'Insurance News' commented:

> 'The Essex & Suffolk can claim, in its own sphere, to be one of the greatest successes the insurance world has ever known.'

---

13 See chart p122.

7 THE PARISH COUNCIL FIRE BRIGADE

When the Parish Council met on 22nd June 1903, they had a formal and final offer from the Essex & Suffolk to, 'hand over the engine now stationed in the parish'. As we know, previous efforts to assemble a brigade had failed dismally but now a knight in shining armour appeared in the form of Frederick Baylis of the White Hart Hotel. He had been hard at work canvassing for recruits, perhaps netting them postprandial in the bar when at their most vulnerable. He had found eight men ready to join him in forming a new brigade. There were plenty of public houses in Coggeshall where working men gathered but the White Hart Hotel was not one of them. As a result, the new brigade had a clear social character. The eight recruits were: William Desborough Bright who was 29, the fourth son of Mr William Bright the Coggeshall Brewer of Stoneham Street. He had worked in a bank before becoming secretary of his father's business. Richard Bridge Appleford was 28, a member of a prosperous local family of farmers and millers of the Abbey Mill, West Mill and Abbey Farm. Appleford was responsible for the dairy and the cattle at Abbey Farm. Walter Brown was 27 and with his brother, the owner of a seed business, established by his well known and respected father. He lived in the family home, 'Claremont' in Church Street. Steward Gooch, 45, had returned from Peru in 1892 where the eldest of his three children had been born. He had first taken on the Bird in Hand on East Street but in 1903, was the publican at the Portobello Inn on Bridge Street. Gooch was also a manufacturer of mineral water with a bottling plant also on Bridge Street. Hubert Harry Saward (called

Minutes of the 135th meeting of Great Coggeshall Parish Council at the Lecture Hall on Monday 20th July 1903. 'The Clerk reported that on July 3rd the Secretary of the Essex and Suffolk Fire Insurance, came over for the purpose of handing over of the Engine and appliances which had been presented to them by the Directors of the Insurance company.' Reproduced by courtesy of the Essex Record Office [ERO D/P 36/30/01]

Harry) was 25, a young man with a mechanical aptitude who had a cycle shop in East Street. Harry Joyce was 43 years old and a friend of Fred Baylis. His butcher's shop at Market End was just a couple of doors away from the White Hart, his previous shop having being destroyed in the Lion Inn fire. Walter J Brown, (no family connection with the other Walter Brown) was 32, a seedsman's traveller and a lodger at the White Hart Hotel. Charles Clark was an architectural draughtsman, 22 years old and living with his parents in Church Street. A keen cricketer, he was Secretary of the Coggeshall Cricket Club where Walter Brown was the Captain.

Setting up and Equipping the Brigade

The council expressed themselves 'greatly indebted to Mr Baylis for all the trouble he had taken (hear hear!).' [MBI 22/06/1903] The proposal to form a brigade was unanimously accepted and a Fire Brigade Committee of three Parish Councillors and all the firemen was established to manage it.

Mike Dalton, the parish clerk, had been in touch with his counterpart at Kelvedon and found that their brigade cost just under £11 a year. Frederick Baylis thought that the cost of the uniforms might be raised by voluntary subscriptions. However, the joy of forming the new brigade could not have been universal because the subscription was not taken up. The overriding feeling was probably one of relief at a problem overcome rather than enthusiasm for the project itself. The contrast with Kelvedon is marked, if understandable, after all Coggeshall had 'always' had an engine.

The Essex & Suffolk Secretary, Robert Anderson, had retired after thirty-four years and Sidney Claridge Turner appointed in his place. He came to Coggeshall on 3rd July 1903 and officially handed over the engine and appliances. A brass plaque had been commissioned by the Equitable and fixed to the side of the machine:

Sidney Claridge Turner
Secretary of the Essex & Suffolk from 1902-27

'Presented to the
Parish of Great Coggeshall by the
Essex & Suffolk Fire Office
on the disbandment
of their brigade'.

The Minutes of the Parish Council record and detail the gift:

'Great Coggeshall Parish Council

Received of the Essex & Suffolk Fire Insurance company, on behalf of the above named Council, the Fire Engine and appliances as mentioned below,

Engine, Suction pipe, 2 nozzles, 4 Spanners, Pole & Chains, Pair of Shafts, Pair of Lamps, 1 Hand Lamp, 11 Buckets, Suction Basket, 1 Nozzle raiser, 8 lengths Cotton Hose, 4 Lengths of Leather Hose, 4 Leather Belts, 3 Hatchets, 1 Spike, 2 Ladders, 2 Large Hatchets, 1 Brass Nozzle, 7 Long and Short Leather Bands, Tortoise Stove.

M Dalton, Clerk to the Council'

The Fire Brigade Committee had its first meeting on the 6th July. Frederick Baylis was appointed Captain, Desborough Bright Vice-

*The refurbished engine and most of the Parish Council brigade in their new uniform.
The four belts inherited from the Equitable are on show, the other firemen had to wait until late 1904.
The Equitable presentation plaque is behind the second figure on the left. This is almost certainly the same engine that was bought
new from Merryweather's in the 1830s and had already been in service in Coggeshall for seventy years.
Best guess left to right Richard Appleford, Harry Joyce, Frederick Baylis, Harry Saward, Desborough Bright, Steward Gooch, Walter Brown.*

Captain and Steward Gooch the Engineer. His first job was to inspect the new machine. The key to the Engine House was handed over to Baylis with 'the power to act' in case of fire. The only items of uniform passed on from the Insurance Brigade were four leather belts.

Mr George Braddy, the Kelvedon Captain, came over on Thursday 9th July to supervise the brigade's first drill and test the Engine and Appliances. He reported that although basically sound, a number of small matters required attention to bring the engine into full serviceable condition. He drilled the new brigade and he expected a high standard of discipline and competency and this set the pattern for the future. *[MB1 06/07/1903]*

The Fire Brigade Committee met again on 26th July and recommended suppliers for the new uniform. Several businesses had submitted quotes to supply nine sets of uniforms and boots. Mr Browning Smith thought that £50 should be raised for repairs to the engine and new equipment for the brigade. When the Parish Council met, there was as always, when expenditure was involved, some dissent. Frederick Smith questioned if it were necessary to fund uniforms – surely boots were enough? Ernest E Surridge thought that 'the parish would

*The Parish Engine fully horsed.
Taken in Abbey Lane.*

not wish the brigade who gave their services with very good heart to risk spoiling their clothes when doing good service to the town'. To resolve the problem a Parish Meeting would be called with a recommendation that the sum quoted should be earmarked. *[Haines]*

The meeting was held on 4th August, 1903 and it is clear that there were still reservations. Mr Smith, perhaps the chief of the penny-pinchers, asked if members of the brigade had volunteered for any set length of time, evidently fearing that they might leave as soon as they had their uniforms. Mr E Surridge, the deputy Chairman replied: 'A number of gentlemen had volunteered their services with a very good heart and that the least the parish could do was to supply them with uniforms'. Mr S Jarvis reminded the meeting that a subscription had been suggested for the uniforms and Jonathan Cook thought the equipping of the brigade should have been put out to tender. Replying, Fred Baylis said that he had obtained estimates from two firms for uniforms and three for boots. On a vote, an expenditure of up to £60 from parish funds was agreed and the contracts were awarded to Messrs Folkard of Market Hill for uniforms and to Messrs Pocock & Sons in Market End for boots for a total price of £43 1s 0d.

The uniform included helmets – black leather for the men and a silver plated brass helmet for the Captain. An extra item 'Plated Epaulettes for the Captain' meant the invoice was 5s over the tendered price. It was over a year later in September 1904 that five sets of belts and axes were ordered from Merryweather at 12s 6d each, which meant that for the first time all nine members of the brigade would be fully equipped.
[MB1 26/09/1904 & Haines]

Apart from this specialist equipment, everything else was bought locally. The

*C & H Warren's Carriage Works
Bridge Street.*

*Refurbishing the Manual Engine
Invoice from C & H Warren
9th November 1903
Gt Coggeshall Parish Council*

*July 9   Taking off wheels to Fire Engine
            Cleaning & greasing ditto
            2 new shoulder collars. 1 new linspin*
            Taking away front carriage, 1 new collar
            & greasing down bolt.
Oct 30 Rubbing down old paint &
            painting with Vermillion
            & re-writing names on Fire Engine
            & Varnishing ditto
Nov 9th Fitting match lined covers to pumps
            in fire engine by order of Mr Baylis*

*Linspin *is an Essex dialect word for Lynchpin: a pin inserted in the axletree to keep the wheel on.*

Market End c1905
Showing Messrs Pocock Brothers shop with Joyce's Family Butcher on one side and the White Hart Hotel on the other. On the right is the house newly built by the Doubledays on the site of the Red Lion Inn.

Invoice from Pocock's for '9 Pairs Firemen's Boots at 21s 3d a pair'
9th October 1903

Fires, Firemen & Other Mishaps

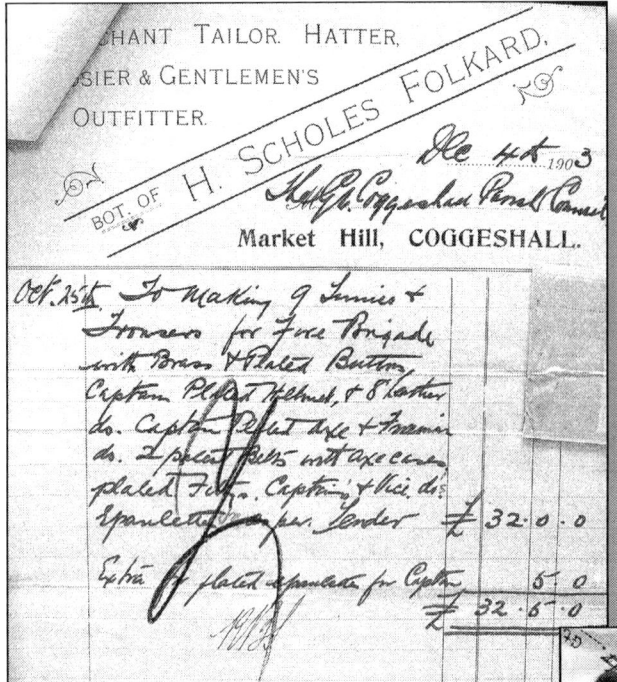

*Invoice from H Scholes Folkard
4th December 1903
The Gt Coggeshall Parish Council*

'Oct 25th
To making 9 Tunics &
Trousers for Fire brigade
with Brass & Plated Buttons,
Captain Plated Helmet, & 8 leather
do. Captain Plated Axe & Firemen
do. 2 plated belts with axe cases
plated Fittings. Captain & Vice do's
Epaulettes as per Tender

Extra for plated epaulettes for Captain'

('do' is an abbreviation for 'ditto')

*All invoices are courtesy of the Essex Record Office
[ERO D/P 36/30/19]*

Invoice from Frederick Baylis December 1903
'Parish Council of Gt Coggeshall

July 10 Paid to J Sprawling for cleaning Fire Engine
Hoses &c
Nov 21 Paid to J Sprawling for cleaning Fire Engine
& new Candles for lamps'

*Invoice from 'The Padlock', Thomas R Rackham,
Church Street, Xmas 1903
Aug 25 Fitting & Keys to lock
    of fire engine station.
Oct 31   Brass Screws'*

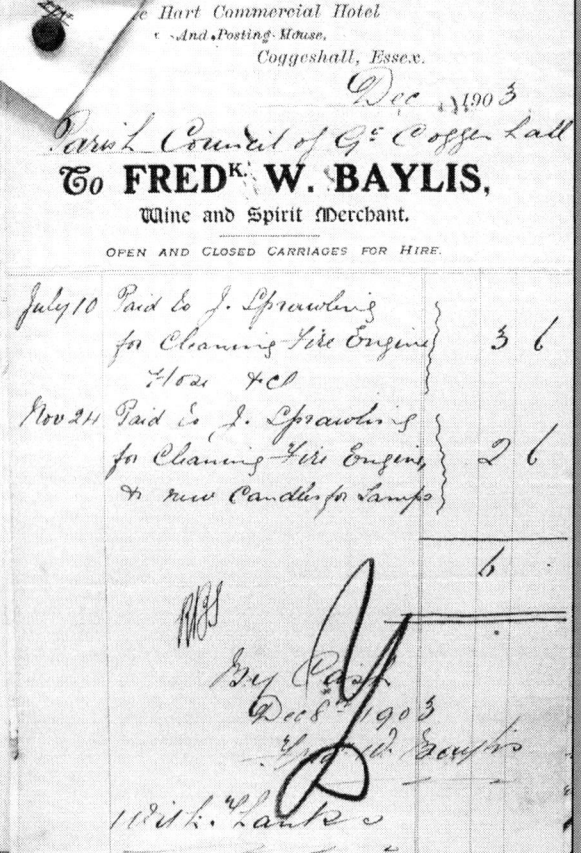

fire engine was serviced, repaired, sign-written and varnished by a local carriage maker, C & H Warren, who had premises in Bridge Street and the 'Padlock' on Church Street provided locks and keys for the station: all the 1903 invoices have survived and in their day-to-day ordinariness, bring something of that time back to life.

Rules and Regulations

The 'General Rules for Coggeshall Fire Brigade' were approved by the Parish Council in December 1903. (See Appendix XI). The engine was to be free to any fire in the parish of Great Coggeshall, although the working expenses were to be paid by the owner of the property where the fire occurred (in practice this usually meant the insurer). Drills were to be held monthly and a fireman absent for three would be subject to a fine or dismissal. The engineer's role was not to fight the fire; 'the engineer shall not leave the engine during a fire but should devote his whole time to the working of the same'. On receiving a call to a fire 'the member shall repair to the Engine House in full working uniform and under the direction of the Officer in Command, get the engine, hose and all necessary tools and when ready, proceed without delay to the fire'. The important question of drinking was also addressed: 'No refreshments to be procured or provided without the order of the Officer in Command'. There was also guidance on how the firemen should deport themselves; 'Members are expected to perform their duties as silently as possible, order, coolness, promptitude and dispatch are indispensable.'

A scale of charges was attached: two guineas for the hire of horses, officer in command, 2s an hour, the firemen 1s, the pumpers 6d, cleaning the engine and equipment after use was 10s. Outside Great Coggeshall, an extra charge of £2 was levied for the use of the engine and hose. These charges were the same as those previously used by the Essex & Suffolk and were generally accepted by many fire offices.

Some Parish Councillors continued to grumble about the ongoing cost of the brigade. These included the expense of maintaining the engine and buying hose and other equipment which had to be found from the rates. The only income generated by the brigade that could be used to offset this was the levy of £2 made when attending fires outside the parish boundary. The Essex and Suffolk may have stopped funding their brigades but they and the other fire offices continued to pay the costs of putting out fires.

First Fire

It was May 1904 before the brigade saw their first action. They were called to a fire at Raincroft on the Colchester Road. There was a quick turnout and the brigade got to work within three minutes of arrival – the practice drills had paid off. A large stack was well alight, other stacks, a large thatched barn and farm buildings were threatened. The engine was set into a roadside pond but when this was emptied, the brigade could do little to stop the fire spreading, first to the stacks and then the barn itself. Although a horse and the other livestock were saved, nearly everything else was lost:

> '....a large double bay barn, a straw stack the produce of six acres, two stacks of pea straw, two tons of trifolium hay, a quantity of timber, agricultural implements, wheelwrights tools and a wagon.' [Haines May 1904]

Perhaps a more experienced crew might have used the water more sparingly and to better effect. It was a rather unsatisfying first outing.

After every fire an account was drawn up as it had been in the days of the Essex & Suffolk brigade; this listed who was present, how long they worked and what payment they were due, the hire of horses and the cost of refreshments. This was presented to the Parish Council who drew a cheque for the Officer in Charge to distribute. The council then applied to the insurer

*Colchester Road looking towards Tollgate Hill and Coggeshall.
The roadside pond on the left provided some water. Raincroft barn was behind it, out of shot on the left.*

for reimbursement. The bill for the Raincroft fire was just over £9, but recovering this was not straightforward as three separate fire offices were involved; The Essex & Suffolk, the Hand in Hand and the Royal. To sort out this unexpected complication and deal with future claims, the Parish Council appointed a Finance Committee.

Captain Baylis Moves On

Having attended just one fire, Frederick Baylis tendered his resignation. He was selling the White Hart and leaving Coggeshall. Harris Smith, the Parish Council chairman, thanked Baylis 'for the very great trouble he had taken in the formation of the brigade' and another councillor hoped that the brigade, 'would be a useful one and that their services would seldom be required, (hear hear!)'. Frederick Baylis continued in the licensed trade, first moving to Earls Colne and then Chelmsford and he eventually retired to Bury St Edmunds where he celebrated his golden wedding anniversary in 1942. His was not the first resignation, that honour went to the engineer, Steward Gooch, who left after the first practice drill under captain Braddy. Harry Saward had been elected to take his place and George Paterson, who was 31 and the manager of J K King's seed warehouse, had volunteered to fill the Baylis vacancy. The Fire Brigade Committee met to elect a new captain, the young Richard Appleford was proposed but with no seconder, he withdrew. After due process, Desborough Bright was voted Captain and Walter Brown promoted to Sub Captain. The committee also recommended that a 'skid' be procured for the engine. This was a metal shoe that could be slipped under the wheels and held

in position by a chain. The contraption slid along the road surface with the wheels on top and acted as a brake when descending hills.
[MBI 30/05/1904 Cuttle 30/05/1904]

The next fire in July 1904 was at Purley Farm, occupied by the seedsmen, John K King & Sons. The farm is a mile and a half outside Coggeshall just off the Earls Colne Road and it gave the brigade their first opportunity to prove themselves. Mr Leonard Hull discovered the blaze in the stackyard and cycled to Coggeshall to raise the alarm. The engine was horsed by the new owner of the White Hart, Mr Isaacs, late of the Pier Hotel Felixstowe and there was a 'prompt muster'. The brigade set off with Sub Captain Walter Brown in charge and found two hay stacks burning fiercely and the farm buildings and several more stacks of seeds, under threat. With a 'capital supply of water', the brigade worked well and after 'several hours hard work' the remaining stacks and the farm buildings were saved. [CC 05/08/1904]

Double Tragedy

In November 1904, Miss Florence King was playing the piano in the drawing room of her home at 'Woodlands', in Church Street:

> 'Shrieks were heard and there was a smell of fire which attracted the attention of her mother and brother, who rushing in found the room full of smoke and Miss King laying on the floor. Mrs King and Mr King succeeded in putting out the flames about Miss King and managed to get her out of the room into the hall where she was found to be badly burnt.'

Stanley King, himself burnt from rescuing his sister, sent for the fire brigade and Desborough Bright and some of the firemen quickly responded and put out the fire in the room while medical aid was summoned for Florence. [Haines 23/11/1904] In great pain, she succumbed to her injuries some eleven days later. The inquest was held in the same room as the accident, the ceiling and walls still blackened by smoke, the door charred and the furniture damaged.

Dr J A Salter, the family doctor reported:

> 'I found her severely burned all over her face, left side, neck and chest and the lower part of the body. The left arm was burned and charred above the elbow and the fingers more or less destroyed... Everything possible was done for the patient.'

Subject to fainting fits, it was thought that Miss King may have fainted and fallen onto a paraffin stove, the verdict was accidental death. [EN 10/12/1904] One of the firemen who rushed to help Florence was the young Richard Appleford. He was taken ill later that same evening with what turned out to be Typhoid fever. The disease was not uncommon in Coggeshall, whose water and sewerage system was something of a scandal. Tragically, Richard Appleford died on the same day that Florence King was buried. He was 29 years old, a well known and popular young man, a keen sportsman and a corporal in the Essex Yeomanry 'one of the smartest in the troop'. The funeral was on Saturday 10th December and nearly a thousand people attended. On top of the coffin, as well as his Yeomanry Cap, were his fireman's helmet and accoutrements and the funeral procession was led by his comrades in the brigade. [CC 09 & 16/12/1904]

There had been changes in personnel in the year or so since the brigade was established, but there were always men waiting to fill the vacancies. The immaculate appearance of the engine and the well-drilled firemen in their smart uniforms and black helmets must have had an effect. The new recruits were Robert Southgate aged 37, married with two children, he was newly arrived in Coggeshall and had opened a fishmonger's shop on Stoneham Street. The other recruit was 32-year-old Alfred Birkin, a Coggeshall man who was married with three children. He had started out as a plasterer and paperhanger but in 1904 had a growing business as a plumber, painter and decorator based at Market End.

More Expense

In January 1905 the brigade were called out to 'Miss Raven's house' much to her surprise, as there was no fire, the first recorded false alarm. Mr Isaacs from the White Hart horsed the engine and sent in a bill for the usual two guineas. The Parish Council were rather put out by the turn of events because as there was no fire there could be no claim against the insurers, leaving them out of pocket. They decided to try and negotiate with Mr Isaacs and sent the Parish Clerk, the wily Mike Dalton, with an offer of one guinea for the horses but he must have had a dusty response because a cheque for two guineas was later drawn in favour of Mr Isaacs.

June 1905 brought more bad news. The leather hose inherited from the Essex & Suffolk was at the end of its working life and needed replacing. Three one hundred foot lengths of 'A1 Brand' hose were ordered from Merryweather's at just under £5 a length. Shand Mason sent in a cheaper price but their couplings were incompatible. *[MB1 19/06/1905]* Then, realising they might be liable in law if one of the firemen had an accident on duty, the Parish Council took out a policy with the Yorkshire Insurance company. At a cost of 7s per man annually, this gave a payout of £250 if a fireman was killed on duty, £125 if he was permanently disabled or a weekly allowance if temporarily disabled. Later the insurance was extended to include the pumpers. *[MB1 19/06/1905 & MB 2 06/07/1908]* Insurance was also taken out on the Engine House, Fire Engine and appliances and this policy, with the Essex & Suffolk Equitable, has survived. It details 'The Engine House, Brick built and slated' and was valued at £50 and the 'Manual Fire Engine and appliances consisting of hose, buckets and the like therein' at £200. The annual premium of £5 was due on Lady-day, 25th March.

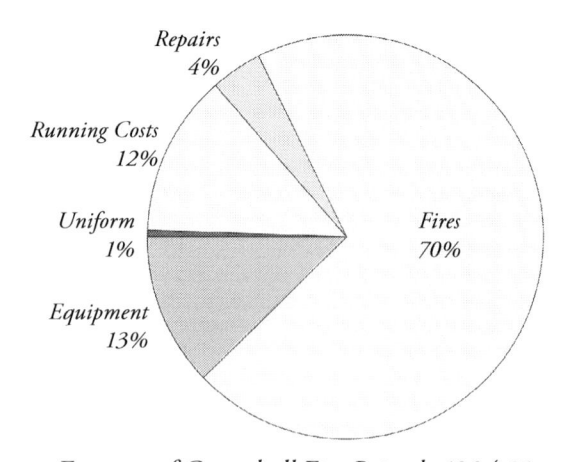

Expenses of Coggeshall Fire Brigade 1904-23
The 1904 start was chosen to exclude establishment costs.
Source: Gt Coggeshall Parish Account Book [ERO D/P 36/30/9-13]

The Cost of the Brigade

The first year's account included establishment costs but the final figure in March 1904 was £49, rather less than the £60 which had been set aside. The first two 'normal' years, seemed to prove the sceptics right with costs averaging £22, double what was expected based on the Kelvedon brigade. In fact much of the equipment was worn out and needed replacing and this inflated the figures in the first few years. By far the biggest expense, amounting to 70%, was in attending fires and in most cases these costs were reimbursed by the insurers. The remaining 30% included running costs (mainly gas and insurance), equipment, uniforms and repairs to the engine and engine house. Looking at the first twenty years 1903-1923 the cost of the brigade, (expenditure less income) averaged a modest £10 a year.

The firemen were growing in experience and the brigade had become a cohesive unit. In March 1906 the Captain, Desborough Bright, entertained them all to a dinner at the White Hart Hotel where 'an excellent repast' was served by Mr Isaacs. The dramatic events of January 1907 were to prove the new brigade's professionalism and worth.

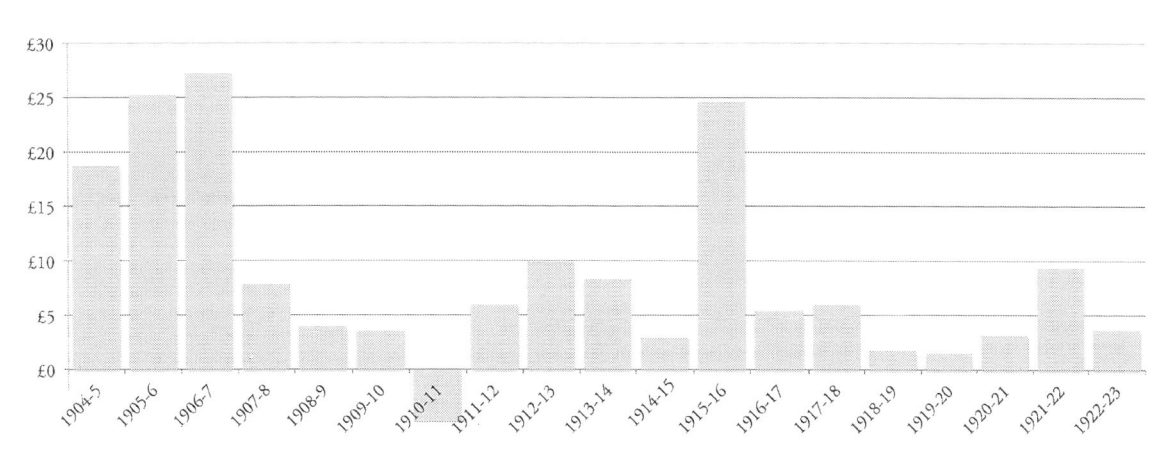

Annual Cost of the Coggeshall brigade 1904-1923 (expenditure less income)
The high figure of 1915-1916 included the cost of extinguishing a fire which was not reimbursed by an insurance company.
Source: Great Coggeshall Parish Account Books [ERO D/P 36/30/9-13]

The Great Fire at Sach's 1907

The fire which broke out in the early hours of the morning of 5th January 1907 became the biggest on record for Coggeshall. Edward Sach, builder and contractor, had premises covering a large area between Back Lane and Church Street. This was a warren of adjoining and abutting buildings, which included other business premises, a range of outbuildings and a children's home, which were detailed in a report after the fire:

> 'Steam saw mills, carpenters and joiners shops, paint shop, stores, offices, stables, machinery (including a recently installed gas plant), a huge stock of timber, tools and other stock in trade. Also involved was another stable, a chaise house and a large builder's workshop: further stables, a cart shed, a store house and other premises: the property of Mr H Mathams, a Baker. Also involved were stables attached to the co-operative bakers store and Hope Lodge, a home for children on Church Street. Sleeping there at the time of the fire were Mr Harri Oliver, Congregational Minister, Miss Cook the Matron and 24 children.'

A contemporary newspaper report vividly describes events:

> 'Mr Mathams states that just after half-past one he heard a crackling noise and going out into his yard, he found the corner of Mr Sach's premises on fire. He at once released his pony from the stable and removed the cart and harness. At the same time Pc Wedlock who was on duty in the town, observed the flames gave the alarm and called up the firemen. With commendable speed they soon got together, rushed to the engine house and themselves ran the machine up to St Peter's Well, about 150 yards from the conflagration. The engine was set in and the supply of water proved efficient. In the meantime the inmates of Hope Lodge, which abuts on the builder's premises, had been assembled. The building was a home for children rescued by the Royal Society for the Prevention of Cruelty to Children[1]. The Rev H Oliver, the matron and Mr E Edwards quickly removed the children (whose ages range from 6 to 12 years) wrapped in blankets and bedclothes and they were given sanctuary in the house of J W Clark, [the architect, surveyor and Overseer and father of one of the firemen], who lived opposite.'

The buildings, for the most part constructed of timber, were now one huge burning mass. A large number of people had assembled, among them two of the Parish Councillors, Mr Ernest Edwards and Mr Ernest E Surridge. Anxious at the size and ferocity of

---

1   The aim was to 'train the children into good and useful men and women, giving them remembrance of a really happy home when they have to go out into the world to earn their own livelihood'. *[CC 23/05/1902]*

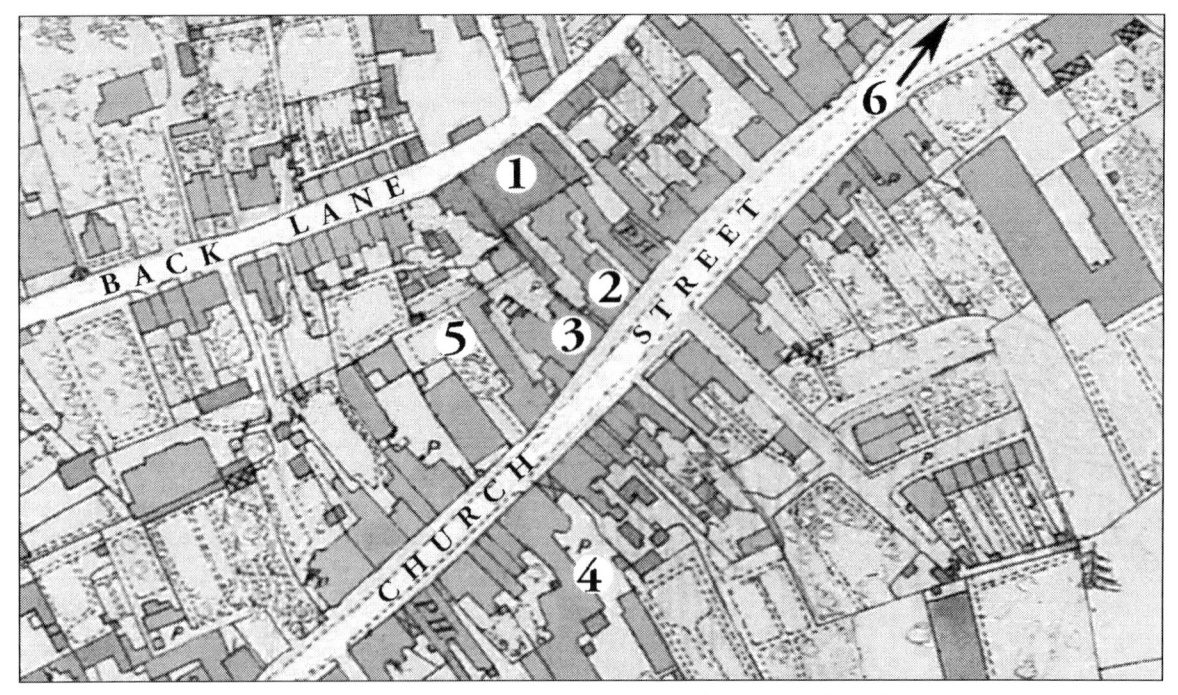

*1. Sach's Main Works 2. Hope Lodge 3. Premises of J W Clark, Mr Mathams & Co-op Stores
4. Fairheads Maltings Yard & Well 5. Matravers Stables etc. 6. Direction of St Peter's Well.*
Reproduced by courtesy of the Essex Record Office

the fire and without consulting the Captain, they decided to send a message to the Kelvedon brigade requesting their assistance.

'Great consternation prevailed and residents in the vicinity moved their belongings to places of safety. With difficulty, Mr Sach's horse was removed from its stable and Mr Matravers, fearing the fire would reach his premises, released his horses. Captain George Braddy and his Kelvedon brigade quickly arrived and fixed their engine in Church Street, they obtained a supply of water from Fairheads Maltings and the well belonging to Mr Matravers and rendered valuable assistance in keeping the fire within bounds. Meanwhile Captain Desborough Bright and the Coggeshall brigade were working hard and effectually and merited the greatest praise. Within two or three hours they had the fire well under control. At one time it looks as if the whole block of buildings including Hope Lodge, J W Clark's offices, Mr Matham's House and the Co-op stores must come down. The tact and perseverance of the brigade alone saved them. A breach was made in the buildings at the North end of Hope Lodge and the progress of the flames was thus stayed. The paint at the end of Mr Sach's residence and the cottage opposite was much damaged. Fortunately there was very little wind blowing that night. There was a large number of willing helpers who rendered very effectual assistance. The cause of the fire was not known. The damage is estimated at £2,000'. *[EN 19/01/1907]*

The Coggeshall engine had been set in to the ancient, spring-fed, St Peter's well just off Church Street. It was 4.30pm the next afternoon, fifteen hours after the fire started, that the order came to cease pumping. Despite pumping something more than sixty gallons of water a minute for all that time, the level in the well had not fallen an inch. In 1876 the well was said to be producing 27,000 gallons of water a day, the overflow running down a culvert under Church Street where it can still be heard in the quiet of the night.

5th January 1907, the morning after the Great Fire at Sach's. The view is taken from Back Lane with the houses on Church Street on the skyline. On the left is 64-year-old William Dyer, a carpenter employed by Sach.
Reproduced by courtesy of Doug Judd

Mr Bright's Corns

Although the fire was a great success for the new brigade, the Captain was infuriated that the Kelvedon brigade had been called without his knowledge. At the next meeting just over a week later, the Parish Council were anxious to mollify him. The Chairman, Mr E E Surridge, thought that the town was to be congratulated by the efficiency shown by their fire brigade at the recent fire and everyone who saw them agreed that they had worked well. Their Captain was to be congratulated on the results and he should also like to thank the Kelvedon brigade for their great assistance. Several outsiders had also provided great help especially Mr Sexton, the proprietor of the Chapel Hotel. Mr Bright thanked the Chairman for his remarks before coming to his point:

'At a fire with the engine and brigade, was he in sole charge or not and why was the Kelvedon engine sent for?'

'Certainly you are in charge but any member of the Council, or any citizen seeing the town in danger is at liberty to send for twenty engines if necessary.'

Mr Bright: 'Who is responsible for paying for the same?'

The Chairman: 'Not you Mr. Bright.'

Mr E Edwards said that the Sub-Captain and another member of the brigade came up to

The Horse, the Pig and the Perambulator

February 1906

Mr James Payne, farmer, was returning home to Coggeshall from Kelvedon Market when his horse bolted up Church-street and ran over a pig. Turning the corner at Dead-lane the reins broke and Mr Payne was thrown out. He sustained a severe concussion and a nasty scalp wound. He was picked up in an unconscious condition and taken into Mr Appleton's house. Meanwhile the horse continued its mad career through Dead-lane and turning into the Colchester-road, it knocked over a perambulator in which was a child belonging to Mrs W Goodey. Fortunately the child was not hurt. The horse ran up the bank opposite the Toll House Inn, became entangled in some wire fencing and fell, damaging the cart and harness, It was afterwards extricated with some difficulty. Mr Payne was able to walk with some assistance and is progressing.
[EN 17/02/1906]

The Wind and the Cyclist

April 1906

As Mr Phillip Wade was cycling on Whites-hill, a gust of wind blew off his hat. In trying to recover it he fell from the machine, severely injuring his left knee. [CC 20/04/1906]

'Poor Bunny's End'

September 1906

Mr Willie Appleford was cycling home from Stisted rather late at night, when in Doghouse-lane he saw a rabbit in the road. It was evidently frightened by the light from the cycle lamp, for it made a dash to cross the road and in doing so ran into the cycle, its head became fixed in the spokes and was drawn up into the chain. Fortunately, Mr Appleford was able to dismount and he caught the rabbit which weighed 3lbs.13ozs. [EN 08/09/1906]

A Pair of Organ Grinders

March 1908

The wife of Thomas Laurence, a horseman of Pointwell-lane, fell while walking on the Kelvedon-road and broke her leg just above the ankle. Two organ-grinders conveyed her home on a wheelbarrow. [CC 13/03/1908]

him and others and said they had more than they could cope with and it was suggested that assistance should be obtained and a message was sent to Kelvedon. Mr Bright said it was casting a slur upon him. It looks as if they thought him incapable and when they took the matter out of his hands his responsibility was at an end. The Chairman said that no-one had interfered with Mr Bright's work on the engine, the Kelvedon Captain went to Mr Bright for instructions and he was treated with courtesy.

> Mr Bright: 'I hope I shall never be wanting in that. But out of courtesy, you should have consulted me before sending to Kelvedon.'
> Mr Edwards: 'When the fire was at its height your brigade was helpless to stay it.'
> Mr Bright: 'How was it if they were helpless they conquered the flames?'
> Mr Edwards: 'The wind changed.'
> Mr Bright said he considered that they had overridden his authority.
> Mr Jervis: 'It was the general opinion that it was the right thing to do to get assistance from Kelvedon.'
> Mr Edwards: 'The Kelvedon engine arrived at 3.35am and played on the fire until 6.00am.'
> Mr Bright: 'The fire was well under control before the engine arrived.'
> Mr Beard: 'The whole thing was done so well. Let us have no bickerings.'

They had tried praise, now they tried bribery, perhaps a longer suction pipe might be provided and an accommodating length of hose. When asked for his view, Mr Bright replied, 'I would have nothing further to do with it', his resignation would take place from that evening and he would send in his uniform in the morning. He was asked to reconsider but when Messrs Surridge and Edwards said that in the same circumstances they should do the same thing again, Mr. Bright responded, 'That cements my decision', he left his seat on the Council and walked out of the room.

The Chairman summed it up:

'As a matter of courtesy it would have been better if

Fireman and watchers at a stack fire in the Coggeshall area c1910.

they had spoken to him. If however, they thought it proper to send for help, they were at liberty to do so. They were sorry to tread on Mr Bright's corns and if they were to ask whether or not to send for assistance, they were in a very weak position.'

So for the moment matters were left.
[MB1 14/01/1907 & CC 18/01/1907]

At the end of January the two councillors involved had a meeting with the fire brigade and expressed regret:

'If anything they had done should have hurt Mr Bright's feelings, they should state that should another fire occur they would not send for an outside engine without first consulting the captain.'
[CC 01/02/1907]

In February Bright received a 'memorial'[2] from the inhabitants and a letter from the brigade asking him to reconsider the resignation. Unable to attend the next council meeting due to ill-health, he wrote saying that in view of recent events he 'could do no less than withdraw his resignation'. *[Haines]* On the 19th February, members of the fire brigade entertained him to a dinner at the White Hart Hotel. *[CC 22/02/1907]* At the Parish Council elections in March, Bright came top of the poll and at the first meeting of the new council, he was elected its chairman.

---

2   What would now be called a signed petition.

Farm Fires

A fire in the stackyard at Griggs farm, attended on New Year's Day 1908, elicited a graphic account in the 'Essex Standard'. The family were asleep when the fire was discovered and the water supply, from a pond in the yard, was limited:

'On Wednesday night January 1st, a fire broke out on the premises at Griggs Farm occupied by Mr Alfred Bright. The fire was first discovered by Mr Thomas Brown who was driving home from Braintree. He at once called Mr Bright and his son and the latter cycled into the town to call up the fire engine. In the meantime Mr Bright had liberated all the stock and turned them adrift in the meadow adjoining the premises. The fire brigade were quickly on the spot and soon got to work. Captain Bright, however, soon saw that it was useless trying to save any of the stacks: he therefore directed the attention of the brigade to saving the buildings and in this they were successful although at one time it looked as if the buildings would be destroyed. A strong wind was blowing at the time and pieces of the lighted stacks were blown onto the roofs, but happily, burnt themselves out without doing much damage. Fortunately, the buildings all had tiled roofs.' *[ES 03/01/1908]*

A report in the 'Chronicle' said the

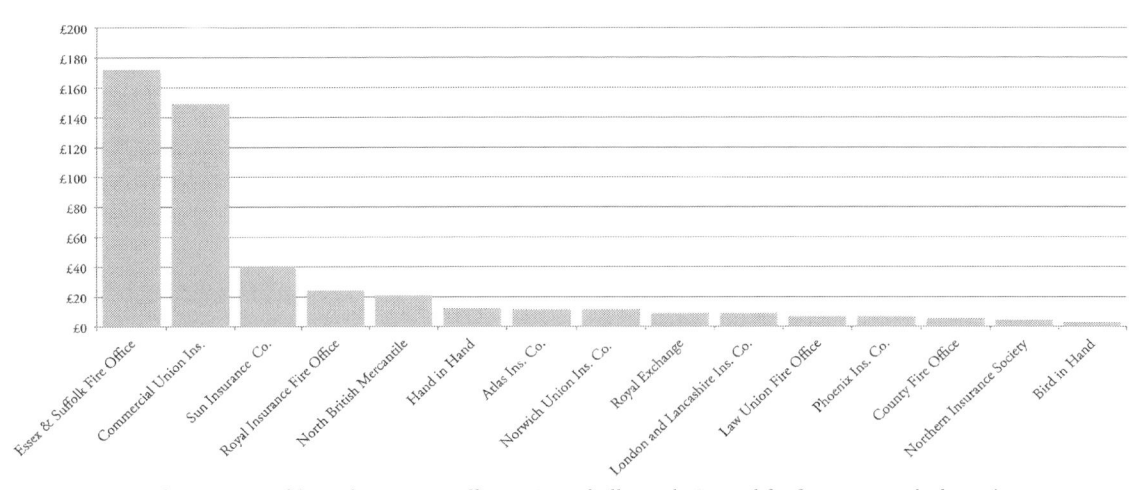

Total amounts paid by each insurance office to Coggeshall Parish Council for fires extinguished 1904-1922.
Source: Great Coggeshall Parish Account Books [ERO D/P 36/30/9-13]

'Fire Brigade had rendered splendid service' in saving the house and several other valuable stacks of seeds. *[CC 03/01/1908]*

In early 1908 the brigade attended two farm fires in Feering. At Maltbeggars, a strong wind fanned the blaze, four straw stacks were destroyed but the farmhouse and outbuildings were saved. The cause of the fire was unexplained at the time but was probably deliberate – it was not to be the last fire at the farm. The other fire at Church Farm was spotted by a couple of boys who ran and told the foreman. The Kelvedon brigade arrived with their famed promptness in just twelve minutes, the Coggeshall brigade thirty minutes later. A range of buildings were alight and a large number of animals including forty-three cattle and nine horses were taken to safety.

The next night saw another fire at Church Farm. This time a stack of pea and barley straw was alight. A 23-year-old labourer and habitual drunk, William Chaplin was arrested at the scene and claimed: 'I have a first class heart and a fourth class head and the two don't go well together'. The resulting court case reveals, in a small way, the tragedy and comedy of the human condition.

'The prisoner had been in the employment of the prosecutor for some 18 months before the fire took place, but had been discharged. On the night in question, the prosecutor came upon the scene at about 8.40 and found the prisoner by the burning stack. A policeman also came up, but directly the prisoner saw the officer he went off somewhat quickly. The prisoner appeared to have stated at first that he set fire to the stack accidentally, that he had a doze by the stack and lit his pipe. But evidence would be given to show that the prisoner left a certain house at eight o'clock and that at 8.19 the stack was alight so the prisoner had no time for a doze. Evidence would also be tendered to show that the prisoner stated that "if one side would not burn he would set the other alight".'

As the jury was not able to agree a verdict immediately, it was sent off to consider the matter in an adjoining room. In the meantime, the court enjoyed a thirty minute adjournment. When the court resumed, one of the jurors was missing but soon reappeared and when the judge asked him to explain, he said that he had 'been to luncheon'.

'His Lordship reprimanded him for not keeping with the other jurors and said that the result was, the prisoner would have to be tried again. He fined the offending juryman £5, a fresh Jury was empanelled and the prisoner was re-tried. In the course of the new proceedings the prosecutor [the farmer, William Moss] explained that a good feeling existed between himself and the accused who only three days before the fire came to him and promised to try and reform from his drinking habits by going away to a situation for six or twelve months.

His Lordship in summing up remarked that he was rather glad that the case had to be re-tried through the carelessness of a juror, because Mr Moss had, greatly to his credit, thrown further light upon the case which he had not done in the previous hearing, as to the prisoner's relations with him.

The prisoner was found guilty. The police officer informed the Judge that the prisoner went on drinking bouts. His Lordship said that he should have sentenced the prisoner to a much heavier sentence, did he not believe that his position was due to drink. He sentenced him to nine months' hard labour.' *[ES 08/02/1908]*

Hard Lessons

A third fire at Sach's in March 1908 reinforced the suspicion that the business was being targeted by an arsonist. The fire itself was unremarkable, but the aftermath provided a salutary lesson for the Parish Council.

> 'An alarming fire broke out on the premises of Mr Edward Sach, builder, about 11.30 on Thursday night….the engine was on the spot in a very short time and soon got to work on the burning buildings, rendering valuable assistance in saving the residence of Mr Sach which adjoins the timber yard. The fire appears to have originated in a wood stack in the timber yard. This was soon one mass of flame. The flames next caught the roof of Mr Sach's residence, but happily the fire brigade were able to extinguish this without great damage. A small store adjoining was also destroyed and considerable damage was done to the greenhouse. The cause of the fire is unknown but is believed to be the work of an incendiary. Mr Sach and his family were away at the time. The fire broke out in the same place as the one which broke out at Mr Sach's in January 1907.' *[CC 20/03/1908]*

The Captain reported the expenses to the Council, £6 15s 10d, a cheque was drawn and application made to the insurers. In May nearly £3 of the total had still not been paid. The Council applied to Mr Sach and he directed them once again to his insurers. With the amount still outstanding in July, the Council decided to press the matter and perhaps unwisely, wrote a threatening letter to the insurers, the London and Lancashire:

> 'Unless the amount allocated to them be paid the brigade will not attend any fire that may occur on premises insured by their company.'

This elicited the following response:

> '….re. fire at Mr Sach's premises…as we have already intimated there is no liability attaching to us for the account rendered and we are therefore unable to recognise same. With regard to your last remark we assume you are aware that the ratepayers, as supporters of the brigade, are entitled to the benefit of the appliances whether they are insured or not.' *[MB2 06/07/1908 & 07/09/1908]*

Although the Parish Council had no legal obligation to provide a fire engine and brigade, having formed one and used the rates to pay for it they were obliged by law to provide fire cover for all ratepayers. Which means that as soon as the Parish brigade was formed, people in Coggeshall for the first time had a *right* to fire protection.

The refusal of some insurers to reimburse expenses was of course exactly the same problem the Essex & Suffolk had experienced. They had no legal requirement to use their engines and could carry out the threat. It was ethical considerations that stopped the Essex & Suffolk and legal considerations that stopped the Parish Council.

In March 1908, the Parish Council tried to further offset the cost of the brigade by raising their prices: a new charge of £2 for the use of engine and hose within the parish and an increase to £4 if used outside. The new fees were advertised in the 'Essex Weekly News' and the 'County Chronicle'.

A survey of the brigade's hose found that there was 920 feet of good hose and 420 feet in poor condition. The committee advised that another 300 feet of hose and a new hard suction hose was needed. The old couplings were sent back to Merryweather for re-use saving 5s per hose. The brigade committee also recommended additional hinged extensions to the pumping arms of the engine so they folded out at the front as well as the back to enable even more pumpers to work it. This made the engine more powerful when needed and with more pumpers, less tiring to pump at the normal rate. [MB2 19/03/1908]

These expenses only inflamed the head-shakers and tut-tutters on the council who continued to grumble about the expense of the brigade. When estimates for two new suction hoses were received in July 1908, £4 15s 10d the pair, only one was bought and Parish Councillor Mr Edwin Fairhead, commented, 'It would have been a good thing if they never had the engine.' [Haines 10/07/1908] Poetic justice would be visited on that particular councillor[3].

A second fire at Maltbeggars Farm in September 1908 provided an opportunity to levy the new £4 charge for the use of the engine outside the town.

'On Friday evening September 11th about 7 o'clock a fire broke out on the premises of Maltbeggars Farm in the occupation of Mr Rann. The farm is situated in an isolated spot on the Tey Road about two miles from the centre of town. On receiving the call, the fire brigade very quickly proceeded to the spot where it was found that a stack of Oats which was situate in the centre of other stacks and near to the farm buildings, was on fire. The brigade however quickly had the flames under control and stopped the fire from spreading. The damage is covered by insurance in the London and Lancashire Fire Office. [ES 19/09/1908]

The council duly submitted the claim to the London and Lancashire and included the new charge. The attempt cut no mustard with the insurance assessors:

'Although your council may have passed a resolution increasing the charge to £4 outside the Parish of Great Coggeshall it is a charge that has not before been made to me for a manual engine – and it is one I certainly cannot recommend the Companies interested to pay - particularly in the case of attendance at the fire in question..we will be willing to apportion the account on the same basis as was charged on the previous occasion when attending this farm.'

The council considered applying directly to the owner for the extra £2 but this proposal was not seconded and the matter allowed to drop. However, in money matters, the council were not easily discouraged and they continued to levy the extra £4 charge and sometimes did receive payment from the insurers as a result.

The new £2 rule was applied in November 1908 for the first time to a fire inside the parish. The Captain reported that the brigade had been called to a fire at Raincroft Farm on the Colchester Road and the expenses totalled £6 7s 10d. The application to the insurers for this, plus the additional £2, met the following response from the assessors:

'We think the office interested would be disposed to agree thereto, less the charge of £2 for the use of engine which it is not customary to pay when the fire occurs in the area controlled by the Council.'

When the Council protested, a more robust reply came back:

'As you are aware, generally speaking Offices are disposed to pay reasonable out of pocket expenses ... but it must not be forgotten that any such payment is purely 'ex gratia, there is no legal right of recovery against either Owners, Occupiers or Offices....and it is universally contrary to the practice of Offices to pay for the use of engines and appliances within the district....We will in the course of a few days apportion your brigade account less the charge of £2 for engine etc.' [MB 2 28/01/1909]

Perhaps for the first time, the Council realised that the financial basis of the Coggeshall brigade rested entirely on the good will of the Fire Offices. The legal position was clarified after a judgement against Harlow Parish Council in

---

3   There was a fire at his farm in March 1916. Fairhead did not refuse the services of the engine.

June 1911. The Council had sent a bill for £35 to one of its own Councillors, for the expenses of a fire at his farm in Harlow. He thought the charge excessive and sent a cheque for £15. The Parish Council took him to court and lost. Just like Coggeshall, they had adopted the Lighting and Watching Act in order to pay for the brigade:

> 'And this made them responsible for the extinguishing of fires and that the expenses of the brigade should have been met out of the rate raised under the act.' [EWN 30/06/1911].

Harlow Council went to the trouble of obtaining counsel's opinion and he agreed with the ruling:

> 'The Parish Council are not, in my opinion, entitled to charge the owners of premises within the parish, the costs and expenses of the voluntary fire brigade or other helpers at a fire on such premises.' [EWN 10/11/1911]

The Council had already seen that their claims for fire expenses were only paid at the whim of the fire offices they now discovered that they could not legally charge a ratepayer for the use of the engine. For a council disinclined to expenditure, these were chilling developments.

Guy Fawkes Arsonist

Guy Fawkes night 1908 proved to be the most destructive to date with four deliberate fires. It would also lead to a court appearance which contributed to the downfall of a well respected family.

> 'The evening of the fifth opened quietly at Coggeshall. There was a small bonfire on the Market Hill and a number of squibs and crackers were discharged. At about ten o'clock however, a fire broke out at Wisdoms Barn, on the Colne road. The building being constructed from timber, was soon burnt to the ground. A newly erected shed and pigsties, were destroyed. Soon after, a fire broke out on the Colchester road, a barn, piggeries, two stacks of mangold seed, one stack of swede seed and a stack of straw were destroyed. As these premises were close to a cottage occupied by Mr Hunwick,

---

Double Whammy   November 1907

Harold P Bright was riding home from Kelvedon when opposite the Half-Way House, the horse he was riding became restive and he was thrown to the ground. The animal galloped away into Coggeshall and was stopped by Mr D Pudney jnr. approaching Stock Street Farm on the Braintree-road. Mr Bright was taken into the Inn and was attended to by Mr and Mrs Elliott. A messenger was dispatched to Coggeshall for a conveyance and Mrs Bright sent a dogcart by Hart, her coachman accompanied by Mr A Turall, a clerk at the brewery. Proceeding home with Mr Bright about a half a mile further on the road, three heifers were encountered. At these the horse took fright, the cart was overturned and the three occupants thrown out. Mr Bright who had already seriously injured his leg, sustained further injuries but Hart and Turrall escaped with a shaking. Mr Bright had to be assisted into a cottage nearby and stimulants administered. a cab was sent for and he reached home without further mishap. Mr Bright is confined to bed. [CC 22/11/1907]

Terrific Report   January 1910

A young man named Leonard Potter, living in Stoneham-street, after lighting a cigarette, threw the match unknowingly into a tin of gunpowder, weighing about a pound. A terrific report ensued and neighbours running into the shed, found that Potter had received a severe shock and some of his hair was burnt off his head. [CC 07/01/1910]

An Elephant and Two Dromedaries
                August 1912

As Fossett's Circus were making their customary mid-day procession around Coggeshall, a horse and cart belonging to Mr Arthur Hutley was driven around Stoneham-street and encountered the tail end of the procession consisting of an elephant and two dromedaries. The horse took fright at these animals and bolted down the street amongst the crowd. It knocked down several people in its mad career, included among them being a seven-year-old boy named Leonard King. He was taken home and shortly afterwards expired as a result of the injuries received. The horse and cart were eventually brought to a standstill by Sergeant Everard. [EN 17/08/1912]

the Coggeshall Fire Brigade, under Captain Bright, made successful efforts to keep the conflagration within bounds. Then in quick succession two old cottages a further 50 yards up the road, were discovered ablaze. Fortunately this outbreak was extinguished by the prompt application of buckets of water. While the latter was being extinguished, a stack belonging to Messrs J and F Rayner, in a field about 50 yards higher up the road was seen to be on fire.' *[EC 23/11/1908]*

Another stack was being watched that night and this led to an appearance at Witham Petty Sessions. The court heard that there had been a custom for some years at Coggeshall of having fires on bonfire night in the 'market-square' and there had been some horseplay, the young men not being very particular where they got the material to start the fires.

Frederick Alston, a land foreman, employed by Messrs E W King stated that he was set to watch a stack of pea-sticks on the night of 5th November. At 11.45 pm he saw two men approach from the direction of the church. They stopped and looked about, then got through the barbed wire fence and walked up to the stack. One of the men stood a few yards away and the other crouched close against the stack. A match was lighted and the flames sprang up a yard high, from which it appeared that oil had been poured on the sticks. Alston ran up to the stack and put the fire out. The two men ran away, one going towards the church and the other (who had lighted the match) getting through the barbed wire fence and crouching down. It was a bright moonlight night and Alston walked up to the fence within two yards of the man, to whom he said 'That is you, Brown, making these fires: you may just as well come out of it, because I know you.' The man made no reply, but remained where he was and [Alston] called to another man named Potter, who had been watching his property, to come and assist. Brown then got up and ran away as fast as he could in the direction of the church and witness called out to him 'That is you, Brown and don't forget it!'

The accused was Ernest Brown, brother of Walter, the Coggeshall brigade Sub Captain. They were partners in the seed business started by their late father. Alston had known Brown all his life and was sure he was the man who put the match to the sticks. He could not identify the other man who ran away.

Mr Jones addressing the Bench said the defendant was a respectable man, who had been in business at Coggeshall for some years and far from his having any malice against Mr King, the two firms had business transactions and were not even rivals. The whole story of the fire was an hallucination on the part of the one man who said he saw it, for strangely enough, no trace of the alleged fire could afterwards be found.

The defendant, on oath, said he lived with his mother at Claremont House, Coggeshall. He did business frequently with Mr E W King and was on the best of terms with him. On 5th November he went to a sausage supper at the Cricketers Arms and left there when the landlord cried 'Time'. On the way home he called at the Locomotive Inn where Renwick bought eight bottles of beer which they carried to witness's house. He went straight to bed at about 11.20. Early next morning he found Renwick in bed with him and they were called to go to another fire[4]. He did not leave the house during the time he stated he was in bed and he emphatically denied that he had ever seen the stack of pea sticks. Supt. Lennon – 'Was it not strange that after you had assisted to take these bottles of beer home you should go to bed without drinking any of it?' Defendant – 'Not at all: I had had enough Scotches that night'. – 'You told the police sergeant a deliberate lie when he spoke to you the next day?' – 'I did not know what I told him: as I was not cautioned.'

Brown was committed for trial at the

---

4   They were probably employed as pumpers on the engine (Brown certainly was at another fire in 1911), so would have gained financial benefit from the fires they attended.

Quarter Session in January where the Grand Jury threw out the Bill for lack of evidence. However, the damage was done, the episode did nothing to further the prospects of the family seed business, which in the hands of Walter and Ernest had showed no signs of prospering. *[Cuttle 25/12/1908]* Whether or not Ernest Brown was the Guy Fawkes arsonist, those fires of November 1908 were to be the last.

Tragic Accident at Feering

At 8.45 in the morning on 4th January 1910, two men, James Evans and George Burton, were engaged in digging a well at Gore Pit in Feering. Burton was a labourer and Evans was a bricklayer and a fireman for the Kelvedon brigade. Burton was 30 feet down at the bottom of the well when he heard a hissing noise and thinking that water was coming in, quickly climbed out. After a while, the hissing stopped and he went back down:

> 'But before he reached the bottom, he seemed to be affected by foul air and on reaching the bottom, he collapsed. He struggled and breathed heavily and his mate Evans, quickly slipped down the rope to rescue him. Evans seized hold of Burton, then he himself collapsed and fell on top of Burton. A man named Clough, who was at the top of the well, called out to Evans, but got no answer. Assistance was called and a doctor summoned. Pc Tucker arrived and about twenty minutes after the two men collapsed at the bottom of the well, their bodies were brought to the surface. Morphia was injected and artificial respiration was tried, for an hour and a half but unfortunately without result. The dead bodies were sorrowfully removed to the homes from which the men came and Pc Tucker advised the coroner, Dr. Harrison of the sad occurrence.'

Burton was 23 years old, Evans 32. At the inquest the Coroner asked:

> 'In the morning was there any precautions taken, to see if the air in the well was clear – was a candle let down. "No. Sir". The Coroner – "All experienced well sinkers know that is necessary to put a candle down the well each time before descending."
> Mr Surridge, (representing Mr Osborn): No danger had ever been experienced in connection with the sinking of three other wells near the well in question. Mr. Fred Osborn said that Evans had been in his employ for six years as a well sinker and was an experienced man.'

Pc Tucker deposed to the efforts made to recover the bodies. He put a lighted candle down the well and when six foot from the top of the well, the candle went out. The coroner recorded a verdict of accidental death with no blame attributable to anyone and commented:

> 'Evans lost his life entirely through his own bravery. [Applause] When he saw his mate in difficulty he did not hesitate, but went at once, down to his death. It was the act of a brave man. [Applause]'.
> *[EN 08/01/1910 & 15/01/1910]*

Captain Bright and the Coggeshall firemen joined the Kelvedon brigade to lead the funeral cortège to the church where 'a great crowd' had assembled. Afterwards sprigs of Thyme were dropped onto the coffins, a tradition of the 'Oddfellows' of which both men had been members[5].

Water

Coggeshall was notorious for its poor water supplies and its endless debates on the subject. In 1900 large numbers of people still had drinking water supplied by the water cart seven pails a week, left at the roadside. It was reported that some of these were left out uncovered all day and a visitor noticed a dog drinking out of one pail. Many areas had no supply of water for fire-fighting and buildings had been lost or badly damaged as a result. In 1902 the Parish Council

---

5   The deaths were probably caused by methane. An odourless gas, which when inhaled displaces oxygen, rapidly causing confusion, unconsciousness and death by asphyxiation. The gas, a natural product of decay, may have been connected with the gore pit after which the area was named, a pit into which (usually) the waste of a tannery was thrown, covered with lime and later filled in. A 'Gorepytt' at Feering was recorded in 1570. *[Reaney p391]*

Friday 3rd February 1911.
First test for the new water main and a jet of water is thrown over Coggeshall's tallest building to demonstrate the pressure. Mr Cobey has just opened the valve on the hydrant. A cast iron hydrant plate is fixed above the shop window on the right.

finally managed to agree on a scheme only for it to be rejected when put before the public in a vote. The 'no' vote was considerably boosted by the threat that rents would go up if the scheme went through. As a result Braintree Rural District Council (RDC) imposed a scheme on the town. The Braintree Clerk, Alfred Hills, later recalled: 'We were opposed tooth and nail by the Parish Council and the ratepayers of the town. When we arrived at the public inquiry .... we found a barrister awaiting us briefed by the parish, and two solicitors representing indignant ratepayers.' [CC 08/03/1940]. The opposers were unsuccessful and in 1909 work on the scheme was underway. A borehole was sunk on Dead Lane with a pumping house above it, a large brick reservoir was built on the Colne Road, the water mains laid and the houses connected up[6]. By early 1911 the town had a proper, pressure fed mains supply, fitted along its length with fire hydrants, marked with cast iron plates. Sadly, most have now been replaced with metricated plastic excrescences.

The arguments did not stop when the job was finished. The Parish Council fell out with the District Council over plans for a grand opening and the three hundred invitations which had

[6] The reservoir contained 136,000 gallons of water and the pumps on Dead Lane could supply it with up to 12,000 gallons an hour if required. There were nine miles of mains in the system which also supplied Kelvedon.

already been sent out, were withdrawn and the ceremony cancelled. Instead, one damp morning in February 1911 and without ceremony William Cobey, Coggshall's new water man, opened a hydrant for the first time[7]. To demonstrate the pressure in the mains, a jet was directed over Coggeshall's tallest building – Mr Dodds premises. A fireman ran out the hose, another braced himself at the branch and Cobey slowly opened the valve. The pressure increased until, spitting like a cat, the water shot majestically high into the air and right over the building, nothing like it had ever been seen, churchgoers crossed themselves. Robert Howard, the courteous engineer who carried out the works, had become very well liked in the town for the way he had gone about his job and when all was finished he was presented with a gold watch and an 'illuminated address' by the grateful inhabitants.
[ES 24/06/1911]

It was a month after the not so grand opening, in March 1911 that the RDC gave the brigade a standpipe and key which allowed them to use the hydrants for the first time. As the demonstration showed, the mains pressure gave such a good fire-fighting jet that the firemen only needed some basic equipment and a hand cart to carry it and the engine could stay in the station. A second-hand 'truck' was bought from Warren's of Bridge Street in July 1911. It was refurbished and fitted out to carry the standpipe, hose and branch, then painted, lined and varnished with 'Coggeshall Parish Council' written along each side. The total cost was £4 5s 0d. It was kept in the Engine House with the old manual which now slumbered in its vermilion glory, only needed for outlying fires.

Although Coggeshall was paying for the water scheme, by law it was managed by Braintree RDC and they were going to be very careful with 'their' water. On 12th June 1911 they wrote to the

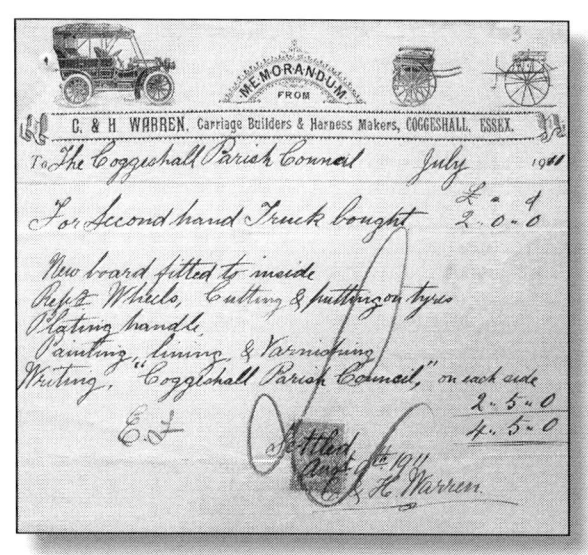

Receipt for the brigade's refurbished new truck from C & H Warren of Bridge Street, July 1911.
Reproduced by courtesy of the Essex Record Office [ERO D/P 36/30/19]

brigade Captain:

> 'I am now desired to state that the Council have decided to make a small charge of 2s 6d for each fire practice to include the attendance of the Council's turn-cock. The Council consider it very desirable that in every case of practice or fire the Council's man should be there to see the water is not unduly wasted: also to assist the brigade in getting a maximum pressure in the mains at the point desired. In the event of a fire occurring the Council do not propose to make any charge at all for water. In reference to the tools[8] which the council understands have been entrusted to you I am further desired to state that the Council consider these should not be used except in an emergency, in any ordinary case, the Councils' men should be asked to do what is necessary.'
> [MB1 12/06/1911]

Desborough Bright reported that the council's man, William Cobey, 'objected to be present after 6pm', which was exactly when the firemen would want him as drills were organised in the evenings, after their day's work. As Captain Bright put it with admirable restraint this 'made it very inconvenient for the brigade to arrange practices.'

---

7 'Mr Cobey was not a big man but sat very upright on his high stepping bike with the hydrant key strapped to the crossbar and sticking out behind like a propeller.' *[Stan Haines]*

8 The standpipe and hydrant key.

The Engine House at Crouches showing the new truck with rolled canvas hose and the standpipe slotted into its box alongside. Behind and seen 'head on' is the manual engine. The quality of the finish can be imagined by the reflection of the hard suction hose in the underside of the footrest. The oval design above is the maker's plate.
The fireman is the then Sub-Captain, Robert Southgate.

Coronation Day 22nd June 1911.
The parish fire engine is waiting to lead the procession off with Harry Saward on the reins. Half hidden to his right resplendent with his silver fire helmet is Desborough Bright, Captain of the brigade and Chairman of the Parish Council, he was also chairman of the organising committee for the day's celebrations. Ignorant of the nightmare of the war ahead, this is surely the epitome of Edwardian England and of a community who celebrated together.

1911 The Parish Brigade at Work

In 1911 the Parish brigade was in its prime. Led by a confident and influential Captain and Chairman of the Parish Council, Desborough Bright, it had a full complement of well-drilled firemen and a first rate engineer in Harry Saward. With the new water main, the brigade could tackle any fire in the town, confident of a reliable water supply. For fires outside the town, the manual engine could be quickly horsed and pumpers were always available, so that given a decent water supply, effective action could be taken.

The brigade attended two farm fires with the manual engine in 1911 which are unique because the detailed expenses for both have survived. The first was at Popes Hall, in the village of Chappel, about six miles north-east of Coggeshall. The fire only merited a two-line report in one newspaper with no mention of the work or even the presence of the brigade.

'A fire at Popes Hall, Chappel in the occupation of Mr Cheffins, destroyed three haystacks.'
[CC 01/09/1911]

The other fire was at Maltbeggars Farm, just outside Coggeshall – the third fire at the same farm. This one was fully reported.

'On Wednesday September 13th a fire broke out at Maltbeggars Farm Coggeshall situate about a mile on the road leading to Great Tey and in the occupation of Mr Watson. The fire was first discovered about 6.15 am when a dense volume of smoke was seen to issue from the barn. Within

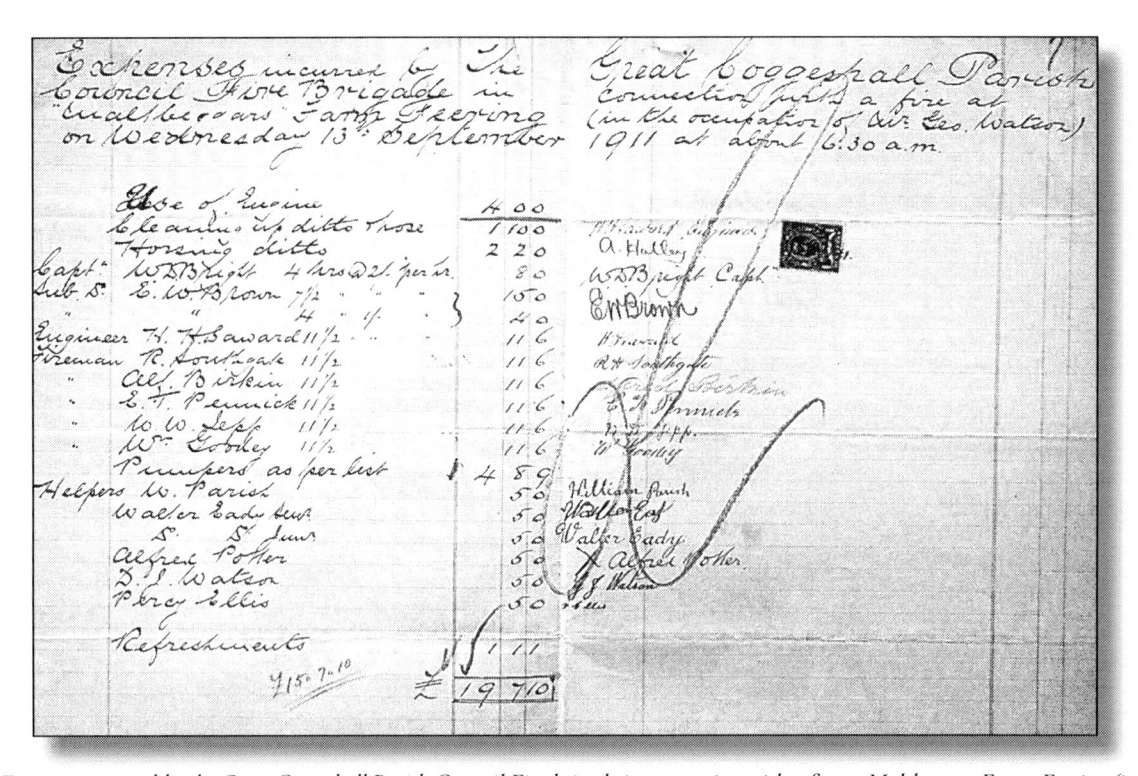

Expenses incurred by the Great Coggeshall Parish Council Fire brigade in connection with a fire at Maltbeggars Farm, Feering (in the occupation of Geo Watson) on Wednesday 13th September 1911 at about 6.30 a.m.
Reproduced by courtesy of the Essex Record Office [ERO D/P 36/30/19]

a few minutes the roof had burst into flames which quickly spread to the stables, cowshed, piggery etc. Word was sent to the Coggeshall Fire Brigade about 6.40 am and before seven o' clock under Capt. W D Bright they were pouring water onto the flames. Finding it impossible to save the buildings which were already alight the brigade turned their attention to saving the stacks and cart shed and in this they were successful. The barn, stables, cow shed and piggeries were destroyed together with the produce in the barn which was filled with corn, two wagons which were loaded with straw ready for thatching and a quantity of farming implements. The men employed on the farm were successful in saving the horses, cattle etc. The fire is supposed to be the work of an incendiary. The damage is estimated at from £800 to £1000 and is covered by insurance.'
[ES 00/09/1911]

This was a substantial but unexceptional, farm fire, lifted from obscurity by the chance survival of the Captain's accounts. Following normal procedure, the fire was reported to the Parish Council so that a cheque could be issued by the clerk. The fire was minuted at a Fire Brigade Committee meeting in September:

> Mr D Bright (Captain) reported that the fire brigade had been called to a fire at Maltbeggars Farm Feering in the occupation of Geo Watson on Wednesday 13th September and incurred expenses of £19 7s 10d including £4 for use of engine.
> [MB2 undated entry in Sept 1911]

This report to the Parish Council summarised a detailed account Captain Bright had made, of the expenses of the fire. Using this, we will look at the Maltbeggars' fire in more detail, making reference to the Popes Hall fire as appropriate.

*List of Pumpers at the Maltbeggars Farm Fire on Wednesday 13th Sept 1911.
Most of the pumpers worked for 10½ hours at 6d. (2½p) an hour.
Reproduced by courtesy of the Essex Record Office [ERO D/P 36/30/19]*

Who's Who at the Fire – The Brigade

William Desborough Bright, the Captain, was 38 years old, secretary in his father's brewing business. Walter Brown, Sub-Captain, 35 years old, a seedsman. Harry Saward, the Engineer was 33 and had a cycle shop on East Street. Robert Southgate, a fireman, was 44 years old and had a fishmonger's shop on Stoneham Street. Alfred Birkin, fireman, a 39 year old had a plumbing and decorating business at Market End. Edgar Pennick, a fireman, 48 years old, the publican of 'The Yorkshire Grey' in upper Stoneham Street. Walter William Jepp, a fireman, 57 years old and a self employed bricklayer from Knights Square, Robinsbridge Road. William Goodey, a fireman, was the publican of 'The Royal Oak', Stoneham Street.

The Helpers

William Parish was 24 and usually worked on his father's farm at Cranmers Green, Great Tey. Walter Eady, a coachman from Farm Hill cottage, Kelvedon was 55 years old, a member of the Coggeshall Working Men's Conservative Association and a singer of songs. Walter Eady jnr 25, was a son of the above and worked as a carpenter. Alfred Potter, a farm labourer from Queen Street with a wife and three children and one of only two men at the fire who left a mark instead of signing for their pay. George J Watson, son of the farmer, was 31 years old and Percy Ellis, 22 was an agricultural labourer and nephew of George Watson, the farmer and tenant of Maltbeggars Farm.

The Coggeshall Parish Engine (ex Essex & Suffolk Fire Office) with a crew of pumpers.
The amount of water lying around and the smoke over the rooftops suggest this was taken after a fire and the rolled leather hose which leans against the barn on the left points to an early date as it was later replaced with canvas hose. Might this be after the great fire at Sach's workshops in 1907? Two pipes are laying on the foot-rest of the engine on the right, perhaps put down for the photograph. The engineer, Hubert Saward is third from the right.

The Pumpers

Harry Saunders was a furniture broker, 46 years old and only lasted an hour at the pump. Ernest Brown, 31 was in the seed business with his brother, Sub Captain Walter Brown. His presence as a pumper might be seen as evidence that their business was not prospering but he only remained for two hours, perhaps he found pumping too much like hard work. It was not unknown for pumpers to just go through the motions at the pumping arms but letting the others do the work. Saward would have been on the lookout for shirkers and they were usually found out and if unreformed, dismissed from the crew. Walter Cutmore was 28 and a farm labourer living in Gardners Row, Back Lane. William Willsher, was a 43-year-old general labourer from Beards Terrace, Walter Sharpe, 36 years old, a hay cutter from the Colne Road, Coggeshall. William Sharpe probably a relative of the above did not live locally. Alfred Cook 29, was the

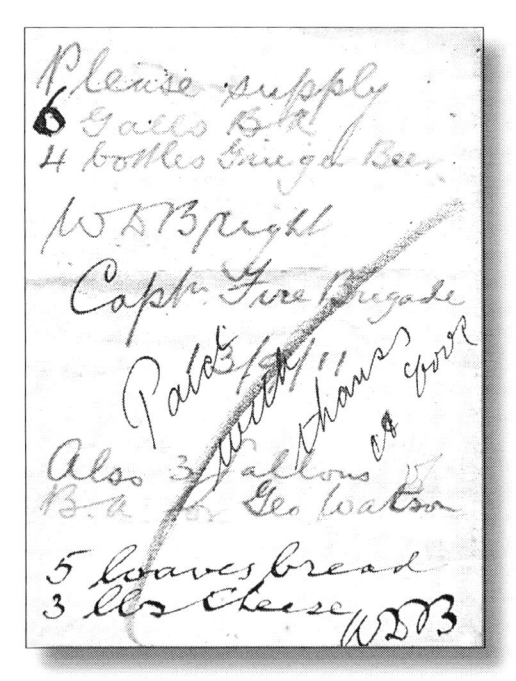

Maltbeggars Farm Fire.
Beer and Refreshments order from Captain Bright who arrived at the fire at about 1.30pm,
seven hours after the brigade were called. Please Supply
6 Gallons of BA [Best Ale] 4 Bottles Ginger Beer
WB Bright Capt Fire brigade
Also 3 Gallons BA for Geo Watson (the tenant of Maltbeggars)
5 loaves bread 3 lbs cheese WDB
Reproduced by courtesy of the Essex Record Office [ERO D/P 36/30/19]

proprietor of the Alexandra Inn on the Colne Road where the refreshments were procured. William Shelley was a labourer. In July 1899 he lost his right eye after a fight at the Wolf public house on Tilkey Road and in February 1900, he was convicted of trespass in search of conies at Markshall. *[ES 13/07/1889 & 17/02/1900]* In December 1907 he was convicted of being disorderly and refusing to quit the Yorkshire Grey public house. *[EN 21/12/1907]* James French was 59, an agricultural and builders' labourer from Tilkey Road. Harry Lawrence, aged 23 was an agricultural labourer and lived with his family at Mill Lane, Robinsbridge Road. Alfred Leatherdale was 30, a farm labourer from Coggeshall Road, Great Tey. William Prew was a 29 year old farm labourer from Ivy Cottage, Colchester Road. William Eve was once a general labourer and painter, now described as a smallholder. He lived with his wife and two children in four rooms in Church Street. A Smith, was a Chauffeur at Holfield Grange and a seedsman of Robinsbridge Road. H Ruffle, 28, a general labourer living in Church Street. George Payne was 16 and still living with his parents and three siblings on Grange Hill.

The farmer, George Watson, was 52 years old and had formerly been a platelayer for the Great Eastern Railway. He was married and both his son George and nephew Percy Ellis worked on the farm.

Thirty-three men were involved in the Maltbeggars' fire, eight firemen, six helpers and nineteen pumpers. All but two were able to sign their name. At the Popes Hall fire, there were twenty-eight men working at the fire, six firemen and twenty-two pumpers. Two of the pumpers could not sign their name, but marked an 'X' instead.

The brigade was called to Maltbeggars at 06.30am on a Wednesday morning and left the farm nearly 12 hours later, returning home at 6.00 that evening.

The call to Popes Hall was received at 4.15 pm on Sunday and the crew returned home nearly 17 hours later, on Monday morning at 8.45. At Maltbeggars nearly all the pumpers had worked for 10½ hours. At Popes Hall most Pumpers were on duty for 11 or 12 hours and one, Mr J W Bearham, was paid for working 16 hours.

The pumpers were almost exclusively agricultural labourers. As for the firemen, they were largely self-employed. The Captain was absent for most of the Maltbeggars' fire, arriving after eight hours at 2.00pm. Both Captain and Sub Captain were absent at Popes Hall, so the Engineer Harry Saward took charge and was paid the Captain's rate until the Captain arrived when he reverted to the fireman's rate.

The 11½ hours at Maltbeggars earned

the firemen 11s 6d and most of the pumpers 5s 3d. At Popes Hall the firemen took away 15s 6d and the pumpers, on average about 5s 6d. Agricultural labourers at the time earned 2s 6d a day. [EC 16/02/14] So for the pumpers, working at the fire may have doubled their usual daily earnings and they had free beer, fifteen gallons of it at the Maltbeggars' fire. The Popes Hall fire was not so well lubricated but the six gallons of beer ordered there may have been supplemented from Mr Chiffin's own stock. At both incidents, bread and cheese sustained the men.

The total bill for the Popes Hall fire was £16 0s 2d and a cheque was drawn from the Parish Council account on 1st September. The insurers, the North British Fire Office paid up in November. The Maltbeggars' bill amounted to £15 7s 10d and the three insurance offices involved, the Essex & Suffolk, the Sun and the County Fire Office reimbursed the Council during October. As both fires were outside the parish, a £4 charge was levied and paid by the insurers without comment, giving the Parish Council a 'profit' of £8 on the fires.

The insurance loss at the Maltbeggars' fire was estimated at '£800 to £1,000' and the extinguishing costs of under £16 amount to less than 2% of this. The three stacks at Popes Hall may have been worth around £400 making the extinguishing costs of £16 something like 4% of the loss. At both fires the relatively low cost of putting out the fire compared to the value of property destroyed, meant that saving even one stack would represent a substantial gain for the insurers and shows the economic benefit of paying for fire extinction.

Whilst the engine and firemen were at Popes Hall, Coggeshall had no fire protection for the best part of twenty-four hours. Banning attendance at such out of town fires was out of the question because this would remove the Council's biggest source of income for the brigade. The hand cart had been available but the only standpipe and nozzles had been taken to the fire. A request was made to the Braintree RDC for a second standpipe and the Council ordered two new nozzles from Merryweathers. For the safety of the town, a rule was brought in that 'two members of the brigade should remain at home in the event of the brigade going out of the parish.' [MB1 08/11/1911].

Captain Desborough Bright

On 16th October 1911, Captain Bright told the Fire Brigade Committee of his intention to resign from the brigade. He was in poor health. On 6th November the Parish Council thanked him 'for the Services that he had rendered to the town and neighbourhood for several years past in connection with the brigade'. Mr Bright thanked them and said he was pleased to have done his best for the welfare of the town. Bright continued as Chairman of the Parish Council and in 1913 joined the Fire Brigade Committee. At the start of the war in 1914, he left the family brewing firm and returned to banking, taking up an appointment at Parrs Bank. However he grew increasingly unwell and after resigning from the Parish Council in 1916, he left Coggeshall and moved to the south coast but his health continued to deteriorate and he died in Weymouth in 1920 at the age of 46. In 1900 he had married the eldest daughter of Reuben Hunt of Earls Colne ironworks but he died childless. [CC 26/11/1920]

Following Bright's resignation Walter Brown was elected Captain and Robert Southgate to Sub Captain. A new fireman, Joe Green, was taken on. At Walter Brown's request, new tools, a hose bandage[9] and lamps for the cart were bought. The Engine House was repaired by Alf Birkin's firm and a new 'Tortoise' slow burning stove purchased from Portways of Halstead. This kept the hose dry and the engine and cart ready for use in cold weather.

---

9   A length of fabric with ties attached and wrapped round a cut or damaged hose on the fire-ground as a temporary repair, until the hose could be replaced.

Harry Saward, Engineer

Harry Saward became the engineer after Mr Gooch's brief occupancy of the role in 1903. A cycle and motor engineer by trade, he had premises in East Street. A skilled cyclist himself, in 1902 he won first prize in the Coggeshall Cycling Gymkhana in the event called 'tent-pegging and tilting the ring' but he disdained to enter the cycling 'egg and spoon' event. Coggeshall rates had risen to pay for the water scheme and used to justify other price rises; cashing in on this, Saward advertised: 'The new water scheme has not put up the price of cycles… they are cheaper than ever'. In the fire brigade as Engineer, he did no fire-fighting and was only responsible for the engine. As the Rule 11 stated:

> The engineer or fireman in charge of the engine shall have the management of the engine, seeing it is placed in a proper position and prepared for working, he shall not leave the engine at a fire but shall devote his whole time to the working of the same and the signals. *[MB1 04/01/1904]*

Once set in to a water supply and with the pumpers ready for action, the order to start was: 'Down With Her!' or 'Down With the Pump!' With a number of enthusiastic men working the dry pump, the first few strokes could be damaging, so 'down with the pump' would be followed by 'easy lads, easy', until the pump was primed and a steady rhythm set up which would continue until the fire was brought under. The order 'Down with the Pump!' was used until 1941, when it was replaced in the drill book with 'Water On!'

With his mechanical aptitude and professional qualifications, it is not surprising that Harry Saward came to have a lot to do with the maintenance and repair of the engine and the appliances. A surviving invoice details his day to day maintenance of the engine over a year from October 1910 – October 1911, during which he carried out hose repairs, shortened hose to remove damage, re-affixing the unions and fitted unions to new hose. There was no standardisation and many sorts of unions (now called couplings), so hoses of different brigades would often not connect. Canvas delivery hose was in general use by 1911, four times lighter and four times less bulky than leather, its main drawback was that it was easily damaged, by falling debris, hot brands or by being dragged over rough ground and this explains the hose repairs detailed on the invoice. Many of the old firemen stayed loyal to leather delivery hose believing that there was nothing better, it would take a lot of mistreatment before failing and if well maintained it would outlast canvas hose many times over. Early canvas hose was of the 'percolating' type, when charged, water would seep through the material causing it to expand and form a watertight seal. After use, both leather and canvas hose had to be cleaned and allowed to dry to prevent moulds from forming, or eventually they would cause the hose to fail. 'Neatsfoot Oil' appears on the invoice.

Harry Saward in 1904.

Fires, Firemen & Other Mishaps

Transcript; Shortening 1 length hose & refitting unions - cleaning & drying hose & fittings - cleaning engine &c - fitting unions to new hose - cleaning hose & fittings - 3 cotters & rep[air] hose - 1 pint neatsfoot oil - polish - rep[air] hose - rep[air] bucket - rep[air] hose - candles - lamp oil - neatsfoot oil - rep[air] hose - new shackle pins to pump - oil - time, filling gasometer baunds*, cleaning & drying hose.
*The water filled circular pits in which the gasometers floated.
Reproduced by courtesy of the Essex Record Office [ERO D/P 36/30/19]

*Harry Saward's shop on East Street.
Fifty years later another fireman, Fred Tilbrook a cobbler, had a shop along here.*

Unlike many other oils, it remained liquid at low temperature and was used to condition leather, in the hose, the seals in the pump, in the harness, straps and other fittings on the engine[10]. Lamp and lubricating oil are self explanatory, the candles bought were probably for the lamps on the hand-cart. Saward also carried out maintenance on the engine.

Harry Saward was a crack shot, a member of Coggeshall rifle club and by 1911 he was hard to beat. In May that year after scoring the 'highest possible' in a match between the Coggeshall and Witham clubs, he was presented with a gun-metal watch and not for the first time, won the Holfield Cup. Saward was on the committee organising the annual Coggeshall show, he organised concerts as secretary of the Coggeshall String Band (he also played the violin) and was known to provide 'amusements' for the children of the National School at their annual treat.

---

10   Neat comes from an old name for cattle, the oil was made from the shins and feet but not the hooves of cattle.

Fire in Church Street

It was June 1913 before the new hydrants were used at a fire, at the warehouse of William East's shop on Church Street (currently McColl's). Men from the butchers shop next door threw buckets of water at the blaze until the fire brigade arrived with the new hand-cart and fireman Pennick in charge. Ps Everard and two of his constables also turned up and helped. The firemen quickly set into the hydrant and brought the hose to bear. The fire had such a good hold by this time with flames roaring twelve feet into the air, that it was an hour before the fire was fully extinguished. Most of the damage, estimated at £700, was to the stock and the warehouse which is still there today and still used to store goods. [EC 11/06/1913] With no natural source of water nearby, the fire would have been very difficult to deal with before the hydrants came into use and demonstrated the value of the water scheme.

1913 saw the departure of Sub Captain Robert Southgate. A native of Ipswich, he had decided to return to his home town. Friendly and sociable, his colleagues were sorry to see him leave and treated him to a farewell supper at the Chapel Hotel on Market Hill. After the meal Captain Walter Brown expressed the regret of the brigade and Southgate responded, 'I will always remember the friendly relations that had existed between members of the brigade and himself while acting as fireman and as Sub Captain.' [Haines 10/09/1913] Southgate's son had his own business, a fish shop on Kelvedon High Street and years later his grandson became an officer in the Essex Fire Brigade.

One of the founder members of the brigade Charles Clark, was elected Sub Captain. He was still living with his parents at Ivy House on Church Street and was employed as an architectural draughtsman in his father's business there.

8 THE FIRST WORLD WAR

In September 1914 barely two months after the declaration of war, a thousand people packed into Market Hill. It was the first recruitment meeting in Coggeshall and 'several young fellows' signed up to serve King and Country and there would be many more before the war's end. *[Cuttle 11/09/1914]*

For the first time, it was not just the soldiers who risked injury and death. On 9th October 1914 a letter from the Chief Constable instructed the Parish Council to take '....immediate steps to reduce all lights to a minimum between sunset and sunrise'. *[MB2 07/09/1914]* The fear at first was of an attack from the sea, but there was an increasing anxiety about air raids, particularly from Zeppelins. Just three weeks into the war a raid on Antwerp had killed six people in their homes. A partial blackout was brought in with an order to, 'Hide Your Lights'! The Parish Council responded by turning off most of Coggeshall's gas street lights for the duration of the war, although at first, seven were left on. The council, always cautious with its money, told the gasworks that their contract was void due to circumstances 'beyond their control', which gave the town a saving of £29 on the gas bill. A local paper reported that in Coggeshall, the 'Hide Your Lights' order was, 'made tangible by the Parish Council, who turned the idea into hard cash'.[1] *[EN 06/03/1915]* To help people in the dark, the Post Office whitened the telegraph poles but not surprisingly, the Parish Council could not get the gas company to paint their lamp standards. The highways authority was also asked to whiten the kerbs.

---

[1] In fact, the eventual loss to the gas company was much more dramatic - the annual bill was £143 in 1913-14 and zero in 1915-16. *[ERO D/P 36/30/]*

The concern was not just for bombs, fires were also predicted. When the subject was discussed by Braintree Urban Council, Mr Bartram thought that, 'There might be several fires at the same time and they would want several responsible officers to be in charge, the special constables would be summoned to keep order in the streets, which meant they would not be able to help the fire brigades'.*[CC 04/06/1915]* In this rather fevered atmosphere, more towns made a rule that a contingent of firemen should remain at home if the engine was called away. In Coggeshall, as we have seen, there was a rule for two firemen to remain and an extra standpipe, hose and nozzles had been obtained. Braintree decided that an officer and four men should always be available but wartime inflation in the price of fire equipment cut back their plans to fully equip them. *[CC 04/06/1915]* Other towns refused to take the chance and prohibited their brigades from attending any 'outside' calls. Among these were Colchester, Halstead and Sudbury. Chelmsford had a 'six-mile' limit for its brigade. The inevitable consequence happened at Fordham, near Colchester in 1917, when a serious fire broke out at a farm. Urgent requests for help were sent to the Colchester, Halstead and Sudbury brigades 'and in each instance, aid was refused, in accordance with the rules established by those authorities.' At the farm, nearly everything was destroyed, stacks, barns and outbuildings, but the farmhouse was saved by the efforts of an 'enterprising young naval officer', who happened to be nearby and directed the many willing helpers at the scene. *[EN 01/12/1917]*

When the Navestock post office caught fire

West Street c1910.

in 1914[2], the Brentwood brigade were called, but refused to attend because they had a rule that requests for the engine outside the town should be either in writing or by telegraph. This was to ensure someone could be charged for their attendance. The post office burnt to the ground. The telegraph machine was probably inside.
[CC 04/09/1914]

1914 was a busy year for the Coggeshall brigade. In April there was a fire in a clover stack at Highfields Farm, caused by a spark from a traction engine. The brigade attended under Captain Walter Brown and prevented the flames from spreading to adjacent buildings. In June a row of old poplar trees along West Street caught fire and the brigade responded. Many of the trees were dead or dying and there were demands to chop the rest down. In August there was a second fire at Highfields and the brigade was in attendance with Harry Saward in command. In September a more serious fire broke out in outbuildings at the Queen's Head on the Colchester Road. The locals were attacking the blaze with buckets of water when the brigade arrived. A cowshed, piggeries and cart lodge were destroyed before the fire was out.

The Coggeshall Air Raid

Churchill had promised that 'any hostile aircraft...would be promptly attacked in superior force by a swarm of very formidable hornets'. *[Blackstone p327]* Unfortunately, like hornets, our aircraft did not come out at night they could only take off in the dark with luck and landing was seldom successful. As a result, when a German raider flew over Coggeshall on a February night in 1915 he could operate with some degree of leisure. Mr Cyril Webb saw the plane: 'It was up against the moon so high it looked no bigger than a pigeon.' Mr Bertie Clarke was standing near the parish church with Pc Tyrell:

'We heard the whizz of an engine and the policeman said "It's an aeroplane". The constable

---

[2] 'Timid people attributed the outbreak to German spies or suffragettes'. In fact the fire was started by an exploding oil lamp next door to the post office.

The Coggeshall Air Raid.
The local police and officers from the Royal Warwicks inspect the crater, 21st February 1915.

got upon the wall but could see nothing, then a bright red light appeared in the sky among the clouds for a few seconds. The driver of the aeroplane shut his engine off for an instant. We could not see the aeroplane but we could hear the ever increasing buzz of the bomb as it dropped and approached the earth. We knew we were nearly beneath the red light – we were standing near the church wall – and at once thought the church was the target of the bomb, so we lay down quickly on the path to avoid being hit. The next instant there was a terrific explosion in the Starling Leeze field, 100 yards from where we stood. Instantly the sky was lighted up by a great red flash from the bomb, just like lightning but red in colour. Every house in Coggeshall was shaken and the inhabitants rushed out. Doors and windows were shaken two miles away. The explosion was so violent as to be heard four miles away at Stisted, the Colnes and Great Tey ....the bullets [shrapnel] from the bomb flew in all directions and did a lot of damage to buildings nearby, besides cutting through a wood fence. Handfuls of brass screws, bits of iron, &c, were picked up near the spot where the bomb exploded.'[3]

'One missile went through the cowhouse and smashed a window in Abbey View just missing a cow. Mr William Williams, the gardener at Abbey View showed our representative round the house and buildings. Bullets from the bomb were so powerful that they cut through two or three wooden walls in succession and some penetrated even an iron roof.' *[From CC 26/02/1915]*

There were indirect casualties. A horse attached to a wagonette of soldiers in Church Street, startled by the explosion, bolted down the

---

3   This raid in which Colchester and Braintree were also bombed may have been the first time that bombs were dropped on Britain from an aircraft. In a raid on Dover at Christmas 1914, the bombs only fell into the sea.

Soldiers of the Royal Warwicks filling in the bomb crater on Starling Leeze, February 1915.

street until it reached the junction at Market End, where it collided with the doorpost of Messrs Stead and Simpsons shop. The soldiers were pitched out, one of them was seriously hurt and the horse fell, breaking one of its legs and had to be put down. Mrs Eady who lived on Tilkey Road, was knocked down by soldiers trying to stop the horse. When she was taken home it was found that her right thigh was broken.

On the following Monday evening Mrs Parker died. She was the wife of Thomas, an agricultural labourer at Surrex. It was said that she never recovered from the shock she suffered from the explosion. Mr Joseph S Surridge was lying ill in bed at Abbey House when the bomb fell and from that time, his condition worsened. He developed bronchitis and died a few days later, aged 55 years. A very well respected man he was proprietor of J S Surridge & Son estate agents and auctioneers. *[Coggeshall Almanack 1916]*

The remaining seven street lights were now turned off. Air raid warnings continued to be a feature of life in Coggeshall for the rest of the war and news of Zeppelin raids elsewhere meant that tension remained high. The first raid was in East Anglia, four people were killed in Yarmouth and Kings Lynn in January 1915. The first in London was in May when seven were killed and raids on 13th and 14th October 1915 killed a total of seventy-one and in 1916 a Zeppelin was brought down just a few miles away at Great Wigborough. In 1917, people in Coggeshall were regularly taking shelter when the air raid alerts sounded. The Parish Council wrote to the Superintendent of the police in Witham:

> 'To advise the Coggeshall Police after air raids when the "all clear" is given, as Coggeshall people are kept up very late not knowing whether the raids were over or not.' *[BBA 10/10/1917]*

The Parish Council Minute Book records that this was to 'remove the unnecessary strain upon them'. *[MB2 02/10/1917]* The air raid sirens were themselves the cause of a certain amount of anxiety. At Grays in south Essex, the siren 'was doing more harm than good and a source of annoyance to nervous people'.

The Royal Warwicks

The 8th Battalion, Royal Warwickshire Regiment arrived in Coggeshall in 1914 and were billeted here for some time. They brought economic and social benefits and generally got on well with the townspeople.

When there was a gas explosion and fire at W G Smith's shop on Church Street several soldiers came to help. The gas men were making a new connection when there was an explosion and the gas meter burst into flames. The gas could not be turned off so the foreman draped his coat over the flames and Mr Smith added a 'motor rug'.

> Some men of the 8th Royal Warwick Regiment and Ps Everard organised a hand-to-hand service with pails of water, whilst others removed the stock and a serious conflagration avoided. A large quantity of stock was damaged by water. [EN 23/01/1915]

When the Council heard about 'the narrow escape from fire' they wrote to Mr Worthington Church of the gas company, requesting 'to place stop cocks at given points in the town'. Worthington Church was not a man to be trifled with and he was already smarting from the loss of income from the street lighting. He wrote back expressing his 'incredulity' at the Council's lack of understanding of gas, telling them that 'the danger of explosion would be increased, not reduced, if the gas could be turned off to several properties at the mains'. He ended the rant by politely declining their request.

Arthur Smith lived in a decayed thatched house in Robinsbridge Road. In early March 1915, some linen airing in front of the kitchen fire caught alight and the room filled with smoke. His daughter, confronted by the scene shouted for help, just as two soldiers from the Royal Warwicks were passing by. Privates Albert Horner and William Grimloy immediately ran in to assist and managed to put out the blaze, undoubtedly saving the house. [EN 20/03/1915]

Something similar appeared to have

Early Closing in Coggeshall
November 1915
In view of the need for more restrictive lighting, a meeting of the tradesmen was held in the Lecture Hall and it was agreed to close at eight o'clock on Friday and Saturday evenings and to urge upon the public to shop as early as possible [EN 13/11/1915]

---

happened at another fire in March:

> 'On Monday evening a fire broke out in a hay stack in Tilkey belonging to Ernest Goodman, Cowkeeper. Several men of the Warwickshire Regiment stationed in the town kept the fire under control by beating out the flames. The fire brigade was summoned and under Captain W Brown the fire was soon extinguished.' [CC 02/04/1915]

However, things were not quite as simple as they seemed:

> 'At Witham Police Court on Tuesday William Frank Stuchfield 27, William Frederick Goldsby, 21 and Walter Mathews 25, Privates in the Warwicks Regt., stationed in Coggeshall, were charged with setting fire to a haystack, the property of Ernest Goodman, Farmer, Tilkey, Great Coggeshall on March 29th and doing damage to the extent of £25. The prosecutor stated that his haystack was situate in a field beside the road. He saw it at 4pm when it was all right: at 9pm he was sent for and found his stack in flames. A fire engine was there and the fire was eventually put out. Henry Wade, bricklayer, said he was at the Lamb public house on the evening of March 29th. The three soldiers charged were there also. At 8.30pm they left and went towards Coggeshall[4]. Just as they left he heard one of the soldiers say they would have their revenge on anything they came across. About a quarter of an hour after he heard a call of fire, he ran to the spot and there saw Goldsby on top of the stack, trying to put the fire out. Harry Potter, labourer, Coggeshall, stated that he was walking along the road near the haystack at about 8.50pm and saw three soldiers standing in the road close

---

4   A stranger might think that Tilkey was part of Coggeshall, to locals the two were distinct and separate.

East Street. Ahead of the coal cart is Abbey View.
The bomb fell behind the outbuildings in the field where the trees are growing. Then called Starling Leeze, the field was later bought as part of the Coggeshall war memorial and known since to locals as 'The Rec'.

to the stack. They were singing and "carrying on" and appeared to be under the influence of drink. When he had gone 50 yards along the road he heard someone shout out "fire!" from the direction of the stack. He went back and found the three soldiers trying to put out the fire in the stack. There were only the three soldiers in the field. [Later] Pc Carver .... went to the guardroom of the 2nd 8th Warwick Regt at Coggeshall and there he saw Stuchfield and Goldsby, who were identified as two of the three soldiers who were seen at the Lamb public house. They were arrested. Witness subsequently arrested Mathews. The three soldiers were remanded till April 20th and were admitted to bail on their own recognisances.' *[EN 03/04/1915]*

At the next hearing only Mathews turned up and a warrant was issued for the other two. In May the matter was dropped through lack of evidence and the continued absence of two of the defendants whom the army did not seem anxious to find.

When the Parish Council presented the account to reclaim the expenses of the fire the insurers 'declined to recognise liability'. The Council were somewhat taken aback as, 'out of pocket expenses' had always been paid in the past. A letter was sent listing previous claims and the full amount was eventually paid, a year after the fire. *[MB2 19/04/1915, 13/03/1916, 27/03/1916]*

Cause for Concern

Things were not well with the fire brigade and by 1915 the deterioration was becoming obvious. Walter Brown, the Captain, was almost certainly suffering some kind of breakdown. After the stack fire at Tilkey in March 1915, his name seems to disappear from the record. The seed firm he and his brother had inherited from their father was declared bankrupt in February 1915 and it was Ernest Brown, the younger brother, whose name appears in reports. The bankruptcy and the death of his mother (a strict Baptist) in March that year must have had a profound effect on Walter and it seems that he never fully recovered.

In June 1915 the Fire Brigade Committee expressed its concern to the council. Mr East, talked of 'the need of the fire apparatus being kept in working order'. The Committee, which included the ex-Captain Desborough Bright, was asked to carry out an inspection of the hose and appliances.

On 26th June 1915, a fire broke out four miles from Coggeshall, at a farm near Marks Tey on the Colchester Road. It involved a range of farm buildings, including two barns, stabling, several stacks, with two cottages under immediate danger. An army officer was passing by in his car and drove quickly to Coggeshall for the brigade. When he arrived he was told that the brigade could not attend; 'as they had no horses'. Back at the fire, local policemen, farm labourers and other villagers were desperately trying to save the cottages. Ladders were pitched and buckets of water flung over the walls and roofs. After Coggeshall's refusal, the Kelvedon brigade was called and the contrast is telling. The brigade received the call at 06.34, the bugler sounded the alarm, the brigade 'turned out smartly' and were working on the fire, four miles away 28 minutes later at 07.02. They managed to save the cottages. The Moore brothers who horsed the Kelvedon engine were carters and hauliers by trade, so their horses may have escaped the requisition which had removed most of Coggeshall's non-essential horses for service with the army. *[EN 03/07/1915]*

Back at Coggeshall, the brigade Committee reported their findings in July 1915. Although a new one hundred foot hose and a breeching[5] was ordered from Merryweather[6], the impression is that they did not or could not get to the heart of the problem which was about people, not equipment.

In January 1916 the 'fire engine shed' was vandalised by children. The Parish Council were understandably upset and ordered that if the miscreants were caught, the clerk 'would see them prosecuted.' Alfred Birkin carried out repairs but the damaged building seems symbolic of the brigade's decline. At a meeting of the Parish Council in March 1916, it was reported that:

> 'The fire brigade had been somewhat depleted and the Captain was non resident.' *[Haines 10/03/1916]*

It is not clear what had happened to Walter Brown following the bankruptcy of 1915. He left the town, but never officially resigned from the fire brigade. His name crops up next in 1920 when he came to Harry Joyce's funeral (as did Fred Baylis). Heartbreakingly, Walter ended up living in a ramshackle shed with no door alongside the Tey Road in Coggeshall. Towards the end of his life, unable to look after himself, he was taken to Braintree Poorhouse[7]:

> 'Where he remained amiable and cheerful to the end. When a visitor, who came to see him just before he died asked "Do you regret your life?", he replied firmly and in some surprise, "No, I enjoyed it".' *[Roper p91]*

At the start of 1916, Coggeshall Fire Brigade had just five firemen and no Captain. Across the country, many firemen had volunteered or were called up to fight in France,

---

5   A Dividing Breeching which converts one line of hose into two.
6   At a cost of just under £9 plus 1s. for carriage on the Great Eastern Railway.
7   The Witham Union Workhouse closed in March 1880. Coggeshall people were then sent to the Braintree Union Workhouse.

Bridge Street, the Royal Warwicks leaving Coggeshall, three Sergeants in the lead.

with the result that most brigades were short of men. The London Fire Brigade for example lost a third of their men between August and December 1914, from 1,251 down to 800. By 1916 the situation was so serious that all professional firemen were given exemption from military service. However, this did not cover town, parish or volunteer firemen, so many of those brigades continued to have problems. Southend started the war with fifty-four volunteer firemen, this was down to thirty-five by the end of 1916 and despite a population of 90,000 the Borough said that they found it impossible to recruit replacements. *[CC 15/09/1916]* The Billericay Fire Brigade started the war with twenty-four men but in October 1916 they were down to five and this did not stop two of them being called up, despite an appeal. *[CC 28/10/1916]* The Kelvedon brigade were also short of men and although the Parish Council gave them leave to recruit they were unable to find anyone to join them. The Council Chairman who also chaired the Rural Tribunal where he ruled on appeals to the call up, suggested that any Kelvedon man granted exemption from military service should be conditional on his joining the fire brigade. *[KPMB 12/01/1917]* As the war continued, appeals against the call up became frequent with a variety of reasons offered for exemption. Mr J Crisp appealed to the tribunal on the grounds that he was the driver of the Braintree fire engine. This was supported by the captain of the brigade and his employer at the Horn Hotel where Crisp was an ostler. Originally accepted, the military appealed and Crisp was told to join up. *[BBA 07/05/1917 & 11/07/1917]* One of Alfred Birkin's employees had been exempted from military service because he was 'the only plumber' in the firm. The military appealed against that decision and at the hearing Alfred had to admit that he was a plumber himself 'but needed to supervise his business'. The plumber was sent off to the war.

New Appointments

It was March 1916 before the problems at Coggeshall were formally addressed. The fire brigade committee met with Mr Edwin Fairhead in the chair. It recommended Alfred Birkin for the post of Captain, to be elected by members of the brigade and suggested that a Sub Captain and three new crew members be appointed to fill the vacancies. Four days later, Harry Saward was made Sub Captain and two new firemen had been recruited, George Alston and Ernest Styles. Alfred Birkin was a member of the Parish Council and had joined the brigade in December 1904. In 1916 when he became Captain, he was 44 years old, with a wife and three children. He had started out as a plasterer and paperhanger, then a plumber and had built up his own business which grew to include house building, employing several men. His steady hand and natural authority were exactly what the brigade needed.

Captain Alfred Birkin

Mr Edwin Fairhead

A few days later, the brigade was called to the farm of the Chairman of the Parish Council, Edwin Fairhead.

> 'A fire broke out on Sunday evening March 19th on Stock Street Farm in the occupation of Mr E Fairhead, where a quantity of straw which had been prepared for the Army, was burnt. The fire was discovered by Mr Fairhead's servant, who gave the alarm. Information was at once sent to the fire brigade who shortly afterwards put in an appearance and quickly got the flames under. Fortunately there was no wind at the time and the other stacks which stood between two and three yards of the burning straw were not touched by the fire. The cause of the outbreak is unknown.'
> [ES 25/03/1916]

It might be recalled that Edwin Fairhead, now Chairman of the Parish Council and the Fire Brigade Committee, was the very same chap who in July 1908, thought that it would have been a good thing 'If they never had the engine'.

The parish accounts show that Captain Birkin paid out almost £7 to those who worked at the Stock Street farm fire, but only 12s seems to have been repaid by insurers. Fairhead may have been under-insured and would have known that the council had no legal authority to claim back the money from him. The Parish Council ended up more than £6 out of pocket, by far the largest loss they had taken to date after extinguishing a fire.

Brigade Improvements

After the fire, Alfred Birkin held a meeting with the brigade to discuss how things might be improved. Their thoughts were considered by the brigade committee on Monday 5th June 1916 with Edwin Fairhead in the chair. Six recommendations were agreed subject to the approval of the full council:

1. That double pay be paid for the first hour.
2. That the Police be asked to pay more attention in calling out the firemen.
3. That firemen be paid for practices at 10s per practice these not to exceed two per year.
4. That name plates for firemen's doors be supplied.
5. That the waterworks man be asked to see that all hydrants are in working order.
6. That three or four Respirators be supplied for the use of the brigade.

As they were often first on the scene, the police had an understandable habit of trying to extinguish fires themselves. The question of responsibility for the hydrants was not so simply resolved. As most hydrants were seldom if ever used, the hydrant pits were sometimes found filled with debris and the valve seized up, but the simple requirement to service them turned into a typical Coggeshall mini-saga which ran for nine years. More of which later.

Before any changes could be agreed, the brigade was called to a fire at Grange Farm, the third of only three fires for which the detailed expenses have survived.

	£. s. d.
To use of hose &c	
Cleaning and drying Hose	10 .0
Captain A Birkin	10.0
Fireman H Saward	5. 0
" J Green	5. 0
" S Green	5. 0
" W Goodey	5. 0
" G Alston	5. 0
" E Prentice	5. 0
" E Styles	5. 0
" E T Pennick	5. 0
To Pumping W Cobey	4. 0
Calling Firemen A Beaumont	2. 0
Refreshment J Sexton	2. 4
	£ 3. 8. 4

*Great Coggeshall Parish Council
To Expenses incurred by Fire brigade at a fire at the Grange Farm Little Coggeshall in the occupation of Mr James Parish,
on June 2nd 1916*

Reproduced by courtesy of the Essex Record Office
[ERO D/P 36/30/19]

Grange Farm Fire, June 1916

'A fire occurred at the Grange Farm near the residence of Mr J Parish, seed grower. The outbreak was near the stack yard buildings and residence, a large portion of a clover haystack being on fire and burning vigorously. The Coggeshall Fire Brigade quickly arrived and a plentiful supply of water was obtained from a hydrant. The Kelvedon brigade, with their engine, also attended, but their services were not required. The property destroyed comprised the part stack of clover hay, the chaff cutter and a large rick cloth.' *[CC 09/06/1916]*

Two years into the war and the average age of the firemen is 46 up from 32 when the brigade was established; it was a brigade of the middle-aged. Conscription had started in January 1916, the upper age limit of 41 meant that all but one of the Coggeshall firemen were too old to be called up. Alf Birkin was 44, Joe Green was 45 and lived on Market Hill, he directed the town brass band and was in business as a plumber & decorator. (His son William known as Billy, was 23 at the time and years later joined and became captain of the brigade.) Sam Green, Joe's brother, was 35 years old and a cabinet-maker from Orchard Cottages, West Street; William Goodey was 45 and a self employed bill-poster living with a wife and seven children at the Old Oak on Stoneham Street; Ernest Prentice was 43, a boot repairer who lived and worked in Stoneham Street; Edgar Pennick was 53 and a publican at the Yorkshire Grey on Stoneham Street. The new recruits were Ernest Styles, 53 a brick and tile maker who had taken over the brickworks on the Colne Road and George Alston a 43-year-old bricklayer from Church Street.

Because the fire was in the area covered by the water main, the manual engine was not needed, neither were the horses to draw it, nor the pumpers to pump it, so this time there was no work for agricultural labourers. Instead there is an item 'to Pumping, Mr Cobey', the turncock

A stack fire somewhere in the Coggeshall area c1910.

of Coggeshall Waterworks. His name was so synonymous with the new water supply that some called the tap-water 'Cobey's ale'. The firemen may well have resorted to this, as the total bill for refreshments only amounted to 2s 4d. At 4d a pint, seven pints in total, for a ten man crew, this is very modest if not downright disappointing by Coggeshall standards. Joseph Sexton, the proprietor of the Chapel Hotel on Market Hill supplied the pittance.

Sub Captain Harry Saward was listed as a fireman and paid at that rate, 1s an hour, only the Captain was paid at the higher rate of 2s. The duty lasted five hours. The council did exercise proper oversight of the account and questioned Saward's charge of 10s for cleaning and drying the hose, double the usual cost. Saward told them that this was due to the additional lengths of hose that were used at the fire. *[MB2 03/07/1916]* Alfred Beaumont a 43-year-old carpenter from Gravel End was paid 2s for calling out the firemen.

The Parish Council approved all six of the brigade Committee's recommendations shortly after the fire. *[MB2 05/06/1916]* The well-known firm of 'Gamages' was approached for the respirators but nothing seems to have come of it, probably because they would not have been suitable for fire-fighting.

The brigade attended several fires in 1917, including Gambrel House and Cromwell House, both in East Street and a small fire at the Hamlet, thoughtlessly extinguished by bystanders before the brigade arrived. The fire at Gambrel House was thought to have started from a bathroom gas 'water geyser' used to heat water and spread through the ceiling and into the roof. The brigade arrived with the hand-cart under Captain Birkin and the hose was attached to the nearest hydrant. Despite the copious water supply it was two hours before the fire was brought under.

During a fire at Teybrook Farm, Great Tey, in September 1918, the brigade made use of and paid, 'five German prisoners of war'. When presented with the account for the fire, the insurers, the Essex & Suffolk Equitable, refused to pay for them and offered £10 against a total claim of over £20. The Parish Clerk was instructed to inform them that the 'amount was to be paid to the Commandant of the military at Halstead for services rendered by the German prisoners as per an account sent in by the military'. A month later the insurers paid up in full. *[MB3 05/11/1918]*

Kelvedon firemen at the Scrip's Farm stack fire, May 1916.
Reproduced by courtesy of the Kelvedon Museum

Summoned by Bells

In May 1916, a fire broke out at Scrip's Farm. This belonged to Mr James Parish who farmed on 1,200 acres, employed forty-six men and was one of the few people in Coggeshall who had a telephone. Although the farm is in Coggeshall, it was the Kelvedon brigade who attended, summoned for the first time in this part of the world by telephone.

> 'Men on the farm were chaff-cutting when a spark from the engine set alight to the top of a wheat stack and the straw being very hot and dry was soon ablaze. It spread very quickly and the Kelvedon Fire Brigade was telephoned for and under Captain George Braddy quickly put in an appearance. The flames, however spread to the adjoining stacks and the fire was not got under control until two wheat stacks and a straw stack had been destroyed. The fire brigade succeeded in saving the remaining stacks. The damage which is estimated to be £700 or £800 is covered by insurance.' *[ES 27/05/1916]*

Coggeshall was somewhat behind the times. The telephone had arrived in the town in 1908 but it was eighteen years later, in January 1926, before the Coggeshall brigade could be called out using the device.

Another tragedy hit the brigade in 1918 when Sub Captain Harry Saward died. Just 41 years old, he was one of the founder-members of the brigade and succumbed to meningitis on 27th August. At his funeral in the Parish Church, his coffin was drawn on a hand bier by his colleagues in the brigade. The Parish Council at their next meeting sent their condolences to his widow.

In November the war came to an end. Seventy-nine Coggeshall men never came home.

9 THE END OF AN ERA

The large building was the seed warehouse which was entirely destroyed in June 1920. The range of buildings running at right angles which included the original boiler and engine house were saved. Only the centre two-storied building still survives.

The Great Fire at King's Seeds

J K King had received a royal warrant in 1885 and at the turn of the century was the largest seed growing business in Britain. Their premises in Coggeshall were extensive, the biggest building, the 'General Farm Seed Warehouse', was built in 1837-39 as a silk mill, its machinery dismantled by Tansley & Son in 1886. It was on three floors, two-hundred feet long, fifty feet wide and ran from the rear of Orchard House just behind West Street, to the footpath at Crouches.

The business was about to experience a period of tragedy and great ill fortune and as is often the way, it came in three parts. The first was the sudden death in March 1918 of George Paterson, just 45 years old and the irreplaceable Manager of the Seed Warehouses. Then on 13th June 1918, Mr Herbert T King the owner of the business, was killed by a bomb whilst inside

King's seed warehouse after the roof had fallen. This is the end of the building shown on the illustration opposite. The watchers are on the Crouches footpath, many on the bridge that crosses Robin's Brook.

a train in Liverpool Street Station in the most lethal raid of the War[1]. King and his manager Mr J H Millard were in the dining car of the train when the bomb fell and King was killed instantly. A Sergeant of the City Police found him and carried him out on to the platform as the carriage was on fire. 'I spoke to him and he did not answer. I felt sure that life was extinct and carried him to the waiting room where the doctor after examination said the death had been instantaneous.' *[Evidence to the Inquest quoted in the Bocking Advertiser 04/07/1918]*

'King's companion, the seventy year old Mr Millard the manager of the firm, was not hit but reeled forward and on regaining himself he looked around and saw Mr King in a pool of blood. He was in the act of lifting his friend up, when another bomb dropped closer, when he fell unconscious with a wound in the back of his head from which blood was streaming. Mr Millard remained in this position for some time, but was ultimately picked up and taken to St Bartholomew's Hospital where the wound was dressed and bandaged. Mr Millard subsequently made search for his friend among the killed and wounded at several London Hospitals and it was only during the evening that he found Mr King's body at a mortuary. With Herbert's death, the line of Kings in the firm came to a dramatic end.' *[Bocking Advertiser 04/07/1918]*

The final blow fell on 6th May 1920. At about 1pm a young girl playing in the yard of St Peter's School noticed a few wisps of smoke emerging from one of the windows of the Seed Warehouse. By the time she found someone to tell, the smoke was billowing and several people had seen it. The Coggeshall brigade was called and a message sent to Kelvedon for assistance. With the fire developing rapidly, heavy smoke began to envelop the school, making it impossible to reopen for the afternoon session, much to the delight of the children. Most of the boys ran

---

1   162 people were killed in the raid and 432 injured when 20 planes dropped 4,400 kgs of explosives. It was the largest number of casualties in a single raid of the whole war.

Coggeshall fire brigade break for a photo in front of the remains of King's seed warehouse, May 1920. Captain Alfred Birkin in the centre, the two Green brothers can be identified, Joe seated and Sam far left.
Photo by courtesy of Sam Birkin

down to Crouches bridge to watch the spectacle develop. The 'Essex Chronicle' takes up the story:

> 'A disastrous fire occurred at Coggeshall yesterday afternoon involving the destruction of the seed warehouses of the firm of Messrs John K.King and Sons, the loss of vast quantities of pedigree seeds and damage estimated at not less than £50,000.
>
> The fire apparently broke out in the lower floor of the large seed warehouse which comprised three floors, while the employees were at dinner. Smoke was seen issuing from the building about a quarter-past one by two of the workmen who live near by. The alarm was given and the fire brigades from Coggeshall and Kelvedon were summoned. There was a high wind at the time and this caused a rapid spread of the flames and within twenty minutes the roof, 200ft long and 50ft wide, fell in. Sparks and flames rose to a great height and could be seen from a long distance. The interior of the building became a veritable furnace, thousands of pounds of pedigree seeds adding fuel to the fire. All the seeds were destroyed - an irreparable loss. At one time it looked as if the private residence, occupied by Mr H T King[2], would become involved, but the united efforts of the fire brigades were instrumental in saving this, although a great deal of furniture was removed to a place of safety. The huge warehouse on the North side of West Street was completely gutted and the adjoining

---

2   It was the residence of his widow.

The Coggeshall brigade turning over and damping down after the King's seed warehouse fire. Mr Cobey stands next to Captain Birkin with the hydrant key in his hands.

stores and seed testing house were also destroyed. The firemen were unable to stay the course of the conflagration until it reached the base of the large chimney shaft on the East side of the premises. The detached offices were not damaged. The big warehouse was packed with seeds from top to bottom. Great praise is due to Captain Birkin of the Coggeshall brigade and Captain Doughton of the Kelvedon brigade together with their men who worked assiduously in checking the flames.'
[CC 07/05/1920]

The brigade had the advantage of a good water supply from a hydrant on site and William Cobey, the water man, helped to maximise the flow. The Crouches side of the fire was too far from a hydrant so the Kelvedon brigade set their manual into Robin's Brook and employed pumpers to provide the jet. There was never any chance of saving the warehouse but the adjoining Orchard House and the building which linked the warehouse to the Engine House, once called the Reel Room, were saved.

The Coggeshall brigade was on duty from the 6th to the 10th of May, day and night, and the bill was just over £145. This account included payment for the pumpers who worked the Kelvedon engine – the last occasion that pumpers and a manual engine were employed at a fire in Coggeshall. Other expenses included an account for twenty-three gallons of mild ale 'supplied to the men whilst on duty'. This notable level of consumption was impressive enough to be reported in the London 'Times' and forms part of the proud record of the Coggeshall brigade.
[The Times 14/06/1920]

Coggeshall's first speed limit, 1914
'Speed Limit 10 Miles an Hour For Motors'.
This one is opposite Paycocke's.

The brigade earned considerable credit for the efficient way it handled such a major incident. Perhaps on the back of that, at the next council meeting it was proposed to double the levels of pay; the Captain 8s for the first hour and 4s for each subsequent hour, firemen were to be paid 4s for the first hour and then 2s, all had an allowance per hour for refreshments. Although the first hour's pay had been doubled when Captain Birkin took over in 1916, this increase had been overdue as wages had increased dramatically during the war.

Coggeshall had a fire brigade that they could be proud of, well-led and effective. Although the Parish Council had modest means and was averse to spending, it kept the brigade up to scratch and on such a big occasion, it did not let them down. It was to be their finest hour.

The Age of the Motor Accident

The first Coggeshall incidents with a motor car also involved a horse. In 1899 a horse and trap containing Frank Beard and the auctioneer Mr J W Clark were travelling on the Braintree Road when a car passed them at speed, 'Mr Beard's horse was greatly frightened and jumped clean over the hedge'. Horse, trap and occupants managed to get back on the road without major damage. *[ES 22/07/1899]* The horse in the second incident in 1903 had a different response. A Benz belt-driven car capable of 18mph was driving along near Coggeshall, when it was spotted by a horse which 'jumped over a wall and ran after the car and tried to bite it'. *[Recounted in CC 02/08/1935]* The first collision involving a motor car was in 1905 when a trap on its way to Kelvedon was hit by a motor, throwing out the occupants and leaving it badly damaged. The report did not see fit to disclose the fate of the car or its occupants. *[CC 30/06/1905]* In April 1917 Miss Rose and Mrs Maria Burton were passengers in a wagonette which overturned after a double hit by 'a runaway horse and car colliding with it.' The ladies were thrown out, rendered unconscious and detained in hospital after treatment. *[EWN 17/04/1917]*

As early as 1906 the Council received a letter complaining of 'the reckless manner in which motors were driven through the town'. *[Cuttle 16/07/1906]* It was not just cars, the appropriately named Charles Sparks, a traction engine driver, was fined 10s with 4s costs for driving a traction engine at excessive speed in Coggeshall, Ps Saunders stating that the engine was going at five miles an hour, the speed limit for a town being two. *[CC 7/08/1906]* In April 1914, after correspondence with the Highways Department, signs were installed limiting the speed of motors to 10 miles an hour.

The first fatality was probably in 1913 when an old man, Mr H Sexton, walking in the road near the Horse and Hounds at Coggeshall Hamlet, was run over on a windy and wet

Market End c1900.
At the top of Bridge Street are the shop and the premises behind soon to be demolished to widen the road.
On the right is Doubleday's shop, also now gone.

January evening and died the next day. The car involved was owned by the Moore brothers of Kelvedon, driven by Bert Doughton and George Braddy was a passenger. Mr Sexton had been to Coggeshall to collect his old age pension. *[CC 17/01/1913]* Another notable fatality involved Miss Janet Stephens, organising Secretary to the League of Nations in Essex. Too impatient to wait for a bus she was half a mile out of Coggeshall, walking towards Braintree at 7.45 pm on 1st May 1927 when she was struck and run over by a car and died a few days later. The car driver, Miss Vaughan, said she had not seen Miss Stephens and was fined the maximum £20 and her licence suspended for a year. *[CC 20/05/1927]*

Motors also heralded a new class of fire. What may well have been the first of these in Coggeshall was reported in October 1921:

> 'Mr Owers landlord of the Foresters Inn was driving his motor car along the Feering Road on Wed October 26th when near the lane leading down to Threadkells Mill, the car by some means caught fire. Mr Owers found himself unable to extinguish the flames and the motor was almost entirely destroyed.' *[ES 29/10/1921]*

In 1925 the increased traffic prompted the Coggeshall brigade to order a set of hose ramps. These are used to protect the hose from damage as vehicles drive over. *[MB3 06/12/1925]*

Vehicles also began to shape the appearance of the town itself. The main road through Coggeshall narrowed charmingly near the Bridge Street junction but was the scene of several accidents and close escapes. The matter had been referred to the County Council in 1919 and referred again after another accident in May 1920. Eventually the old buildings were demolished, the road widened and a little bit more of our idiosyncratic past was lost.

Horse to Petrol

It was getting to be impossible to find horses for the engine, a problem which started during the war when huge numbers of horses were sent to France and continued as they were replaced by motor vehicles. In April 1918, even the Moore brothers had to give up their contract to supply horses for the Kelvedon engine. The Council advised; 'Anyone living outside Kelvedon must send their own horses at the time of making the call'. *[KPMB 18/03/1918]* Braintree had the same rule and missed two major fires through the lack of horses. In April 1922 the Coggeshall Fire Brigade Committee approached Arthur Hutley, a haulier from Church Street who agreed to make his lorry available and within a couple of weeks a draw-bar was fixed to the manual engine so that it could be towed. As a result 1922 marks the end of the horse-drawn era for Coggeshall Fire Brigade. Kelvedon's manual was similarly adapted in 1923 and Braintree's in 1924. *[EWN 04/01/1924]* In all cases the move from horse to motor was made by necessity not choice but these tinkerings were only an interim solution. The age of horse-drawn manual engines was numbered, new motor fire engines were taking over, they were immediately ready, faster on the road, more powerful, did not need pumpers and were increasingly reliable – but they were very expensive. Coggeshall Parish Council were well aware that they had to do something if they wanted to keep a brigade in the town. The problem was, in 1922 the total cost of the brigade to the Parish Council was a little over £9 and with a new motor engine costing anything between £400 and £1,000, it was difficult to see how things would pan out.

Fire at Houchins Farm

The farmhouse at Houchins was already old when it was used by General Fairfax during the siege of Colchester in June 1648. On the afternoon of 8th August 1921, Frank Ham a thatcher was at work at the farm with his son when he happened to look up:

'They saw a barn on fire and quickly gave the alarm, but the whole building was enveloped in flames within a few minutes. The premises immediately adjoining which were mainly thatched and tarred soon caught and fanned by the wind, the flames spread to the stackyard and within a very short time were ablaze. A strong breeze was blowing from the north-west: otherwise, nothing could have saved the old farmhouse. It was deemed necessary to remove the furniture to a safe distance. The Coggeshall and Kelvedon brigades attended and devoted their energies mainly to preventing the fire spreading. The cause of the outbreak is unknown. The damage estimated at £6,000 is covered by insurance.' *[EWN 12/08/1921]*

The brigade remained at the fire for some considerable time, which combined with the new rates of pay and the additional expense of the Kelvedon brigade, made the Houchins fire the second most expensive to extinguish in the brigade's history at just over £102. The biggest was the King's fire a year earlier. Commercial Union, the insurers, paid up promptly.

Despite the difficulties between Captain Birkin and the Council, when it came to fires, the brigade continued to work well. During a fire at Bryan Saunder's workshop on Stoneham Street, in September 1922, one of the councillors, Mr Austin, watched them at work and 'spoke in approval of the fire brigade' at the next Council meeting. A letter from Bryan Saunders was read out to the Council which paid tribute to the 'excellent work accomplished by the fire brigade'. The fire itself, had the makings of a farce. The workshop involved was upstairs at the rear of the building, an inflammable mix of timber, lath and plaster as well as wood shavings, varnishes and spirits used in the trade. It started when Bryan went out and although smoking was banned, the apprentices decided they would take the opportunity to enjoy a pipe of tobacco. A discarded match set a bin of wood shavings alight and there was panic and mayhem as the lads realised they had set the building on fire. They reacted by running around and shouting. This caught the attention of several passers-by and buckets of water were carried upstairs and thrown on the blaze. Someone went for the brigade, who brought order to the scene and soon extinguished the fire with only minor damage caused to the fabric of the building. *[MB3 02/10/1922 & Rose 1995]*

Eccentricity at Kelvedon

In 1923 a serious fire broke out in a row of cottages at Kelvedon and the bugle summoned the Kelvedon brigade under Captain Doughton. Helpers started to remove the furniture from a cottage next door to the burning building, the home of a woman only just delivered of a child. After carrying her to safety, a brandy was thought advisable to revive the lady but 'none could be obtained from the usual sources' – the pubs were closed. Kelvedon was rife with tee-total mania and no-one was ready to admit they might have their own supply. Eventually an unreformed 'private resident in the street' came up with the reviving spirit. Whilst this humanitarian work was going on, the fire threatened to get out of hand and Captain Doughton wanted the Coggeshall brigade to assist. Although the situation at the time was described as 'touch and go', a rule had been brought in that no such message could be sent without the consent of the Parish Council. Eventually they were tracked down and the invitation dispatched. A correspondent reported that 'Flames were shooting high in a stiff breeze and the burning wood and sparks were thrown off to a great distance'. The Kelvedon men were hard pressed and it was, 'more by luck than anything else'

> ### No Horses, Mansion Destroyed
> #### February 1918
> *When a fire broke out at Easton Lodge word was sent for the Braintree brigade not once but twice, at midnight and at 2am and both times the brigade said they could not attend as they had no horses, as did Saffron Walden brigade. Chelmsford brigade refused because the lodge was outside their six miles rule. The Dunmow brigade did attend and saved part of the Hall. The people from Easton decided that in future they would help themselves and when the church bells rang, every man and woman who answered the call would take a pail.*
> *[Leeds Mercury 23/02/1918]*

that the row of cottages and other property were saved. When Captain Birkin and his men arrived, the crisis was over. Unsurprisingly at this point, the subject of beer came up – but the outlook was grim. Relief came when another unnamed resident heard of the difficulty and had a cask to hand. He quickly ran it down to the fire in his car 'where it was thankfully accepted'. No doubt an atmosphere of fear prevailed among the Kelvedon licensees under the malevolent gaze of the tee-total Mafiosi. The law might have been sympathetic as there was a legal precedent which involved firemen near Sheffield, who after working at a fire, were found drinking in a public house outside hours and the landlord prosecuted. The defence claimed that the landlord was 'performing a charitable act in supplying the men with a glass of beer' and that it 'would be a hardship to firemen if they were not allowed to obtain a beer'. The judge decided the publican had been quite justified in giving them a drink after their hard work, but the firemen should understand that they had no right to demand it. The case was dismissed and gave legal authority to the argument that nothing should stand in the way of a fireman and his beer.
[Sheffield Evening Telegraph 05/10/1897]

Hydrants, Engine and Engine House

The relationship between the Parish Council and Captain Birkin played out over a number of events during the 1920s and was one of the factors that influenced the brigade's future. The need to service the hydrants was first identified in 1916, although nothing seems to have been done. The subject came up again in 1922, when the Fire Brigade Committee[3], recommended that the brigade 'ease and oil' the hydrants as part of their 'thrice yearly practice'. In December 1922 the Council agreed to this, paying the brigade £1 for each practice but they also wrote to Braintree RDC hoping that they might pay or carry out the servicing in future. There was no reply and the brigade neither practised nor cleaned the hydrants. Eighteen months later there was a fire near Osha Smith's cottage on Robinsbridge Road:

> 'The discovery was made about 2 o'clock and although the Coggeshall Fire Brigade were summoned they found on arrival that the premises including the stables, piggeries and other outbuildings could not be saved but they were successful in preventing the flames from spreading to a thatched cottage which was only about ten yards away. The fire was supposed to have been caused by small boys playing with matches near the buildings.' [EWN 08/08/1924]

The brigade found the hydrant blocked with stones and this delayed their efforts to fight the fire. In his letter detailing the expenses, the Captain complained to the Council about the hydrant. This was a bit rich considering that he was supposed to have serviced them, on his own committee's advice, two years before. In a second letter read out at the same meeting, Alf Birkin announced his resignation from the Parish Council and this was accepted without the usual courtesy of thanking him for his service. Other than for reason of health, a resignation mid term was not usual and suggests a falling out.

Alfred Birkin seems to have had little interest in the more prosaic parts of his role because at the same meeting it was the Chairman of the Council who reported that the 'fire engine station'[4] was in need of attention. The roof and ceiling were subsequently repaired and barbed wire put up, 'to prevent boys climbing onto the roof'. [MB3 01/09/1924] After a further inspection the doors were painted 'with one coat of paint'. As for the hydrants, it took yet another letter to get a response and it was not what they hoped for, as the RDC thought that the brigade should attend to the hydrants. The Clerk was sent to Captain Birkin and this gives further evidence of the increasingly distant relationship, 'to ascertain if the brigade were agreeable to accept and carry out the Council's recommendation of December 4th 1922', some two years before. [MB3 01/12/1924] Captain Birkin reported back that they were agreeable, but then again did nothing. In September 1924 the Council decided to pay someone to carry out the work and finally in October 1925, over nine years from the first report, the hydrants were cleaned and serviced. [MB3 05/10/1925] The contrast with Kelvedon is telling; it was the end of 1926 before they noticed the problem, 'the hydrants in the parish are in a bad state through rust and dirt'. They asked the Braintree RDC to 'put the hydrants into working order' at the Council's expense and then the brigade would look after them. This was one year later but nine years faster than Coggeshall. [KPMB 26/11/1926]

Fire at The Old Maltings

Despite all this, the brigade remained an effective fire fighting force. In August 1923 a fire broke out in the stables behind the Greyhound Inn on Church Street, which had been in the hands of Daniel Leaper's son William some sixty years earlier. Access was gained through double gates

---

3   This comprised all the firemen (including Captain Birkin, who always attended) and three Parish Councillors.

4   This was the first Coggeshall use of the name 'fire Engine' and 'Station', previously the 'engine' and 'engine house'.

Osha Smith's Cottage Robinsbridge Road - looking over Robin's Brook from near the ford. The buildings on fire must have been to the right, largely hidden here by the hedge.

on Church Street, passing underneath a first floor room to the yard and stables beyond. The fire was serious, not just in its intensity but in its potential to spread. When the brigade arrived, Captain Birkin sent word for the Kelvedon brigade to assist. The fire spread northwards from the stables into the adjoining building, called the Old Maltings, once part of Mr Beard's premises. These joined the Conservative Club, so its survival was in the hands of the firemen.

> 'Yesterday afternoon a fire broke out in some stables at the rear of the Greyhound Inn, Church Street, Coggeshall. It spread to the adjoining building known as the old malting, owned by Mr. Edwin Fairhead JP CC and contained mangle, swede and turnip seed belonging to Messrs. E W King & Co. These premises were completely destroyed. The fire burned furiously for about an hour. The Conservative Club, which it joins, was in danger but the fire brigade who were quickly on the scene in the command of Mr. Alfred Birkin, saved the situation.' *[EH 10/08/1923]*

With the hydrants providing an inexhaustible supply of water and a well-led and experienced brigade, a potential disaster in the middle of the town had warranted just a few lines in the newspaper.

The Modern Age Arrives

The world was changing and there was no disguising the fact that the Coggeshall brigade with its hand-cart and manual engine was looking decidedly tired and out of date. To see the future we have to look, of all places, to Bocking. This town, six miles west of Coggeshall, had a fierce rivalry with its close neighbour, Braintree. The spirit of competitiveness between the two extended to their fire brigades, both of which had a long and proud history. It will be remembered that both attended Richard White's 1777 Church Street fire. Both brigades had manual engines, but in January 1925, Bocking was able to steal a march on its neighbour:

> 'On Saturday a new motor fire engine, purchased by the Bocking Parish Council was handed over to the Captain of the Bocking brigade. The new engine is an 8hp Gwynne standard attached as a trailer. It is capable of pumping 140 gallons a minute and throwing a three quarter inch jet 80 feet into the air. The engine, which takes the place of two old manuals, is complete with all the necessary equipment. The towing vehicle was based on a Ford 'TT' One Ton chassis, fitted with a purpose-designed body, provided for the rapid conveyance of the firemen with accommodation for equipment.'

The scene after a barn fire. Taken in the Coggeshall area but date and location unknown.

The towing vehicle and trailer pump cost Bocking something over £500. Taking their cue from the lifeboats, Bocking called out their firemen with a Maroon – a rocket which exploded with an almighty bang high in the air. New 'Fire Brigade Regulations' were published which might give an insight into Bocking's past malpractice:

> 'The Engine when on the way to a fire is not to be stopped for the purpose of picking up men who fail to respond to a fire call in time to start with the engine.'

> 'Any member of the brigade guilty of insubordination, practical joking, neglecting to attend a fire … shall be subject to immediate dismissal.'

They were also careful to look after the new machine:

> 'A practice run shall not exceed four miles and on every occasion the trailer pump shall be attached and used alternatively from a hydrant and from the river. Every care shall be taken of the machines and when at practice, water must not be pumped from the hydrant for a longer duration than one minute or from the river for a longer duration than three minutes (this is considered to be sufficient to ensure the proper working of the pump).'

[Attached to Bocking Parish Council Minutes ERO D/J 138/2/5]

Braintree Council were confounded by this unexpected development but gathering themselves, soon saw the solution – they must have a better and bigger engine than Bocking! Officials looked at fire engines made by Merryweather and Dennis which cost almost £1,000 but were able to pump 300 gallons a minute, a very satisfying double the amount that the Bocking pump could manage. At a meeting in August 1925 one of the Braintree Councillors, Mr Ransom, (who was against the proposal to buy a new machine) asked if:

> 'Braintree were considering spending a thousand pounds on a fire engine because Bocking had spent just over half that amount and it was felt that "Braintree could not allow Bocking to do it on us".'

Mr F C Brand no doubt spoke for the overwhelming majority of the town and the council when he responded:

> 'That is the general idea.' *[CC 21/08/1925]*

The Bocking Brass Hats

While Braintree was still debating, Bocking was not content with having the best fire engine, they also wanted to flaunt it in the face of their rivals:

'An entertaining situation has arisen between Braintree and Bocking over fire appliances and it serves to illustrate how far competition may run between two neighbourly towns with a little parochial pride on each side. Until the present year both Braintree and Bocking each had a manual fire engine, the full service of which required about a score of able-bodied men. The engines began to get old: pumping by hand was found to be slow and old-fashioned and men were not so eager to pump as their fathers had been, while horses got so scarce that an edict was issued to the effect that those who needed the use of the engine at a distance, must send horses to draw it!

So early this year, Bocking took the forward step of purchasing an up to date motor fire engine capable of travelling at forty miles an hour and of pumping any pond dry in a very short time. The Bocking firemen, resplendent in bright brass helmets and proudly mounted on their red engine with brass bells clanging made a very fine sight as they went round the parish. To cap the lot, Bocking brigade recently appeared in a Braintree procession and were promptly dubbed "the Bocking Brass Hats". The Braintree brigade with only their manual would not turn out beside their Bocking neighbours' motor engine. Local wags enlivened the procession with a comic take off of the Braintree brigade![5] The anticipated result has come about for it was not to be expected that Braintree were to be humiliated at the expense of Bocking. So Braintree Urban Council are within an ace of buying a brand new motor fire engine which will cost £1,000 and will be capable of doing nearly double the duty of the Bocking engine, because it will cost so much more money.'

[Undated Essex Chronicle article pasted in the minutes of Bocking Parish Council Minutes]

---

5   An old 'trench truck' bearing the inscription 'Braintree Fire Brigade 1926' containing several buckets one of them labelled 'Beer', escorted by two be-whiskered ancients.

A Whole New Ball Game

With no horses to collect, the new engine was quick to get on its way and its unprecedented speed meant it could be in attendance at outlying farms and villages in what must have seemed the blink of an eye. Once on site the engine was very effective, its pump could be got to work immediately without the need to organise pumpers and powered by petrol rather than beer, it worked tirelessly throwing out copious amounts of water.

Bocking had taken out a loan to buy their new engine and the repayments added to the rates. It did not take a genius to come up with a way of reducing the burden – Bocking offered their fire protection services to the wider community. Local parish councils were invited to a conference where the new appliance was demonstrated and 'ways & means of placing the new fire engine at their disposal' were discussed. This meant that for a modest fee, Bocking offered to provide fire cover. Several neighbouring parish councils liked the look of the proposal and signed up for the service. In many cases this was the first time that these villages could feel properly protected against fire – and at a cost which could be met even by their modest means.

On the 14th February 1925 there was a celebration dinner at Bocking, when the new machine was officially handed over by Mr Courtauld. One of the Bocking Councillors, a Mr Golding, said to much laughter, that 'He would be tempted to hope that there would be lots of fires, or at least a jolly good blaze so the engine would show off its capabilities to its utmost'. *[EWN 20/02/1925]*

His wish would soon come true, but no-one would have thought that the graphic demonstration of the new engine's capabilities would be at the expense of the Coggeshall brigade.

Meanwhile....

The Coggeshall brigade turned out in May 1925 to a fire in the office and seed store of James Parish in the yard of Abbey View, East Street. Running to the scene with the handcart, the firemen found that the fire had a good hold and threatened to spread to the house itself. A message was sent to the Kelvedon brigade but good work and a plentiful supply of water meant that by the time they arrived the danger was over. *[EWN 05/05/1925]* James Parish claimed that the fire was a body blow and cited it when his business failed five months later, although the figures do not really support the claim. Parish owed nearly £6,000, the fire destroyed 'Stock and other trade effects to the value of over £1000', he recovered £820 from the insurers leaving him just £180 down. *[EWN 01/01/1926]*

The owner of the property was Mr E E Surridge a solicitor who in 1914 had been sensationally arrested, held in Chelmsford gaol overnight and brought to trial accused of misappropriating a client's money but then found not guilty[6]. He was declared bankrupt in March 1915 and left the country. Surridge objected to the brigade's charges at the fire and to the Kelvedon brigade charging a full fee when they were simply standing by. An investigation found that 'the fees per hour were not considered excessive compared to other brigades'. Although the insurers, the 'Sun' and the 'Northern' eventually paid the bill, Surridge's dissatisfaction and influence was such that in September the Fire Brigade Committee requested permission to 'prepare a set of rules and regulations for the future working of the brigade together with a list of charges for the engine and fees to be paid'. The brigade charge for the Abbey View fire was less than £10. *[MB3 06/07/1925, 10/08/1925 & 07/09/1925]*

Brass Hats Triumphant

Pattiswick is an ancient settlement, a scatter of farms and houses adjoining Coggeshall to the west. In July 1925 during a violent thunderstorm a large barn at Pattiswick Hall was hit by lightning. The farm blacksmith, Mr Cutmore, was watching from one of the farm buildings and saw the bolt strike the thatched roof of the barn, close to the weathervane. The thatch burst into flames and within a short time, the whole barn was alight. As a result of recent publicity, it was the Bocking brigade who got the call for help and they responded despite the fact that Pattiswick was not one of the parishes that had signed up for the engine. The Kelvedon brigade was closer and was on the telephone but it only had a horse-drawn manual engine. Coggeshall was still not on the phone, but one of the farm workers was sent to call them out. The call to Bocking was sent via Braintree police station:

> 'The message was received at Bocking at 8.35am and so expeditiously did the brigade respond that they were playing on the blazing barn at 9.10am. From a large pond the engine pumped powerful sprays onto the fire and the pond was emptied in a couple of hours. The engine was then moved a quarter of a mile across the farm to another pond and within five minutes was pumping water through 500 yards of hose. It was undoubtedly due to the splendid performance of the new engine that Pattiswick Hall was saved as the wind was carrying the flames and tufts of burning straw onto the farmhouse. This was the first test of the new engine and the result exceeded all expectations.

Mr Harris Smith, the farmer had been ill in bed for some days but he at once got up on the alarm and assisted in saving the contents of the doomed barn which burned fiercely. Mrs Smith also helped and a piece of burning thatch singed her hair but fortunately this was quickly extinguished and Mrs Smith was not hurt in any way. There were also plenty of village helpers and the Coggeshall Fire Brigade arrived with their manual drawn by a motor lorry but by this time the Bocking engine had saved the situation. Captain

---

6 On a technicality; his solicitor said that no written request had been made for the money which he said Surridge was ready to return. As the repayments led to Surridge's bankruptcy, the client's money probably was being used inappropriately.

The famous Bocking Brass Hats in 1925.
The towing vehicle is based on a Ford TT one ton lorry, the bodywork purpose designed following the Braidwood pattern with the firemen on the top facing outwards. Behind is the Gwynne pump mounted on a specially made trailer.
Reproduced by Courtesy of Braintree Fire Station

J Lawrence was in charge of the Bocking brigade and Captain Birkin of the Coggeshall brigade. A traction engine and threshing tackle were drawn up to the destroyed stack of wheat preparatory to threshing. When the fire spread to the stack the engine was not running, but it was quickly got under steam and was drawn away just as the flames reached it, the driver being scorched in his efforts, but he stuck to the task and succeeded.'[7] *[CC 24/07/1925]*

The Coggeshall brigade stayed at the fire for some time turning over and damping down, doing the dirty work long after the Bocking heroes had left.

For the Bocking brigade, the fire proved a wonderful demonstration of their new engine and of their ability to provide fire cover over a wide area. What were the thoughts of the Coggeshall firemen when they returned home?

---

7   I understand that this engine has survived to this day, owned by an enthusiast and in working order.

Back in Coggeshall, the Parish Council was apparently more concerned about the way the brigade was being managed than about its outdated equipment. Alfred Birkin had other priorities and little concern for the niceties of protocol. After the Pattiswick Hall fire, he sent the account of expenses directly to Harris Smith, the owner, instead of to the Council as was usual. At another fire in December that year, something similar happened and the insurance company cheque went directly to him, rather than to the Parish Council. *[MB3 02/12/1925]*

These actions were probably not deliberately discourteous, they were rather a busy man's expedient. Deliberate or not, they were provoking to a Parish Council already concerned about his management of the brigade. In December 1925, they sent a formal request that the Captain of the fire brigade should 'furnish the council with a complete list of all hose and appliances and the condition of the same'. *[MB3 06/12/1925]*

A month later the Captain reported that there was a problem with the engine but otherwise the equipment was in good order and there was enough hose for normal requirements. A local firm, James Potter & Sons was contracted to 'attend to the valves of the engine &c'. The work may have been substantial because the engine was away for five months, not returning until June 1926. *[MB3 07/06/1926]*

The declining status of the Coggeshall brigade was demonstrated again in late June 1926. A fire had broken out at Deal's seed warehouse in Kelvedon. Norman Deal tried to fight the fire himself, before calling out the Kelvedon brigade and when more help was needed, the Colchester brigade was summoned. The Coggeshall brigade, just three miles away was not wanted. *[CC 25/06/1926]*

The situation was not helped by the brigade's lack of a telephone. Although the first lines reached Coggeshall in 1908, there was still no official way of calling out the brigade by phone[8]. In January 1926, the Colchester Telephone Exchange asked the Parish Council:

> 'If any one connected with the fire brigade was on the phone, whose name could be hung in the exchange for use in case of a fire call.'
> *[MB3 04/01/1926]*

After some enquiry, it emerged that no one in the brigade had a telephone. Lakes Garage on East Street had one (Coggeshall 23) and Mr Lake was used to being called out in an emergency for breakdowns. He was approached and proved amenable. An agreement was drawn up on 11th January 1926:

> 'I beg to confirm our verbal arrangement respecting the use of your telephone for fire calls viz:- to allow your name to be used for fire calls and on receipt of call you to inform the Captain and for each call the Council to pay you a fee of two shillings and sixpence.'
> *[MB3 01/02/1926]*

---

8 Coggeshall's first telephones, Coggeshall 1 & 2, were taken by John K King & Sons. *[Francis Nichols]*

The Last Laugh

Braintree Council, after investigating the alternatives, bought a £1,000 'Dennis Turbine' Fire Engine. It was handed over to the brigade on 18th January 1926, a year to the month after the Bocking engine. The Council chairman said:

> 'It is only right that a town of the size and importance of Braintree should have the finest and best fire fighting apparatus they could afford'.
> *[EWN 19/01/1926]*

Having laid out all that money on the new engine, Braintree, like Bocking, wanted to maximise their income. They were also considering the wider question of fire protection across the whole rural district for which they had jurisdiction.

At a meeting of the Coggeshall Parish Council in October 1926, it was announced:

> 'The Chairman reported that he had received a notification from the Braintree Urban District Council of their intention to give a demonstration with their new fire engine at Coggeshall on October 2nd.' *[MB3 04/10/1926]*

The demonstration (which actually took place on the 9th) followed the format of an earlier one at Braintree:

> 'A large number of the townspeople assembled to witness the ceremony, which was preceded by a demonstration of the capabilities of the engine, a suggestion having been made in some quarters that the pressure of the water from the hydrants alone is sufficient to cope with fires in the town. This was tested by comparison demonstrations with the help of the engine and the efficiency of the new method was proved beyond question. Whereas the hydrant threw up a jet of water to only 30 feet or so, with the help of the engine, four jets were thrown up 3 or perhaps 4 times as high and the pressure of the water was far greater.' *[EWN 19/01/1926]*

Coggeshall Parish Council was under some pressure itself. The manual engine, now almost a hundred years old, was coming to the end of its useful life and they could not easily afford to replace it. Coggeshall rates had already increased[9] to pay the continuing costs of the water scheme and would soon rise again to pay for the proposed sewerage scheme[10]. The Bocking, Braintree and Kelvedon fire brigades had become symbols of civic pride which encouraged expenditure. In Coggeshall, reluctantly formed and never embraced, the brigade served a necessary, utilitarian function, which gave no incentive for frivolous gestures.

The fire at Pattiswick had convincingly shown that a modern motor appliance, based some distance away, could put out a fire before the old fashioned local brigade arrived at the scene. The logic was inescapable: if Braintree could offer an affordable arrangement, the Parish Council was going to be listening.

The End of an Era

On 18th May 1927, the brigade was called to a fire at the charmingly named Trumpingtons, a farm in Great Tey a couple of miles from Coggeshall in deepest countryside. No account of the fire has come to light, but it must have been both serious and protracted, as the expenses amounted to £77, the third most costly fire in the history of the Parish brigade. It was also to be the last recorded occasion when the Manual Engine was used at a fire. It performed well, but by the time it returned, a day later, it was badly damaged:

'Serious damage was done to the Barrels of the Engine Pumps by stones being put into the box with dirty water.'[11]

Repairs were organised but it was never used again. Perhaps fittingly, at the same meeting,

Stack fire near Coggeshall c1912.

steps were taken that would effectively bring about the end of the brigade itself. The future of Coggeshall's fire protection was put into the hands of the Fire Brigade Committee. They were given a simple instruction:

'To investigate the Fire Engine Business and report to the Council.' *[MB3 13/06/1927]*

The Fire Engine Business

It is a curious fact that as the nineteenth century drew to a close, apart from London, the fire brigade business remained virtually unregulated. Without either political leadership or legal direction, the system of fire brigades and fire protection across the country was in a chaotic state. Numbers of towns and villages made no provision at all for fire fighting whilst others had engines that were old or badly maintained and were found to be useless when wanted. With the decline of the insurance brigades, more reliance was placed on public bodies and this seems to have made the situation worse because their responsibility was only to their own ratepayers. Towns which spent money on a fire engine usually brought in rules to prohibit them from operating outside the town without prior authorisation or guaranteed payment.

---

9   The water rate had doubled in 1919 due to 'excessive wages, new plant and the cost of fuel' *[MB3 11/08/1919]*
10   Finally completed in 1932.
11   The Box was a cistern in the engine where the buckets of water were poured to feed the pumps. As water was scooped out of a pond, stones and mud from the bottom could easily be picked up. A coarse filter in the engine stopped larger stones, smaller stuff could be drawn in and, as in the Trumpington's fire, cause damage to the valves, cylinder and pistons.

It was just such a circumstance that led to an infamous case in 1897. Wolverhampton town council had come to no agreement to provide cover for the surrounding rural area and as a result left strict instructions that their brigade should not venture beyond the town boundary. When a fire broke out at Wrottesley Hall, four miles from the town, Lord Wrottesley sent a messenger to call out the brigade – and they refused to attend. The house was destroyed in the fire, as was its famous library with a first folio Shakespeare and one of the most complete sets of ancient English Chronicles in existence. The incident caused a national furore but except for an amendment to the Lighting and Watching Act clarifying the legality of a council making a payment where agreement had been reached, there was no change in the law.

An attempt was made in 1899, when 'The Fire Brigades Bill' had been proposed and debated in Parliament. The modest proposals in the Bill sought to regulate the existing brigades so that:

> 'We may rely with the same confidence on the fire brigades of the country as we do on that magnificent service, the Metropolitan Fire Brigade.'

At the second reading, evidence was presented as to the present position:

> 'The House will remember the great fires at Sunderland, Newcastle on Tyne and Norwich and in many other places .... which have taken place in the last three years.. these fires would not in all probability have been so disastrous but for the deficiency in appurtenances and equipment of the brigades that had to deal with them..Local Authorities too often rely on water pipes and hydrants ...and neglect to provide a fire engine as a second line of defence.. I was staying a few weeks ago down in the country.. the local authorities having put up hydrants in the village.. considered that there was no use for a fire engine...In one place the engine is a hundred years old and the urban district pays £5 a year to maintain the brigade and pay the rent on the engine house. In another, the date on the engine is 1768... and the Urban District Council allow £10 to maintain the brigade. So egregious has been the neglect of the local authorities in many districts, that ratepayers have held indignation meetings.'

The MP for Stowmarket in Suffolk had inspected 'some score of brigades' and found 'constantly' that drills were very irregular, the appliances often dangerously defective and expert instruction totally deficient:

> 'Yet it is to these bodies that the fate of villages, of factories, of small towns, of historical buildings and pictures is complacently left ... One rate-supported engine I found standing rusty, as it had stood for months, on the village green, with weeds growing in rare profusion upon its wheels. Another engine lashed down by ropes and rings to the floor of its shed, making a swift departure impossible in an emergency. Or to find the brigade horses employed during the day carting dust or stones or watering roads away from the fire station. *[Hansard 12/05/1899]*

The evidence was regarded as 'anecdotal', the Bill withdrawn and a select committee set up to gather evidence. Their report was published in July 1900 and shelved.

In the 1920s the expensive move to motor fire engines both encouraged and enabled town and borough councils to sell fire protection beyond their borders – or to withhold it. As we have seen locally, the Bocking and Braintree brigades having spent a lot of money on new fire engines, tried to recoup some of it by inviting neighbouring parishes to contribute. Billericay did the same when they took delivery of their new motor engine in 1925. Several nearby parishes signed up but there was something rather sinister in the comment of the council's chairman who hoped that those parishes who had failed to contribute would soon 'come into line' and added: 'it would be unfortunate for a fire to occur in a non-contributory parish and that parish to be refused'. *[CC 20/02/1925]* This veiled threat was sharpened because Billericay had 'history'. A year earlier when a fire broke out in nearby Basildon they had refused to send their engine (then an old manual). Adverse comment prompted them to explain; 'When the Basildon Parish Council were asked to make a contribution towards the upkeep of the brigade and appliances, they refused to do so.' *[EWN 23/05/1924]* Exactly why some parishes without an engine would refuse to join a scheme is a mystery, as the contributions were usually fairly modest.

Some parishes had more than one offer and saw an opportunity to be exploited. In 1924, Rainham Parish Council put the matter succinctly:

> '....a letter had been received from the Clerk of the Barking Urban Council offering the services of their fire brigade in the event of fires at a retaining fee of £50 per year plus fire brigade expenses. In October 1921, the chairman pointed out, Barking offered their brigade services at a retaining fee of £100 per annum plus expenses and that the council declined. Before that in September 1919, Tilbury offered the use of their brigade at a retaining fee of £7 10s 0d a year and expenses and that was refused. As they knew in 1921 the Romford Urban Council had expressed their willingness to enter into an agreement with Raynham to attend local fires for expenses only, they did not want a retaining fee and the parish council had accepted the offer..... now the Barking people were evidently trying to look for fresh customers and wanted Raynham to send them £50 a year to help them. He thought they were well protected with Romford on one side and Hornchurch on the other....in two years time, if we leave it, Barking will come for nothing. [Laughter] *[EWN 07/02/1924]*

Maldon Borough Council had a strict rule that its brigade should only attend fires beyond the borough boundary to those parishes who had paid a fee, so when their brigade attended a fire in a non-paying parish in March 1924, there was a calling to account:

> 'Alderman Turner asked for an explanation as it was against the rules and regulations for the engine to go outside the borough. Councillor Granger [Chairman of the Fire Brigade Committee]....said the police were not conversant with the rules and on receiving information of the fire he rang up the brigade and himself used the pretext of bringing a scheduled Drill forward a couple of days in order to call out the brigade. On arriving [the brigade] found that the fire was threatening the farmhouse so decided to go on and save the house. A letter was received from the occupier .... thanking the council for the services rendered by the brigade and stating that ....had it not been for the prompt action of the brigade the fire would have reached his house. Alderman Black said that he was glad the fire brigade had been able to help the poor farmer. [Laughter] The Mayor said they recognised that Mr. Grainger was a most hard working chairman but the rules must be obeyed: they had asked outlying parishes to pay a retaining fee for their services of the brigade in cases of fire and it was not likely they would do so if they found they could get such services for the asking.' *[EWN 28/03/1924]*

Chelmsford Town Council debated the question of attending 'outside' fires in 1922. They had received letters from several parish councils requesting fire cover. These they agreed to, on receipt of payment plus expenses should a fire break out and if they were 'within six miles of the fire station.'[12] *[CC 01/09/1922]*

The Council also agreed that unless arrangements had been made, 'the Council's brigade and appliance would not in future be permitted to respond to calls to fires at premises situate outside the borough'. The town developed the concept further in 1925, by signing up almost thirty individual people and properties outside the town at a cost of a guinea a house per year. When a councillor asked if these were within the six miles radius he was answered 'If they are a few yards out what does it matter?' *[CC 28/08/1925]*

So it was against this background that in June 1927 the Coggeshall Fire Brigade Committee began to consider how the town might be protected in the future. Realistically, there were only two options: either buy their own motor appliance, or seek the protection of Braintree RDC. Before the decision was made, the Parish brigade was to have a last triumph.

---

12   The amount was based on the number of ratepayers and capped at £25 a year.

Paycocke's House at about the time of the fire.

Paycocke's

Paycocke's House was given to the National Trust in 1924 and is probably Coggeshall's most famous building. When it caught fire on Tuesday 23rd October 1928, the prompt and effective action of the Coggeshall Parish brigade led by Captain Birkin, greatly limited the damage and may even have saved the building.

> 'On Tuesday at about 8.30pm, a fire broke out at Paycocke's House... It appears to have originated in an upper storey of the east wing of the building and was discovered by one of the maids in residence, who quickly gave the alarm. The news spread rapidly, with the result that a large gathering was soon on the scene. There was a high wind blowing at the time and as the flames burst through the roof it was feared that the building was doomed, but the old oak of which the house is chiefly composed, burnt slowly. Fortunately, the fire brigade soon put in an appearance and with a plentiful supply of water from a hydrant close at hand got the fire under control very quickly. In the meanwhile, a telephone message had been sent to the Kelvedon Fire Brigade, who are to be commended for the very prompt manner in which the call was answered. Fortunately their services were not required. The Braintree Fire Brigade arrived shortly after the fire had been extinguished. The damage, which is estimated at several hundred pounds, is covered by insurance and was chiefly confined to the staircase, an upper room and to the roof at the back of the east wing. Very little damage is apparent from the front view.' *[ES 27/10/1928]*

This was the last fire for Coggeshall's Parish brigade and perhaps a fitting memorial. The fire was also important in another respect – three brigades and two engines were in attendance within a short time. The combination of telephone and the rapid attendance by Braintree's new motor appliances showed how it was now possible to provide an unprecedented level of fire protection. The pattern for the future was clear and the autonomy of the parish brigades was coming to an end.

November 1928 – The End is Nigh

Less than two weeks after the fire at Paycocke's, Braintree RDC organised a meeting for representatives of Great and Little Coggeshall and Kelvedon to discuss the 'better and more modern protection in case of fire'.

Mr Fellows, the Assistant Clerk for Braintree RDC outlined the proposed scheme. This came about, he said, through the need to do something about the Bocking brigade. Having attended twenty-five fires, 'six of them bad ones' since they bought their new engine, the charge on the people of Bocking had become very heavy. The Rural Council had decided to create a more comprehensive and equitable scheme which would better address the fire-fighting requirements of the whole district. It would relieve individual parishes with fire engines of meeting the expenses of fire extinction and distribute costs equally and fairly to the whole district by paying for the service through the rates.

A new, up-to-date and 'powerful' Morris fire engine had been bought for the Bocking brigade as 'they had a bigger district and rather more hilly country to cover'. The Bocking brigade's towing vehicle and trailer pump (the same one that had put Braintree's nose out of place) was only four years old and in perfect condition. Under the plan, it would be transferred to Kelvedon and provide cover for the surrounding area including Coggeshall. It was suggested that Coggeshall might continue to use the hose cart as a first response until the Kelvedon Area brigade arrived. The Coggeshall representatives apparently raised no objections to this downgrading of their status.

The final act in the Bocking Brass Hats saga is poignantly recorded in the minutes of Bocking Parish Council: 'Bocking brigade and equipment would be stationed at Bocking as at present but that the Rural Council would now own and control all equipment'. *[22/04/29]*

The Foundation Stone of Kelvedon Fire Station 1912.

In Coggeshall, the Chairman of the Parish Council outlined the new scheme, rather appropriately, on Guy Fawkes Day, 1928. The town would benefit by having fire cover at a fixed and affordable price with no administrative responsibilities. A motion 'That the Rural District Council be asked to carry out the scheme as outlined' was proposed, seconded and carried. That was that. After one hundred and fifty years, Coggeshall would no longer have its own fire engine. *[MB3 05/11/1929]*

Why Kelvedon?

In 1931 the population of Kelvedon was about 1,700 and that of Great and Little Coggeshall 2,700. On this measure the engine should have been based in Coggeshall – so why did it go to Kelvedon? The difference between the two fire stations was important. Kelvedon's Fire Station, opened in 1912, was remarkable, brick built on two floors in the Italianate style it was complete with a tall campanile for hose drying. The contrast with Coggeshall's tiny, prosaic, aged and vandalised brick box with barbed wire on the roof could hardly have been greater. A direct comparison can be made; in 1924 the Coggeshall engine house door was repainted with one coat of paint, in 1922 the Kelvedon station repainting specified: 'three coats best oil paint outside and two coats inside.' *[KPMB 01/08/1922]*

Drawing of Kelvedon's Italianate Fire Station built in 1912 by George Braddy for £220.

The Kelvedon station had room for a modern fire engine, Coggeshall's did not. The stations also symbolised the status of the two brigades. Since the appointment of Bill Doughton as Captain, the Kelvedon brigade was winning a reputation for their fast turnout, smartness and efficiency and was held in high regard by the people of Kelvedon, their pride given substance when the new station was built. Although the Coggeshall brigade was well led and worked effectively at fires, the Captain was disengaged and left the Parish Council to sort out any problems, not even aware, for example, that the station roof was damaged and water was coming in. Perhaps this would have changed if Coggeshall had been gifted a modern fire engine. Instead it went to Kelvedon and they offered a modern fire station, an excellent record, proven leadership, committed firemen and a real appetite to take on a new challenge.

Last Rites

On 7th October 1929 Coggeshall Parish Council heard that the arrangements had been finalised. There would be a small 'Supplementary brigade' in Coggeshall with the hose cart and four men to serve as firemen. The hose cart was described as 'fully equipped' but in fact it was the same hose cart with the same equipment as before. So – 'four men and a handcart', a sorry excuse for a fire brigade. The four were, Captain Alfred Birkin and his son George, Frank Weinrich and Billy Green.

The Parish Council sent a letter to the firemen, thanking them for their services and requesting the return of their uniforms. The old manual engine was sold to Alfred Birkin for £3. The council thought it not worth the expense of advertising. Sam Birkin, Alfred's grandson, can remember the engine standing at the back of a building at Crouches. Unfortunately it has now gone and Sam could not recall its fate.

The Parish Council tried to palm off the Engine House to the RDC. They declined and thought the building should remain with the Parish Council.

On Saturday 23rd November 1929 representatives from Bocking, Kelvedon and Coggeshall parish councils attended a ceremony to officially hand over the new fire engines to the Bocking and Kelvedon brigades. Captain Lawrence of the Bocking brigade, Captain Doughton from Kelvedon and Captain Alfred Birkin from Coggeshall were all present and when the ceremony was over, everyone sat down for a nice cup of tea. James Parish, Chairman of the Rural Council praised the quality of the engines and the economic advantages of the 'comprehensive scheme' and concluded with the hope 'That the parishes which hitherto had been without appliances of their own would appreciate what the council was endeavouring to do for them (Hear Hear)'. *[EN 30/11/1929]*

Braintree RDC Kelvedon area engine and crew c1930, Captain Doughton with the peaked cap. This is the Gwynne trailer pump and Ford TT based Towing Vehicle inherited from the Bocking brigade.

The Wilderness Years

During the next nine years, the Braintree RDC Coggeshall Supplementary brigade declined into obscurity. The Kelvedon brigade did make an effort to include them, Alfred Birkin attended their annual dinner in February 1933. The gesture was a kind one but the Coggeshall brigade were not really part of the club. The Braintree, Bocking and Kelvedon brigades regularly met at fires and attended each other's summer carnival, the engines often leading the procession. Reporting on the 1931 Coggeshall Church Parade, the 'Chronicle' mentions that brigades from Braintree, Bocking, Kelvedon and Coggeshall attended but it seems unlikely that our four firemen appeared in the procession, pushing their handcart and sucking in the noxious fumes of the sleek machines of the brigades in front. *[CC 24/07/1931]*

Fires at Pattiswick Hall

The first major fire under the new order was another at Pattiswick Hall, in January 1930. A motorist driving along Stane Street, saw flames and drove up to the Hall to give the alarm. As he turned in to the farm he saw that there was a stack alight and hammered on the door to rouse the occupants. The owner, Mr Kerr and his family were away but a servant answered the door unaware of the fire. The brigades at Kelvedon and Bocking were quickly summoned by telephone.

Although there was a good supply of water, the wind had strengthened to a gale which fanned the flames so that all six stacks in the yard became involved. The countryside all around was lit up with the glare and upwards of six hundred people were reported to have assembled from places as diverse as Braintree, Kelvedon and Witham. Three stacks were saved and both the house and the farm buildings (which had been

Two of the Braintree Rural District Council brigades, c1930 showing fire appliances for the Kelvedon and the Bocking areas. Nearest the camera is Captain Doughton with the Ford TT and Gwynne trailer pump inherited from the Bocking brigade. On the left is the new Morris fire engine and the Bocking firemen with their Captain, Harry Lawrence.

rebuilt after the last fire) were out of the way and not at risk. When the fire was at its height, a heavy fall of rain drenched the firemen and drove away the spectators but had no effect on the blaze. The brigades remained fighting the fire all night and right through the next day.
[CC 17/01/1930]

The fire-prone Edward Sach had another blaze in one of his workshops in Back Lane in March 1930. First noticed at 10.30 at night, the Kelvedon and Bocking brigades attended. The workshop was completely burnt out but the nearby timber yard and houses were saved, largely because the night was windless. The Coggeshall Supplementary brigade was not mentioned in reports, so the plan that should have seen them attending first may have been forgotten.
[CC 07/03/1930]

A farm fire at Feering in 1931 showed the new regime working at its best. Called out to a fire involving several haystacks and farm buildings at Church Farm, Feering, the Kelvedon brigade had trouble securing an adequate water supply. The Bocking brigade was summoned and they set into the River Blackwater, a quarter of a mile away. Drawing a plentiful supply the two crews were able to attack the fire and prevent it from reaching the few buildings that remained.
[CC 30/10/1931]

The Bocking brigade was still being summoned by a maroon. In the dead of night, the sudden explosions were alarming the more sensitive residents. Evidently, the Rural Council had been 'experimenting for some time at Kelvedon and Coggeshall' with an alternative method of calling out the brigade with a system of electric bells using the telephone lines. Such a scheme had been used elsewhere for at least fifty years but clearly involved a cost and was not universal. In Braintree, a tradition had grown up that the Crittall factory hooter was sounded three times to call out the brigade. When the homes of Braintree firemen were first fitted with fire bells in 1937, someone forgot to tell the hooter–man. This caused some slapstick confusion and rushing about with two calls, received, one on the bells and one on the hooter, some minutes apart, which were eventually found to be to the same address. The problem of the Bocking maroons did find a solution, as we shall see, but it was not to come in the form of an electric bell.

Pattiswick Hall seems to have been dogged by bad luck – or someone with a grudge, because a third fire broke out there in July 1933. John Kerr saw flames as he was returning one evening after shutting in his poultry near the rectory. He called out and people quickly got up and followed him to the Hall where the family were asleep in bed unaware of the drama outside. Kerr phoned for the brigade and then joined the locals trying to release the livestock trapped in the burning buildings. Several heifers and a bull succumbed in the dense smoke.

The Bocking brigade were summoned by the firing of maroons at 11.45pm and it is said that they were 'playing on the burning buildings before midnight' – if true, an extraordinarily quick turnout. Several sheds and barns were destroyed but others saved and again the house was untouched. [CC 14/07/1933]

The fires at Pattiswick Hall gave the Bocking brigade its first triumph and may also have marked its demise. With the formal amalgamation of Braintree and Bocking into one town, there was no reason to maintain both brigades. The Bocking brigade was disbanded and the maroons finally silenced. Bocking fire station was closed in March 1934 and its Morris engine transferred to Kelvedon. The decision seems to have been accepted with no evidence of dissent[13]. Captain Lawrence had served the Bocking brigade for 25 years and had attended every fire during that period. Another milestone should also be recorded; George Braddy, Kelvedon's first Captain, died suddenly on Friday 13th October 1933, aged 70 years. He was buried at Kelvedon church with the brigade in attendance. [EN 14/10/933]

Kelvedon Fire Station needed some minor alterations to house Bocking's engine, completed in time for the transfer in March 1934. The Kelvedon brigade attended their first major fire with the new machine in November when it was called, with those from Maldon, Witham and Colchester, to a serious fire at the Anchor Press in Tiptree. They were quickly at the scene and prevented the fire from spreading. The response demonstrates the increasing connectedness and co-operation among the different brigades aided by the telephone and the motorised engines. [CC 09/11/1934]

Kelvedon's quick turnout was evident at a fire at Easthorpe in September 1936. Lightning had set two stacks ablaze and put the telephones out of order, so a lad was sent by bicycle to raise the alarm. The engine left the station 'within two and a half minutes of receiving the call'. The men worked 'smartly' to prevent the fire from spreading and remained on duty for 20 hours before returning to Kelvedon. [CC 11/09/1936]

Harry Osborn joined the Kelvedon brigade in 1932 and eventually became Sub Captain under Bill Doughton. Recalling those days he said 'I can only say they were very happy years and we had a lot of fun'. The engine was kept spotlessly clean and polished. Bill Doughton and Harry Osborn had a telephone, the rest of the crew were summoned by the fire horn.

> 'When there was a fire, my wife took the call while I fell out of bed and dragged on some trousers. Sometimes the person calling was so panicked they forgot to tell us whether the fire was at Church Street Kelvedon or Church Street Coggeshall. Fun it may have been but the brigade took great pride in its record of extinguishing fires quickly and efficiently.' [BWT 01/05/80]

The Kelvedon brigade under Bill Doughton thought itself the equal to any.

---

13   The Courtaulds factory at Bocking had its own brigade, so the fire fighting tradition continued in the town for a while longer.

West Street, showing Paycocke's on the left then the Fleece and beyond that, the row of cottages affected by the 1937 fire.
Photo by courtesy of the Coggeshall Museum

Fire in West Street

It was about noon on Friday 14th May 1937 when a fire broke out in a row of seven cottages next to the 'Fleece' public house on West Street in Coggeshall. The Coggeshall Supplementary brigade were first in attendance and turned out in their fire gear, drawing the hand cart with a 'Birkin's' builders ladder perched unsteadily on top. There was a good hydrant nearby but just as they were making a start, the Kelvedon fire engine drew up and their brigade somewhat ostentatiously it was thought, played the part of the professionals. Windows were broken in the attempt to get a jet to play inside and knock back the fire which was burning with great ferocity in the first two cottages. Mr Cowell lived in the first and the other was a small 'general' shop kept by Mr George Smith a basket maker whose work was on display on the pavement outside. Stanley Haines then a young lad, remembers seeing the black smoke from the fire when he was playing with his friend Ronald Tansley. They both ran down to West Street by way of the Crouches path to find the houses on fire and a crowd gathering to watch. Stan remembers the polished brass helmets as the Coggeshall firemen got to work. *[EN 22/05/1937]* The fire was also recalled by one of the Kelvedon firemen who was present, Jim Parish:

> 'The funniest thing that ever happened, I never shall forget it, we got called out to a fire and it was over Coggeshall, up West Street .... just past the pub,.... it was a house on fire, the fire was in the roof and the Coggeshall Fire Brigade were there putting it out or trying to, when Kelvedon turned up. I can't think of the name of the captain of Coggeshall Fire Brigade, but he come along and this was getting on for lunchtime and he said "Hello Bill" because this was Mr Doughton "Pleased to see you" he said, "you can take over now we're going home to dinner" He called all his men away and left the Kelvedon men to put it out.'
> *[ERO SA 44/1/49/1]*

As for the fire, neighbours worked to remove the furniture from the third house, while the firemen fought and eventually brought the fire under control. The two cottages including the shop were completely gutted and the next, occupied by Mr and Mrs Lawrence, although badly damaged by water was saved. The gutted

The fire engines of the Braintree RDC brigades. Coggeshall Church Parade on Market Hill, probably in 1931. In front is Braintree's Dennis Turbine fire engine with Captain Dinsell, behind it is Bocking's Morris engine with Captain Lawrence and at the back is Kelvedon's Ford Towing Vehicle with Captain Doughton.

buildings were demolished and the gap in the frontage remains to this day. *[CC 21/05/1937]*

The West Street fire marks the low point of the Coggeshall Supplementary brigade which had in truth become almost irrelevant. However, the world was changing and the decision to accept the transfer of the fire engine to Kelvedon nine years before, increasingly looked like a big mistake. If there was to be a war as many people thought and the Kelvedon and Braintree brigades were tied up with their own troubles, who would come to Coggeshall's aid?

The West Street fire was to be Alfred Birkin's last, he was 65 years old and had served the community both as a Parish councillor and for thirty-three years as a fireman. He died eight years later, in 1946.

In October a rather singular fire occurred in Coggeshall Hamlet. Mrs H Lucas was lighting a fire in her front room, probably using paraffin, when a sudden burst of flame set fire to both her and the room. She rushed outside with her skirt and apron alight, which she managed to tear off as she continued on to the telephone box to call the brigade. Upstairs in bed was her partially disabled husband and her two children, John, 12 and Nancy, 6. The house quickly became smoke logged and Mr Lucas thinking they were trapped, started to knot together sheets and blankets to let the children down to the ground. The indomitable Mrs Lucas made her way back inside and reaching the bedroom, assisted her husband and children to safety. Her hair and eyebrows were singed and both arms suffered burns. The neighbours formed a bucket chain and managed to control the flames, so the Kelvedon brigade when they arrived, had little to do. *[CC 22/10/1937]*

10 THE SECOND WORLD WAR

Coggeshall Parish Council, relieved of the day to day burden of managing the fire brigade, had been quiet on the subject for some time. This changed as anxiety grew about the possibility of war. March 1937 provides the first evidence of this when the Council considered the condition of the engine house at Crouches where the fire cart was kept. After discussion with Captain Birkin, repairs were put in hand. *[MB4 22/03/37]*. Then in June, concerned once again about the hydrants, the Council wrote to Braintree RDC suggesting that a six weekly inspection was needed to ensure that they were always ready for action. This interval was so short that it probably says more about the councillors' anxiety than the condition of the hydrants. *[MB4 07/06/1937]* A gas powered air raid siren had been installed in 1938 next to Mr Birkin's shop but when tested in late 1938 hardly anyone heard it. The Council officially described it as 'very inadequate' and complained to the District Council.

At a Parish Council meeting on 5th December 1938 the councillors finally confronted the real matter of concern – the town had no fire engine or proper fire brigade. If incendiary bombs fell as everyone feared, Coggeshall's fire cover until, and *if,* the Kelvedon brigade arrived was dependent at best on four firemen and a handcart. After discussion, the Council resolved that the brigade 'both as regards personnel and equipment was very deficient'. They appointed a committee to meet Mr Fellows, the Assistant Clerk of Braintree RDC who had responsibility in the matter. *[MB4 07/11/38 & 05/12/1938]*

The fire services were a subject of keen national debate at the time, because of the Fire Services Act 1938. For the first time this made the provision of fire services a legal requirement. *[ES 14/01/1939]* It also brought to an end the long-standing practice of charging the insurance companies for the expense of putting out fires. The local authorities were now going to have to bear the whole cost and they were not well pleased:

> 'Braintree Urban Council have passed a resolution protesting against the serious burden to be thrown upon the ratepayers as a result of the Fire Brigades Act 1938 and pointing out that hitherto volunteer fire brigades have been largely maintained by contributions received by owners of properties concerned in fires, usually through insurance companies, but under the provisions of the Act, no claim against an owner will lie, so that in the absence of a voluntary offer from the insurance companies, the whole of the maintenance, costs etc., of the brigades, which in rural districts must be considerable, will fall on the rates.'
> *[BWT 16/02/1939]*

As a first step in carrying out the requirements of the Act, local authorities were instructed to carry out a survey and inspection to assess future fire-fighting requirements and to:

> 'make provision for the extinction of fires and the protection of life and property.'
> *[Hansard 20 July 1938 Vol 110 cc992]*

When the Parish Council Committee met Mr Fellows that December, they found that Braintree RDC had the matter well in hand. Plans had been drawn up to reorganise fire services across the district and a Chief Fire Officer, Mr Lewis White, had already been appointed. *[MB4 02/01/1939]* White was the District Surveyor for the RDC so this was his second job. Under the scheme although the 'regular' fire engine would stay in Kelvedon, Coggeshall was

Braintree Rural District.

FIRE BRIGADE SERVICE.

A fully equipped Fire Brigade is located at a Fire Station at

KELVEDON.

The Telephone Fire Call is Kelvedon 54 and 86.

The Brigade will primarily serve the following Parishes North of the Railway from Braintree to Witham:

Great and Little Coggeshall,
Kelvedon,
Marks Hall,
Feering,
Pattiswick,
Stisted,
Bradwell,
Cressing.

In the event of fire no other Brigade must be called, and if more than one Brigade is necessary, it will be the responsibility of the Chief Officer of the Kelvedon Brigade to summon any such additional help.

The Fire call telephone number should be kept for ready reference by the side of every telephone.

H. E. FELLOWS,
Deputy Clerk of the Council

24th July 1939

Poster issued 24th July 1939 by Braintree RDC. Published as a result of the Fire Services Act 1938, this specifically brings fire protection under the control of the Braintree District Council.
The poster is now much faded and the date, bottom left although correct, is recent and pasted over the original.
Reproduced by courtesy of Kelvedon Museum

to have a new 'Auxiliary Fire Service' brigade and appliances, paid for by the Government. The Auxiliary Fire Service (the AFS) was created to help the regular brigades fight fires caused by air raids but they were strictly not to be used for normal 'domestic' fires. When the committee reported back to the Parish Council, the plan was well received and seems to have answered their concerns. The fact that the regular brigade would remain in Kelvedon seems to have been accepted.

In July 1939, Braintree RDC issued posters to publicise the new arrangements for fire brigade services. As far as Kelvedon was concerned, there was little apparent change as the brigade was to keep using the Morris fire engine inherited from Bocking. However, they were now officially responsible for a large area, which as well as Coggeshall, included Feering, Marks Hall, Pattiswick, Bradwell, Stisted and Cressing. The other change, and this would prove to be significant, was that they were brought under the command of the new Chief Fire Officer, Lewis White.

The familiar '999' number for the emergency services was not in common use at this time, hence the telephone numbers shown and the suggestion that they should be kept by all telephones 'for ready reference'[1]. The numbers were for Bill Doughton and Harry Osborn, Captain and Sub Captain of the Kelvedon brigade whose phones had been installed at the expense of the RDC. In Coggeshall, the plan was for maroons to be sounded as a fire warning.

Bill Doughton had invented his own novel system for calling out the brigade. This was rigged to the front of his house in the High Street and took the form of a tall gas cylinder with a huge horn attached. Above it a sign read:

BRAINTREE RDC
FIRE ALARM
TO CALL BRIGADE
TURN KNOB 'A' AND WAIT
Penalty for improper use £20

Apparently ear-plugs were not supplied! Even at the time this was regarded as so idiosyncratic that it was featured on a short Pathé News film[2]. As the commentary says 'That's the way they go to blazes in them there parts!'

At this stage, the plans for protecting the

---

1 The 999 system was introduced in parts of London in 1937, following a fire in November 1935 when five women were killed. A neighbour tried to phone the fire brigade but was held in a queue by the telephone exchange. He wrote a letter to the editor of 'The Times', which prompted a government inquiry. The use of 999 only became widespread after the war.

2 This very short film can be seen online with a bit of a search, try 'Curious Fire Alarm'.

public from bombs were very basic. In February 1939 Coggeshall was offered 'a trench to accommodate fifty persons....if the parish thought it desirable'. The Parish Council did think so but pointed out; 'That as 1,000 or more refugees were likely to be sent to Coggeshall, in an emergency, a trench accommodating fifty persons would be quite inadequate'. They suggested Crouches Meadow (where the surgery now stands) or the Recreation Ground as the best sites. *[MB4 06/02/1939]*. In March, obviously convinced by the Parish Council's logic, Braintree agreed on a seventy-five person trench. It was probably never constructed as the fashion moved towards the greater protection offered by covered shelters.

Lewis White

Lewis White, the new RDC Chief Fire Officer, probably knew nothing of fire brigades or fire fighting when he was appointed in 1938. He had some experience of the army and this would have counted in his favour but his appointment would have been recommended by his character and bearing. He could be convivial, enjoyed a drink and good company and for some, was a kind and loyal friend. His style though was military, disciplined and authoritarian, he knew his mind and did not take to being contradicted.[3] On appointment he probably took a training course in fire brigade practices, drills and procedures, whose style would have been familiar to him from his time in the army. White would prove to be a very able fireman and later achieved the lofty rank of Column Officer in the nationalised fire service – but that was in the future. In 1939, with no previous experience, his task was to bring the Braintree RDC brigades to a state of war readiness.

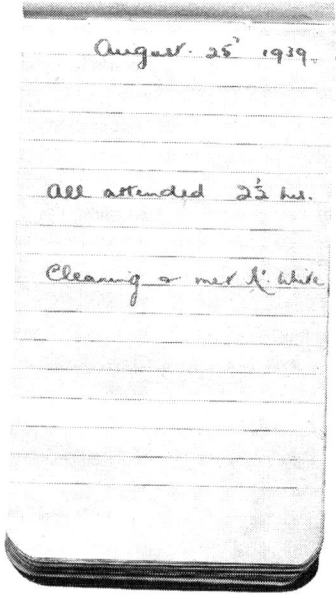

---

3   Some years later, when a Braintree Council meeting was interrupted by a 'journalist from an ultra left paper', of all those present, it was Lewis White who was asked by the chairman to 'check the man's credentials'. There was no further trouble with the journalist after that. *[B&WT 09/09/1950]*

Kelvedon Fire Brigade Log, August 25th 1939. 'Cleaning & met Mr White' - the meeting which resulted in the end of the Kelvedon Fire Brigade.

Kelvedon Fire Brigade

In 1939, the Kelvedon Fire Brigade had provided fire cover for some fifty-two years and with the approaching war, looked set to write a new chapter in its history. We know something of those times because Captain Bill Doughton kept a logbook in which he recorded the names and times of those who attended fires and drills. The first record begins on Monday 31st July 1939 and the eight strong Kelvedon brigade were carrying out routine duties, pumping out the sump at the Recreation Ground for the parish council and cleaning the fire engine. The next entry is for Friday 25th August 1939, which was not their usual training night and reads 'All attended 2½ hrs Cleaning & met Mr White'. On that fateful day when he introduced himself to the Kelvedon brigade he was in no doubt about what he wanted and how he was going to run things. The Kelvedon brigade had always set their own high standards and were proud of what they had achieved. Bill Doughton had years of experience,

Kelvedon's Morris Commercial fire engine & some of the crew in happier times. Probably Kelvedon Carnival in the summer of 1938.

he was boss of his own building business and respected in his community. When Lewis White turned up and instructed them on how things were going to be, Doughton and the Kelvedon crew would have none of it, they were not going to be told what to do by some jumped up official with no experience, there was a heated argument, the men resigned on the spot and walked out. Forty years later, Harry Osborn the Kelvedon Sub Captain, remembered what happened:

> 'We didn't like being told what to do by someone who knew little or nothing about it.....When the authorities started taking over and bossing us about, we left. They tried to tell us what our hours of drill would be and how much time we should spend cleaning the engine. We were all terribly keen but we wouldn't be told what to do – not after all that time. We walked out, we left everything.'
> *[BWT 01/05/1980]*

As Lewis White closed the station that night, the dying echo as he turned the key effectively marked the end of the Kelvedon brigade. Braintree RDC was then confronted with a real problem; war was imminent and their well laid plans for the area looked to be in ruins. It was soon apparent that the Kelvedon crew were not going to back down, there was no way that Lewis White was going to change his position and the Braintree RDC had to support the authority of their new Chief Fire Officer.

Sometime in the following week, someone must have had a word with the Kelvedon men because they agreed to carry on for a short while until a new brigade was trained. In Bill Doughton's log book entry for the 25th August (see illustration), Lewis White is politely but icily referred to as 'Mr White' not the correct but unsayable, 'Chief Officer White'. The next training night was missed but the crew reassembled on Monday, 4th September 1939, the day after war was declared. They enlisted and began training Kelvedon's Auxiliary Fire Service crew. They drilled again with the Auxiliaries on 11th September at Swan Street and that was the last entry.

As well as the resignation of the brigade, Braintree RDC had another problem. In order to get Government funding for the Auxiliary Fire Services at Coggeshall and Kelvedon, the RDC had to show that they already had adequate peace-time fire cover in those places. This provision was brought in to stop local authorities using the government funded AFS to subsidise 'normal' fire services which should have been paid from the rates.

Coggeshall was the only place where the RDC could recruit and establish a new brigade for the area. Perhaps against expectation, when the call for firemen was made, there was a ready response, the men encouraged no doubt by a genuine desire to contribute to the war effort and to keep Coggeshall safe.

Apart from the interview with Harry Osborn some 40 years later, no written record has yet been found of the Kelvedon 'mutiny'. A few insiders did know what happened, Ken Thomas, for example, who became a member of the Kelvedon AFS knew that 'there had been a row'. *[Recounted by his friend, Bryan Everitt in conversation with the author 2011].* The official line taken at the time was that the move had been planned.

An official announcement was made at a meeting of the Rural District Council in late September 1939:

> 'The Chairman reported that it had been decided to abolish the fire station at Kelvedon and have one at Coggeshall. Mr H E Fellows said it was proposed to build a new station on Market Hill, Coggeshall at an inclusive cost of £150. It was decided to proceed with this and to have an auxiliary brigade at Kelvedon.' *[CC 29/09/1939 & EN 30/09/1939]*

The extraordinary choice of the word 'abolish' may well reflect the Council's true feelings over the episode. At the Council meeting where the announcement was made, no questions or discussion were reported so the Councillors (and the Press?) must have known what had happened but were unwilling to say anything which might bring the unsavoury episode to public attention. The Minutes of Kelvedon Parish Council are also notably silent on the matter. It was an extraordinary event at a time of national emergency when everyone was supposed to be pulling together.

The 'hush up' was successful. In Coggeshall the explanation given that Kelvedon could not find enough men to crew the engine, was accepted. 'Losing' the fire engine to Kelvedon in 1929 had become a sore point, the event had somehow diminished Coggeshall, so there was more than a little triumphalism when news got around that the engine was 'coming back' and little interest in how it had come about.

As well as recruiting a crew, a new fire station would have to be built. The old Engine House was too small and there was no other suitable accommodation. The matter of finding a site and building a new station was given the highest priority. The Kelvedon 'mutiny' took place on 25th August and by 23rd September, a site for the new station had been chosen, plans drawn up and the contract agreed.

Training

As there was nowhere suitable in Coggeshall, on the 9th September sixteen Coggeshall men reported to Kelvedon Fire Station for initial instruction. Some were there as potential Coggeshall RDC firemen (regulars) and some for the Coggeshall Auxiliary Fire Service. Among the squad were three of the old 'Hand Cart brigade', Alfred Birkin's son, George (who soon dropped out), Billy Green whose father Joe and uncle Sam, had both been in the brigade in 1916 and Frank Weinrich, all the rest were newcomers. Chief Fire Officer White's plan was to complete preliminary

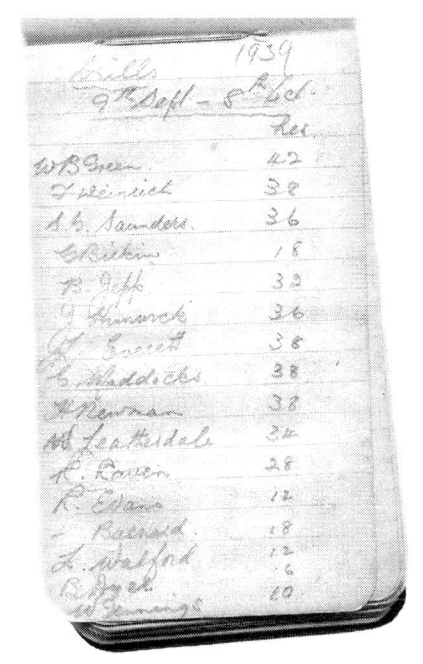

Coggeshall Fire Brigade & AFS Initial Training. This shows the total hours training for each man for the month 9th September – 8th October 1939.

> **Policemanism - The End of a Tradition**
> **November 1938**
> Polite society had always abhorred the rowdiness and mis-rule of the Coggeshall Guy Fawkes celebrations and slowly managed to stifle it:
> 'William Everett, summoned for letting off a firework at Great Coggeshall on November 4th, did not appear. Pc Lewis stated that he saw a number of persons standing outside the Conservative Club at Coggeshall, where two fireworks exploded with loud reports. He went to the persons and saw the defendant throw a firework on to the roadway, where it exploded with loud report.
> The Chairman: "Was it a cracker?"
> Pc Lewis: "No it was a large firework which would cost 6d."
> Assistant Clerk: "Do you know anything of the record of Coggeshall for fireworks."
> Pc Lewis: "In the past this fireworks business was very serious at Coggeshall and I am doing my best to stop it. In previous years fireworks were thrown about indiscriminately and people walking along the streets had to look after themselves."
> "Is the defendant a man or a boy?"
> Pc Lewis: "He is a man, 30 years of age".'
> "Defendant is fined 10/-." ' *[EN 19/11/1938]*

training by the 8th October, just a month away and the date when the new fire station should be ready. In the meantime, the engine remained at Kelvedon. As all the recruits had regular jobs, training was done in the evenings and at weekends, with most men putting in six to eight hours a week. Billy Green, who was to become Coggeshall's new Captain, completed forty-two hours of training in the month and most of the rest were not far behind. Bill Doughton's logbook was now being used by the Coggeshall brigade and this provides a insight into the brigade's activities during the early months of the war. There was some theory work but most of the training involved running out and making up hose, getting one or more deliveries to work, pumping from hydrants and from open water, ladder drills, knots and lines.

On Saturday 14th October 1939 the new crew was judged to be ready. Tony Saunders well remembered the day when his father Stan (one of the new firemen) asked him if he wanted to come along to get the fire engine and they went to Kelvedon with Billy Green. 'It was all arranged to pick it up on Saturday. We didn't see any of the Kelvedon men, they had all finished and gone. Someone came with the key and opened the station and we started the engine, it didn't have a battery, we just gave the handle a turn, then rode back on it, my father on one side, Billy Green on the other and me in the middle, it was wonderful'. *[Tony Saunders Autumn 2010]*

The engine was taken down the Abbey Lane and set in to the deep water of the mill pond. The rest of the firemen joined them there and the afternoon was spent in pumping practice. Billy Green had seven firemen under his command, Frank Weinrich, the brothers Stan and Bert Saunders, Lenny Walford, Bob Evans, Bill Jennings and Jack Hunwick. So it was Saturday 14th October 1939 that marks the foundation of the next Coggeshall Fire Brigade - the Braintree Rural District Council brigade.

184   *Fires, Firemen & Other Mishaps*

John Sach demolishing the shops on Market Hill for the new fire station, September 1939.

The fire station on Market Hill, built in the autumn of 1939 and pictured here c1965.
Note the wartime siren mounted on the twin poles which was still used at this time to call out the brigade during the day.

The New Fire Station

Things moved with impressive speed. The site chosen was right in the centre of the town on Market Hill where a range of shops was demolished to make way for it. The buildings were occupied so the residents were compulsorily moved out at very short notice. Aesthetically the demolition was a disaster, that such a thing was done at all, tells us a lot about those times and the sacrifices that were thought to be necessary to survive.

The old buildings were demolished by John E Sach who probably also built the new station, a simple 'L' shaped building in brick, with a pitched roof over the appliance bay and a flat roof over the office, store and lavatory. There were wire hooks for fire gear down one side and a Tortoise stove to heat the place. A door at the back led out to Church Street with the key on a hook next to it.

The new Coggeshall brigade cut quite a dash in the town. Owen Martin recalls:

> 'I remember Billy Green then, they had the old brass helmets and they used to sit alongside on the back and the ladder on the top. I saw them go out to fires with the old bell ring ringing, it was a lovely thing, all red and brassed up.' *[Owen Martin interview]*

Denis Wood has a similar impression:

> 'You saw those men with their brass hats sitting each side and the bell ringing, it just looked a picture and really impressed me as a young lad.' *[Denis Wood interview]*

The crew had bought their own brass helmets so when some time later, the order came through to paint everything in drab, it did not go down well. Not just the helmets but the fire engine and the brass fittings all had to be a uniform grey, the paint supplied free of charge. Billy Green definitely did not want his helmet painted and resisted, as he said at the time, 'I paid a lot of money for that hat!' *[Peter Hale interview]*. For the raiders high overhead, the glint of moonlight on Billy Green's helmet would have been all

The new poster issued in October 1939 following the Kelvedon 'mutiny'. 'Amended Notice - It has become necessary to transfer the fire engine from Kelvedon to a new station at Great Coggeshall'. The telephone was that of Billy Green on Stoneham Street. The poster has faded almost to invisibility.
Reproduced by courtesy of Kelvedon Museum

they needed to press home their attack. Despite this, it was more than a year later and after direct experience of the Blitz that the brush was regretfully applied to the Coggeshall machine. *[Recounted by Fred Moss to the author]* Although looking the part, by 1939 the traditional brass helmets were 'old hat'. (Sorry!) The brass conducted electricity and its shape could snag draping cables to lethal effect.

In October 1939 four months after the original issue, Braintree RDC published an 'Amended Notice' detailing the new arrangements and phone number for the fire brigade, because, as they succinctly put it: 'It has become necessary to transfer the fire engine from Kelvedon to a new fire station at Coggeshall'.

The new brigade training at Pointwell Mill with the Morris Commercial fire engine October-November 1939. Billy Green, Bob Evans, Stan Saunders, Bill Jennings, Bert Saunders behind, Lenny Walford, Jack Hunwick and Frank Weinrich. The sashes worn by Bob Evans and Bert Saunders probably indicate that they are Leading Firemen.
Photo by courtesy of Mick Barnett

Preparations for War

With the new brigade established and the station finished, drills continued on Saturdays and Sundays every week. With raids expected daily, there was a sense of urgency in the exercises and practices. The brigade also spent time learning their new home ground - locating and testing the hydrants across the area for which they were responsible. On 21st October 1939, they were at Feering, on the 29th at Pattiswick, at Stisted on 12th November and Cressing on the 18th. They practised hose running at Scrips and Highfields Farms and pumping from open water at Abbey Lane and Pointwell Mill and at the ancient St Peter's Well on Vane Lane in Coggeshall. The Parish Council were not happy about the size of the area covered by the brigade, fearing they may be miles away when needed back home. They wrote to Braintree RDC and suggested that the home ground be limited to Coggeshall, Kelvedon, Feering, Bradwell and Pattiswick. *[MB4 08/01/1940]* Although no reply is recorded in the minutes, Stisted and Cressing have long been part of Braintree's ground so there may have been a change at this time.

The brigade began to practise at night and in December had their first 'blackout' drill, working in the dark or with shielded lights, trying to achieve complete familiarity with the equipment and the engine. Safety was a problem for everyone during the Blackout, there was much use of white paint: stripes were painted on the kerbs and telephone poles, even by one Essex farmer on his cows. The fire engine headlights were shielded down to a thin rectangle in the centre of the lens which allowed only a meagre glow of light to emerge. A document 'Blitz Hints' offered useful advice on the subject:

'Do not use your masked headlights unless you

Pumping practice alongside the Blackwater at Pointwell Mill, drawing water from the millpond. October-December 1939
Photo by courtesy of Mick Barnett

must. Vehicles which will be used in raids at night should have all chromium or bright parts painted over or blacked out. This applies to brass on trailer pumps or any reflecting surfaces which would give away the presence and position of fire-fighting units to the enemy above'.

Even with the new 20mph speed limit, traffic accidents were regular and local papers of the time had a weekly list of those killed and injured on the roads. One accident helped resolve the issue of the air raid siren.

A local man, Doug Potter, who was in the army and desperate to get back to see his family, 'borrowed' an army lorry and drove home from his base one weekend. Reaching Coggeshall in the early hours, he drove up Bridge Street, failed to stop at the top and ran smack into the sturdy but inadequate air raid siren outside Birkin's shop, flattening it.[4] There had been some debate over where best to site a new electric air raid siren. The Parish Council thought the town clock tower was

not strong enough, so the big grain silo of John K King was suggested. This was the tallest building and in the centre of the town (where Kings Acre is now). When the new station was complete the electric siren was installed on its roof.

The siren was operated remotely by land-line from Braintree, a rising and falling note sounding the warning and a continuous tone for the all clear. The line was damaged by 'enemy action' in February 1941 and temporarily operated manually from Coggeshall until repaired. It remained well after the war, fixed high above the station between two telegraph poles. Used to call out the brigade during the day, its deafening sound was familiar in the town until the 1970s. Kelvedon must have been regarded as low-priority, because despite requests from the Parish Council, it was not until June 1944 that it was granted an air raid siren. In the meantime, as resourceful as ever, the village had installed one of its own at the gasworks. *[KPMB 08/06/1944]*

---

4   This is the siren that few could hear when it was tested.

The Auxiliary Fire Service

One of the provisions of the 'Air Raid Precautions Act' of December 1937, was 'to extinguish fires likely to result from an attack'. This brought about the creation of the Auxiliary Fire Service, the AFS. In 1938 there were estimates that Germany could drop 3,500 tons of bombs on Britain on the first day of war and with the evidence from Spain on the effects of small incendiary bombs, it was thought that the regular fire brigades would be overwhelmed when the raids started.

AFS firemen and women were volunteers and paid £3 a week (women were paid £2). A publicity campaign encouraged people to join and do their bit for the war effort. It was also a way for those in reserved occupations to help. The entrance requirements were simple: applicants should be between 25 and 50 years old, pass a medical and be prepared to be on duty in an emergency.

A year before the Coggeshall Auxiliary brigade was established Stan Barnett had enrolled in the Colchester AFS. He signed up on 10th October 1938 at the then brand new fire brigade headquarters on Cowdray Avenue in Colchester. He trained both there and at the AFS centre in St Peter's Street in Colchester. Stan transferred to Coggeshall and was alongside when the Auxiliaries and the regular brigade men signed up on 9th September 1939. A standard sixty-hour training programme had been created for the AFS recruits and this, for the first time, brought a degree of common practice for drills and fire-fighting procedures across the whole country. As the Coggeshall 'regular' brigade was a new unit, they may well have been the first of the regular brigades to use the AFS training programme and drill book.

George Maddocks, Coggeshall AFS 1939 - 41
His AFS badge seems to have been painted out so the photo may date from his enrolment as a full time fireman in July 1941, just before the new NFS insignia and uniforms were issued.
Photo by courtesy of Bunty Moss

The AFS had a smart uniform in a dark blue material which was claimed to be 'nearly 100% waterproof'. It comprised a double breasted tunic with special 'AFS' buttons, trousers in blue serge with a red stripe, a peaked cap and rubber boots. For fire-fighting there were oilskin leggings, webbing belt, axe pouch, axe and a Brodie[5] tin hat. *[EN 15/10/1938]*

The tunic was distinctively marked with an 'AFS Braintree RDC' badge in red on a dark blue background. Mr Saunders, Chief Air Warden for Braintree, claimed that 'the uniform had proved a great attraction and had helped recruiting and

---

5 'Brodie' helmet, named after its designer H L Brodie a Londoner who patented it in 1915. There had been some changes by the 2nd World War with an improved liner and an elasticated webbing chin strap.

No photo of the Coggeshall AFS has so far come to light, so this will have to do - taken in October 1939 it shows another Essex group, from Ilford. A builder's lorry is being used as a towing vehicle for the trailer pump just visible on the left. The lorry also carries a standard 35 foot ladder and a smaller extension ladder. Four of the crew are wearing leggings and boots.

was the envy of the air wardens'. *[CC 06/12/1940]*

Coggeshall had eight Auxiliaries in July 1940: Len Everett (who was probably Section Commander), Stan Barnett, Bob Raven, Bill Leatherdale, Bert Dyer, Bernard Jepp, John Willsher and George Maddocks.

Because they had trained together and were equally inexperienced, there was an equality and respect between the two Coggeshall brigades that was not always the case elsewhere in the country. Regular firemen often regarded the new Auxiliaries with some disdain. In Coggeshall, the circumstances of their creation and the immediate crisis of war threw both groups together. When Frank Weinrich of the regular brigade married in St Nicholas Chapel, Little Coggeshall, in November 1940, both brigades were in attendance and both gave wedding presents; a silver teapot and a silver cruet.
[ES 23/11/1940]

Instead of fire engines, the AFS was equipped with trailer pumps, officially described as a 'Home Office emergency fire-fighting appliance'. Some brigades, like Bocking had tried these out in the 1920s, as a cheaper alternative to a 'proper' fire engine but they had never become popular with the regular brigades. With the war emergency the government had placed orders for thousands of these pumps.

Equipment for the Coggeshall AFS was slow in arriving. In January 1940 the Clerk to the Parish Council wrote to Braintree RDC that 'all possible steps should be taken to obtain the necessary equipment for the Auxiliary Fire Service as soon as possible'. In the meantime the AFS crew were keen to practise hose running and branch technique with 'live water' so when someone suggested giving the old manual engine a try, they were ready to give it a go. The engine, still in Mr Birkin's barn at Crouches and thick with dust, was pulled clear and taken down to the river at Bridge Street where it was run into the ford. Willing hands enthusiastically pumped the engine but the fireman at the branch looking down the dry nozzle reported, 'Nothing this end!' Pumping continued a little more tentatively until with a shocking bang an explosion of water soaked the crew. The old engine, 103 years after it first came to Coggeshall, had rewarded them for their impertinence. It went back into its barn, never to pump again.

Stan Barnett
Photo by courtesy of Mick Barnett.

During 1940 the trailer pumps began to arrive in numbers so that by December that year Braintree, emphatically putting themselves first, had nine pumps to themselves, leaving the Coggeshall AFS to wait another six months until June 1941 before their trailer pump finally arrived. Nationally it had taken a while for production to build up but by May 1941 25,000 trailer pumps had been distributed. *[Hansard 20/05/1941]* These pumps could be manoeuvred by hand and taken across fields and into places inaccessible to a fire engine. The Auxiliary machines had standard and interchangeable fittings and equipment, so could be used with other AFS units anywhere in the country. Among these was the 2½ inch fire hose with instantaneous couplings which are nowadays standard equipment. The regular brigades had enormous problems in this respect because of the sheer variety of equipment carried that was not interchangeable. Even within London the 95,000 fire hydrants had six different types of outlet all needing their own special standpipe.

Although the Home Office supplied the Auxiliaries with a trailer pump it did not provide a vehicle to tow it. Instead an allowance was given to find a suitable vehicle locally. In Coggeshall an old Humber car was bought and painted grey with the running board and wheel arches outlined in white to aid visibility in the dark. The trailer pump was first kept in the old Engine House at Crouches but this was inadequate as a base for the new brigade, so the Auxiliaries moved into an old barn on the south side of the Gravel (now demolished).

Additional fire-fighting equipment was supplied in the form of stirrup pumps. These were very effective hand-powered pumps, drawing water from a bucket and producing a jet or spray from a rubber garden hose. Simple, robust and effective, they are still standard equipment on many fire engines for dealing with chimney fires. In August 1940, the Parish Council suggested that fifty be supplied to Coggeshall. *[MB4 08/01/1940]* They were to be distributed around the town to attack small fires at an early stage.

In the smaller villages without regular firemen, the Auxiliaries were the only fire brigade. William Drane of Great Tey (four miles east of Coggeshall) remembers how he got involved as an Auxiliary:

'A chap came down to help fit everyone with gas masks and he said, "if you are interested there is Civil Defence[6] and Fire Service and First Aid: join up and get some training in". I wasn't old enough to get into the Civil Defence[7] so I filled up the Fire Service papers and I got a good years training in, you know, part time. When the war come I tried to get into the Fire Service regular but I was classed as a key man on the land and they wouldn't take me. Well I had some exciting times in the Fire Service, we went to different turn outs. I used to go round demonstrating different things helping to form out fire parties, it was all voluntary I wasn't forced to go. Being a small village, there was only five of us firemen, well we arranged a system so there was always two of us out all night.' *[ERO SA 12/574/1]*

---

6   The ARP was renamed the Civil Defence Service in 1941 to more accurately reflect its many roles.

7   Wardens were ideally 'at least thirty years old'.

Felix Hall c1900. The two outer curved wings had been demolished before the fire of 1940.

The Coggeshall RDC Brigade

The AFS and regulars shared some training and took part in joint exercises but officially, they were supposed to be kept apart when it came to 'peacetime' fires. However, in many places AFS men would join the regulars to gain experience. The first call to the Coggeshall regulars was not the heroic action the crew may have been hoping for. On 27th November 1939 they were called to pump out the flooded Kelvedon Sewage Works. They were called there again the next day and spent a total of nine hours pumping. An unromantic and tedious introduction to the fireman's life. It was more than two months before the brigade had their first 'proper' call. This was on 17th January 1940 to Barclays Bank in Kelvedon High Street. An oil heater had exploded and set two outhouses alight behind the bank. The bank manager and two shopkeepers 'kept the flames in check' until the brigade arrived and it was three hours before the men were able to return home. *[CC 26/01/1940 & Log]* The men did not have to wait long for the next fire, just four days later they were called out again and it was a big one.

Felix Hall

Felix Hall was a country mansion just west of Kelvedon and perhaps four miles or so from Coggeshall. It was probably the largest building in the district at the time. The weather in January 1940 was bitterly cold with a severe and penetrating frost and in the Hall, the water pipes had frozen up. Builders had been called and used a blowtorch to free up the frozen pipes. The owner of the house was away shooting in Scotland so as dusk fell, everyone left, the key was turned in the lock and the empty house settled into silence. The effort to defrost the pipes had started a tiny smouldering fire that at first could have been extinguished with a pinch of the fingers but over the dark hours of the night this grew into crackling life, as first one and then another of the many rooms caught fire. The Hall was isolated in its grounds but was visible from one of the estate houses:

> 'Mother came down the stairs and looked through the landing window and shouted "the hall's alight, the hall's alight!" Us kids jumped out of bed and saw the flames coming out of the windows and the roof. The fire brigade arrived after about half an

Felix Hall today

hour[8]. It was a howling wind and freezing cold. As the water from the hoses went up the spray came back over the firemen and they had icicles hanging from their helmets' *[Kelvedon Speaks 1999 p 305-6]*

The 'Essex County Standard' reported the fire in the next edition:

'The hall was in the course of reconstruction and repair and builders had been actively engaged on it for about a year. Repairs and restoration had almost been completed, only interior paintwork being left to do. The hall is owned by Mr Houghton Brown and he left Felix Hall on Thursday for a short stay in Scotland. The blaze was first noticed shortly before 8am by Mr George Aves, a gardener at the Hall. He noticed a curious light in two windows from the cottage where he was about 300 yards away. He hurried over and soon saw what was wrong – the flames were leaping from the roof by that time and nearly all the windows were lit up by the fire – he hurried across the fields and called the fire brigade.

So intense was the heat that scaffold poles lashed to the portico and several feet from the face of the main building were charred by the heat and the ropes broke away causing the poles to crash down. Every window in the house was burnt out and the roof and upstairs floor as well as those on the ground floor, collapsed into the large cellars. Coggeshall Fire Brigade were working on the scene until 7pm and the remains were still smouldering throughout Monday. It is thought the building had been smouldering throughout Saturday night and to such an extent that when the flames eventually burst out, the whole interior of the building which was already very hot, was involved in a few minutes.' *[ES 27/01/1940]*

'That morning we all went to the 11 o'clock church service and walked to the hall afterwards. Even though it was still smouldering there were huge icicles hanging outside the building on the window sills.' *[Kelvedon Speaks 1999 p 305-6]*

The brigade log puts the time of call on Sunday 21st January at 08.05am, the brigade left at 08.15 and arrived by 08.26 to find that the place was a ball of fire, all the windows were

---

8   The time from call to arrival was 21 minutes.

The New Braintree RDC Coggeshall brigade, Winter 1939.
Seated on top Stan Saunders and Jack Hunwick
Billy Green Bill Jennings Lenny Walford Bob Evans Bert Saunders Frank Weinrich

gone and the roof had fallen in. Billy Green was quoted as saying, 'It is a mystery how such a fire escaped notice for so long.' The men were at the scene until 23.30 but then returned in relays to turn over and damp down the remains until the evening of the next day, Monday, at 7.00pm when they finally went home. A duty totalling some 35 hours, literally a baptism by fire. The loss was estimated at £15,000 and would have been immeasurably greater had the house been furnished. It is ironic that after the Kelvedon 'mutiny' and the transfer of the engine to Coggeshall, the first three calls were all to Kelvedon and the last resulted in the destruction of the principal mansion in the village. The slower turnout and travelling time of the Coggeshall brigade had no effect on the outcome, the Hall was doomed and was never rebuilt.

The Phoney War and the AFS

The expected onslaught following the declaration of war in September 1939 did not take place. Days turned to weeks and then months with nothing but false alarms. Across Essex, the Auxiliary Fire Service were on duty at their stations throughout the night, but by April 1940 with no bombs falling, this had stopped. There were some red faces in Saffron Walden when part of the fire station used as the Auxiliary sleeping quarters caught fire, causing considerable damage to the interior and to ARP bedding and clothing.
[CC 12/04/1940]

Nationally, with little to do, morale in the fire services began to fall and the Auxiliaries in particular were criticised in the Press and widely thought to have been a waste of money and its men 'army dodgers'.

'Action stations' for the Auxiliaries had been called on 1st September, two days before war was declared. At that date the Coggeshall crews were still being mustered and as we have seen, it was over a month later in mid October 1939, before the RDC engine was transferred and the Regular and Auxiliary crews became available. The phoney-war period gave both crews a much needed opportunity to practise together and build up their familiarity with their new equipment and working as a team.

Some parts of Essex had problems recruiting Auxiliaries. In January 1940 there were just 6 recruits for the whole of the Chelmsford rural area where the requirement was for 289. They had seven trailer pumps and no-one to man them. Maldon Council thought that a great deal of time and money was wasted on the Auxiliaries when in six months 'many of the men would be called up'. Our own Mr Fellows from Braintree said that they were careful to select personnel for their Auxiliary Fire Service 'who were the least likely to be called up'. By this he probably meant those in reserved occupations rather than the ancient and the decrepit that no army would have a use for. *[CC 26/01/1940]*

The Coggeshall brigade had their first Gas Practice on 8th January 1940, getting used to the practical difficulty of very limited vision through the mask, especially in the blackout. Although it must have been tempting, the respirator was not designed to be used in the dense smoke and low oxygen levels of a house fire. It was rumoured that an AFS crew died when using their gas masks in this way and a memo was circulated to all personnel warning them against this practice.

The brigade continued to train at least once a week and responded to a number of peacetime fire calls; chimney fires, grass fires and one or two minor house fires. The first fire brigade ARP (Air Raid Precautions) practice was in March 1940 and the brigade watched an ARP demonstration in Braintree in April. This pattern of weekly practice, hose running, pumping at the river, viewing hydrants, blackout and gas drills continued without any sign of enemy action all the way through until June 1940.

On 18th June 1940, the Regular brigade joined the Auxiliaries to test their pump at the river bridge. This time when the sirens sounded, the drone of enemy aircraft could be heard. The Regular crew quickly made their way to the station where they remained until the all clear sounded at 4.15am the next morning. Instructions were received to begin 'picquet duty', in other words to standby at the fire station overnight, ready to roll immediately they were needed. The next night there was another air raid warning and the crew was again on duty from 01.30 until 04.00 and on the 21st for more than fourteen hours from 13.00 – 02.15. No bombs fell on Coggeshall so the brigade was not called out, but it was clear that with jobs to go to, the men could not all be on duty like this every night. A Fire Brigade Circular of the time warns that:

> 'Repeated attendance of part-time personnel in response to recurrent air raid warnings will cause fatigue and where such conditions obtain… make arrangements if possible for the institution of a rota system.' *[Fire Brigade Circular 01/08/1940 No 79 ERO A12987 Box 8 File 73]*

A rota was introduced, at first two men from the brigade and four from the Auxiliaries went to the station on standby every night but from 6th July, a 'night duty' was established. A metal framed bunk bed was brought in so that two men could sleep at the station, one from each service, and this duty probably continued until the end of the war. The siren would not be used for domestic fires, so the men on night duty would have called out a crew the old fashioned way. It was vital that 'domestic' fires were quickly extinguished so as not to become a marker for the bombers above. If the air raids were especially intense, both crews would still turn out in full. On 11th July 1940, for example, all sixteen men were on duty from 01.10 until 02.45 and

Coggeshall Air Raid Precautions (ARP) Wardens E65. Standing are Messrs Brown, Sellars and Arnold and seated are Messrs Pease, Browning (both with white helmets for Chief Wardens) and & Mr Shelley. All carry gas masks. Equipment includes whistles, a rattle, stirrup pump, hand bell, metal buckets and a paraffin lamp.

they all turned out again at 05.08. No doubt as their experience of the raids increased a more sustainable routine developed.

During this time it was the job of Tony Saunders (the son of Stan, one of the firemen), to light the stove so the station would be warm for the men reporting for duty each night. The 'Tortoise'[9] stove at the back of the station which burned coke, heated the radiators and a kettle on top provided hot water for tea.

So began the most intense and dangerous period in the history of our brigade. The central role of the fire brigades in what was to come had not been fully appreciated at the start of the war but in the words of Herbert Morrison the Home Secretary 'It became apparent that fire was perhaps the biggest single element in the enemy's attack.' *[Hansard 20/05/1941]*

---

9   These famous stoves had been made by Charles Portway in Halstead, since 1830.

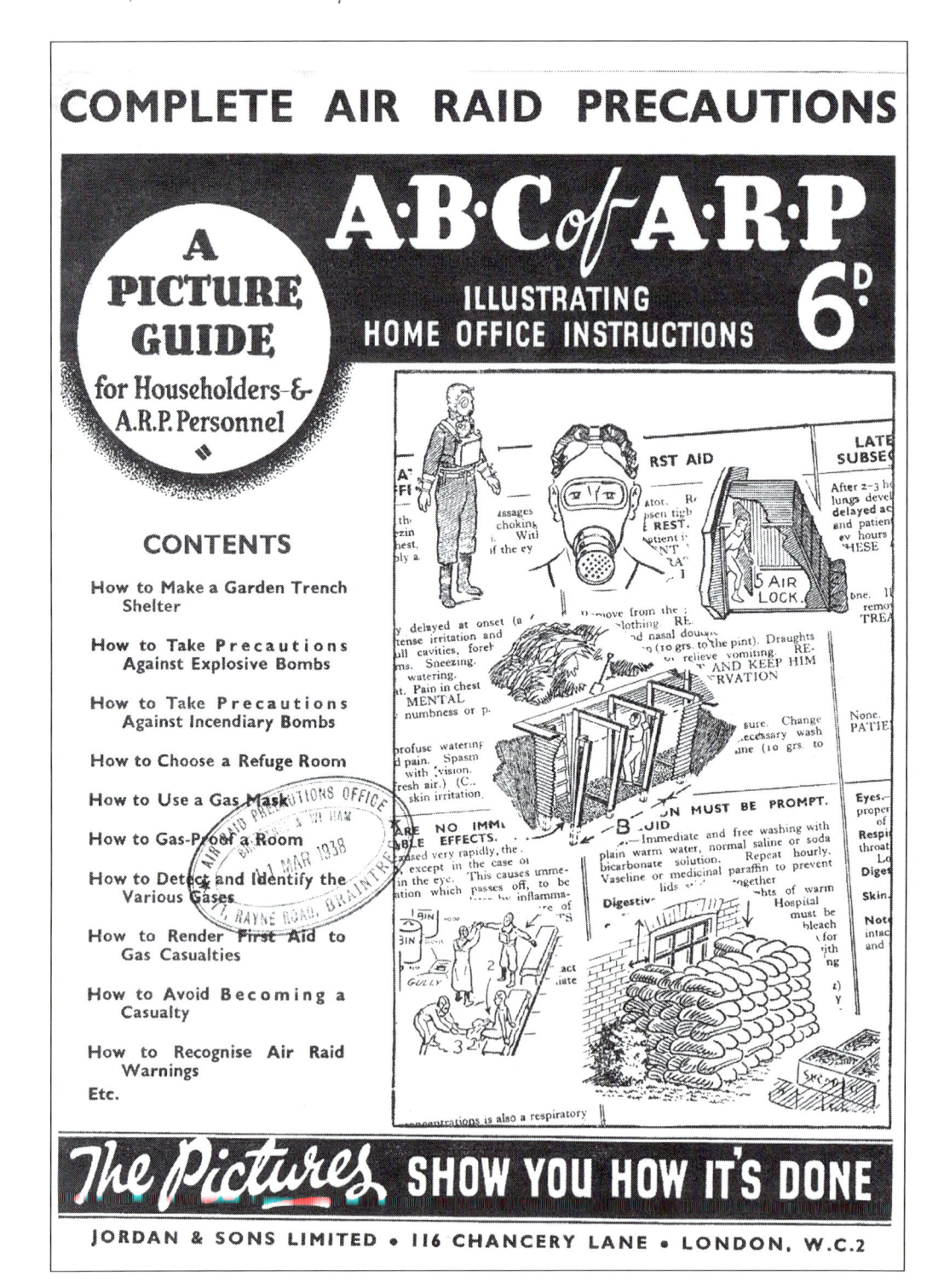

An early Air Raid Precautions Leaflet for householders and ARP personnel, issued from the Braintree ARP Office on 1st March 1938. Includes instructions on Explosive, Incendiary and Gas Bombs.

The ARP Organisation

As well as the regular firemen and the Auxiliary Fire Service, a third organisation played a key role in fire protection (among its other responsibilities), the Air Raid Precautions service usually known as the ARP. Their brief was to protect civilians from the danger of air raids and key to this were the ARP wardens. Established in 1937 these were volunteers, men and women, and wore an overall topped with a metal Brodie Helmet marked with the letter 'W'. Regional and local ARP control centres were established with access to a range of resources. As well as the wardens, the ARP had Heavy and Light Rescue Units to release people trapped in collapsed buildings, mobile first aid posts (FAPs) and repair gangs were on standby to repair damage to roads and railways and other infrastructure as a matter of priority.

Reports from the Coggeshall ARP were sent on to a permanently manned centre at Braintree and then to the regional centre at Cambridge. Warnings of air raids came in the other direction – from Cambridge to Braintree and it was they who operated the Coggeshall Air Raid Siren via a land line, a dedicated telephone line. Coggeshall was on the boundary between divisions, just outside the parish to the east, Great Tey was part of the Colchester division.

The ARP were on duty at various locations around Coggeshall looking out for bombs and fires and reporting on what they had seen and heard.

The ARP trained their own 'first aid' or first attack, fire service. Wardens were expected to deal with incendiary bombs and minor fires, before they got out of hand. The regular brigade and the Auxiliaries only attended the bigger and more developed blazes. Covering as it did an extensive rural area, the authorities did not want the Coggeshall brigade away fighting a distant fire in a field which could perhaps have been left to burn out when the greatest threat was from an uncontrolled fire in the centre of a town.

Reproduced by courtesy of the Essex Fire Museum

Early experience of incendiary bomb attacks raised an unlikely piece of firefighting equipment to near heroic status. A circular sent out to all brigades in August 1940 stated:

> 'As the result of experience so far obtained in dealing with enemy attacks by incendiary bombs, it has been decided to increase the supply of stirrup hand pumps for use in connection with air raid fire precaution schemes. It is clear that the stirrup hand pump is a very effective appliance for dealing with light incendiary bombs which have been used in large numbers by the enemy: and it is important that as many of these appliances as possible should be quickly available at the scene of any attack.... For this reason it would be desirable to carry two hand-pumps on each first line unit. ...it would also be desirable to have means of conveying a number of the hand pumps speedily to any part of a town where they might be required. These pumps would supplement any such appliances already on the scene (whether carried with the regular or emergency fire brigade units...) and could be made available for use by fire brigade or auxiliary fire

*German Incendiary Bombs, before and after.
The bombs are just over 12 inches long.
Reproduced by courtesy of the Essex Fire Museum*

service personnel.' *[Fire Brigade Circular 01/08/1940 No 79 ERO A12987 Box 8 File 73]*

The ARP were very successful in dealing with incendiary bombs. The combination of watchers to locate a fire and a quick response with tongs, bucket and stirrup pumps, proved to be a potent combination, so that by 1941 fire watchers were required by law, fire parties were organised and marshals recruited in their thousands, to catch fires at an early stage. This considerably reduced the demands on the then overstretched Auxiliary and regular brigades.

As the war progressed ARP training became quite intense. Competitions were organised between different warden groups to raise morale and promote high standards. These included a fire test where two incendiary devices called 'fire devils' were set alight inside a hut. When these had achieved a good hold, a team was sent in first to find and rescue an 'unconscious' person, before going back to subdue the fire and finally deal with the 'bomb' itself. Each team was marked out of a possible 450 points and the winners were sent on to the next round. *[CC 06/02/1942]*

A memo from Lewis White, the Braintree RDC Chief Fire Officer, dated February 1941 offered information and advice:

'The Germans have followed the logical course of first attacking with H.E [High Explosive], so driving everyone underground and then using Incendiary Bombs to start fires. This has necessitated a large number of people being above ground ready to fight these fires. A possible further development might be the use of particulate Arsenical Smoke Bombs'.

Our boffins were up to these tricks and recommended the firemen to 'draw an old woollen sock over the gas-mask container to act as a prefilter' and thus mitigate the effect.
[Circular from the Office of the Regional Commissioner in a Memo to all Chief Officers Braintree RDC Fire brigade Service 10/02/41 Author's collection]

As well as reporting the fall of bombs, ARP wardens enforced the blackout and manned the First Aid Posts. They also warned people of air raids with whistles, gas attacks with rattles and sounded the 'all clear' with hand bells.

Fines for those showing a light at night were dealt with at Witham Court. The fines for private houses with defective blackout were usually between £2 and £3. The cases give an

Phyllis Wood, a Coggeshall native, applied to join the ARP in 1938 when she was 20. She kept a list of the air raid warnings in the early part of the war.
Illustrated above is the period from 31st August–25th September 1940 when there were forty alarms.
A note next to 16th September states 'Church Bombed'.
Between 7th June-19th October when she left the town, she recorded a total of 151 air raid alarms.

ARP Warden's helmet

insight into the atmosphere of the time. Bob Brown a Coggeshall ARP warden was on duty in Church Street at 12.15am on an October night in 1940 when he 'heard the cry of fire'. The glow was tracked down to a bonfire in the garden of Percy Surridge, a retired bank manager. In court Surridge said that he had instructed his gardener to light the fire earlier and twice went to see if it was out, he claimed that a gust of wind must have re-ignited it. He was fined £1. William Cobey, the engineer in charge of Coggeshall's water supply was summoned in August 1940. An ARP warden had seen lights shining out of the windows and door of Feering pumping station from two hundred yards away. He did not know who to contact and was unable to break in, so the lights were on all night. Cobey stated that he had used an inspection light down the well the previous day and must have inadvertently left it on. He was fined £5.

Other lighting offences in Coggeshall included Francis Hill of Holfield Grange who was fined £1 for having 'undimmed sidelights, no rear light and the running boards on his car not whitened'. Hill claimed that the rear lights had shorted out and the paper covers on the sidelights had been displaced when he went to have a look. *[EN 09/12/1939]* Jack Manning was fined £1 for not having an 'authorised front light' on his bike and Stan Saunders, one of the firemen, was fined £2 for not having any lights on his car. *[EN 31/01/1942]*

Brick and concrete air raid shelters were built all around the town. They proved hard to demolish and a few still remain. Anderson shelters, which people built in their own gardens, had to be applied for and were means tested, some were had for nothing, others paid £7. In most of Coggeshall those who lived any distance from one of the shelters or who would not leave their house, took cover as best they could, usually under the stairs which was considered the safest place in a house. Owen Martin who lived out in the country at the Cradle House remembers:

> 'During the raids we used to go under the stairs, we were in there night after night and went to school tired and you couldn't learn anything, just too tired. We had no shelter to get to—there was one just down the road but we thought we might be

killed on the way there.'

Many people were involved in protecting the town. The Kinema on East Street did a roaring trade during the war, playing to packed houses. When an air raid warning was sounded a sign was illuminated next to the screen with the word 'Alert' and all those who were needed, would leave their seats and make their way out, the rest staying put to enjoy the film.

The Incident Reports, Bombs over Coggeshall

It soon became clear that Coggeshall was in the firing line as it came under an extraordinary barrage from the air. The ARP observations, timed and dated were logged in Cambridge as 'Incident Reports'. There was a fixed format to these: the location, what had fallen, what damage had occurred, any persons known to be involved, hurt or killed and whether or not a road or railway was affected or blocked. The range of objects falling from the sky included aircraft, High Explosive Bombs (HE), Incendiary or Oil Bombs (IB) and Parachute Mines (PM). Quite often these did not explode and would either be described unexploded or UXHE or UXPM.

The incident reports paint a very vivid picture of the times and show what the ARP wardens, the Regular and the Auxiliary Fire Brigades were dealing with day to day whilst in most cases, still carrying on with their normal day time jobs.

The following notes are taken from the reports, with a narrative inserted as appropriate.[10]

18th July 1940
At 00.45 1 HE Bomb exploded in field at Sky Green Road Feering. No Casualties, no fire, 2 windows broken and ceiling damaged in nearby house.
10.55 60yds to left of Cockrels [Cockerals] Farm &

---
10 This is not a definitive list. There were more incidents than are mentioned in this account including aircraft crashed or crash landed. For those interested see ERO Incident Reports D/BC 1/7/3/1-10 and Situation Reports C/W 1/5/1-9 etc

60 yards from Sky Green Road.

15th August 1940
One Incendiary bomb at Langley Green Kelvedon. 00.57, 500yds east of Langley Green, fire Burnt out in Field. Coggeshall Fire Service on the spot.

26th August 1940
Crashed plane in field near Tey Road Coggeshall Burning Furiously, Time of Occurrence. 15.25. 16.59 Now reported at Baldwins Farm Gt Tey Road. Outside Braintree & Witham Sub area.

27th August 1940
Frame Farm Feering, One Incendiary Bomb, fire under control. No damage. Dropped in garden
Stocks Green Feering, Two Incendiary Bombs, No Damage, fire Extinguished.
Hovels Farm, Two incendiary bombs time: 22.30, No damage done bombs extinguished.
Potash Farm, Three Incendiary Bomb's 22.30, No damage bombs extinguished.
Domsey Farm Feering, One Incendiary Bomb near Curd Hall, burning in field no damage.

31st August 1940
British Fighter plane crashed at Palmers Farm Coggeshall at 16.45, Crew of two [sic] baled out and are reported safe. Two Haystacks fired were extinguished by the Fire Services of Braintree RDC.

It was the Coggeshall brigade who attended this fire. Billy Green, off duty at the time, followed on in his Austin car and arriving at the farm he retrieved his fire gear stored in the boot and then, dressed in full regalia, he walked over to the fire to take charge. *[Stan Haines]*

The crashed plane was a Hawker Hurricane flown by Flight Officer (later Wing Commander) 'Jumbo' Gracie DFC who as soon as he landed, thumbed a lift to Colne Engaine to see the Heinkel aircraft he had just shot down. Next day it was discovered that he had broken his neck in the crash. Gracie was one of the 'aces' of the war, leading a squadron in Malta but was killed in action in a Mosquito aircraft in 1944.

A Fire Brigade Circular offered firemen some advice on crashed aircraft:

There have been one or two cases of the

unnecessary loss of life when tackling fires in crashed and burning aircraft ..... it will often be difficult to decide whether to tackle a burning crashed aeroplane, one of the main questions being whether the fire should be extinguished in order to prevent bombs from enemy aircraft in the vicinity, or valuable property being set alight. If not, consideration should be given to leaving the fire to burn out especially if there is any question of unexploded bombs or a mine still in the aircraft.
[FB Gen 16/12 19th June 1941]

The Blitz - Coggeshall to Docklands

The huge fires caused by incendiary bombs often needed more fire appliances than any local area could supply so a Regional Plan was developed enabling extra firemen and fire appliances to be brought in when required. The real problem though proved to be command and control. All the brigades had their own officers but outside the biggest cities there were no higher ranks to take overall charge. By tradition, the senior officer of the brigade where the fire had broken out would be in charge but because of the number of engines and men involved this was an organisational challenge for which most firemen were unprepared and some incapable.

On 7th September 1940 soon after 17.00, enemy raids targeted the Docks on both sides of the Thames involving the East and West India Docks, Surrey Commercial and Millwall Docks. At Purfleet the Anglo American Oil Works and other industrial buildings were hit. The Regional Plan was initiated and on the night of the 7th-8th September, Coggeshall's engine and brigade was one of some 600 fire appliances called into action. In Coggeshall, the flash of bombs and the glow of burning fires could be seen along with the deep rumble of distant explosions. The call came to report for duty at Thameside and the crew of regular and Auxiliary firemen, set off with some trepidation. The remaining crew of both brigades were left to guard the town.

The Coggeshall brigade made the journey to the docks on their open top fire engine, and for the best part of a week, reported to locations alongside the Thames ready for the night time raids. As the day dawned they would use the heat of the fires to dry their soaked fire gear. Bert Saunders recalled a giant oil storage tank splitting and men engulfed in the flames and another crew member, Bob Raven, saw the Thames itself on fire. On one occasion, Bert entered a building to check for fire, not realising it was in use as a temporary morgue. Shining his fading lamp around the dim interior he suddenly realised the lines of dark shapes were dead bodies and shot out of the place as white as a sheet.
(Recollections of Tony Saunders, Mick Walford and Janet Tansley, all children of wartime Coggeshall firemen)

Still resplendent in pre-war red, gold and chrome and helmeted in polished brass, the Coggeshall crew cut quite a dash among the almost universal grey of the London and Auxiliary Machines. When the Coggeshall brigade arrived at one incident, the firemen respectfully opened ranks to let them through, mistakenly thinking that Billy Green's splendid uniform meant someone of high rank. The crew felt compelled to advance and disappeared into the smoke only to reverse tracks and reappear, somewhat abashed, almost immediately. *[Fred Moss]* Back home, the families did not know where the men had been sent and it was at least a day later before Billy Green managed to make a telephone call to Joe and then the news soon spread. When the firemen eventually returned home, exhausted by their efforts, half the town was waiting on Market Hill to welcome them back. It was an experience that none of them would ever forget.

Command and control may not have been up to the enormous challenge of the Blitz but the determination and spirit of the firemen themselves and their many acts of heroism was well recognised at the time and both the regulars and the Auxiliaries enjoyed the esteem of the public as a result.

On the 17th October 1940, Billy Green

Letters of thanks for the work of the Coggeshall brigade at Thameside in September 1940.

Top: From Percy Garon then Chief Officer of Southend-on-Sea Fire Brigade and later to be Commander of Fire Force 11 of the National Fire Service.
Below: From Mr Fellows, Clerk of Braintree District Council.

COUNTY BOROUGH OF SOUTHEND-ON-SEA
FIRE BRIGADE

PHONE: MARINE 6222/3
P. G. GARON
CHIEF OFFICER

FIRE STATION
TYLERS AVENUE

YOUR REF
OUR REF   C/ET

18th September, 1940.

I welcome this opportunity of asking you to accept, and to be good enough to convey to the Members of your Brigade concerned, my grateful thanks and appreciation, also of the Members of all the Brigades in this area, for the magnificent help rendered to us at the fires during the last few days.

It was my first experience of the Regional Scheme working from places long distance, and I assure you that the knowledge of such assistance being available when our nearer comrades are heavily engaged is a great comfort.

The keenness and enthusiasm shown by all concerned was a credit to the Fire Services.

Again thanking you, and with kindest regards,

I remain,

Yours truly,

District Officer.
No.1 District.
No.4 Region.

Braintree Rural District Council,

Telephone:
BRAINTREE 260.

Official Communications should be addressed impersonally to "The Clerk of the Council."

HEF/OR.

St. PETER'S CLOSE,
BOCKING, BRAINTREE,
Essex.

17th October 1940.

Dear Sir,

At a recent Meeting of the above Council Mr. White, the Chief Fire Officer, reported upon the splendid work of your Brigade when you responded to a Regional fire call at Thameside.

The Council wish me to write and say how much they appreciate the ready response of the members of the Brigade and they are very proud indeed to learn of the wonderful assistance which was rendered.

Will you be good enough to convey the Council's message of appreciation to all the members of the Brigade, and their sincere thanks to you as their captain.

They feel they can rely with great confidence on your continued good work whenever the need arises.

These are difficult days and if everyone make up their minds to lend a helping hand on such occasions of emergency they can safely feel that much valuable work is being done in the common effort to bring this ghastly war to a victorious conclusion.

Yours faithfully,

Mr. W. Green,
Chief Officer,
Coggeshall Fire Brigade,
Coggeshall,
Essex.

received a letter from the Braintree Council:

> 'At a recent meeting of the above Council Mr White, the Chief Fire Officer reported on the splendid work of your brigade when you responded to a Regional fire call at Thameside. The Council wish me to write to you to say how much they appreciate the ready response of the members of the brigade and they are very proud indeed to learn of the wonderful assistance which was rendered. Will you be good enough to convey the council's message of appreciation to all members of the brigade and their sincere thanks to you as their Captain.' *[Author's collection]*

Regular and Auxiliary brigades across Essex were called in to provide assistance on many occasions but there are few surviving records. Essex appliances were called in to London in April 1941 for example but this is only known because of an accident; Fred Everson from Dovercourt 'after a severe air raid by the enemy', was ordered to tow the Dovercourt AFS trailer pump to London but collided with a bus in Romford and was charged with driving without due care and attention. His trailer pump must have been part of a considerable convoy of vehicles heading for the capital as the paper reported that this was just one of three accidents to AFS vehicles at the same spot that morning. Everson was fined £2 with 27s costs. *[CC 23/05/1941]* At Corringham, lines of fire engines would pass by on the way to the docks, their bodywork and polished brass fittings gleaming, only to return the next day smoke blackened and filthy. *[Recounted by Bryan Everitt]*

When the fire engine was away, the AFS manned the station overnight ready to respond to the telephone. Roy Maddocks, then just a lad, spent a night in the top bunk at the station with his father George, an AFS fireman, in the lower berth. At the time he thought it was fun but a bit odd because 'the engine was away and the place was empty.' *[Roy Maddocks interview]* In fact he played a key role, if a call had come in, he would have run round to call out the crew while his father made his way to The Gravel to open up the AFS station.

Coggeshall Church September 1940.
The turret stairway collapsed the day after the bomb fell.

Coggeshall Church

Incident Report: 16th September 1940:

> Coggeshall Church 5 miles east of Braintree struck by HE Bomb at 21.15. No casualties but church extensively damaged. Report states that two bombs exploded and perhaps unexploded bombs still in debris...

Denis Wood was looking out that night:

> 'It screamed as it came down, a terrible row right overhead then I saw it hit with a flash and a ball of flame. I thought all the trees were on fire but there was no sign of that the next day. There were two bombs that fell together, the other one at the top of the Churchyard. George and Phyllis [two of his siblings] were halfway up Church Field the next day when it went off. They flattened themselves and decided not to go any further.'

The brigade had been called out to standby at the station by the siren. That night because an enemy aircraft could be heard circling overhead, they decided to mobilise the appliance so it was

September 1940, Coggeshall Church.

immediately on hand if any bombs fell. However, for the first and only time as far as we know, the fire engine would not start. It was always left with the starting handle in position to 'catch' but that night, when they turned the engine over, nothing happened. When it did start, the bombs had already fallen. It was thought then that fate had intervened to keep the men safe.
[Recollection of Mick Walford December 2010]

The Vicar, Norman Brown, wrote this account:

> 'On 16th September 1940 Coggeshall suffered a major loss. London was the chief target and its defence was the first consideration. This allowed lone bombers to cross our shores with comparative impunity and it was such a lone raider that was heard circling Coggeshall. It was the night of Monday the 16th September 1940, shortly before a quarter past nine o'clock, when two bombs were heard to fall. One fell in Butt Field and exploded the following afternoon, no-one was hurt and there was no obvious damage. The other fell in the church yard close to the north-west corner of the church, penetrating at an angle so that it must have been directly below the tower before detonating. Later, rods were put down the hole made by the falling bomb: they were 25 feet long and failed to reach the bottom. The depth at which it exploded probably accounted for the noise which was heard more clearly at a distance than near at hand. In the church the walls were pushed out by the blast so the roof was unsupported and came crashing down, the roof of the Nave dragged down the north arcading and so the roof of the north aisle. Further east, although the walls were strained outwards the roof maintained sufficient force to hold.
> On the day following the bombing, the turret stairway collapsed and the masonry fell onto and smashed the roof of the western bay of the south aisle. During the following week the south west corner of the tower collapsed.' [Brown, 1956]

Two soldiers were on lookout duty on top of the church tower that night but amazingly both were unhurt.

Incident Reports

20th September 1940
Coggeshall 22.25, High Explosive & Oil Bomb.

20th September 1940
Several Incendiary Bombs near Marks Hall, Coggeshall, No damage, no fire time of occurrence 22.56. 23.15 reports all bombs burning out without doing any damage.

25th September 1940
One High Explosive at Coggeshall 23.05 apparently between Abbey and Sewage farm. No casualties or damage.

2nd October 1940
Ten High Explosive and One Oil Incendiary Bomb reported to have dropped at 12.10hrs in ploughed fields south of Purleigh [Purley] Farm, Feering. No casualties or damage.
Oil Bomb was burning but has been extinguished by wardens.

8th October 1940
Message from police 09.45 Roads blocked due to air raid damage A120 Braintree-Colchester Rd near the Queens Head public house:
I beg to report that an enemy bomb was dropped on the verge of the Braintree-Marks Tey Main Road A120 about 200 yards east of the Queens Head Inn, Feering, on the morning of the 8th inst. The road was subsequently closed by the police owing to the suspected presence of unexploded bombs in the adjoining meadows. The crater formed by the explosion of the bomb is approximately 15 feet in diameter and 8 feet deep. Nine yards of granite Kerb has been displaced and the 6 foot concrete haunch fractured and raised for approx 6yds. The 2" asphalt surface has been cracked across the entire width of the carriageway. 20 feet. A 1" water pipe has been broken.

29th October 1940
Three HE Bombs dropped at approx 18.15hrs at Feering near Domsey Farm adjacent to A12. No damage to road or casualties

5th November 1940
03.38, Report from Warden E64 Coggeshall, Position of occurrence, Purley Farm Coggeshall, Type of bomb HE. A bomb has demolished a farm house where 3 people are known to be living, no fire, no other damage to property, no road blocked no report as to position of UXB. Time of occurrence 02.15 services on the spot or coming. We have dispatched One Ambulance, One Rescue, One First Aid Post and the Coggeshall Ambulance is on its way.

Air raid damage at Purley Farm Feering at 02.15 05/11/40 H.E. Bombs, Number not known. Farmhouse completely wrecked, three persons trapped but now released, these have been relocated to relatives house, Doctor in attendance injuries not serious. Services attending included one Ambulance from Coggeshall, one Ambulance from Braintree, one F.A.P. Braintree, one Rescue Party Braintree. Police report that 7 H E Bombs were dropped.

Owen Martin remembers:

'They got bombed right out but they were alright, Tony Bower got thrown right across the room but he was alright. We took a collection at school, they had lost everything. The next day Jack Bowers and Harry Bowers found a hole, there's two gateways on the right hand side and there was a hole there, it looked like another bomb had gone in and they just filled it in and it must be there to this day'.
[Recounted to the author]

9th November 1940
Hawkes Hall Pattiswick Two High Explosive both unexploded. Time of Occurrence 19.00 on or near farm buildings. People have evacuated. Military at Coggeshall have been informed.

15th November 1940
14.52 Warden E64 reports Ten Incendiary Bombs dropped in meadow North of Houchins Farm House Feering, Bombs scattered harmlessly on Meadow-land. All burnt out. No Damage. Time of Occurrence. 02.15.

15th November 1940
22.52 High Explosive Little Tey. No report yet of casualties or damage.

The Tilkey Brigade on Duty

16th November 1940
Two Paramines dropped 200yds NNE of end of Tilkey Road Coggeshall. Extensive damage to property. Three cows destroyed. One slight casualty. Time of Occurrence, 20.14 hrs.

One Paramine fell not far from the Red House otherwise known as the Pest House at Tilkey where Denis Wood lived, he recalls:

'The "Tilkey brigade" [an ad hoc group of locals] were out and saw the parachute falling near the Red House. It came down very flat, they said it just cleared a little stack up by us, so it must have been low, we were lucky. Old Shovel Wade, Siddy and Stack Wilsher, they saw the parachute and thought it was a German, so armed with clothes props, they went away after him. Well, it went up – and they went down. The cows were hit but weren't killed outright Mr Browning the butcher dealt with them. They were butchered in the field and the remains thrown into the crater. When the by-pass was built it went right through it.'
[Denis Wood]

15th February 1941
Bomb at Bank Street & Coggeshall Road, Braintree. Confirmed Three Killed. Two x male One x female, Five in hospital, Seventeen minor. Lloyds Bank demolished & other buildings damaged. Road blocked, open to single line traffic at 12.05 & fully repaired on 22/02/41.

15th February 1941
22.00, Pattiswick High Explosive.
02.40, Siren at Coggeshall, operated by remote control from Braintree, failed to sound the 'Raiders Passed'. This was probably due to enemy action.
15.55 The Coggeshall Siren is being operated by hand, remote control being out of order.

18th February 1941
20.15, E67 PC63 Lewis reports, Dornier 17 flying E.N.E. passed over Searchlight post at Bradwell-juxta-Coggeshall came out of low cloud and went slightly past. Machine gunned the post and military personnel, re-entered cloud and continued on still flying E.N.E., No casualties.

Gatehouse Farm bomb crater c1985

Gatehouse Farm

26th February 1941
23.12, One Paramine reported 150yds N of Gate House Farm Coggeshall. Time of Occurrence. 20.45. Police and Wardens on the spot.
PM fell in open field causing damage to farm buildings Two flashes seen and Two explosions heard.

Owen Martin lived nearby at the Cradle House and ran up the track to the farm with his father to see if everyone was alright As they approached in the dark they heard a great rushing of water coming down towards them, which swept past leaving them even more shocked. Luckily everyone was safe at the farm but a water tank, high up in one of the barns was dislodged in the blast and tipped its contents onto the track causing the sudden flood. Markshall Rectory was also close by and shaken by the blast but although windows were broken there was no major damage. The crater was enormous, eighty-six feet across and forty-one feet deep, 'big enough for a London bus'. It was said that experts who were called in to examine it concluded that the size resulted from unusual ground conditions. The crater is still there and can just be seen from the Old Rectory Road.

28th February 1941 20.41 Owing to proximity of UX Parachute Mine, B1024 Earls Colne to Coggeshall Rd blocked from Bullocks Cross Feering to Bird in Hand Public House, Earls Colne. Open to traffic 20.25.

Braintree RDC brigade's Coggeshall engine c1940, the Morris fire engine, still in pre-war red livery. Pictured having just pulled out of the station on Market Hill.
Front: Capt. Billy Green, driver Bob Evans, Top: Bert Saunders with Lenny Walford standing behind him. On the back is Frank Weinrich and behind him, Stan Saunders. Note the white painted curbstones to improve visibility in the blackout.

13th March 1941
Found in a field beside the R Blackwater at Feeringbury 16.00 13/03/41 part of a Parachute Flare that was dropped at Feering on Feb 26th 1941.

14th March 1941
Two Incendiary Bomb's have fallen between Feering Bury and Toll House Coggeshall. No fires Police and Wardens on Spot. Time of Occurrence 22.25.

12th May 1941
05.12, About Four High Explosive and 100 Incendiary Bombs Witch Wood, Two miles from Coggeshall along B1024 to Earls Colne
00.15 hrs. Fifteen Incendiary Bombs and One Oil Bomb all unexploded have been removed to Kelvedon Police Station. No damage caused beyond fire in the wood which has been extinguished.

19th June 1941
00.37 Incendiary Bombs dropped near Isinglass Factory West Street Coggeshall, No damage.

An Ominous Instruction

With an invasion expected at any time, Billy Green, the Coggeshall Captain, received instructions on the procedures to be followed when it happened. These were passed on with some degree of secrecy because of its potential effect on morale. Control of the Fire Services would be maintained, it was hoped, by devolving it to the regions. However, any equipment that could be of use to the enemy had to be put out of use and this included the Coggeshall fire engine. Captain Green was instructed that if the worst happened he was to permanently disable the engine. There was an envelope, pinned to the station notice board and cryptically labelled 'Emergency Fire Brigade, Label for Fire Engine'. The label was to be attached to the engine in

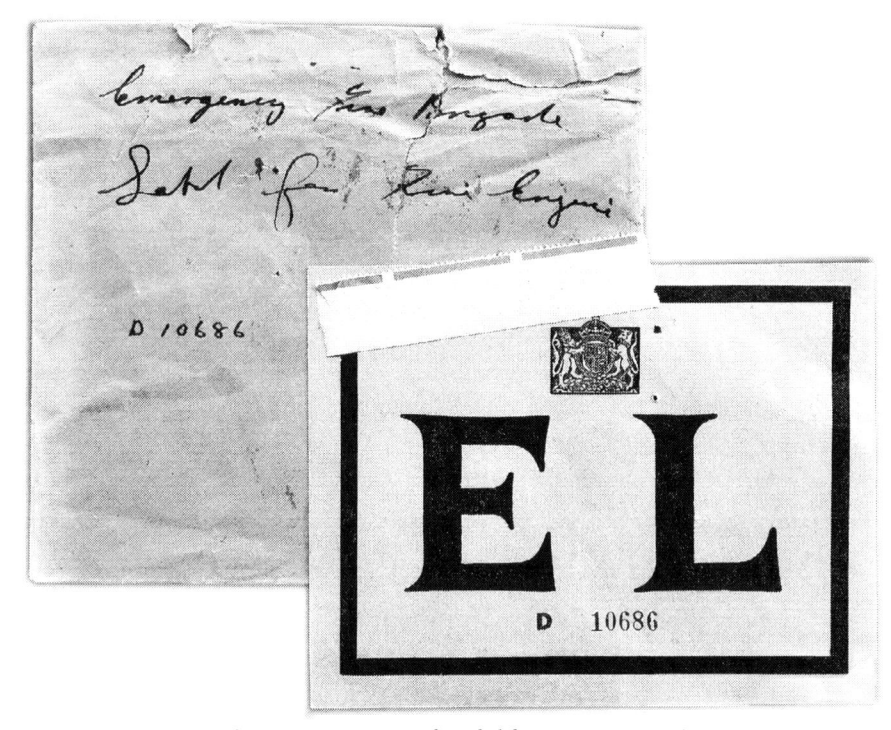

'Emergency Fire Brigade Label for Fire Engine' 1941.
The emergency would have been the imminent arrival of German troops following the invasion.
Under these circumstances the fire engine was to be fatally damaged so as not to be of use to the enemy and this label usually kept in its envelope in the office, would have been fixed to the screen and the station abandoned.

extremis to verify that the destruction had been officially sanctioned (see illustration).

[The label was in the possession of Bert Saunders who passed it and the story to the author c1989].

These were perhaps the worst days of the war and invasion seemed certain. Farmers had already been warned that their stubble fields, if more than 300 yards long would make an ideal landing ground for enemy aircraft so it was recommended that furrows should be ploughed between the lines of sheaves, before they were removed. *[CC 09/08/1940]*

In the summer of 1941, there had been reports of enemy bombers apparently targeting the harvest fields with incendiary bombs. This, together with the fear of enemy paratroopers is evident in a letter that arrived at the fire station from Major McKerrow, Commanding the 42nd Divisional Supply Column. *[Roneo letter in the author's possession dated 18/08/1941]* This informed him that from the 19th August 1941, an 'Inlying Picquet - Prevention of Fires in Crop-Growing Areas' was to come into force. This comprised nine men and a Non Commissioned Officer and was to assist farmers in preventing fires which may break out in their corn-fields and to act as an immediate 'strike-force' against airborne troops. The police or fire brigade could call on these soldiers by dialling Braintree 379. The men were issued with basic fire-fighting equipment: sacks, axes, shovels and beaters. To fight the paratroopers they were also issued with 20 rounds per rifle and 12 magazines for their bren gun. They were thus better equipped for fighting fires than they were for fighting paratroopers.

1941 National Fire Service helmet badge and woven cloth uniform patch of Fire Force 11 which had its headquarters in Southend and covered most of Essex, including Coggeshall.

Nationalisation

During the heavy raids of April 1941, the fire service was showing the strain. In London officers had been on continuous duty, many had been out for fifty-eight nights running and doing paperwork during the day. The Home Office had no direct chain of command to the 1,450 separate brigades across the country, there was no national co-ordination, equipment was not standardised and neither was the command structure. The astonishing achievements of the regular and AFS brigades during the Blitz were more about individual determination than a planned response. Firemen with minimal experience would find themselves in charge of what would in peacetime have been enormous fires.

The chaotic nature of command and control meant that experienced AFS crews might find themselves under the command of a regular fireman fresh from training, who may never have attended a fire. Although London had a big regular brigade with experienced officers, the same did not apply elsewhere. The Coventry raid in November 1940 caused huge fires which the local fire brigade and AFS units held for four hours and were then overwhelmed. There was a complete breakdown of command and control and no co-ordination or direction given to the units called in to help. The raid vividly exposed the absence of strategic organisation and command capable of responding to such a devastating attack. Herbert Morrison, the Home Secretary, debating the Fire Services (Emergency Provisions) Bill said:

> 'In these weeks and months of heavy fire fighting the regular and auxiliary firemen and firewomen have done a magnificent job of work of which this country can be proud. Fire-fighting .... is now an operation of war.....The fundamental difficulty in the present arrangements is the relatively small basic unit upon which the whole fire-fighting machine must be built so that even very small plans of operation and mobilisation may involve 20 or 30 separate local authorities and chiefs of fire brigades'.
> *[Hansard 20 May 1941]*

The Bill was passed and in just 13 weeks the process was complete.

Billy Green the Coggeshall Captain officially heard about the change two days after it happened. A letter from his Chief Fire Officer, Lewis White dated the 20th August informed him that:

> 'As from 18th August 1941 the whole organisation of the fire service throughout the country was to be taken over by the government and was to be known as The National Fire Service.'
> *[Author's possession, see illustration overleaf]*

A Fire Brigade Memo No.83/1941 had been sent out on 15th August:

> 'As from midnight on Sunday/Monday 17th/18th August, the members of the fire brigades maintained by the local authorities and the appliances, vehicles and property used by the fire brigades pass from the control of the local authorities to that of the Secretary of State.'
> *[ERO: A12987 Box 8 File 73]*

So it was that in August 1941 the Regulars and Auxiliaries were combined and the National Fire Service (NFS) came into being, under the new Chief of the Fire Staff, the marvellously and fortuitously named, Sir Aylmer Firebrace. At a stroke the number of fire brigades in the country fell from 1,450 to 39 and were renamed, 'Fire Forces'. The NFS was regionally organised with between two and four Fire Forces in each region, each under a Fire Force Commander.

Braintree Rural District Council.
(FIRE BRIGADE SERVICE.)

Telephone: No. 260.
(2 Lines.)

L. A. B. WHITE,
CHIEF FIRE OFFICER.

St. PETER'S CLOSE,
BOCKING.
Essex.

LABW/GR.

20th August 1941.

Memorandum to All Chief Fire Officers.

NATIONAL FIRE SERVICE.

I have to inform you that as from the 18th August 1941, the whole of the Fire Brigade Organisation throughout the country will be taken over by the Government and will be known as The National Fire Service.

I enclose herewith a copy of a message received from the Minister of Home Security and I shall be glad if you will arrange to pin this up in your Station.

"CONFIDENTIAL" INFORMATION.

In connection with any confidential information which is passed on to you for your guidance and in some cases for the guidance of the general public, it has been brought to my notice that this has been circulated in a manner in which it did not comply strictly with the instructions given. If any such instructions are received it will be quite in order for the notice to be posted in the Fire Station but any further information given to the members of the general public should be given verbally. In future, any communication passed on to you marked "Confidential" should be treated in this fashion, but of course any technical details should be strictly for information of the Fire Brigade personnel only.

Lewis A. B. White

Mr. W. Green,
Stoneham Street,
Coggeshall,
Essex.

A letter from Chief Fire Officer White informing Coggeshall's Captain that he and his brigade were now part of the National Fire Service, dated 20th August 1941, two days after the event.

Fire Force 11 had its headquarters in Southend and was responsible for most of Essex from Southend to Thurrock and Saffron Walden to Harwich. The former Chief Fire Officer of Southend-on-Sea, Mr Percy Garon, became its Commander.

At the end of September 1941 the Braintree Chief Fire Officer, Lewis White, was promoted to the senior rank of 'Column Officer' in the Norwich NFS.

Coggeshall probably became a 'Section Station' with Billy Green its Section Officer. The Kelvedon AFS also became an NFS station and joined with Coggeshall, Witham and Hatfield Peverel to form a 'Company' under a Company Officer, P C Evitt. *[CC 28/11/1941]* Appointed in December 1941, Evitt had formerly been Captain of the Witham AFS. He was of the 'officer class', scion of a respected and prosperous Witham family; his father had been Chairman of the Urban Council and his mother Chairman of the women's section of the British Legion. Evitt's elder brother George, a Flying Officer in the RAF, was killed in action during the battle of Britain in June 1940.

Two Coggeshall firemen, Stan Barnett and George Maddocks, had begun training as whole-time firemen a month before nationalisation, in July 1941. Both served for a time in Colchester before Stan was posted to Saffron Walden and George to Halstead NFS fire stations.

The new NFS uniform included a dark blue double breasted tunic. The peaked cap of the AFS was adopted instead of the peakless sailor-type cap favoured by many pre-war brigades. For fire-fighting, Brodie steel helmets replaced the traditional brass ones and were the same as those previously issued to the AFS. An old Coggeshall helmet shows the initials 'AFS' ghosting through the coat of drab paint on one side and the 'NFS' logo on the other. The Coggeshall part-time NFS firemen may only have been compensated for the pay they lost when called to duty. Bob Raven worked as a bricklayer for Mr Birkin and his pay was stopped the minute he answered a fire call.
[Janet Tansley]

Coggeshall's 'Morris Commercial' fire engine was replaced by a second-hand Dennis 'G' type 25cwt appliance, dating from the 1930s. Still on the 'Braidwood' pattern, the new appliance carried a water tank and a high pressure hose reel, which enabled fire-fighting to start immediately on arrival without first having to find water. The hose reel was a very effective tool that answered for all but the biggest fires. The Braidwood design gave the firemen no protection from the elements and this was a problem on long journeys in cold and wet weather hence its nickname, 'the pneumonia wagon'. Firemen had also been killed or injured falling off a Braidwood engine. Designs with enclosed cabs were available but the tradition of the Braidwood pattern was deeply engrained and not easily given up.

Coggeshall's Regular and AFS firemen, already working well together, were now merged into one unit and may eventually have had two fire appliances at their disposal, the new Dennis and an Auxiliary Towing Vehicle or ATV pulling the trailer pump originally issued to the AFS.[11] Using borrowed or rented vehicles to tow the trailer pumps had proved a failure. During an air raid on Manchester in December 1940 so many towing vehicles were unserviceable that crews resorted to pushing the pumps to the fires.
[Blackstone] In early 1941 an order was placed for 2,000 two-ton vans for use as towing vehicles. These were fitted with a thick iron roof to protect the crew from shrapnel and inside there were benches for the men and stowage for hose and small gear. Some 5,750 were eventually built.

The creation of the NFS coincided with a reduction in bombing raids, evident in the local 'incident reports' which show that fewer bombs and mines fell as time passed. Despite this the Coggeshall firemen maintained night duty at least until mid 1944.

---

11   So far, the only evidence that Coggeshall had an ATV is Tony Saunders' recollection of it.

As all the brigades now used a standard drill book and with a reduction in raids, timed drills became part of the training process and competition against neighbouring sections encouraged. Coggeshall's success in such competitions was modest. In September 1943 they achieved the distinction of third place out of seven in the 'Light Trailer Pump' section behind Silver End (first) and (annoyingly) Kelvedon (second).

The 'call-out' system for 'civilian' fires had changed little since Daniel Leaper's time. Billy Green took the call and while he made his way down Stoneham Street to the station, his father Joe, now getting on and rather portly, trundled around alerting the crew. Janet Tansley[12] remembers him 'running' up Queen Street to their house shouting 'Bob, there's a fire!' Joe carried on to Bill Leatherdale's, 'Bill, there's a fire!' then via Vane Lane to Church Street and the Conservative Club where Les Spry was the landlord 'Les, there's a fire!' On to Frank Weinrich's shop 'Frank, there's a fire!' Finally to the Chapel Hotel where Bill Jennings was landlord. By then the messenger was the message! Janet said 'Sometimes, Joe used a bike.'

In May 1943 Earls Colne airfield became operational. Built on farmland between Coggeshall and Earls Colne it was home first to B17 Flying Fortresses, then B26 Marauders of the USAF and in 1944, Halifaxes from the RAF.

In 1943 a Flying Fortress which had taken off from the airfield suffered an engine failure while circling to gain height. The pilot attempted to land but lost a second, then a third and finally the last engine also failed. The aircraft narrowly missed the roof of Herons Farm where Mrs Blackwell was hanging out the washing. At Whitegates Farm Mr Sillitoe and his son Hector were on top of a haystack and saw the aircraft coming straight towards them. They got down and managed to run clear as the B17 went through the stack and demolished their farmhouse before finally coming to rest. *[Andrew Webb & Cecil Blackwell]* The crew survived the crash and got out but fearing the fuel and bomb load would go up at any second, they picked up Mr Sillitoe senior and ran for their lives, reaching the Bird-in-Hand before the explosion. The Halstead and Coggeshall brigades were called out to deal with the fire, and found yellow lumps of unexploded ordnance lying amongst the debris. The animals in the barn were killed instantly in the fireball, the carbonised body of a horse was found still standing in its stall and the pigs in a row in their sty. *[Roy Maddocks interview]* The house was never rebuilt and the site is now an overgrown copse.

The sight of aircraft flying out and struggling back badly damaged became an abiding memory for many.

The St Botolph's Raid

Although enemy activity had diminished, one of the biggest raids in our area took place in the winter of 1944. Colchester had escaped relatively lightly in bombing raids (not so in casualties: thirty-eight people were killed when bombs fell on Severalls Hospital in August 1942). On 23rd February 1944 a raid originally thought to be heading for London was diverted to Colchester. Some 1,400 incendiaries were dropped in what became known as the 'St Botolph's Raid'. Fire engines were mobilised across the county. Archie Warren was a Column Officer in the NFS and responsible for Colchester. He recalls

> 'I went to the top of a hill on the outskirts of the town and saw what appeared to be fires from one boundary of the town to the boundary on the other side. For the one and only time of my life I had to request "make one hundred pumps", I got sixty.' *[Leete]*

St Botolph's Church was hit by several incendiaries and saved by two schoolboys who climbed onto the roof and used stirrup pumps to

---

12   Then Janet Raven, her father, Bob, was a wartime fireman.

control the fires. Coggeshall's George Maddocks was given a more prosaic task. He followed a 'hose layer'[13] as it made its way from the river, up East Hill and then towards the St Botolph's area. His job was to catch the couplings as they unrolled out of the lorry to prevent them being damaged when they hit the road.

The NFS 'Commandos'

In March 1944, a circular was sent out inviting firemen from the National Fire Service to join a new elite fire-fighting unit[14]. Plans had been drawn up to send four columns of specially trained NFS firemen behind the advancing troops as part of the then top secret D Day landings. Volunteers applied from every corner of war-torn Britain and went through a stringent selection process. Once through that hurdle they went off for arduous and specialised fire-fighting training, fitness work-outs and long route marches. They were later sent to the coast to practise driving fire appliances and pumps on and off landing craft, sometimes under gunfire.

Stan Barnett who had joined the AFS in October 1938 and was one of the Coggeshall Auxiliaries during the Blitz, applied to join the new column. At this time, 1944, he was working full-time with the NFS in Saffron Walden. Stan passed the interview and entrance tests and successfully completed the rigorous training process which in addition to fire-fighting instruction and drills, included a military assault course and route marches in full gear, all under army instructors. He joined 'A' company of The National Fire Service No4 Column, Overseas Contingent. Five columns were formed in all and they were fully trained by D Day. Their job, once they were across the Channel was to assist the armed forces by fighting fires, military

Stan Barnett during his service with the NFS Overseas contingent 1944.
Photo by courtesy of Mick Barnett

and domestic, alongside the advancing troops. However, things did not turn out as planned and the elite of the British Fire Service waited with increasing impatience in their barracks for a call that never came. For reasons still disputed, in November 1944 the Columns were stood down – except that is for Stan's unit, the 4th. They were chosen, it is said, because they were the most representative of all parts of the country, with firemen from the North, Scotland and Wales as well as Suffolk and Essex. In January 1945, the 4th finally moved from their bases at Ipswich and Lexden near Colchester[15]. On the 24th January, the coldest night for 80 years, No 4 Column, some five hundred and fifty men, with their pumps and vehicles, sailed from Tilbury to Ostend to assist the American Army. They became the only unit to take the Fire Service's colours into battle.

The 4th had sixty pumps plus support

---

13   A lorry loaded with hose which ran out continuously from the back as it drove along, in London this was, 'at a steady 20mph'. Perhaps Essex was more careful of its couplings so the hose layer was limited by how fast George could run.

14   Nicknamed the 'NFS Commandos' in the Press.

15   Now the Essex County Fire & Rescue Service Workshops.

vehicles including hose laying lorries, a mobile kitchen and dispatch riders. Column Headquarters and one other company went to Namur in Belgium, two companies to Liege, one to Verdun and one to Etain in France. Within a few hours of arriving at Verdun, the company was in action fighting a severe roof fire in a hotel being used by American troops. In the main, the NFS units were with the Twelfth (US) Army Group and the Quarter Master Corps, others were attached to the US Ordnance Corps. After a period with the Americans, the Column was transferred to the 21st British Army Group under General Montgomery. On 17th March 1945 the first NFS crews crossed the Rhine into Germany. By July, after an extraordinary six months, it was over. The Column had dealt with 195 fires in the American Sector and 94 in the British area.

A document in the Essex Record Office, *[ERO C/DB 8/13]* probably issued to all the firemen on the disbandment of the unit in July 1945, provides a contemporary description of the Column and its work:

> 'In a few days the crews were scattered far and wide behind the battle fronts. France, Holland, Belgium, Luxembourg and Germany all saw the grey tenders and blue-clad firemen in action. Petrol oil, ammunitions, explosives. These were the fires that the Column fought and vanquished.'

The document also includes endorsements, one from Brigadier General Plank from the office of the Commanding General of the US Army reads:

> 'The work that your column did was invaluable in minimising loss by fire of critically needed and irreplaceable equipment and supplies. Your men constantly demonstrated their ability, skill and courage in the Liege area during the V-1 attacks and in other areas when the necessity arose.'

There are several other testimonials praising the work and skills of the Column.

The Column returned from Ostend on 15th July 1945. Stan Barnett was discharged from the NFS in November 1945 and rejoined as a part time NFS fireman at Coggeshall two weeks later. The business he established with his brother, selling war-surplus materials and tools, in Queen Street, Coggeshall, became famous in the district. Stan was promoted to Sub Officer in Charge in June 1951 a position he held until his retirement from the service in February 1969. At his funeral Coggeshall firemen acted as guard of honour.

In June 1944 a strange new machine appeared over the town. Tilley Wilsher lived near the top of Tilkey, an ex-Londoner she had a voice which carried well. Overheard from two hundred yards away 'there goes another one with its arse alight!' That was a V1 flying bomb. From September 1944, Essex became 'Doodlebug Alley' with a total of 412 flying bombs falling on the county up to the start of 1945. They were a regular sight over Coggeshall, everyone fearing the engine would cut out as it passed overhead. One or two did fall locally, the remains of one lay for a while in a ditch near Purley farm and another fell in Jays Lane, Marks Tey on 8th October and seriously damaged more than thirty houses. In September the even more lethal V2s began to fall and more than a dozen came down in Essex. Launched from Holland they mostly passed high over Coggeshall and at three times the speed of sound, it was impossible to hear them coming. None fell after 12th October 1944.

Stan Haines lived at St George's Terrace on Tilkey Road and worked for a time as a trainee fitter at Earls Colne airfield. He vividly recalls one night in late 1944: 'My mother shouted up the stairs - there's a plane crashed at the top of the field!' The aircraft was a four engined Halifax bomber with a crew of six, probably on an SOE (Special Operations Executive) mission and carrying 'light' 500lb bombs. One of twenty-nine Halifaxes that had taken off that night from Earls Colne airfield, it had failed to gain height, hit some power lines and came down in a field on Fabians farm. As Stan and his brother looked there was an explosion and as they got outside they heard something that they could never

Coggeshall's NFS fire engine, a Dennis 'G' type 25cwt appliance, pulling out of the station on Market Hill. The photo probably dates from after the war as the headlights are unrestricted and the kerbs unpainted. The drum of the high-pressure hose-reel can be seen at the rear of the machine which is painted in drab grey.

forget, the sounds of the airmen trapped inside. As they ran towards the aircraft there was another explosion and the lads were knocked back by the blast. The farmer's daughter, Vera Prentice, was also running towards the crash site. Just two or three of the crew had escaped and one of them, seeing Vera, picked her up and got down into a ditch just as the plane blew up and the trapped men were silenced. 'Herb' Prentice took the survivors to the farmhouse and gave them scotch. The RAF were clearing the site at 7.30 the next morning and by late afternoon all the debris had been removed except for an undercarriage wheel which remained in a field-side pond for years. The airmen returned some years later and were presented with a machine gun from the aircraft which had been ploughed out some time before.

Stan Haines recalls another incident:

'I was riding my bike on the Earls Colne airfield perimeter track heading for one of the petrol dumps when I heard a most terrible bang and saw what looked like bits of corrugated iron roof sheets slowly falling from the sky'. *[Stan Haines interview]*

Two Lancaster bombers had collided in mid air and both crews, fourteen men, had died in an instant. The debris fell over a wide area, some close to the bomb dump in Witch Wood. It was there that an airfield fire engine used the newly developed fire fighting foam to put out the blaze. Several field fires were also started and the Coggeshall brigade were at the scene:

'....we got some of the fires under control, some corn was still in the fields, it was October time and I helped the regulars. [The debris] didn't all fall in one place it was quite a bit of a mess.'

[Transcript William Drain of Great Tey, ERO SA 12/574/1]

The war-work of the Coggeshall brigade continued into 1945 but with the end of the war in Europe, the brigade returned, no doubt with some relief, to normal peace-time activities proud that they had carried out their duty to the considerable credit of the town.

Coggeshall National Fire Service Crew and Dennis 'G' type 25cwt appliance in 1948.
Seated on the pump: Stan Barnett, Bill Huckle, Fred Tilbrook, J Speed, Bill Dale, Les Spry
Standing: Bert Saunders, Bill Jennings, Bob Evans, Len Cheek, George Maddocks, Peter Joyce

Coggeshall National Fire Service Crew 1948.
Back Row: J Speed, Bill Dale, Fred Tilbrook, Len Cheek, Peter Joyce, Bill Huckle, George Maddocks.
Front: Stan Barnett, LFm Bert Saunders, Section Leader Bob Evans, LFm Bill Jennings, Les Spry.
Stan Barnett's 'Overseas' shoulder flash is just visible and of course, the distinctive beret of the Column.

Endings and Beginnings

Coggeshall's new Dennis appliance had made the old Morris fire engine redundant. It was bought by Stan Barnett for £25 and he sold it to Bob Evans, who owned the garage on East Street, for £45. Bob Evans removed the ladder, attached a crane and used it as a recovery/tow truck for the garage. Tony Saunders inherited this vehicle when he took over the garage. He reports,

> 'As a tow truck, it pulled well but wouldn't stop, it only had brakes on the rear wheels. The open cab meant it was very cold to drive in the winter. I towed a car back from Wethersfield one freezing night and thought - that's enough, I put it behind the garage and there it stayed until a chap from Tiptree made me an offer and took it away. I found out later that he had scrapped it'.
> *[Mick Barnett and Tony Saunders interviews]*

With the war at an end, decisions were made as to which of the NFS stations were to remain open and which would not. Closures had begun in 1945, leading to protests from firemen who wanted to carry on and parish councils who were reluctant to see their local station close. Coggeshall was to remain operational but the Kelvedon fire station was marked for closure. With the prospect of losing their fire engine again, Kelvedon Parish Council appealed to the Fire Force Commander at Southend. In the meantime the insurance for the fire station came up for renewal, normally they charged this to the NFS, but thinking this might be inopportune they paid the amount themselves. To no avail as the answer, in February 1947, was a straight refusal. The Council's angry response was 'that the NFS be asked to vacate the fire station and notify the Council when the building is clear'. The Council subsequently wrote to their MP Tom Driburg and then to the County Council on the matter but all was in vain and the station was closed in the spring of 1947. *[KPMB 17/03/1947 & 02/06/1947]* (See Appendix XIV).

Retained Firemen

The larger towns continued to operate much as they had before the war with whole-time firemen working a shift system to give twenty-four hour cover. For the rest of the country and for the first time, an overall plan was drawn up for rural fire stations like Coggeshall to ensure their sustainability into the future. These stations, which provide fire cover to 90% of the area of the UK, were to be manned by 'retained firemen', men and women who had primary employment elsewhere but agreed to turn out with the fire engine when required. For this they would receive a 'Retaining Fee' of £12 a year and a payment of 5s for each call attended.

The war left a much more integrated service with different stations regularly working together. In 1946 for example, the Coggeshall brigade attended stack fires at Felsted with the Braintree and Dunmow brigades and they went to another fire in Colne Engaine with the Colchester and Halstead NFS brigades. *[CC 10/05/1946]* Coggeshall firemen spent seven hours at a stack fire at Bouchiers Grange in October, assisted by the Braintree and Halstead NFS. *[CC 04/10/1946]* The last reported fire for the NFS crew was on the 7th November 1947 when they assisted the Tiptree NFS at a fire which destroyed a stack of linseed at Tiptree Priory worth £700. Well supplied with equipment after the war, they used 1,000 feet of hose to bring water across the fields to the fire. *[CC 14/11/1947]*

So after a dramatic and honourable seven years, another stage in the history of our brigade came to an end. Dated 30th March 1948, the Home Secretary, Mr Chuter Eady, sent out an 'Order of the Day' to the officers and men and women of the National Fire Service, thanking all for what they had 'endured and achieved' and passed on the service 'into the hands of the new Fire Authorities.'

11 A NEW START - ESSEX COUNTY FIRE BRIGADE

In 1948 the Government returned the brigades to local control, not, as they had promised, to the Urban and Rural District Councils but to the County and Borough Councils. There was no appetite to return to the organisational nightmare of the hundreds of brigades that existed pre-war. Funding came in part from the rates and the rest from government grant.

Essex had been covered by two Regions and two Fire Forces of the NFS: Metropolitan Essex was in Fire Force 36, part of No 5 London Region and the remainder was in Fire Force 11 which formed part of No 4 Eastern Region. These two fire forces were merged and on 1st April 1948, the Essex County Fire Brigade was created[1]. It was one of the largest brigades in the country, sixty-five of the NFS stations remained open, twenty-eight permanently manned by whole-time firemen working a shift system and thirty-seven manned by 'retained' firemen. The brigade started with a deficit of a hundred and two whole-time and one hundred and fifty-nine retained men. The whole-time deficiency was soon made up but the retained shortfall became endemic and remains to this day. It was always difficult to find people who at a moment's notice could drop what they were doing and rush to the fire station. Despite the shortfall, retained stations went to great lengths to make sure there were enough firemen available at all times to keep their fire station 'on the run', an imperative that took priority over just about anything else including family and social life. A sense of duty reinforced by wartime service and more readily accepted then than it is now.

---

1   The exception was the County Borough of Southend which had its own independent fire brigade

The fire gear for the new service comprised a double breasted fire tunic with a webbing belt and axe pouch, waterproof leggings with leather boots and (except for senior officers) NFS 'Brodie' steel helmets, painted a distinctive cherry-red.

The brigade was divided up for administrative purposes into six divisions. Coggeshall, Station 74, was crewed by retained firemen and became part of 'F' Division with headquarters at Braintree Fire Station, which at that time had a whole-time crew.

The call out systems for retained firemen was described by the Chief Fire Officer as 'many and varied.' *[CFO Annual Report 1957 ERO C/DB 6/1]* Most operated over rented telephone circuits belonging to the General Post Office which sounded a bell in the fireman's house. The system had been much extended after the war to cover all retained firemen so by 1948 the brigade operated 630 of these bells, mostly in firemen's homes but others were in business premises or works clubs where numbers of firemen regularly gathered. There were also fifty-four wartime sirens, used to call out the men during the day by sounding a continuous tone (previously the 'all clear').
[CFO Report 1948 ERO C/DB 6/1]

Billy Green retired in 1948 and Bob Evans took over to become Officer in Charge under the new brigade. A steady and practical man, he owned a garage on East Street. Bert Saunders and Bill Jennings continued as leading hands. Both Stan Barnett and George Maddocks had left the whole-time NFS in 1945 and rejoined the Coggeshall brigade part-time, Stan immediately and George, encouraged by Bert Saunders, a year later.

At the end of the war, the Auxiliary

*Coggeshall's first Essex County Fire Brigade engine.
Formerly a Second World War Auxiliary Towing Vehicle, this was refurbished and fitted with a water tank, pump and hose-reel at the brigade's workshops at Lexden. This was the first of many conversions, all of them sent to Retained Fire Stations. The controls are for the hose-reel, which was pulled out through the square hole above. Both engine and trailer are marked with Coggeshall's station number, 74. Photograph probably taken in November or December 1948.*

Towing Vehicles or 'ATV's which had provided such sterling service were no longer needed and hundreds became available for sale. Most were Austin K2s, robust vehicles with a two ton chassis and a six cylinder petrol engine. They were not fire engines, being designed to carry firemen and equipment and pull a trailer pump. To make use of these surplus vehicles, the Home Office came up with a design to convert them to 'Hose Reel Tenders'. In 1948 the Essex Fire Brigade planned to convert twelve ATVs using this Home Office approved design. This meant adding a 160 gallon water tank and fitting a pump, driven by a power take off from the engine/gearbox. This supplied water to a high pressure hose-reel, stowed centrally inside the vehicle which could be fed out from either side, through slots fitted with rollers. Controls, pressure gauge and a water inlet were placed on the near side of the vehicle. A trailer pump (ex-war and also in plentiful supply) provided greater pumping capacity for standard delivery hose if required. The conversions were carried out in the brigade's own workshops at Lexden. The period of austerity after the war meant there was little money for new fire engines so the ATV conversion programme provided an affordable short term solution. By the end of 1948, only two vehicles had been converted and the first of them went to Coggeshall. In his inaugural annual report of 1948, the Chief Fire Officer described the new appliance as 'an efficient first-aid type fire engine' and continued, 'one such unit was recently allocated to Coggeshall'. *[ERO C/DB 6/1]*

So by the end of 1948, Coggeshall had a 'new' fire appliance, repainted and lined out in the traditional red livery and with its new Essex Fire Brigade Station number, 74, painted on the

*Rear view of Coggeshall's converted Auxiliary Towing Vehicle (ATV) taken in 1948.
Hose racks were fitted inside the rear doorway, with benches for the crew running along each side.
The vehicle was not fitted with a rear door. Behind is the trailer pump, a wartime Beresford Stork, carried on a BSB Trailer.*

engine and on the trailer. The trailer pump was an ex-wartime Beresford Stork model, carried on a BSB (Briggs Motor Bodies) trailer, Briggs being part of the Ford group in Dagenham.

Conversions of ATVs continued at the Lexden workshops and reached a peak in 1953-54, when the brigade had a total of thirty-one ex-ATV fire engines, all allocated to retained stations. They replaced a 'mixed bag' of ageing fire appliances for which it was increasingly difficult to find parts and maintain.
[CFO Annual report 1949 ERO C/DB 6/1]

The Austin ATV, like many vehicles at the time, had a 'crash' gearbox - one with no synchromesh. This required some skill for successful gear changes (using a 'double declutch'). Mis-timings resulted in the gears grating, a sound often accompanied by ironic jeering from the crew. ATVs were inconvenient when reversing, as the trailer pump had to be detached first. Every time the machine returned to home station the trailer would be unhooked and pushed into the bay before the appliance could be reversed in. The modified ATV's had room for perhaps eight firemen: the Officer in Charge and the driver in the front and six on the benches in the back. The record for Coggeshall though, was fourteen which included the smallest man lifted on top of the hose reel.

Coggeshall's first major fire under the new brigade was at 3am on Saturday 3rd July 1948, to Lake and Elliot's works at Chapel Hill in Braintree. One of the night shift workers in the foundry saw flames and raised the alarm. The Braintree brigade was quickly on the scene and called out the Coggeshall and Halstead brigades because of the danger of the fire spreading to other parts of the works. The building was a

Essex County Fire Brigade Station 74 Appliance and Crew 1948.
Sub Officer Bob Evans, Leading Firemen Bert Saunders and Stan Barnett, Firemen Les Spry, George Maddocks, an unknown whole-time officer, Firemen Bill Jennings, J Speed, Fred Tilbrook, Bill Huckle, Peter Joyce.

hundred feet long and thirty feet wide and used as a carpenters shop and paint store. Good work by the brigades using four jets, saw the fire out in half an hour although 25% of the building was severely damaged and the loss was estimated to have been 'at least £3,000'. *[EN 06/07/1948 and Chief Fire Officers Annual Report 1948 ERO C/DB 6/1]*

After sterling service as a Column Officer in the NFS, Lewis White returned to his job as surveyor to the Braintree Council and also became Officer in Charge at Braintree Fire Station. In 1949 the Coggeshall and Braintree brigades under his command saved the ancient Blackwater Mill alongside the main road at Bradwell by preventing a fire in the garage spreading to 'one of the few remaining wooden water mills in Essex'. The owner, Tom Metson, dashed in through the smoke to rescue his car before the brigades arrived. *[EN 12/08/1949]*

Stan Barnett took over as Officer in Charge in 1951 when Bob Evans retired. Coggeshall and Tiptree brigades attended a house fire in February 1952 which seemed to demonstrate that the Blitz spirit still lingered:

'Mr Eric Taylor a Witham Ambulance driver, was returning from duty to his home at Observer Way Kelvedon, when he saw smoke coming from a downstairs window of the house at No 3 and called the fire brigade. The whole of the downstairs floor was severely damaged before the fire was controlled by the Coggeshall and Tiptree brigades, but the other house in the block of two which was in serious danger of catching fire, was saved. The tenant, Mr J Hunwick a box-maker, was at work and his wife was next door "The first I heard of it was when Mr Taylor shouted 'Your house is on fire!'", Mrs. Hunwick told a reporter. A dish of hot-pot in the oven, ready to be cooked for the evening was stewing merrily when the fire brigade arrived. "One of the firemen said it smelled lovely" said Mrs Hunwick. All that is left of the ground floor of the house, is the charred floor and struts which supported the walls of the rooms'. *[BWT 21/02/1952]*

Looking immaculate, Coggeshall's converted ATV pulling out of the station on Market Hill probably in the 1950s.

The 1950s Auxiliary Fire Service

The Auxiliary Fire Service which had ceased to exist in 1941 was revived in the 1950s[2], because of the 'Cold War' and the fear of a nuclear attack. Recruitment to the new service proved to be a continuing problem:

> 'A visit from an officer of the Essex County Fire Brigade Divisional headquarters, stresses the great need for more recruits to the Auxiliary Fire Service. The serious shortage of volunteers for this service is a matter of great concern for the authorities responsible for the general well being and safeguarding of the people during times of war. The Government has sponsored an intensive recruiting campaign to close the vital gaps in Civil Defence. The peace time fire brigade has prepared itself by special training of instructors for the acceptance and training of recruits. The men and women who come forward will be key personnel if and when an emergency arises. Out of a total population of some 100,000 people in this part of Essex only 20 men and 7 women have joined the Auxiliary Fire Service. It is not intended to build up the Civil Defence Service to wartime strength at the present time but it is essential that men and women come forward to form the framework upon which those services could be rapidly expanded at a few hours notice. As far as time goes, volunteers will be asked to give just two hours each week for instructional training.' *[B&WT 04/01/1952]*

There was a substantial AFS Station at Colchester with its own appliances and a formal training system. After basic training the recruits were allowed to ride to fires on the engines of the regular firemen, widely known as the 'reds', to gain practical experience.

Peter Hale applied to join the Coggeshall Fire Brigade at the very time that Stan Barnett was under pressure to establish an AFS section. 'Stan said that if I wanted to go in the fire brigade, I'd got to join the AFS'. Peter thought that Stan pulled a fast one because, unlike the retained firemen, the AFS men and women were unpaid volunteers. *[Peter Hale interview]*

One of the Coggeshall wartime firemen,

---

2 Under the Civil Defence Act of 1949

The station accident book, issued in 1948 and used until 1997, still with plenty of room so there never was a 74/2. There were only three minor accidents in the first five years and all involved the same man – Fred Tilbrook, who was the Coggeshall Cobbler. The first at Greenstead Hall: 'Leg badly bruised, caused by slipping in mud while manhandling trailer pump in field.' The second at Castle Hedingham 'Caused by falling while hauling hose at fire' and the third at Coggeshall 'Bruised finger whilst manhandling pump'. Fred survived.

Braintree Control Desk c1955.

Les Spry, had reached retirement age and left the service, but agreed to take charge of the Coggeshall Auxiliaries. They trained at the fire station on Market Hill and would take the ATV and trailer pump out for practice sessions with Les driving. The Auxiliaries did not last long in the town, the regulars were short of men and keeping the pump on the run was always the first priority. When Peter was successful in joining the 'reds', he took his AFS number and seniority along with him. The Auxiliaries could never recruit anything like the numbers wanted. Even at its peak in 1952-3 there were 355 Auxiliaries in Essex against a target of over 2,500.
[CFO Report 1952 ERO CD/B 6/1]

Communications

Towards the end of 1950 a new remote control call out and communication system was tested at Coggeshall. Designed and built by the brigade 'Comms' section, it connected the Coggeshall station to the divisional control at Braintree Fire Station. The line could carry a signal test, a call-out operating system, speech and could sound the fire siren in case of a power cut at the control point. The test was successful and a new control desk was installed at Braintree in May 1952 and by 1954 a total of thirteen stations were connected. The merging of divisions in 1956 meant that the Braintree Control was closed and its network of lines were then linked to the new control at Colchester via a 'gizmo' called a 'selector point'. From then on, Coggeshall firemen were called out from the Colchester HQ on Cowdray Avenue.

The Coggeshall brigade earned a mention in the 1954 annual report of the Chief Fire Officer as an incident of note. This was call 186 at 15.20hrs on 27th October 1954:

> 'No 74 Station, Coggeshall were called to West Ford Farm, Rivenhall where the brick wall of a building in the course of demolition had collapsed and a workman was trapped under the debris. The man was extricated by brigade personnel and found to have injuries to his left arm and both legs. Removed by ambulance to hospital.' *[ERO CD/B 6/1]*

Fire at Ken Mower's Shop 1957

In 1957, the year that Peter Hale, David Honey, Fred Moss and Fred Polley all joined the station, there was a severe fire at Mr Mower's general store at Market End in Coggeshall. The fire vividly illustrates the fire-fighting spirit of the time.

A dense fog had settled over the town on a bitterly cold December morning. The bells went down at 04.30, but Ken Mower's shop was already well alight before anyone had noticed at that early hour. Sub Officer Stan Barnett, lived only a couple of doors away on East Street and would have had a good view as he answered the call. He reached the station seconds later, donned his fire gear and without waiting for the crew, opened up the station, drove the engine to the shop and got it to work. He managed to force his way into the building with the hose-reel and started to knock down the fire on the ground floor. As the firemen arrived at the station they found the doors wide open and the appliance gone. David Honey remembers the night and the thick fog 'We could hear the pump running but couldn't make out where it was at first'.

Ken Mower's shop December 1957. The unglazed windows are the only visible evidence of the recent fire.

The crew soon joined Stan and with his loud encouragement, worked their way upstairs to tackle the seat of the fire on the first floor and then cutting away the lath and plaster to attack the fire inside the wall. Afterwards, Ken Mower wrote to the Divisional Officer at Colchester, DO Kehoe, praising the work of the Coggeshall crew and providing the first eye-witness account of the crew at work:

> '..My wife and I would like to express our appreciation and gratitude for the efforts of the Coggeshall Fire Brigade in the early hours of Wednesday December 4th under the direction of Sub Officer Stan Barnett whose lusty voice (and curses) brought a humour which helped to lighten the tragic circumstances.
>
> It is difficult and may seem unfair to single out any particular incident from a crew which worked so splendidly together but we feel we must mention the courage of Sub Officer Barnett who arrived alone and extinguished the fire on the ground floor single handed, also Leading Fireman Tilbrook and the three or four members of the crew who were there in the early stages and prevented what might have been a very dangerous situation…. Ken Mower'

[Courtesy of Mick Barnett]

Fire Brigade Life in the 1950s and 60s

From 1952, all retained recruits were required to have a medical examination. David Honey recalls his at Braintree carried out by Dr Gill. David, Peter Hale, Fred Polley and Fred Moss all took the medical at the same time (all having joined on the same day in July 1957). Redolent of those times, when the men were lined up afterwards and Fred Moss asked, 'Well, have I passed?' he was told, 'You run along, it's nothing to do with you at this stage'. *[David Honey]* The retirement age was set at 60 but an annual medical was required after the age of 55. *[CFO Report 1952 ERO C/D B 6/1]*

New recruits were trained on the station, there was no central training school for retained firefighters until 1963. The station, built in a hurry at the start of the war, had no drill yard and there was no tower for ladder drills. The river was used, as it always had been for pumping practice, the roads, quieter then than now were used for hose running and other stations such as Colchester were visited which had better facilities. The Officer in Charge decided when a new recruit was ready to go 'on the run' - that is to ride the engine to fires and this would be confirmed by the whole-time Assistant Divisional Officer (ADO). Under his watchful eye, the recruit would take part in a drill, be tested on knots and lines, procedures and equipment. Training would continue 'on the job'. It did not always happen in this way, Peter Hale was riding before he completed his basic training, 'We were so short of men you see'. *[Peter Hale interview]*

A Heavy Goods Vehicle licence was needed to drive the appliance and training for this was allowed after a few years' experience, using a spare fire engine and usually done after the working day or on a Sunday. The brigade had its own examiner, DO Harrington. Hearing some noisy gear changes from David Honey, Harrington rather eccentrically advised him to take his time by suggesting he 'read a newspaper' during the procedure.

Ken Mower's shop, ground floor.
Showing how the fire had penetrated through the ceiling and behind the panelling from the room above.

Fire at the Doctor's House, 1958

When the doctor's roof caught alight, there was no fire engine or brigade in the town. Stanley Haines recalled the incident:

> 'There was a lot of smoke coming from the roof and quite a few people had gathered[3]. I asked if anyone had called the brigade but I decided to go down to the station to be sure. I was surprised when I got there to find it empty apart from a couple of firemen who told me that the engine and crew had gone to Braintree.'

The call was relayed to control and the two firemen, David Honey (known as 'Hun') and Ian Chaplin made their way to the fire by bike, to see if they could do anything. Someone was playing a garden hose ineffectively towards the roof and inside the house, the Doctor, brusque at the best of times, was becoming apoplectic. They watched him shouting down the phone and as they backed away, he tore the machine from the wall and flung it to the ground. His gaze then fell on the two firemen 'I need a ladder!!' The Doctor had quite a bit of silverware in the loft and wanted to get it before it was destroyed. 'Well we haven't got a ladder' said Hun, perhaps not too diplomatically, as he backed out the door. The fire engines from Coggeshall, Braintree and Tiptree had been mobilised. The Coggeshall crew received the call at Braintree where they were

---

3   Including the author, eight years old and on a tiny bike belonging I think to Nick Coe.

Fire at Mower's shop.
The room above the shop, cleared of its contents and showing the intensity of the fire of 4th December 1957.

Fire at the Doctor's House, Church Street 1958.
This view, taken from near the Woolpack, shows thick smoke issuing from the roof before the brigade arrived.

being issued with new uniforms. The Braintree appliance had already gone and Coggeshall followed. Fortunately the fire was soon under control and although the roof and first floor were in a mess, the building and the silverware were saved.

The Brigade in the 1960s

Almost a decade after it was established, the brigade was making determined efforts to finally replace the wartime ATVs, with proper fire engines - 'limousine style' Dodge Water Tenders, fifteen of which were ordered in 1957 alone. One of these new engines, allocated to Tiptree, turned out for the fire at the Doctor's house. The war-time appliances of Coggeshall and Braintree looked conspicuously old fashioned in comparison.

Perhaps aware of its coming fate, the trailer pump, by then a Coventry Climax type, made an escape bid. Returning from a call, the ATV was drawn up in front of the station and a couple of men got out to detach the trailer so the vehicle could be backed in. No trailer pump! Everyone got back in and retraced the route along the road to Kelvedon, fearful of the damage that may have been caused when it came off and the paperwork that would have to be completed. The first trip came up blank but on the second it was spotted in a muddy pond at Pound farm on a notorious right angled bend. It was recovered, cleaned up and no paperwork was required.

By 1962 all stations had modern fire engines, then called self propelled pumps and by 1964 all the Auxiliary Towing Vehicles were gone, sold off at public auctions.

Uniforms were issued from a specially made trailer which had been built and commissioned in 1959 and was towed around the brigade by a short wheelbase Austin two-ton van. *[CFO Annual Report 1959 ERO C/D/B 6/3]* This would park up by the

Fire at the Doctor's House, Church Street 1958.
In the centre is Coggeshall's ATV, a little late to the scene, with a hose-reel run out. On the left is an appliance from Braintree, also towing a trailer pump. On the right a motorcycle policeman directs traffic.

water towers next to Braintree Fire Station on a Sunday morning. The fire gear comprised rubber boots, tunic, leather belt and black cork helmet. The black oilskin leggings, pulled on over the trousers, were separate – one for each leg. The gap between the two was invariably the first to get wet during a fire. The 'Undress' uniform was a blue shirt, jacket, trousers, black shoes and a peaked cap. A dark Mackintosh was also supplied of an old fashioned cut. David Honey remembers his first 'clothing parade' during which he was asked for his cap size. A gravelly voiced Braintree fireman by the name of 'Chunky' Moyles, who was assisting, grabbed Hun's backside to test its dimensions and shouted 'Six and seven eighths!' A cap of that dimension was passed down and proved to be a snug fit.

When Jack Parry joined in 1964, he was the first Coggeshall fireman to undertake a Basic Training course. For this he reported to Ilford on Sundays, where the post-war Auxiliary Fire Service Training Centre had been modified and opened for brigade use in 1963. Training Officers entertained the retained recruits with a series of lectures and practical drills. Jack Parry reported every Sunday for four or five weeks:

'We did lessons inside first and then we had to go out, it was January and bloody cold. I remember we had to crawl along a charged hose with the branch flailing about which we had to bring under control. There was also a test: we went into some old wartime huts on the training ground - we were put in at one end in the dark and smoke and you had to get down to the other end and outside as fast as you could.'

David Honey recalled that a training caravan was introduced and made its way around the county's fire stations. It was used to give 'Basic Fire Training' theory and every member of the brigade had to take part and then pass oral and written exams.

Increasingly, the station had to deal with Road Traffic Accidents (RTAs) but in the 1950s, the appliance carried little by the way of equipment other than small tools, such as a hacksaw, a hammer and a screwdriver. Although Coggeshall was not well equipped for such calls,

230   Fires, Firemen & Other Mishaps

Tiptree's new Dodge Appliance at the Doctor's House fire in 1958, looking very modern compared to the Coggeshall ATV. Note also the firemen's fire gear, boots, black oilskin leggings, tunic with leather belt and axe and black cork helmet.

the brigade was. By the mid 1960s, Essex, it seems, was leading the field in this area with two specialist vehicles with the acronym 'PEST' these were sent to all RTA incidents. David Honey recalls:

> 'The Pump Escape Salvage Tender. It was a massive thing, there were two in the brigade, one at Colchester and one I think at Grays. It carried everything you could think of. We were taken down to Colchester on a Drill night to look at it. I remember there was a big fire exhibition up in London, we went to the Essex stand and there it was - this new salvage tender was the latest thing.'
> [David Honey - the Exhibition was at Olympia in July 1965.]

There was no rule then about how many firemen rode on the engine to a fire and this could get a bit out of hand:

> 'We had a fire call one night and the engine pulled out as the last of us threw ourselves on board. There wasn't much room in the back and I guess we were making a bit of noise because we had only got as far as the 'Cricketers' when Stan [Barnett] turned round in his seat to see what all the fuss was about. There were eleven of us in the back. Stan ordered the driver to stop and pointed - "You're out, you're out, you're out!" and so on. We trudged back to the station thinking about the turn-out fee we had lost'. [David Honey]

In the 1960s retained firemen were still being called out using the wartime system of a 'call bell' and day-time siren. The bells were installed within days of a new man joining up. Fred Moss discovered that by completing a form, a telephone could also be installed and with the brigade already paying for the line, it was cheap to run. [Bunty Moss interview] For most firemen, the last three digits of their brigade number became the telephone number[4]. There were three separate, dedicated call bell circuits in the town carried on the telephone poles alongside the public lines and they would be tested weekly from the station by operating them briefly six times, whilst isolating the siren, a job that needed both hands. The bell was very noisy, 'It used to go off like hell!' said Peter Hale, 'and couldn't be turned off', so the whole household was disturbed. The bell was loud enough to wake up the neighbours, which is what happened on Jack Parry's first night in Coggeshall. Living then in Albert Place, he and his wife were woken in the middle of the night by the bell in David Honey's house next door. They wondered what on earth it was. Jack, who had a tobacconists shop on Church Street, was soon recruited. He remembers one night when the bells went down (his bell was fixed in the bedroom), he was hopping about, trying to get his trousers on when he slipped on the uneven boards of the old house and found himself under the wardrobe 'the wife couldn't stop laughing'. [Jack Parry interview]

The siren was operated via a time-switch to prevent it sounding during the night, from 10.30pm to 7.00am. The system was tested weekly during Thursday Drill Night, by request to the Colchester control room and the result relayed back to them by phone and recorded in the station log.

When a fire call was received, the first man into the station would pick up the phone and report: 'Station 74, Coggeshall'. A typical message might be: 'Send your pump to a car fire at West Street Coggeshall, message timed at 05.45'. The message was repeated back and the Officer in Charge would confirm that the appliance was proceeding. There was no appliance radio at this time so when the incident had been dealt with, the 'Stop Message' would be sent by the station phone, on return[5].

The station was 'compact'. When the new Dodge arrived, there was just room for it to reverse inside if the mirrors were pulled in first. A few years later another engine, probably a brigade spare, seemed to go in alright but did not want to come out. Its more steeply angled ladder had compressed the suspension on the way in and the machine 'popped up' once inside. The door frame was cut away at the top and the engine was

---

4   Coggeshall numbers only had three digits then.

5   The phone only had a '4' on it, all the other holes on the dial were filled in.

A fire at Colton & Shearman's scrapyard, looking up the Colne Road. Date: probably early 1960s.

released. Hooks on the bay wall accommodated fire tunics and helmets with the leggings and boots underneath on a board just off the floor. The space was so tight that when there was a call, the firemen donning their fire gear made it difficult for later arrivals to squeeze past and the machine was often moved forward to give more room. The station prided itself on a fast turnout, the firemen running, cycling or driving to the station and abandoning bikes, cars and carpet slippers on the road outside.

To celebrate its tenth anniversary in 1958, the brigade decided to hold an Open Day and all stations were thrown open to the public. This proved so successful that the event has continued ever since, although now stations pick their own day. In 1958, grateful parents were quick to see the opportunity for a bit of free child-minding and dropped their children off at the station, picking them up later in the day. The next year there was a rule that children should be accompanied and this remains in force.

1959 was the station's busiest since the war with 142 calls – at least double the usual total. The summer was hot and dry resulting in many field fires. The brigade budget for the retained service in 1959 was estimated at £25,000, but the bill by the year's end was actually £51,000.

The station was riding high and won the 'A' Division Fire Brigade Quiz in both 1961 and 1962 but probably reluctant to become the object of envy, never featured in the list of winners for the rest of the century.

There was a notable fire in 1961, 'Alarm 418' on 24th February at 04.17 when the station was called out, along with Colchester and several others, to the Weyroc Chipboard factory at Marks Tey. This building, on two floors, measured some 180 feet x 30 feet and contained some 200 tons of chipboard and 24,000 sacks of raw materials as well as other industrial equipment. Twelve jets were at work and the fire destroyed the roof and 50% of the building, the rest severely damaged by water and smoke. The site alongside the A12, was until recently, occupied by Andersons.

On 30th January 1963 two workmen were overcome by gas whilst digging to repair a fractured gas main near the clothing factory in Vane Lane, Coggeshall. Collapsing unseen, they fell unconscious at the bottom of the trench[6]. Two Coggeshall firemen, George Maddocks and his son-in-law Fred Moss had been at the station and decided to walk up and have a word with the men who George knew from his job with the Water Board. Finding them, George and Fred recovered the bodies and moved them to safety before starting artificial respiration. A message was sent and the brigade arrived with Stan Barnett in charge. The workmen began to show signs of life and eventually came round. Later that year a ceremony was held at the fire station and George, Fred and Stan received a Meritorious Conduct Award from the Essex County Council for their actions in saving the men. George retired from the brigade in June 1964 but in October that year he was at it again. An overhead electricity line had fallen on a workman and George used a branch to remove the cable and attempted 'with heart massage' to revive him, despite being told by a watching policeman that he 'was wasting his time'. The man, James Howard, came round and although severely burned, eventually recovered. George received the Royal Humanitarian Society resuscitation award.

In 1963 all 105 front line appliances and sixteen officers' cars were fitted with radios for the first time. A main and several subsidiary transmitters had been set up to provide coverage for the whole county and this went live on 1st April. All firemen were examined and if successful, issued with a certificate of competence as a 'Radio Telephony Operator'. For the first time, crews could communicate while they were on the road.

1964 was a busy year for the station, another long hot summer and stubble burning after the harvest: a total 132 calls were logged, just ten fewer than the record year of 1959.

---

6   The gas at that time was coal gas which was poisonous.

Presentation of the Meritorious Conduct Awards, April 1963.
Fred & Bunty Moss, Stan & Annie Barnett and
George & Amy Maddocks.
Wives and families were very much part of the station.
Photo courtesy of Bunty Moss

Pay and the Ben Fund

The pay system was cash based and as operated in Coggeshall, somewhat idiosyncratic:

> 'The logbook recorded the fires and drills attended and other payments due for each man. When pay-day arrived, Stan Barnett the Officer in Charge, would consult the book and announce the sum due, for example £5 2s 6d. "Right!" he said as he pulled out a roll of notes and licked his thumb to peel off one, two, three, four, five. Then the fist would dig into his pocket and a big handful of change thrown on the table. Half a crown would be picked up and Stan would say "Hang on a minute, I'll toss you for it". The coin would be flicked and examined "Ah sorry that's for the Ben Fund". If the fireman suggested that on the whole he would sooner just have the money, it was reluctantly

234   *Fires, Firemen & Other Mishaps*

Fire at Colton & Shearman's scrapyard. First photos of Coggeshall's Dodge appliance. Probably 1960s.

handed over. We were always paid in cash and other than the book there was never any paperwork involved.' [David Honey]

Stan Barnett was always keen to raise money for the Fireman's Benevolent Fund, as Dave Honey put it: 'It doesn't matter what it was, the Ben Fund always came first'. Stan was nearly always seen with a cigar in the side of his mouth. David Tassel, an Auxiliary Fire Service Sub Officer from Colchester remembers his first view of him.

> 'He was standing in the middle of the road in his fire gear with his tunic undone and a big cigar jutting from his mouth, stopping the traffic to get his fire engine out'.

The cigars were Havanas, specially ordered by Jack Parry at his Church Street shop in boxes of 25. It was on a visit to pick up his cigars in 1964, after the nightime call bell incident, that Stan enlisted Jack into the brigade. When Stan came to retire in 1969 the crew bought him a wooden cigar box as a leaving present, something out of the ordinary, the box had been made by the renowned Coggeshall woodcarver Bryan Saunders. In a scenario known only too well by all retained firefighters, the event was interrupted by a fire call. Wearing their best suits the crew ran out of the Chapel Hotel and across the road to the station. A car had crashed on West Street and was on its roof. Kenny Taylor, the smallest fireman, was pushed into the vehicle and helped its elderly occupant out, apparently unharmed. [Jack Parry interview]

At another crash on the Colchester Road, a few years later, the driver was found to be trapped. A new recruit watched as a hacksaw was requested and then fainted as a human leg was passed out of the vehicle. It was, of course, an artificial leg. A good story but one with the whiff of a fire service myth of which there are many, some true, usually involving naked people trapped in unlikely circumstances and mostly too coarse to be recorded here.

Annual Dinner Dance. The Chief Fire Officer, Jim Ellis, is speaking, Stan Barnett is nearest the camera. 1960s.

The Annual Dinner Dance

The regular money raising event for The Fire Services National Benevolent Fund[7] was the station's Annual Dinner Dance. The first was held in an upstairs room behind the Chapel Hotel and nearly ended in a fight. A cake donated as a raffle prize had been won by the war-time Chief Fire Officer, Lewis White. It seems that White accidentally dropped the cake but then kicked it as it reached the floor as it were a football. Stan took great exception to this and tempers flared, understandably on Stan's part as the cake had been made by his wife. Despite this inauspicious start the dinner dances, continued with great success and were thereafter held in St Peter's Hall in Coggeshall. They were formal affairs, attended by the Chief Fire Officer, whose driver by tradition, was the only person to have a free meal. Tickets were in great demand both locally and among fire service personnel, whole-time and retained and the hall was always full. Caterers provided a three course meal and after the loyal toast (proposed by the most junior member of the crew and a job which many years later fell to me),

7   Now called the Firefighters Charity.

cigars and cigarettes were lit, speeches were made and answered, each finished with a toast. Most important of all, a substantial cheque for the Benevolent Fund would be presented to the chief. Then the tables were cleared, the band struck up and dancing would begin. Many people, including the Coggeshall shop-holders had been approached to donate a raffle prize and this was drawn during a break in the dancing. Through all this, the fire engine stayed on the run (for local calls) and an officer from Colchester would stand by at the station, ready to run up the road and alert the crew if a call came through.

The dinner dances continued over many years and by the time of the last one in the late 1990s, there had been something over forty-four of them, a great and proud tradition.

The Brigade in the 1970s

A solitary logbook has survived from 1970-71 and this gives an insight into the operation of the station at this time. The Officer in Charge was Sub Officer Polley and several of the entries are probably in his meticulous hand. The logbook was a record of the activity of the station and was used to calculate pay. The entries have a standard format. Drill night was on a Thursday evening (as it was in 1939 and remains so to this day). A typical Drill night was recorded on 11th June 1970:

'19.00 On Duty for Drills
In Attendance F/M Moss, Honey, Taylor, Yeo, Speed.
L/F Hale, L/F Gladwin, S/O Polley I/C
Remote control and call bells tested.
Found in order A Div. H.Q. informed.
Men engaged in weekly tests.
Cleaning appliance and equipment.
19.30 Pump and men left for Bridge St Coggeshall
Hose testing and drill.
20.30 Pump returned to station.
Radio tested strength '3' [8]
21.00 Men dismissed.'

---

8   Strength 3 was 'Loud and Clear', 2 was 'Broken' and 1 'Unreadable'.

Fred Tilbrook (left) being presented with his twenty year Long Service and Good Conduct Medal in 1968 by the CFO, Jim Ellis, at the Dinner Dance. Stan Barnett is on the right.

The men occasionally reported to Colchester or Braintree for Drills or lectures. 'Carry-down' drill was practised regularly at Colchester drill tower. In this a live volunteer (later a dummy) was carried down the ladder on the shoulders of a fireman. 'Everest' gear was usually attached in case anything went wrong and this was meant to automatically lock up and prevent the casualty from falling to the ground. Live carry-down drills continued as part of basic training until the 1980s. Whole-time officers would sometimes arrive at the station to instruct the crew on Drill Night. The rather diminutive Station Officer Lufkin, for example, lectured once on 'The Fireman's Lift' and was then challenged to carry Stan Barnett. Lufkin blanched but squared up and tucked his shoulder into Stan's groin. With a mighty effort, a deal of grunting and staggering, he did it. Stan was aloft!

The Chapel Hotel was conveniently placed opposite the fire station on Market Hill and at 9pm after drills, tradition dictated that the men should resort there for a pint or two. The station enjoyed a good social life and both men and wives would regularly meet at the 'Chapel' on a

Crew Photo 1967, Dodge Appliance.
Peter Maddocks, Jack Parry, David Honey, Peter Hale, Ken Speed, Ian Chaplin, Fred Moss
Kenny Taylor, Lenny Gladwin, Stan Barnett, Fred Polley, Royston Yeo.

Saturday night.

The station continued to be called out via the siren and call bells. Responding to a call-out, the details were relayed by telephone ('T' in the logbook). For example, this call on 6th September 1970:

> '08.00 By T from A Div HQ
> Send pump to Stettles Farm Belchamp Otten
> 08.02 Pump and men left F/M Moss, Taylor, Chaplin, Leatherdale, L/F Hale, L/F Gladwin, S/O Polley I/C
>
> F/M Honey station duty
> 08.35 F/M Honey off duty
> 14.25 Pump returned to station
> 14.35 Men dismissed.'

The log shows turnout times of two or three minutes and although this was an accepted convention, it was probably not far from the truth. The turnout was certainly very quick and a welcome entertainment for the locals, recovering as they were from the deafening wail of the siren, painfully loud if heard from close by. In addition to Drills and fire calls, the brigade regularly 'stood-by' at both Braintree and Colchester, providing cover for these towns when their own engines were out.

Although as we have seen, the brigade provided a basic training course after 1963, many firemen who had joined before then had been trained on the station and on the job. In 1970 the brigade caught up with some of them. Ken Speed had joined in 1956 and Ken Taylor in 1957 but after thirteen or more years, both were now required to attend a Basic Training Course. They reported to Colchester fire station or service workshops at Lexden for training on three consecutive Sundays.

The number of crew riding the appliance to a fire call was still not subject to limits. A call to Earls Colne High Street on 14th July 1970 had a crew of nine men and another to Copford Green had a crew of ten! That was the entire Coggeshall brigade at the time. In contrast, three men were mobilised to Tiptree in June and just two for a call to Eight Ash Green, the Sub Officer and a Leading Fireman. By 1981 the maximum number of crew was limited to seven and the minimum four, although a crew of three could proceed but another appliance was then dispatched to back them up.

On two occasions in the log the pump failed to turn out when called. For both calls, just two firemen reported for duty[9]. Such a failure to respond was regarded as a very serious matter, both by the station and by senior officers and an enquiry would follow.

There were many power cuts during the winter of 1970-71 and these had consequences for the station. A power cut on the 8th December, blacked out 'A' Division HQ at Colchester. When this happened, a fireman was required to stand-by at Coggeshall (and every station) to operate the call-out system manually. Coggeshall Fire Station was itself subject to a blackout at 22.00 on the same day. In this case, neither the call-out bells nor the siren could be operated, so a full crew remained on stand-by at the station. They were only dismissed when power was restored, the call bells and clocks were checked and the siren time-switch reset. The siren sounded 'in error' on 7th January, the men turning out with no fire to attend and it stopped working entirely on 10th July, L/F Hale stood-by at the station until it was repaired.

Deficiencies were promptly dealt with. When the appliance failed its vacuum test at the river in Bridge Street, during a drill night in July 1971, it was sent off to brigade workshops in Lexden at 9.10pm with a crew of five and returned after repairs some two hours later.

One or two firemen regularly reported for two hours of station cleaning, this was one of the perks of the job as it provided a bit of extra income. In May 1971, a senior officer after examining the record decided that the cleaning was being overdone and left instructions that it should only be carried out 'If it was essential'. This underestimated the Coggeshall men. From that date, although the entries continued as before, they were now recorded as 'On duty for *essential* station cleaning'. The station was

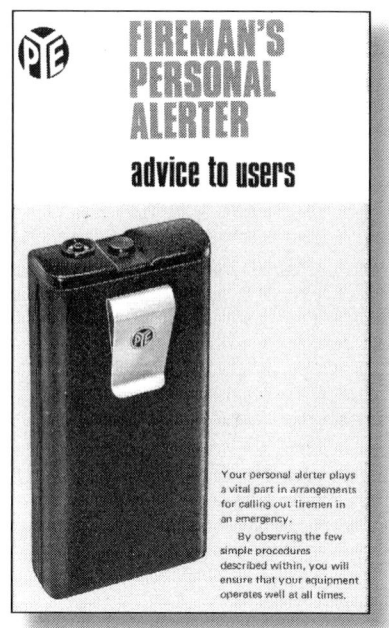

The radio alerter which brought an end to the alarm bells and siren c1973

closely managed, evident in the regular visits of whole-time senior officers, Divisional Officer Hawkins and Assistant Divisional Officers Aspinall and Parish who inspected the station, appliances and equipment before signing the log if everything was found to be in order. The ethos and atmosphere was military, senior officers were saluted, there was a 'parade' on drill night, the men brought to 'Attention!', 'At Ease!' and 'Dismiss!'

Modern Breathing Apparatus (BA) using compressed air was introduced during the late 1960s, first to whole-time stations and then between 1971 and 1973 to retained stations[10]. A record book recording weekly tests and fires show that Coggeshall was using the sets from August 1973. Intensive training was required before BA could be worn and although not then compulsory, most of the Coggeshall firemen

---
9 An Officer in Charge and a qualified HGV driver were needed.

10 Breathing Apparatus first came into use during the 1950s with Essex firemen being trained in the use of the Siebe-Gorman 'Proto' set, which was a re-breather system, using oxygen to refresh and reuse exhaled air. The service upgraded to the lighter and safer Mark V Proto sets in 1962. Proto sets were never carried on Coggeshall's appliance.

Fred Moss, Peter Hale and David Honey after receiving their Long Service and Good Conduct Medals for twenty years' service, in 1977. DO Reg Hawkins is second from the right.

undertook it. David Honey, one of the first to qualify, completed his one week training at Colchester and Clacton where special BA chambers had been constructed. These could be heated and filled with smoke to give a more realistic training experience. At the end of the week there was a theory exam and a practical test.

The days of the call bell and siren were numbered. By 1972 twenty-five retained stations in Essex had been converted to a radio call out system using personal alerters and the remaining fifteen soon followed. The alerters made by 'Pye', were clipped to the belt or pocket and re-charged on the bedside table overnight. Although the Coggeshall siren remained on standby it was never used again in anger.

On the morning of 22nd January 1973 Fred Polley, the Officer in Charge at Coggeshall, was at the station responding to a fire call and about to open the bay doors when he collapsed. An ambulance was called but Fred never regained consciousness. He left a wife a son and a daughter. He was just 52 years old.

The station attended a dramatic fire in the autumn of 1973 at the Woolworth store on Colchester High Street, which eventually burnt to the ground. A fire in the stockroom spread to the restaurant on the upper floor where some customers refused to evacuate even when the flames became visible. One elderly lady insisted on finishing the pot of tea that she had paid for. Fire precautions in the store were poor and it was largely due to the good work of the firemen from Colchester who were first at the scene, that no-one was seriously hurt.

Fire at Bouchier's Grange

'It was the middle of the night when the bells went down, I woke up and looked out and I could see a massive bright light in the sky and I thought good lord! You think and get your bearings and then I realised it was Bouchier's Grange.' *[David Honey]*

An ancient house on the Markshall Road Bouchier's had always been a farmhouse but the tenant farmer, Jimmy Bell, had moved out to a new bungalow opposite and had little affection for the place. The cause of the fire was never discovered. By the time the brigade arrived flames were coming out of the roof. Peter Hale who was OIC made 'pumps five' – two came from Braintree and two from Halstead. Despite their best efforts, by the end, the house was just a shell with a chimney stack standing in the centre. The crew returned to the station, not for the first time, thick with dirt, soot and sweat[11]. *[David Honey interview]* All that remains of the house today is the garden wall and the gate that once led to the front door.

---

11 Retained firemen wore their own clothes under their fire-gear and this regularly meant a lot of heavy-duty washing, not a casual matter in the days before washing machines. Firemen were eventually given a 'washing powder allowance' but it was still (usually) down to the wives to do the work. Because of the pervasive reek of fire, on returning from a call, Bob Raven was instructed by his wife to leave his soiled clothing on the doorstep. On one occasion, finding the pile in the middle of the kitchen floor, she flung it out of the window and into a neighbour's garden. *[Recalled by Bob's daughter, Janet Tansley]*

Crew with the Dennis F38 in 1980.
Steve White, Colin Saxton, Doug Corder, David Salmon, David Gooding
Ian Chaplin, LF Fred Moss, SubO Peter Hale, LF Mark Shearman, David Honey.

The Dennis F38 parked outside the station in 1981.

*September 1981. The Dennis F38 stands in the bay of the Market Hill Station for the last time.
'A 6.5 litre, straight six cylinder Rolls-Royce, Twin Carbs, Twin Coils, it was a wonderful machine.'
An assessment by David Honey in 2012.*

Highfields on fire, May 1977.

Fire at Highfields

At 11.30 am on Wednesday 11th May 1977, fire swept through Highfields, a sixteenth-century, timber-framed building off West Street in Coggeshall. The blaze seems to have started on the second floor of the house where builders were working. Six fire engines from Coggeshall, Colchester, Braintree, Tiptree and Witham fought the blaze but strong winds and low water pressure hampered the firemen. Highfields was owned by Wilfred Bull and his wife Patricia and they had only recently moved in. Onlookers reported that they had heard large bangs and cracks from the farmhouse from over a mile away. Fireman Dave Mayes from Braintree, was injured during the fire and rushed to Essex County Hospital but fortunately suffered only minor injuries. The fire was under control at 1pm but not before the inside of the building was burnt out, leaving only an empty shell. Workers from Mr Bull's antique shop in the village tried to salvage what they could from the house but thousands of pounds worth of antiques were destroyed. The house was later rebuilt.

A New Appliance

After years of active service, by the early 1970s, the Dodge was coming to the end of its useful life. In 1967 the brigade had bought two new 'Dennis' appliances fitted with Rolls-Royce petrol engines. Both carried a 'wheeled escape' a heavy ladder mounted on two big wheels allowing it to be manoeuvred at a fire. One of the engines after serving at Hadleigh fire station for a number of years, was returned to service workshops and converted to a water tender. The vehicle's design allowed the capacity of the internal water tank to be adjusted depending on the ladder carried. Fitted with a more modest 'Ajax' wooden ladder, it could hold three hundred gallons of water, twice the amount as when carrying the wheeled escape. The pumping controls instead of being at the rear, were sited at the sides and this added to the appliance's distinctiveness. After conversion the engine was sent to Coggeshall where it was received with enthusiasm.

The number of calls attended by the station, although very variable, had been steadily increasing, from 23 calls in 1948 to 84 in 1965.
[Figures from the CFO Annual reports]

The Fire Station on Market Hill 1939-81.
Note the limited clearance through the doors and the frame cut away at the top after an earlier appliance became 'stuck' inside.

The Coggeshall crew parade for the last time outside the station on Market Hill, 1981.
Back row: Ian Chaplin, David Honey, Steve White, David Salmon, Mark Shearman
Front: David Gooding, Fred Moss, Mark Chaplin, Colin Saxton.

Ex-firemen, wives and widows meet for the last time outside the Market Hill Station in May 1981.
1. John Leatherdale, 2. Stan Barnett, 3. Stan Saunders, 4. Bert Saunders, 5. Mrs Barnett, 6. Lenny Everett,
7. Mrs Marks (Widow of Lou Marks), 8. Len Cheek, 9. Bill Dale, 10. Mrs Polley (Widow of Fred Polley), 11. J Speed,
12. George Maddocks, 13. Les Spry, 14. Bill Huckle, 15. Vic Lawrence, 16. Frank Shearman, 18. Jack Parry, 19. Chris Evans,
20. Lenny Gladwin, 21. The Bugler, Ken Thomas (NFS in Kelvedon).

The New Fire Station

The fire station on Market Hill was built under emergency conditions on a site which was too cramped to provide anything more than very basic facilities. As early as 1955 the brigade began to look around for a site to build a new fire station. It was hoped that the sale of the town centre site would provide the capital for the project. Various locations were looked at over the years but it was not until the late 1970s that a suitable (cheap) piece of land was found alongside the road to Earls Colne on what was then the edge of town. The land was bought and plans drawn up. In keeping with the long tradition of 'Coggeshall Jobs', in June 1980 before a brick was laid, two painters from the Essex County Council turned up one day 'To paint the new station.'
[Stan Barnett letter to Editor 'Escape' magazine 24/10/1980]

The site on the Earls Colne Road was at one time a clay pit and brickworks known as 'The Brickyard' and owned by Sam Birkin. It was also where co-incidentally in September 1917, Mr H B Saunders, father of Stan and Bert of the wartime brigade, had dug up a whopper of a potato weighing in at 1lb 7½oz. *[BBA 12/09/1917]*

Some of the land had been used as a rubbish dump for many years and by local repute once contained a 'bit of good stuff' discarded by Americans from the nearby air base at the end of the war. There was also some 'bad stuff':

'Edgar Frank Rutkin aged 14 of Mount Road, Coggeshall was seriously injured on Saturday when an object which he had found in a dump on the Earls Colne Road exploded. Edgar and other boys ignored the "Trespassers will be Prosecuted" notices and climbed through the fencing to play. Edgar found what appeared to be a slender, short piece of brass with two lengths of wire attached. Returning home he began to experiment with his find, using a cycle lamp battery. Suddenly there was a violent explosion. His left hand was badly hurt and particles of metal passed through his clothing and marked his body.'[12] *[CC 18/03/1949]*

---

12 Apparently the object was a battery which shorted out when he put power into it. Edgar survived and later joined the RAF. Forty years on his nephew, Andrew Rutkin, became a Coggeshall fireman. *[Thanks to Andrew and his Aunt Eva, Edgar's sister for these details]*

Site of the new fire station c1979. Although the telephone pole is in much the same place this view is nowadays almost unrecognisable as the station is surrounded by houses.

Construction well underway.

The architect for the building was the Huckle Tweddell Partnership in association with the County Architect. The intention was to 'provide a building which relates in character to traditional buildings in the area', which it clearly does not. The builders, T J Evers Ltd of Tiptree, began work at the end of 1980 and the station was completed in nine months at a cost of £151,000. Extensive piling was needed to carry the weight of the station on the unstable ground beneath it. The station includes 'a roomy and well lit appliance bay, office, communications room, a recreation/lecture room with a small refreshment bar, lavatory and shower facilities, drying and cleaning facilities and a dedicated Breathing Apparatus servicing room'. There is a good sized drill yard with an underground static water tank and a substantial drill tower with four floors and fitted out for drying hose. Spacious, clean and modern, it was a huge contrast to the old station.

Last Rites

After forty-two years, time was up for the station on Market Hill. It had served the brigade well through some of the most difficult times and there were many people with fond memories who wanted to bid their farewells. This resulted in a remarkable assembly of retired Coggeshall firemen, wives and widows, several having served in the war-time brigade. Standing in front of the appliance in May 1981 and with Stan Barnett's National Fire Service Flag unfurled, they were brought to attention for the final time as a bugler sounded the last post.

The station closed in September 1981 but stood for many more years, its red paintwork slowly fading to pink. The building provided occasional storage space for the community but was eventually demolished in 1988 and the site rebuilt as shops with flats above, looking much as it did in 1939 before the station was built.

Grand Opening

The opening ceremony for the new station took place on 10th September 1981, the Lord Lieutenant of Essex, Admiral Sir Andrew Lewis, the principal guest, with the Chairman of the Fire and Public Protection Committee, Councillor J V Storey and the Chief Fire Officer, Roger Paramour and other less exalted officers in attendance. The firemen were inspected and then as the daylight faded, gave a demonstration drill. Sir Andrew officially declared the station open and unveiled a brass plaque commemorating the occasion. Long service medals were presented to a number of Essex firemen and then tea and buns were served. The whole thing was judged a great success.

Within a year, two things had happened. The first was my arrival as a new recruit and the second was that the station, convivial as ever, got its own licensed bar. I will leave it to you, dear reader, to guess which was greeted with the most enthusiasm!

Doodley

More than one fireman, working alone at the new station, reported strange noises, or of hearing someone come into the station only to find no-one there. At first this was put down to 'just the station settling' or 'the bay doors rattling in the wind' but although nothing was ever seen, after a number of incidents and shared experiences, it came to be accepted that the station might have a ghost. The site, at the edge of the town, was desolate and remote enough in those days, to work on the imagination - bordered as it was on three sides, by the old brickfield, overgrown and tangled with brambles. Being the last person to leave the station, in the middle of the night after a call, turning out the lights and locking up as the wind whistled through the tower, unsettled many a rational being. Adding to the atmosphere, two fields just along the Colne Road are strangely

The new station nears completion, a view of the rear of the building.

Admiral Sir Andrew Lewis inspects the crew prior to the demonstration drill, 1981. CFO Roger Paramour on the left.
The crew (L to R)
Fm Mark Chaplin, Fm Colin Saxton, LFm Fred Moss, Fm David Gooding, Fm David Honey, Fm Steve White.

The Lord Lieutenant of Essex, Admiral Sir Andrew Lewis, talks to David Honey (Mark Shearman is nearest the camera) and declares the station open.

named, Deadman's Hill and a little further on, Deadwoman's Hill. In the spring of 1883, closer to the station, the body of an old woman was found drowned 'in a ditch on the Colne Road'. The wife of a travelling hawker called Edward Martin, the woman had apparently drowned in sixteen inches of water. *[Inquest EH 24/02/1883].*

    Reports of the station 'ghost' inevitably became a matter of local speculation and as a result a tale did emerge concerning a man known as 'Doodley' who was said to have drowned in one of the pools that infested the old brickworks.[13] Although a search of the records drew a blank with the name, it did come up with an untimely death on the site. In January 1925 the body of Charles Cook, a thatcher and small-holder, was found ten feet under the icy surface of a pond on the brickfield. He had been reported missing by his family and a search soon came across the broken ice on the pond and a hat lying nearby. It was reported that there had been no sign of a struggle. *[EN 17/01/1925]* Although sometimes unsettling, the ghost is not thought to be malevolent and these manifestations, or indeed, any unexpected noise, are always explained as 'It's just Doodley'.

That's it for Now!

With a brand new station and a modern appliance, circumstances had offered the Coggeshall brigade a great opportunity, one that they embraced with some relish. Full use was made of the training opportunities provided by the new drill yard and tower. The station also proved an excellent venue for all sorts of social and charitable gatherings and events. It also grew increasingly busy, the number of calls increasing from 84 calls a year in 1965 to 348 calls in 1989, the busiest year in the station's history to date. There is plenty of stuff for some future chronicler to get his teeth into and I wish him or her well! After all, the 'Longer History of Coggeshall Fire Brigade' is yet to be written.

Trevor Disley, February 2017

---

13   Reported by Brian Humphreys via his father in law, Vic Lawrence, once a fireman at the Market Hill Station, whose house on the Tey Road overlooked the brickfield.

Sub Officer Peter Hale with the Dennis appliance on the day of the new station opening, 10th September 1981. The bell, alas, is no longer carried on fire engines.

Bibliography

Archer, J E
1990
'By a Flash and a Scare' Arson, Animal Maiming and Poaching in East Anglia 1815-1870
Breviary Stuff Publications

Beaumont, G F
1890
A History of Coggeshall in Essex
Marshall Bros & Edwin Potter

Braidwood, J
1830
On the Construction of Fire Engines and Apparatus, The Training of Firemen etc
Bell & Bradfute and Oliver & Boyd et el

Blackstone, G V
1957
A History of the British Fire Service
Routledge and Kegan Paul

Blackwell, G R and Brown, A F J et al
1959
This Coggeshall
WEA Coggeshall Branch

Braggs, A P and Board, B and Crummy, P et al
1994
'A History of the County of Essex Vol 9'
Victoria County History

Brown, A F J
1990
Meagre Harvest
Essex Record Office

Brown, Rev F N
1954
The Parish Church of St. Peter ad Vincula
Rev F Norman Brown,

Brown, Rev F N
1956
The Rebuilding of the Church of St. Peter ad Vincula Coggeshall
Reprinted from the Transactions of the Essex Archaeological Society Volume XXV, Part II, New Series.

Clark, G
Farm Wages and Living Standards in the Industrial Revolution: England, 1670-1850
Department of Economics UC-Davis, Davis CA
http://faculty.econ.ucdavis.edu/faculty/gclark/papers/farm_wages_&_living_standards.pdf

Dale, B
1863
The Annals of Coggeshall
A H Coventry & John Russell Smith

Drew, B
1952
'The Fire Office' The Essex and Suffolk Equitable Insurance Society Limited 1802-1952
Published by the Society, Curwen Press

Dickson, P G M
1960
The Sun Insurance Office 1710-1960
Oxford University Press

Ezra, N
2010
Kelvedon Fire Brigade a brief History
Feering and Kelvedon Local History Museum

Gyford, J
1991
Men of Bad Character
Essex Record Office

Halls, H
1968
'Essex' Copper Plate
[Fire Plates issued by the E&S]
Halls, Henry

Hobsbawm, E J and Rude, G
1969
Captain Swing
Lawrence and Wishart

Holland, M
2004
Swing Unmasked: The Agricultural Riots of 1830 to 1832 and their Wider Implications
FACHRS Publications

Hussey, S and Swash, L
1994
Horrid Lights
Essex Record Office

Kenyon, J W
The Fourth Arm
1948
George G Harrap & Co. Ltd.

Kent, J and Jinks, R and Mays, M (Eds)
Kelvedon Speaks
1999
R Kent

Leete, J
2008
Under Fire, Britain's Fire Service at War
Sutton Publishing

Horton, R (Ed)
2013
Merryweather & Sons Ltd
The Fire Brigade Society

Merryweather & Sons
1901
A Record of Two Centuries. Being a short history of the house of Merryweather & Sons on Long Acre & Greenwich 1690-1901
Merritt & Hatcher Ltd

Noakes, A
1957
The County Fire Office 1807-1957
A Commemorative History
H F & G Witherby Ltd

Peacock, A J
1965
Bread or Blood
Victor Gollancz

Young, C F T
1866
Fires, Fire Engines and Fire Brigades
Lockwood & Co

Roper, E
1989
Seedtime The History of Essex Seeds
Phillimore & Co Ltd.

Rose, Dodo
1995
Bryan Saunders
Round House Press

Reaney, P H
1969
The Place Names of Essex
Cambridge University Press

Williams, B
1927
Fire Marks and Insurance Office Fire Brigades
Charles & Edwin Layton

Workers' Educational Association (Coggeshall Branch)
1951
The Story of Coggeshall 1700-1900

APPENDIX I: List of Fires in Coggeshall 1833–1937

Not complete as many fires went unreported

	Date	Address	Nature of fire	Cause
1	13/09/1833	Cows Hall, Wakes Colne	Double barn & 6 stacks &c	Not known
2	11/02/1834	Great Tey	Person	Spark from fire
3	00/02/1834	Coggeshall	Child, about 6yrs old	Clothes caught from fire
4	01/08/1835	Curd Hall	Hay barn & stacks	Spontaneous combustion in haystack
5	05/11/1838	The Gravel	Window curtains	Firework thrown into upper window
6	27/05/1839	Coggeshall	Child, 3yrs female, died	Clothes caught fire
7	10/06/1839	Barn, Earls Colne	Barn, stacks &c	Wadding from gun
8	09/05/1840	Bridge Street	Bed, bedding	Not stated
9	00/12/1841	Feering	William Rogers, a child, died	Clothes caught alight
10	28/01/1842	Halls Silk Mill	Silk factory fire	Ignited from the steam engine
11	00/02/1843	Coggeshall	Eleanor Amos, a child, died	Clothes caught fire
12	28/01/1844	Kelvedon	Mrs Barns, an old woman, burns	Fell on fire in a fit
13	18/03/1844	Barrack-yard, Braintree off Cog. Lane	19 cottages barn & sheds &c.	Incendiary? 4 Engines including Coggeshall
14	04/08/1844	Pattiswick Hall	Haystack	Spontaneous Combustion
15	21/11/1844	The Mount	House burnt to ground	Arson by thieves - 'Coggeshall Gang'
16	05/05/1844	Vaughan, Grocer	Contents of shop	Not known
17	09/04/1847	Jemima Storehold	Child, 2yrs old girl, died	Unexplained open fire in room.
18	02/07/1849	Thatched Cottage, Coggeshall	Cottage destroyed	Spark from neighbour's oven on thatch
19	05/11/1849	Chickley's Farm, Aldham	Several outbuildings	Accidental, firing a squib from a gun
20	26/09/1850	Isinglass Factory	Boiler house on fire	Accidental
21	15/08/1851	Clover Stack, Pattiswick	Clover stack destroyed	Ashes from a harvestman's pipe
22	09/11/1851	Farm at Feering (Rectory)	Barn &c	Supposed incendiary, domestic arrested
23	23/04/1852	Cottage, Robinsbridge Rd	Contents of room	Soot falling on straw by the fireplace
24	23/04/1852	Cottages at Cockerills Farm Feering	2 cottages destroyed	Spark from an oven falling on the thatch
25	01/01/1853	Buckles (Bucklers) Farm Great Tey	Farm building	Supposed incendiary
26	04/03/1853	Church Street	Mantel on fire	Accidental
27	25/03/1853	Gate House Farm	Shed in a sheep yard	An idle smoker in the hay loft
28	10/06/1853	Cottage, Grange Hill	Room on fire	Children playing with lucifers
29	26/02/1854	11 Crouch Place	Timber in partition wall	Overheating furnace next door
30	14/04/1854	Premises of T Turpin, Inworth	2 sheds, piggeries, stable &c.	Unknown
31	27/07/1854	Church Street	Curtains alight	Candle
32	12/08/1854	Ironmonger, Church Street	Chimney board alight	Careless servant
33	22/08/1854	Cottage, The Gravel	Room alight	Candle
34	30/09/1854	Hammer Barn, Marks Tey	Barn destroyed	Malicious persons assumed
35	29/10/1854	Friends Meeting House	Roof timbers alight	Overheating flue
36	23/01/1855	Black Boy Inn	Not stated	Accidental
37	13/03/1855	Ironmonger, Church Street	Child, hair & face burnt	Fell into fire grate
38	08/04/1855	Friends Meeting House	Roof on fire	Stove overheated
39	11/04/1855	Coggeshall	Child, 4 yrs old girl	Clothes caught alight

ESSEX EQUITABLE INSURANCE SOCIETY.

This engraving adorned the policies of the Essex Equitable Insurance Company, later the Essex & Suffolk Equitable, from 1803 until the early 1820s. It was drawn and engraved by Isaac Taylor a Colchester artist and pastor. Illustration is from a seven year policy dated 21st September 1803.
Reproduced by courtesy of the Essex Record Office

40	29/04/1855	Next Brewery, Little Coggeshall	Thatch on clamp of mangel wurzel	Spark from pipes 'by some means'
41	05/05/1855	Stable at Woolpack Inn	Cottage and stables &c	Probably accidental
42	09/10/1855	House	Window blinds	Candle
43	03/06/1856	Grocer Shop, Coggeshall	Boxes of lucifers in shop window	Not known
44	01/07/1856	Shed 'near this town'	Shed and useful donkey	Children playing with lucifers
45	26/07/1856	2 Cottages, Chalkney Wood, Gt Tey	Cottages destroyed	Pipe smoker?
46	26/07/1856	Cottages, 2 mls from Coxall, Gt Tey Rd	2 cottages destroyed	Some children playing
47	07/02/1857	Velvet Factory	Fire in the factory	Overheating flues
48	19/02/1857	Coggeshall	Bedroom contents	Spark from a candle on a bed
49	22/04/1857	Stoneham Street area	Samuel Andrews, 4yrs, died	Clothes caught fire
50	08/05/1857	Nr Brewery, Coggeshall Hamlet	Straw ricks	Quite a mystery
51	23/08/1857	Hay Ricks, Highfield House	2 ricks & other damage	Lucifer match
52	03/12/1857	Tilkey Road	Emma Saunders, 7yrs, serious burns	Playing with the fire
53	27/03/1858	Robinsbridge Road	Walter Payne, 4yrs, severely burnt	Spark from the fire
54	04/03/1858	Premises of Mathias Gardner, Builder	Woodwork in works	Heat from chimney
55	12/06/1858	Shed in East Street	Shed	Heat from engine
56	23/08/1858	Premises	Bedroom material smouldering	Not stated
57	10/02/1859	Farm at Pattiswick	Stacks of wheat & straw	Supposed incendiary
58	03/03/1859	Hungry Hall, Earls Colne	Barn, piggeries, shed & hen house	Not known
59	06/03/1859	Cottage, Black Brook, Bradwell	2 cottages, floors & thatch	Chimney fire
60	24/12/1860	House & Bank	Large beam under a fireplace	Domestic fire
61	16/01/1862	National School, Church Street	Beam under the hearth	Domestic fire

#	Date	Location	Damage	Cause
62	04/06/1862	St Peter's Brewery, Stoneham Street	Rafters alight	Silly test for gas leak
63	17/12/1862	Church Street	Room	Candle
64	27/05/1863	Godbolts Farm, Little Tey	2 stacks	Deliberate by tramp
65	16/10/1863	Inquest at The Woolpack	Eliz Nicholls, 3½ yrs, died	Domestic fire
66	14/01/1864	Goods Shop, Stoneham Street	Shop & house	Gas explosion
67	28/07/1864	Scrips Farm	Farm premises	Accidental
68	12/09/1864	Colchester Road	Straw stack	Boy with lucifers
69	29/09/1864	Tey Street, Great Tey	2 cottages, barn, stable &c	Candle from lantern
70	20/01/1865	Windmill Great Tey	Windmill destroyed	Overheating during a storm
71	00/01/1865	Pointwell Mill Lane, Cog Hamlet	Siggers, girl, 9yrs	Too near the grate
72	08/10/1865	2 Cottages at Inworth	House fire	Not known
73	21/04/1866	50, Stoneham Street	Outbuilding	Children & lucifers
74	04/05/1866	No address given	Totham, boy 5 or 6yrs, burnt	Fire caught clothes
75	21/05/1866	Tey Road, Feering	2 cottages destroyed	Overheating oven
76	00/07/1866	Cottage at Feering	Thatched cottage destroyed	Not known
77	12/12/1867	Farm at Chappel	Outbuildings and stacks	Tarpaulin on a steam engine ignited
78	16/05/1868	Anchor Inn, Inworth	Part of public house	Not known
79	01/03/1869	Walcott's, Great Tey	2 barns, 3 stacks &c	Bursting steam engine
80	04/03/1869	Church Street, Beard's Maltings	Stable, loft malt & bean mills &c	Gas light in the stable?
81	16/04/1870	J K Kings Seed Farm, ½ mile fr town	Stack	Not known
82	21/09/1871?	Inworth Grange	Large barn, stabling, stacks &c	Possible steam engine, thrashing
83	13/07/1872	Ivy Brook Farm, 4 mls from Coggeshall	Barn	Lightning
84	11/08/1874	Cottage in West Street nr Cricketer's	Kitchen, house	Not stated
85	19/09/1874	Hill Farm (Fabians), Colne Rd	All farm buildings	Supposed incendiary
86	02/06/1875	Adjacent Cog Gas Works, East St.	Timber & brick cattle sheds &c	Spark from furnace
87	27/08/1875	Warren: Grocer & Baker, Lt Cogg	Thatched shed	Not stated
88	06/09/1875	Cottages at Little Tey	4 thatched cottages	Children playing with lucifers
89	00/02/1876	Robinsbridge Road, Drying House	Herring, sprats, harness, horse	Heat from drying house?
90	22/08/1876	Coggeshall Hall	Barn, outbuildings & 8 stacks	Believed a boy aged 13yrs
91	10/03/1877	Frith's, Market End	House & shops	Lamp or beam in chimney
92	05/03/1878	G P Swinborne's Tan Yard, West Street	Sheds	Not stated
93	02/12/1878	Palmers Farm, Tey Rd	Farm building, 8 stacks &c	Threshing machine
94	18/02/1879	Prested Hall, Feering	Barns, sheds &c	Supposed incendiary
95	04/03/1879	Tilkey Windmill	Windmill	Not known
96	21/03/1879	Bradwell Hall	Hall 100% destroyed	Kitchen fireplace
97	12/11/1879	Beard & Bright Brewery, Stoneham St	Thatched roof of brewery premises	Not stated
98	00/09/1880	West St next Mr Wash, Coachbuilder	Shavings in coal closet under stairs	Accidental, child with lamp
99	02/12/1880	Cottage Inworth	Sibley, a child, girl, died	Clothes caught alight
100	04/05/1881	Purleigh Farm	Farm buildings 100% destroyed	Lightning strike
101	14/12/1881	Curds Road	2 stacks of faggots 3000+	Deliberate
102	24/10/1882	Bull Public House, Bradwell	House burnt to ground	Chimney
103	28/07/1883	Chalkney Mill	Barn, cowhouse, 3 stacks &c	Supposed incendiary

#	Date	Location	Description	Cause
104	03/12/1883	East Street, rear of Mr Bucks shop	Workshops &c	Fire used for trade purposes
105	08/12/1883	Old Potash Farm, Pattiswick	Stack of bean straw	Match thrown down
106	13/01/1884	The Lawns, Coggeshall	Nursemaid on fire	Dress caught from fire, burns
107	15/03/1884	Coggeshall Gasworks	Roof on fire	Hot irons
108	22/04/1884	Coggeshall & district	Earthquake	Act of God
109	04/07/1884	Bouchiers Grange	Stabling, sheds, coachhouse &c	Not known
110	11/08/1884	Hay House Farm, Earls Colne	Stack, hay and clover	Supposed overheating
111	15/01/1885	West Street	Workshop on 2 floors	Benzolene lamp overturned
112	14/11/1885	Cooks Field, Coggeshall Abbey	Straw stack	Small boys set fire to stack
113	26/03/1886	Inworth	Louisa Ruffle, 43yrs, died	Lamp overturned whilst filling
114	20/12/1886	Wisemans School, Kelvedon	School 100% destroyed	Flue from greenhouse
115	04/07/1887	Hay House Farm, Earls Colne	Stack destroyed	Pea-picker children
116	21/07/1887	Stack, Griggs Farm	Stack faggot wood	Deliberate
117	11/08/1887	Bird in Hand, Cog'shall Rd, Earls Colne	Cottage, public house, stack	Possibly children
118	01/11/1888	Large Room behind Chapel Hotel	Room on fire	Oil lamp fell
119	07/04/1889	Hay House Farm, Earls Colne	Wheat stack	Supposed incendiary
120	01/08/1890	Coggeshall Hall Farm	8 stacks	Overheating
121	26/10/1890	Church St, residence Charles Poulton	Parlour on fire	Hot coal from fireplace
122	05/11/1890	Windmill Hill, Feering, Offhand farm	Barn and straw stack	Not known
123	19/04/1891	Cottage of Mrs Hughes	Room	Beam in chimney
124	02/01/1892	Cottage, Inworth	Jane Brown, 9yrs,	Fire caught dress alight
125	07/03/1892	Sach's, Back Lane	Workshops	Not stated
126	03/09/1892	Walcotts Farm, Great Tey	Stacks, 2 wheat 2 hay	Unknown
127	06/11/1892	Prospect Place, Tilkey	Bedroom, smoke logged, rescues	Accidental, match
128	07/11/1892	Warehouse, Stoneham Street	Warehouse & contents	Unknown
129	06/07/1893	Farm, Blest End, Bradwell	Farm buildings, stacks &c	Heat of the sun
130	06/07/1893	Herons Farm, Bradwell	2 large barns, cattle sheds, stacks &c	Heat of the sun
131	28/07/1893	Crowlands Farm	Large barn, horseshed, 3 stacks	Child 6yrs playing with matches
132	04/10/1893	Bird in Hand, Cog'shall Rd, Earls Colne	Stable, cartshed, pt barn, storehouse	Not known, possibly children
133	01/12/1893	Beard & Bright Brewery, Stoneham St	Malting kiln	Coal falling from kiln fire
134	08/12/1893	Red Lion, Market End	Outbuilding adjoining	Spark from fire
135	04/04/1894	Red Lion Inn &c, Market End	Inn, shops	Paraffin lamp
136	11/05/1894	Beard & Bright Brewery, Stoneham St	Thatched roof	Sparks from the engine house
137	06/09/1894	Haystack at Tilkey	Stack	Lads returning from circus
138	08/10/1894	Brickwall Farm, Stisted	Large barn	Not stated
139	05/11/1894	Thatched Shed, Tilkey	Large thatched shed	A mystery
140	05/11/1895	Nr The Toll House	Large stack wheat straw	Supposed incendiary
141	08/10/1896	Tilkey	Linen & person	Too near the fire
142	14/10/1896	Nr Hare & Hounds, Little Coggeshall	Stack of hay	Supposed incendiary
143	14/09/1897	Griggs Farm	Stack of hay	Boys with matches
144	19/10/1897	House nr The Gravel	House, stable &c	Accidental, possibly lamp in stable.
145	03/11/1897	On Rd Surrex to Cockerills Farm	Barn, shed &c	Supposed incendiary

#	Date	Location	Details	Cause
146	05/11/1898	Windmill House, Tilkey	2 straw stacks	Supposed incendiary
147	12/02/1900	East Street	Room	Beam in chimney
148	30/04/1901	House at the Hamlet	House 100% destroyed	Not known
149	00/09/1901	Manns Farm, Burtons Green	Farm buildings	Not known
150	23/09/1902	Crowlands Farm	3 stacks	Not known
151	03/11/1902	Nunty's Farm	2 sheds & machinery	Not known
152	03/01/1903	Edward's Farm, Bradwell	Stack	Struck by lightning
153	26/05/1903	Cottage near brook at Stisted	Thatched cottage	Accident lighted paper
154	11/05/1904	Premises on Colchester Road	Double bay barn, stacks &c	Not stated
155	29/07/1904	Purley Farm	2 haystacks	Not stated
156	22/11/1904	Woodlands, Church Street	Florence King, 35yrs, died	Paraffin stove
157	05/12/1905	Tilkey Road	Charles Ransom, 6yrs died	Domestic fire
158	01/09/1906	House at Surrex	Oil-stove explosion	Oil-stove
159	12/01/1907	Sachs' Back Lane	Workshops &c	Not known
160	25/04/1907	Overend Park Farm, Inworth	Warehouses & seed store	Incendiary
161	01/01/1908	Griggs Farm	5½ stacks hay & clover	Not known
162	07/01/1908	Church Farm, Feering	Range of farm buildings	Not stated
163	08/01/1908	Church Farm, Feering	Stack, pea & barley	Deliberate
164	16/11/1908	Hill House, Inworth	Room	Old beam in chimney
165	29/01/1908	Maltbeggars Farm	4 stacks	Not stated
166	01/03/1908	Sewing Factory, Church Street	Flames issuing from chimney	Smouldering
167	12/03/1908	Edward Sach's Premises, Back Lane	Workshops, stores &c	Believed incendiary
168	11/09/1908	Maltbeggars Farm	Stack of oats	Not stated
169	03/10/1908	Tilkey Road	Several stacks	Not stated
170	05/11/1908	Wisdoms Barn, Colne Road	Barn, shed pigsties	Probable incendiary Nov 5th
171	05/11/1908	Barn, Colchester Road	Barn, piggeries, 4 stacks	Probable incendiary Nov 5th
172	05/11/1908	Cottages, Colchester Road	2 cottages	Probable incendiary Nov 5th
173	05/11/1908	Colchester Road	Stack	Probable incendiary Nov 5th
174	21/12/1908	Holfield Grange	Renault car in garage	Not known
175	26/01/1910	Almshouses, Church Green	Mrs Birkin 84yrs	Not known
176	06/06/1910	Kelvedon High Street	Workshops	Not stated
177	05/12/1910	Surrex, J F Church's Farm	Stack	Not known
178	08/12/1910	Gravel House	House, 3rd floor	Not stated
179	05/08/1911	Bright & Sons Brewery, Stoneham St	Brewery	Heat from copper fire
180	27/08/1911	Popes Hall, Chappel	3 haystacks	Not stated
181	13/09/1911	Maltbeggars Farm	Barn, cowhouse, sheds &c	Not known
182	03/04/1913	Cottage, Tilkey Road	Coal place under the stairs	Not known
183	12/06/1913	East's Stores, Church Street	Storehouse	Not known
184	23/04/1914	Highfields	Clover stack	Possibly spark from traction engine
185	27/06/1914	West Street	Trees	Not stated
186	20/08/1914	Highfields	Not stated	Not stated
187	20/08/1914?	Queens Head Inn	Cowshed, cart lodge, piggeries &c	Not known

#	Date	Location	Details	Cause
188	00/01/1915	G W Smith, Church Street	Gas explosion and fire	Whilst new connection made
189	12/03/1915	Robinsbridge Road	Furniture & linens	Linen airing in front of fire
190	29/03/1915	Tilkey	Haystack	Soldiers
191	26/06/1915	Farm Buildings near Marks Tey	2 Barns, stabling &c 3 stacks	Not stated
192	19/03/1916	Stock Street Farm	Stack	Not known
193	02/06/1916	Grange Farm	Part stack, chaff-cutter, rick cloth	Not stated
194	31/01/1917	Gambrel House, East Street	Bathroom	Gas geyser
195	01/05/1917	Cromwell House	House	Not given
196	28/05/1917	Coggeshall Hamlet	Not known	Not known
197	00/08/1918	Teybrook Farm	Farm?	Not stated
198	04/06/1919	Feering Bury	Not given	Not stated
199	18/10/1919	Cottage, Tilkey Road	Cottage, occupied by Mr French	Not stated
200	16/12/1919	Queen Street	William Roy Seex, 2 ½yrs,	Scalds from kettle
201	06/05/1920	Kings Seed factory	Seed warehouse	Not stated
202	08/05/1921	House, Robinsbridge Road	Roof	Chimney
203	15/04/1922	Hill farm, Inworth	Beam in kitchen fireplace	Kitchen fire
204	00/09/1922	Bryan Saunders Shop, Stoneham Street	Woodcarving workshop	Apprentices
205	09/08/1923	Maltings (seed stores), Church Street	Premises 100% destroyed	Not known
206	06/08/1924	Mr A Smith's, Robinsbridge Road	Stables, piggeries, outbuildings	Small boys playing with matches
207	22/11/1924	Thompson's Field, Robinsbridge Road	3 stacks peas, cabg seed, wheat straw	Not stated
208	21/07/1925	Pattiswick Hall	Barn granary stables &c	Lightning
209	18/12/1925	West Street, George Birkin's house	Mantelpiece	Defective flue
210	27/09/1926	Council School, Inworth	Classroom	Overheated chimney
211	16/03/1927	Grange Farmhouse	Beam in chimney	Not stated
212	23/10/1928	Paycocke's House	Interior of house	Beam in chimney
213	09/12/1928	Abbey Mill farm	3 stacks	Not stated
214	00/06/1929	On the Colne Rd, Feering.	Matravers Charabanc, destroyed	Accidental
215	10/01/1930	Pattiswick Hall	6 stacks	Not stated
216	27/02/1930	Mill Lane, Robinsbridge Road	Room	Oil lamp
217	03/03/1930	Sach's, Queen Street	Workshops burnt out	Not stated
218	00/07/1930	Scrips Farm	2 stacks	Not stated
219	04/04/1931	Beside Coggeshall to Earls Colne Road	4 ton stack straw	Not stated
220	00/07/1931	Little Coxall, Kelvedon Road	Sheds, clover & hay	Not known
221	27/10/1931	Church Farm, Feering	Most of the farm buildings	Not stated
222	26/02/1932	Inworth Hall	Chimney	Chimney
223	05/04/1932	Post Office & Gen Store, Feering	Bedroom	Beam in chimney
224	17/10/1932	New Road, Coggeshall Hamlet	Room on fire	Whilst lighting fire
225	06/07/1933	Pattiswick Hall	Barns & Sheds	Not stated
226	13/04/1935	Mill Lane, Robinsbridge Road	Alice Cresswell, 63yrs, died	Fell in fire
227	06/12/1935	Surrex, Feering	James Cowlin, 77yrs, died	Probably candle
228	14/05/1937	Cottages, West Street next to the Fleece	Cottage & shop destroyed &c	Not stated
229	18/10/1937	New Road, Coggeshall Hamlet	Person & room	Accident with fire

APPENDIX II: Roll of Honour

Essex & Suffolk Fire Office Brigade 1849–1903

Mostly unrecorded
Hersom, Samuel
Leaper, Daniel
Leaper, William
Potter, Thomas
Rolph, Mr
Rustell, Mr
Tansley, James
Tansley, William
Webb, Mr

Parish of Coggeshall Fire Brigade, 1903–1939

List may be incomplete
Alston, George
Appleford, Richard
Baylis, Frederick, First Captain
Birkin, Alfred, Captain
Birkin, George
Bright, Richard Desborough, Captain
Brown, Edward Walter, Captain
Brown, W E
Burnham, J
Clark, Charles J, Sub Captain
Gooch, Steward G, First Engineer
Goodey, William
Green, Joseph
Green, Samuel
Jepp, W W
Joyce, Henry
Paterson, George
Pennick, Edgar T
Prentice, E
Southgate, Robert Henry, Sub Captain
Saward, Hubert Harry, Sub Capt. & Engineer
Styles, Earnest
Weinrich, Frank

Braintree RDC Brigade 1939–1941
National Fire Service (NFS) 1941–1948

List probably incomplete
Evans, Robert (Bob)
Green, W (Billy)
Hunwick, J
Jennings, W (Bill)
Saunders, Bert
Saunders, Stan
Walford, Lenny
Weinrich, Frank

Auxiliary Fire Service (AFS) 1939–1941
National Fire Service (NFS) 1941–1948

List probably incomplete but see also next page.
Barnett, Stan
Dyer, B
Everett, Lenny
Jepp, B
Leatherdale, Bill
Maddocks, George
Newman, A (may not have completed AFS training)
Raven, Bob
Wilsher, J

A Short History of Coggeshall Fire Brigade

National Fire Service 1941–48,
Essex County Fire Brigade and Essex County Fire & Rescue Service 1948–2016

Sub O – Sub Officer, Officer in charge at the station
LF – Leading Fireman, now Leading Firefighter
Ff – Firefighter, previously Fireman
s – Still Serving as of 2016

SL – Section Leader (NFS only)
NFS: A starting date of or before 1948 indicates previous NFS service.
List probably incomplete

Rank	Name	Service
Sub O	Adams P	2001 - 2016 s
Ff	Bacon L	2005 - 2010
LF	Baker J	1973 - 1980
Ff	Barnett P	1999 - 2010
Sub O	Barnett S G	1941 - 1969
Ff	Bell A	1998 - 1999
Ff	Bilton M	2016 - 2016 s
Ff	Boyling	2016 - 2016 s
Ff	Brassington M	2005 - 2013
Ff	Briggs R	2011 - 2016 s
Ff	Byford G	2003 - 2016 s
Ff	Cade P	2004 - 2015
Ff	Chantry T	1996 - 2006
Ff	Chaplin I A	1960 - 1983
Ff	Chaplin M	1980 - 2000
Ff	Chaplin T P	1973 - 1974
Ff	Corder D L	1974 - 1980
Ff	Dale A W	1948 - 1956
Ff	Dennerley S	1997 - 2010
Sub O	Disley T H	1982 - 2014
Ff	Drury V D	1955 - 1957
Ff	Dye P J	1997 - 1999
Ff	Dye P W	1997 - 1999
Ff	Edworthy T F	1959 - 1961
Ff	Ellis A G	1951 - 1958
Ff	Ellis G	2016 2016 s
Ff	Evans C	1983? - 1985 ?
Sub O	Evans R	1941 - 1951
Ff	Freeman A H	1948 - 1948
LF	Gladwin L G	1954 - 1977
Ff	Gooding D	1973 - 1984
Capt	Green W B	1941 - 1948
Sub O	Hale P	1957 - 1988
Ff	Hewitt M	1991 - 2005
Ff	Hines R G	1955 - 1961
Ff	Honey D	1957 - 1986
Ff	Huckle C W	1946 - 1950
Ff	Humphreys B M	1986 - 1998
LF	Jennings W A P	1941 - 1951
Ff	Joyce P J	1948 - 1949
Ff	King N	1989 - 2002
Ff	Knights S P	1979 - 1980
Ff	Lawrence V D	1951 - 1954
FF	Knopp J	2009 - 2016 s
Ff	Leatherdale J H	1961 - 1963
Ff	Leatherdale J H	1967 - 1973
Ff	Maddocks G W	1948 - 1964
Ff	Maddocks P H	1953 - 1970
LF	Marks L	1951 - 1965
Ff	Martin D	2011 - 2016 s
LF	Moss F	1957 - 1985
Ff	Parry J W H	1964 - 1973
Sub O	Polley F A	1957 - 1973
Ff	Potter D	1954 - 1964
Ff	Potter E J	1952 - 1955
Ff	Rawlings J R	1982 - 1982
Ff	Repman P	1998 - 2000
Ff	Ritson T R	1951 - 1952
Ff	Rutkin A	1990 - 1997
Ff	Salmon D J	1979 - 1982
LF	Saunders B S	1941 - 1950
LF	Saxton C	1980 - 2007
Ff	Schroder K	2000 - 2010
Ff	Shearman F	1974 - 1975
LF	Shearman M	1975 - 2005
Ff	Shearman P	2015 - 2016 s
Ff	Sim C	2001 - 2006
Ff	Speed K A	1956 - 1977
Ff	Speed J T	1948 - 1954
Ff	Spry L	1941? - 1956 ?
LF	Street I	2010 - 2016 s
Ff	Taylor K	1957 - 1973
LF	Tilbrook F W	1948 - 1964
Ff	Totham H L	1949 - 1949
Ff	Walford L	1951 - 1956
Ff	Webb A	2006 - 2009
Sub O	White S	1979 - 2000
LF	Wilkins P	1988 - 2015
Ff	Wilkinson D J	1962 - 1963
Ff	Wright T	2006 - 2014
Ff	Yeo R L	1964 - 1979

APPENDIX III: Essex & Suffolk disbursements - the losses by fire 1821–1904

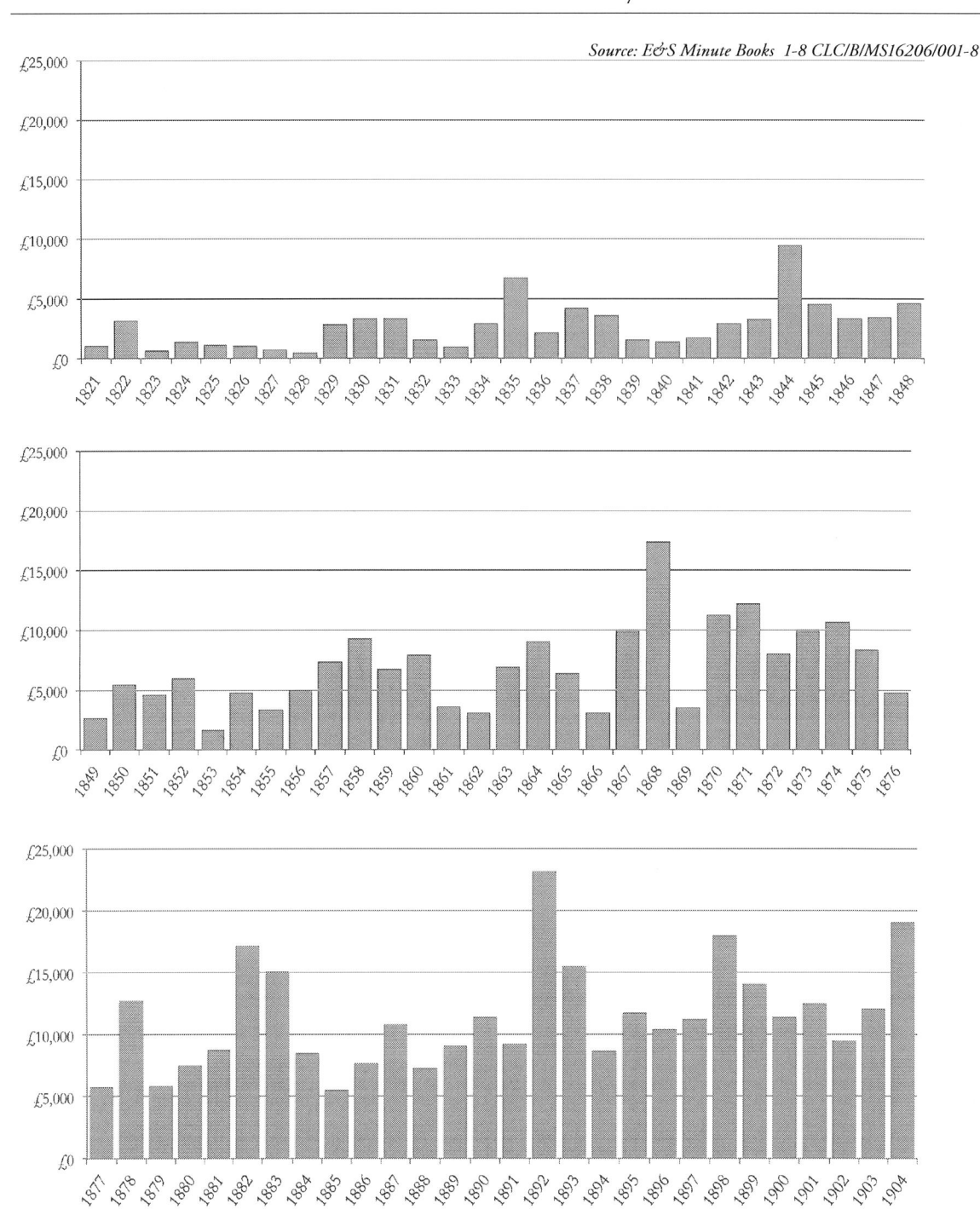

Source: E&S Minute Books 1-8 CLC/B/MS16206/001-8

The graphs show the total amount paid out each year in settlement of fire insurance claims by the Essex & Suffolk. Most of the peaks are a result of incendiarism and these continue throughout the period. The losses of 1892-1893 were due to hot dry weather and lightning. The inflationary increase in the cost of fires through the period is very apparent.

A Short History of Coggeshall Fire Brigade

APPENDIX IV: Value of property insured with Essex & Suffolk agencies 1845

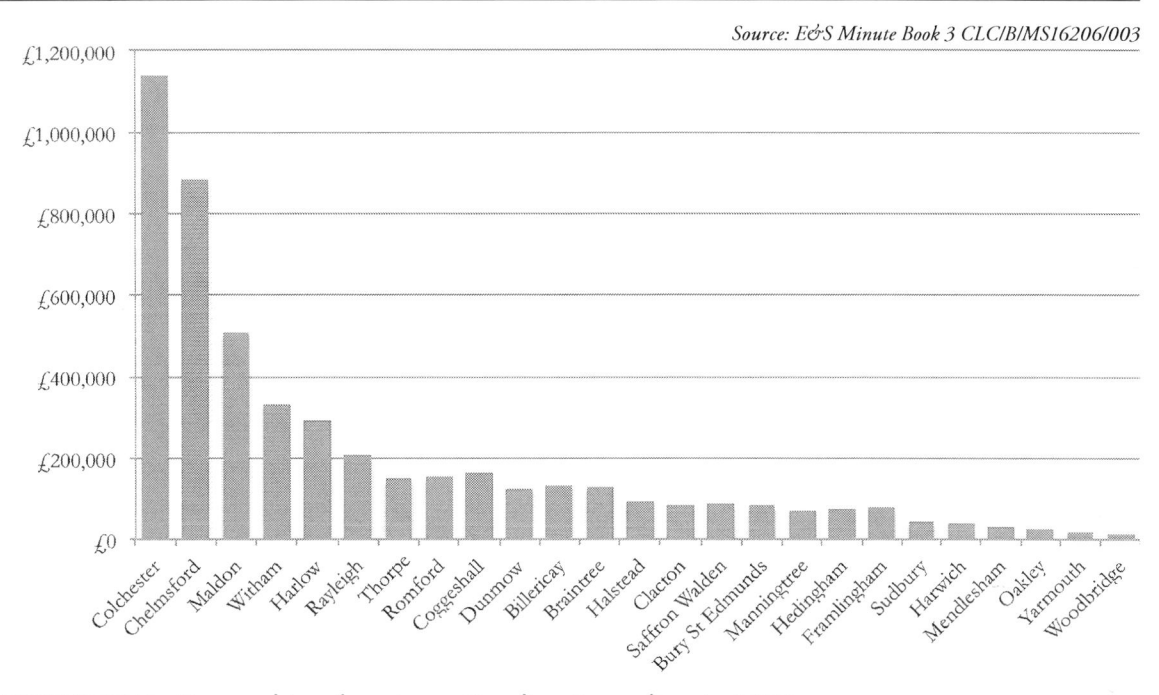

Source: E&S Minute Book 3 CLC/B/MS16206/003

Bar chart showing insured property values by location (descending): Colchester (~£1,140,000), Chelmsford (~£880,000), Maldon (~£510,000), Witham (~£330,000), Harlow (~£290,000), Rayleigh (~£210,000), Thorpe (~£150,000), Romford (~£155,000), Coggeshall (~£160,000), Dunmow (~£125,000), Billericay (~£135,000), Braintree (~£130,000), Halstead (~£95,000), Clacton (~£85,000), Saffron Walden (~£85,000), Bury St Edmunds (~£80,000), Manningtree (~£70,000), Hedingham (~£80,000), Framlingham (~£80,000), Sudbury (~£45,000), Harwich (~£40,000), Mendlesham (~£30,000), Oakley (~£25,000), Yarmouth (~£10,000), Woodbridge (~£15,000).

APPENDIX V: Ownership of engines attending Essex fires in 1868

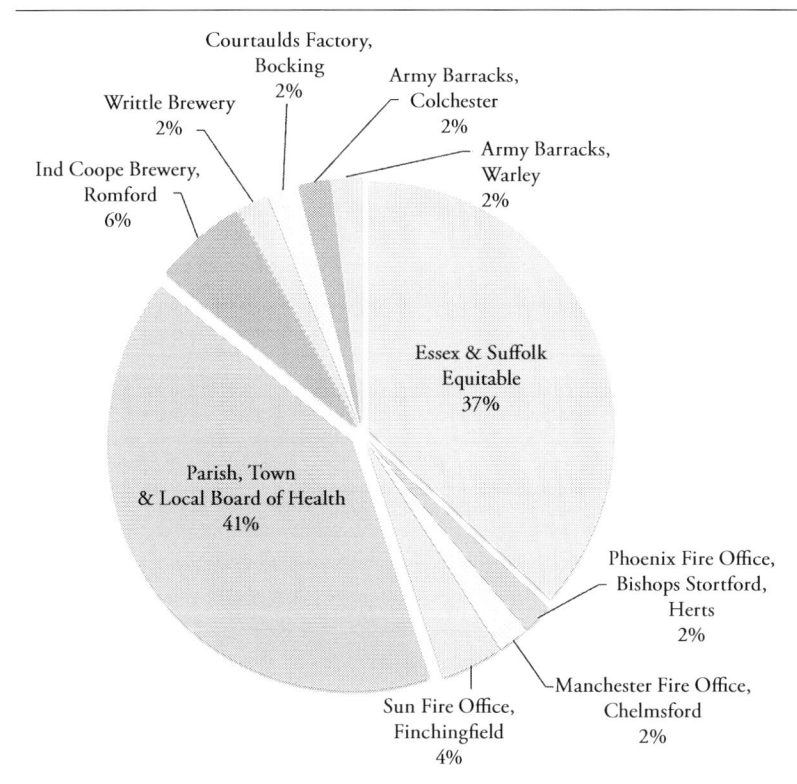

Pie chart:
- Parish, Town & Local Board of Health: 41%
- Essex & Suffolk Equitable: 37%
- Ind Coope Brewery, Romford: 6%
- Sun Fire Office, Finchingfield: 4%
- Writtle Brewery: 2%
- Courtaulds Factory, Bocking: 2%
- Army Barracks, Colchester: 2%
- Army Barracks, Warley: 2%
- Phoenix Fire Office, Bishops Stortford, Herts: 2%
- Manchester Fire Office, Chelmsford: 2%

A survey of engines attending Essex fires reported in the 'Essex Chronicle' in 1868, using the search engine of the British Museum Newspaper Archive. This search engine is not perfect so fires were undoubtedly missed, although these would be unlikely to challenge the broad results. Fires where no engine attended are not recorded. Total of 49 fires.

APPENDIX VI: Essex & Suffolk: income and losses by category 1872–1876

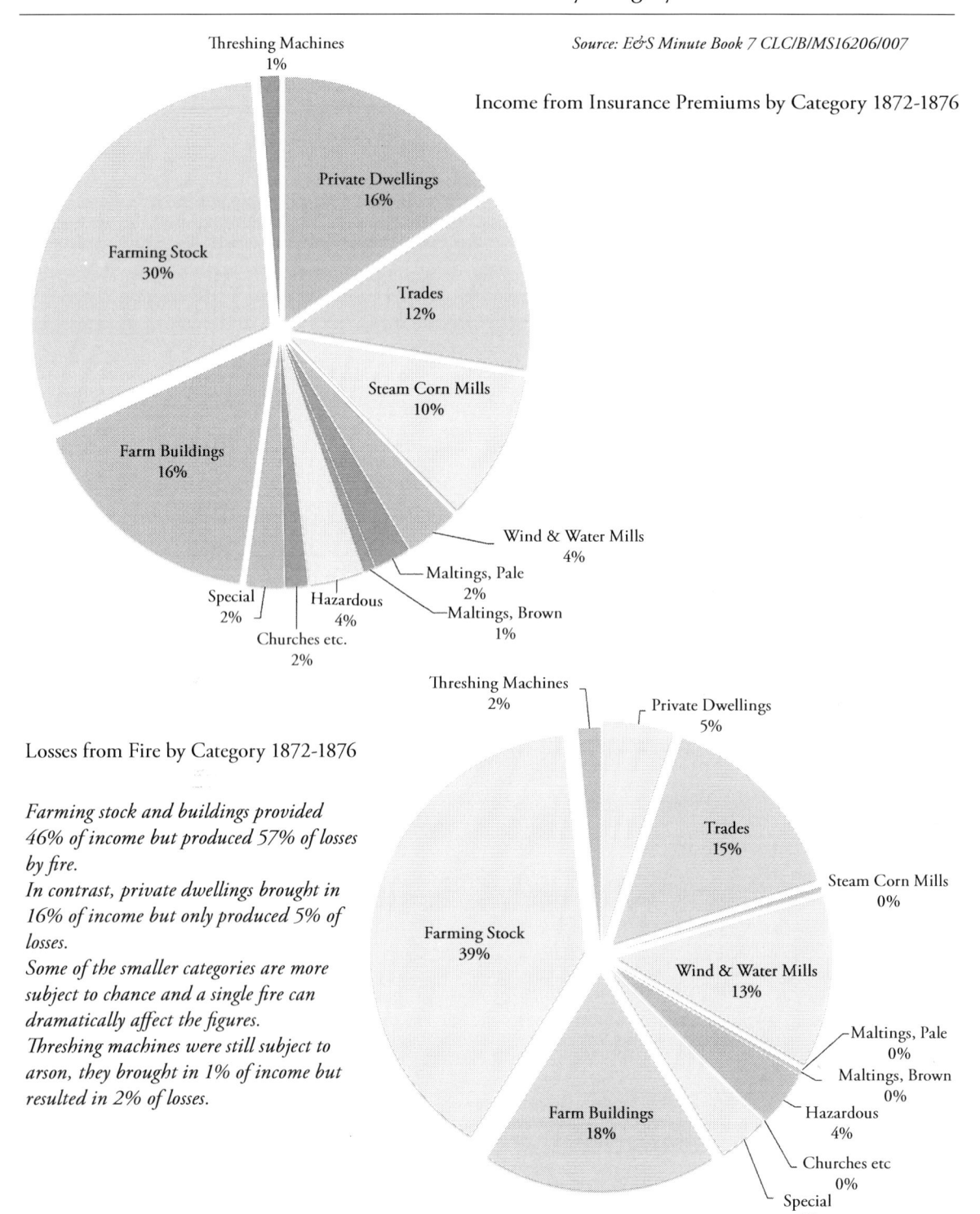

Source: E&S Minute Book 7 CLC/B/MS16206/007

Income from Insurance Premiums by Category 1872-1876

- Threshing Machines 1%
- Private Dwellings 16%
- Farming Stock 30%
- Trades 12%
- Steam Corn Mills 10%
- Wind & Water Mills 4%
- Maltings, Pale 2%
- Maltings, Brown 1%
- Hazardous 4%
- Churches etc. 2%
- Special 2%
- Farm Buildings 16%

Losses from Fire by Category 1872-1876

Farming stock and buildings provided 46% of income but produced 57% of losses by fire.

In contrast, private dwellings brought in 16% of income but only produced 5% of losses.

Some of the smaller categories are more subject to chance and a single fire can dramatically affect the figures.

Threshing machines were still subject to arson, they brought in 1% of income but resulted in 2% of losses.

- Threshing Machines 2%
- Private Dwellings 5%
- Trades 15%
- Steam Corn Mills 0%
- Farming Stock 39%
- Wind & Water Mills 13%
- Maltings, Pale 0%
- Maltings, Brown 0%
- Hazardous 4%
- Churches etc 0%
- Special 4%
- Farm Buildings 18%

APPENDIX VII: Mentions of the word 'incendiary' in local newspapers 1820–1898

Mentions of the word 'Incendiary' in the 'Essex Standard', 'Chelmsford Chronicle', 'The Ipswich Journal' and the 'Bury and Norwich Post' using the search engine of the British Library Newspaper Archive. The final number is the average number of occurrences each year among the four titles.

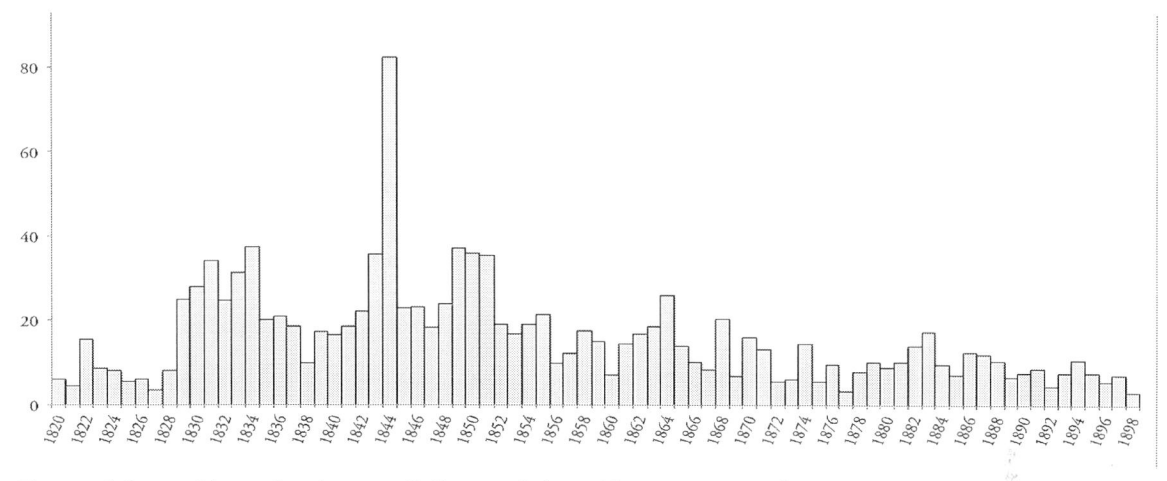

The use of the word 'incendiary' may well illustrate fashionable concern as much as a technical description and the analysis makes no attempt to differentiate between the two, nor to identify misattribution of the cause of fires, or other uses of the word 'incendiary'. Despite these provisos, the resulting graph does seem to have some interest and congruency with other research in identifying periods of rural unrest. The period of unrest around the 'swing' movement of 1829-34 and the major outbreak of 1844 are evident as are the outbreaks of 1849-1852. The declining rate of attacks during the period is also apparent.

APPENDIX VIII: The average value of property insured in each agency in 1840

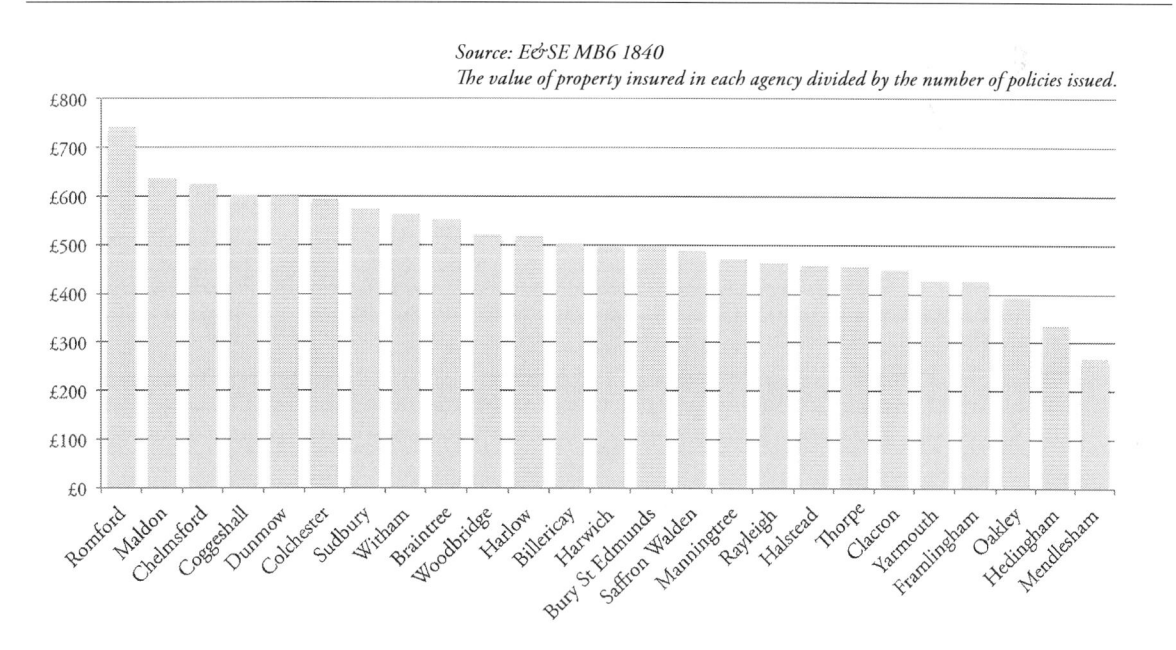

Source: E&SE MB6 1840
The value of property insured in each agency divided by the number of policies issued.

264 *Fires, Firemen & Other Mishaps*

APPENDIX IX: Farming as a % of total insurance in Essex & Suffolk agencies in 1853

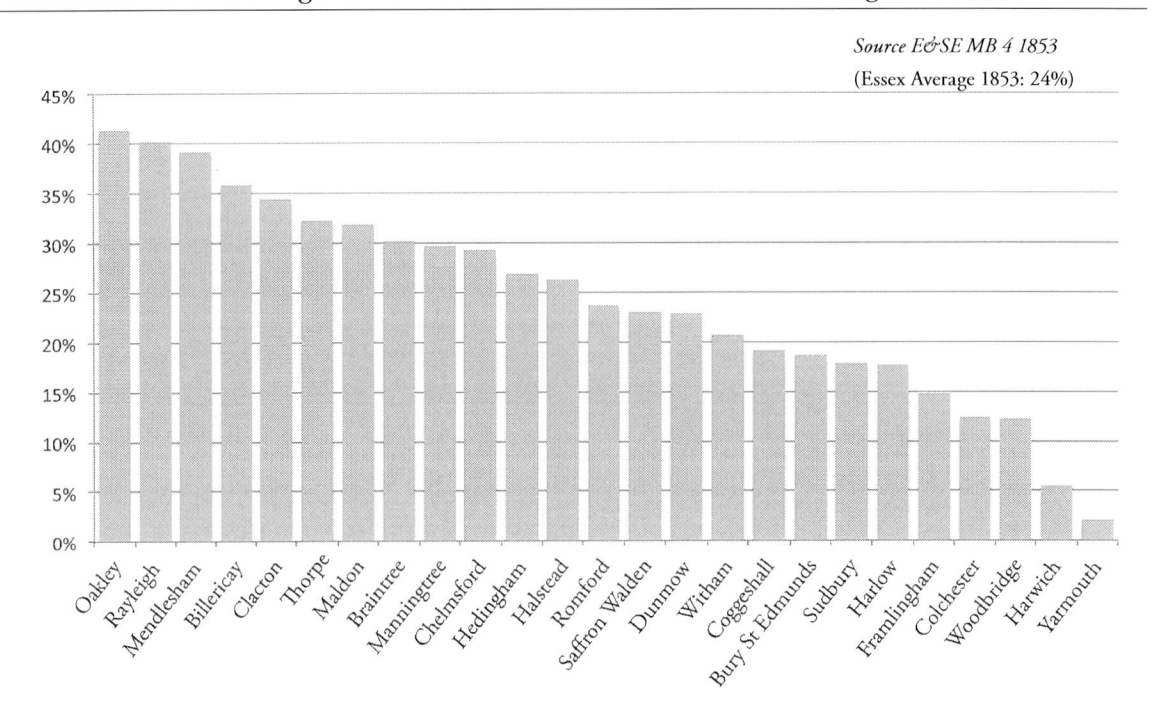

Source E&SE MB 4 1853
(Essex Average 1853: 24%)

APPENDIX X: The number of calls attended by Coggeshall fire station 1948–1972

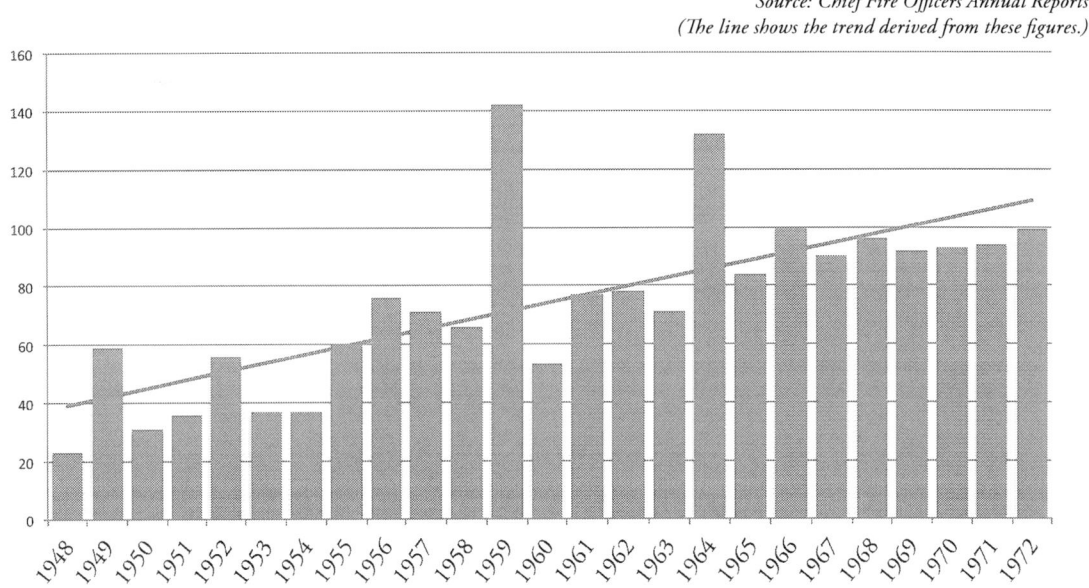

Source: Chief Fire Officers Annual Reports
(The line shows the trend derived from these figures.)

APPENDIX XI: General Rules for Coggeshall Fire Brigade

Source: Minutes of Great Coggeshall Parish Council 07/12/1903 ERO D/P 36/30/1-4

1. The brigade shall be called "The Coggeshall Fire Brigade".
2. The brigade shall consist of a Captain, Deputy Captain and a number of Firemen, to be fixed from time to time.
3. The business of the brigade shall be conducted by the Officers and a Committee of 12 Members to be elected annually.
4. The brigade shall meet for Drill once every month, (date and time to be left to the discretion of the Captain). Special Drills may be called by the Captain as often as he thinks necessary.
5. If a Member does not attend three Drills or Fires in the course of a year, his name shall be struck off the roll of the brigade at the next annual meeting.
6. Any Member being absent from three monthly Drills in succession or neglecting or refusing to attend at a Fire, without giving to the Captain or officer in Command a satisfactory reason for his absence, it shall be laid before the Committee and the Committee shall have power to fine such Member a sum not exceeding 1s: or dismiss him from the brigade.
7. No Member shall appear in uniform except he is on duty.[sic]
8. Each Member shall promptly obey all orders which he may receive from those in authority over him and shall conform himself to all regulations which may from time to time be made.
9. The property of the brigade shall be vested in the Officers of the brigade for the time being and in case the brigade should at any time cease to exist, the whole of the property shall be handed over to the Parish Council of Great Coggeshall.
10. Two days notice at least shall be given to each Member of all meetings.
11. A list of the Members of the brigade shall be kept at the Police Sergeant's House.
12. A Member on reaching the age of 60 years shall not be summoned for active Fire Service but shall be eligible to take relief duty: if he has been a Member fifteen years, he shall be entitled to wear his uniform of the rank he attained in the brigade with the privilege of attending such meetings as he might at the time of his retirement.
13. Immediately on receiving notice of a "Call" to a Fire, the Member shall repair to the Engine House in full working uniform and shall under the direction of the Officer in Command, get the Engine, Hose and all necessary tools etc ready to start and when ready shall proceed without delay to the Fire.
14. The Engineer or Fireman in Charge of the Engine shall have the management of the Engine, seeing it is placed in a proper position and prepared for working, he shall not leave the Engine during a Fire but shall devote his whole time to the working of the same and the Signals.
15. If the Captain should be absent, the next Officer shall take command but in case all Officers are absent the Senior Member present shall act as Officer in Command for the time being, but shall retire upon the arrival of an officer proper.
16. No refreshments to be procured or provided without the order of the Officer in Command.
17. No Member shall leave a Fire (except in the case of injury) without the permission of the Officer in Command.
18. The Members are expected to perform their duties as silently as possible, order, coolness, promptitude and dispatch are indispensable.
19. After any Practice or Fire, three Members of the brigade shall clean up and do all necessary work to Engine by order of the Captain.
20. The Engine to be Free to any Fire in the Parish of Great Coggeshall. The working expenses to be paid by the owner of the property where the Fire occurs.
21. The Charge for brigade to attend a Fire outside the Parish of Great Coggeshall shall be Two pounds and working expenses.

APPENDIX XII: Essex & Suffolk Equitable Insurance Society Fire Marks

(A summary of this account appears in the text.)

There was a tradition for Fire Offices to fix their own signs, called fire marks or fire plates, to the outside of the premises they insured. The Essex fire plates were of sheet copper, which had been pressed into a die to create a raised design, 6½" x 8¼" in size. The plate was probably designed by a local pastor and artist, Isaac Taylor, who also created the engraving which appeared at the head of the Society's policies for the first few years. The die was produced and the plates pressed in Birmingham and by January 1803 the first plates had been delivered to the agents. The Deed of Settlement links policies and marks:

> 'The Badge or Mark of the Society shall accompany every policy which shall be issued by the Society with a view the more publicly to notify the insurance effected by the policy...'
> *[E&SE Deed of Settlement 1804 amended 1807]*

In practice, many more policies were issued than fire marks. For example, in 1803, eighteen policies were issued in Coggeshall but only six plates were provided and between 1805 and 1806, twenty-four policies were issued in Coggeshall but no plates were supplied. A letter written to the new Halstead agent in 1806 explains the matter:

> 'You may deliver a Mark to every person who wishes it and that will put them up in front of buildings that are insured, but we seldom give more than one or two Marks to a person although he insure several Estates, as they cost the Directors 2s. each and we are sparing of them as we can with propriety'. *[Quoted in Halls p15]*

When the Society changed its name from the 'Essex' to the 'Essex & Suffolk' it was decided to issue a new mark, but as a batch of the old ones had only just been ordered, it had to wait. It was thought that more could be made of the original design by embellishing it with colour and gold leaf. A Colchester artist, James Dunthorn, carried out the work. The decorated marks were very striking, the surrounds and lettering in gilt with the Essex shield in red with gilt Seaxes and the background in black. They were popular with some agents who were soon requesting more of the same. Between March and April 1807 Dunthorn decorated a hundred and thirty-one marks at 1/3d each. *[Halls p17]* The directors were unconvinced as to their value and when stocks ran out in 1810, the Secretary wrote:

> 'We have been without Marks for some time now and since the stile [sic] of our Society is altered to the Essex and Suffolk it will be necessary to have a new die sunk, but which at present the Directors have given no order about, nor do they seem very much inclined as Marks are very expensive and of no very great utility. Every Mark we had cost the Society 2/3d[1].' *[Quoted in Halls p21]*

In 1813, there was a change of heart prompted perhaps by the poor 1812 figures which showed that the rate of growth at 5% was considerably down from the 12% growth of 1808-1811. *[E&SE MB annual statements]* The Essex & Suffolk's competitors, (the Royal Exchange, the Norwich Union, the Phoenix and the Suffolk and General Country) seemed to be prospering and they used marks. The Directors decided to order some more, using the old design, saving the cost of a new die, but as they saw it, reinforcing a well-known and recognised trademark. *[Hall p25]* For some people, the marks may have had magical, talismanic properties, important at a time of unrest when incendiaries were on the prowl. Noakes claims: 'In country parts many ignorant people believed that a house bearing a fire mark would not burn. This led farmers to remove the marks from their houses and hang them on the hay ricks'.

Perhaps more reasonably, some thought that the mark might encourage an incendiary to seek another farm, one not protected by insurance, where real damage could be done. *[Noakes p54-5]* The last batch of marks were received in 1818 after which no more were ordered, the Directors having finally decided that they were not worth the expense. Halls estimated that a total of 1,500 marks were produced by the Society, only a very few survive.

---

1   This means that the plate itself cost 1s which is inconsistent with the amount quoted in the 1806 letter to the Halstead agent.

APPENDIX XIII: Fire insurance classes 1854

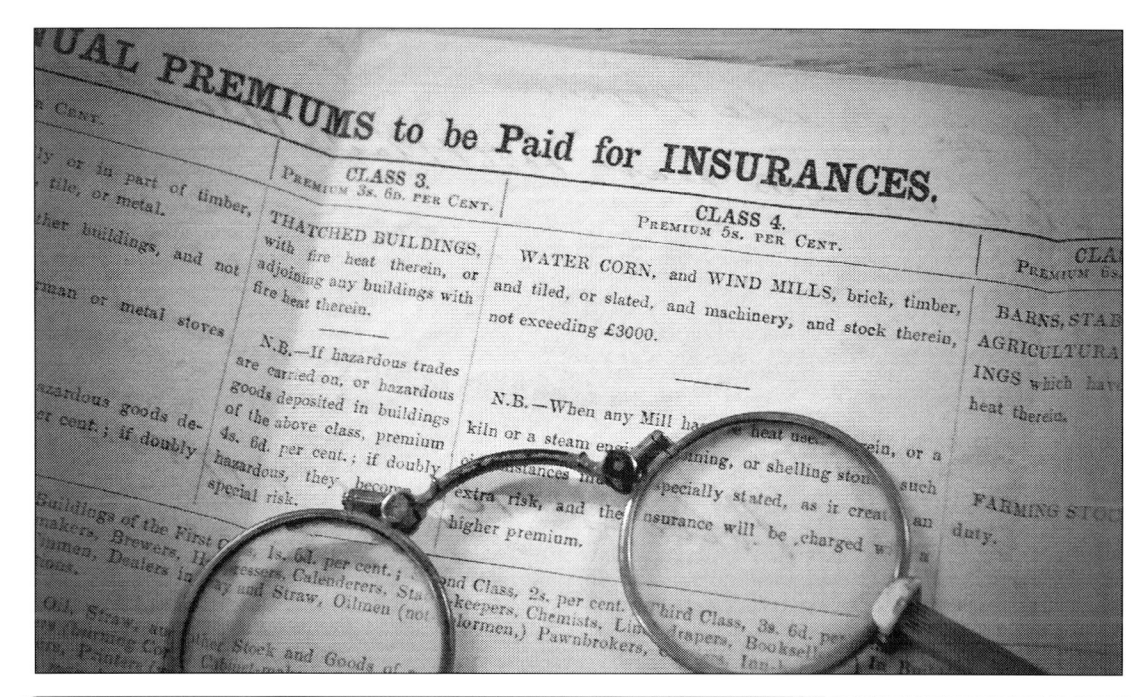

Fire Insurance Classes 1854

This is a Policy of Assurance with the 'Essex Economic Fire Assurance Association' of 25th March 1854 in the name of 'Thomas Wheeler of Gravel Lane Great Coggeshall, Wheelwright', the term 'Per Cent' used in the table means per £100 insured

CLASS 1: PREMIUM 1s PER CENT
BUILDINGS with external walls wholly of brick or stone covered with slate, tile or metal, standing alone or with other buildings separated by partition walls of brick or stone.
N.B. if hazardous trades are carried on or hazardous goods deposited: Premium 1s 6d per cent, doubly hazardous 2s per cent.

CLASS 2: PREMIUM 1s 6d PER CENT
BUILDINGS with external walls wholly or partly of timber, weather board or plaster, covered with slate, tile or metal.
BUILDINGS of the first class adjoining other buildings and not separated by party walls of brick or stone.
Shops or warehouses in which are German or metal stoves with pipes.
N.B. if hazardous trades are carried on or hazardous goods deposited: Premium 2s per cent, doubly hazardous 3s per cent.

CLASS 3: PREMIUM 3s 6d PER CENT
THATCHED BUILDINGS with fire heat therein, or adjoining buildings with fire heat therein.
N.B. if hazardous trades are carried on or hazardous goods deposited: Premium 4s 6d per cent,
doubly hazardous they become a special risk.

CLASS 4: PREMIUM 5s PER CENT
WATER CORN and WIND MILLS brick, timber and tiled and Machinery and stock therein not exceeding £3000.
N.B. When any mill has fire heat used therein, or a kiln or a steam engine adjoining, or shelling stones,
such circumstances must be specially stated, as it creates extra risk.

CLASS 6: PREMIUM 6s PER CENT
BARNS, STABLES and other AGRICULTURAL BUILDINGS which have not any fire heat therein.
FARMING STOCK, free from duty.
DUTY 3s per cent on all Property excepting FARMING STOCK.

APPENDIX XIV: Kelvedon Postscript

This logbook was given to the author by Bert Saunders who was a great collector of all things. It measures 85mm x 130mm and covers the period 31st July 1939 to 11th July 1940. It was started by Bill Doughton of the Kelvedon brigade but after just three entries and the disagreement with Chief Officer White, the book was taken over by the new Coggeshall brigade. In July 1940 the entries stop, no doubt the logbook was replaced with a more official document, now like much else, sadly lost.

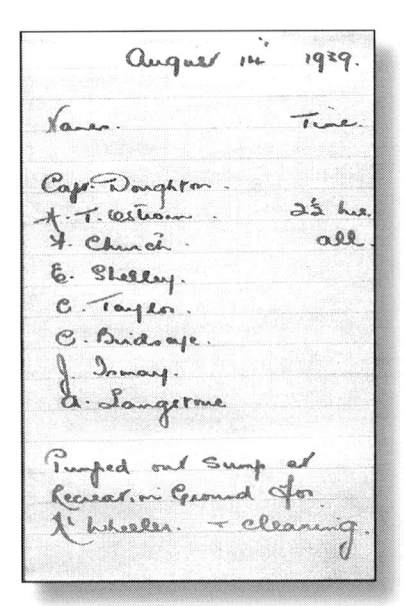

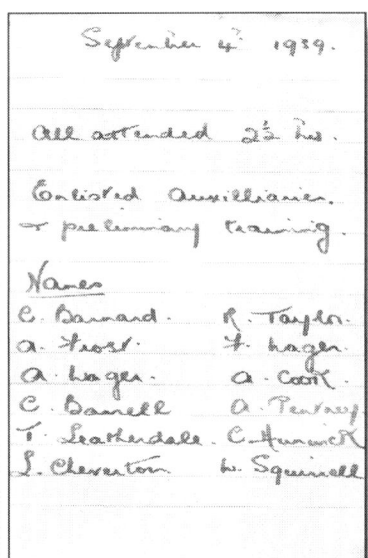

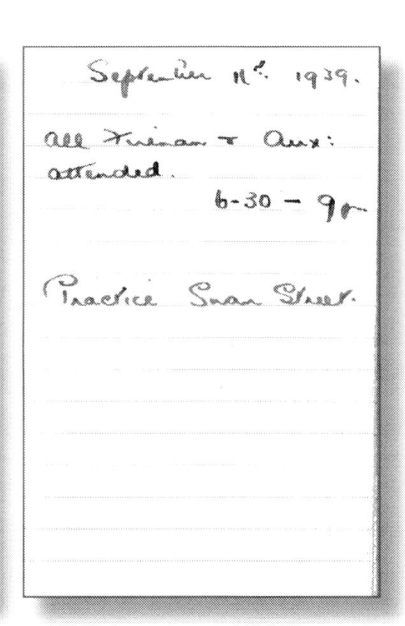

The 14th August was a normal Tuesday drill night for the Kelvedon brigade. They pumped out the recreation ground for the Parish Council and cleaned the station and the appliance.
(*Captain Bill Doughton, Harry Osborn, F Church, E Shelley, C Taylor, C Birdseye, J Ismay, and A Langstone.*)

The drill which should have been on Monday 21st was rescheduled for Friday 25th probably to allow Lewis White to meet the crew (illustrated elsewhere). This was when they all walked out, so there was no drill on the next Monday.

After consideration, the brigade returned the following Monday, having agreed to continue until the new Coggeshall crew could be trained. So on 4th September, the day after war was declared, Captain Doughton and his men enlisted Kelvedon's Auxiliary firemen (*C Barnard, A Frost, A Wager, C Bamell, T Leatherdale, L Cleverton, R Taylor, F Wager, A Cook, A Pentney, C Hunwick, W Squirrell*) and began preliminary training. This continued on 11th September and then the record ends.

APPENDIX XIV: Kelvedon Postscript

Kelvedon Area RDC Fire Brigade, April 1937
Sub Captain Harry Osborn (Centre Left) making a presentation to Captain William Doughton.
J Ismay, F Church, C Birdseye, Harry Osborn, Bill Doughton, A Langstone, C Taylor, E Shelley.
Photo by courtesy of the Kelvedon Museum

Notice of Station Closure

Letter dated 6th March 1947 regarding the attitude of the Kelvedon 'formation' and the intention to close the station.

It seems that the Kelvedon NFS firemen (see letter left) had no desire to meet D O Kehoe. Perhaps it was their way of expressing dissatisfaction at the turn of events, but walking out had become something of a Kelvedon thing. The 1939 walk-out precipitated the relocation to Coggeshall as we have seen. The captain and men had also resigned in May 1928 when they were unhappy about things - although on that occasion they returned when the council responded to their demands. [KPMB]

Illustration courtesy of the Kelvedon Museum

Coggeshall Fire Station 2009
Ff Lee Bacon, Ff Andy Webb, Ff Tim Wright, Ff Paul Cade, Ff Justin Knopp, Ff Mark Brassington, Ff Graham Byford
Ff Karl Schroder, Leading Ff Paul Wilkins, Sub Officer Trevor Disley, Leading Ff Paul Adams, Ff Stewart Dennerley

Index

A

Abbey View
   1915, Bomb 142
   1926, Fire 164
Adams, Paul photo 270
Agricultural labourers 30, 31, 135
Agricultural Labourers Union
   1873, Sackings at Bouchiers Grange 64
   1874, Failure of 65
Air raids
   1914 141–143
   1939-1945 200–214
Alerter, radio 238
Alexandra Inn 135
Allen, Charles 16, 18, 22
Allen, Lewis
   Appointed to Coggeshall Agency 16
   Bankruptcy 22
   Non-payment of rates 20
   Resignation 21
Allen, William FRS 16
Alston, Frederick 126
Alston, G, fireman 148, 149
Amos, Eleanor 252
Amos, William 50
Anderson, Robert
   1868, new broom at the Essex & Suffolk 60
   Portrait (illust) 60

Andrews, Samuel 253
Annual Court 4
Appleford, Richard
   1903, Founding fireman 106
   1904, Died of Typhoid 115
Appleford, Willie 120
Arse alight (Doodlebug) 214
Austin, Mr 158
Auxiliary Fire Service (AFS) 188–191
   1940, difficulty recruiting 194–197
   1950s Auxiliary Fire Service 222
Auxiliary Towing Vehicle 218–219

B

Back Ditch ix, 94, 95
Bacon, Lee photo 270
Baldwins farm 200
Bamell, C, Kelvedon AFS 268
Barber, Police Constable 73
Barnard, C, Kelvedon AFS 268
Barnett, Mrs 244
Barnett, Stan 222–225
   1938, Enlistment in the AFS 188–189
   1941, Joined whole-time NFS 211
   1944, The NFS Commandos 213–214
   1948, Photo NFS 216
   1948, Photo Essex Fire Brigade 221
   1951, Officer in Charge at Coggeshall 221
   1969, Retirement 235–239
Barns, Mrs 252
Bawtree, George 60

Baylis, Frederick
    1901, Bought White Hart 104
    1901, Helped at a fire 103
    1902, Pronounced on Water Supply 104
    1903, Founding Parish Brigade Captain 106
    1903, invoice (illust) 112
    1904, Resigned from brigade 114
    1942, Golden wedding 114
Beard, Barney 67
Beard & Bright's Brewery
    1879, fire 75
Beard, Frank 75
Beard, John 61
Bearman, James & Sophia 68
Beauchamp Roding 15
Beaumont, Albert 150
Beaumont, G F, water scheme 68
Beckwith, Thomas 43
Beckwith, James 17
Beckwith, W 17
Bedposter 3, 7, 26
Beer drinking
    1849, Bill more than fire damage 37
    1854, Pub fire brigade 60
    1897, Legal authority for 159
    1911, Amount drunk at farm fires 136
    1911, Bill (illust) 36, 135
    1916, Very modest 150
    1920, King's Seeds fire 155
    1923, Grim tee-total Kelvedon 159
    Overview 37
Bell, Jimmy 239
Benevolent Fund
    Pay & the Ben Fund 233
Benzoline 79
Beresford Stork trailer pump 1948 220
Bibliography 250
Billericay 4
Bird in Hand (Colne Road)
    1887, Fire 85
    1893, Fire 89
    1941, Bomb 206
    1943, Aircraft crash 212
Bird in Hand (East Street)
    1812, Robert Brightwen 10
    1869, William Leaper 62
    1879, Sold by Wm Leaper 72
    1890s, Steward Gooch 106
    c1900, Illust 40
Birdseye, C 268–269
Birkin, Alfred
    1904, Joined Brigade 115
    1916, Elected Captain 147
    1916, Repairs to engine house 146
    1929, Supplementary brigade 172
    Retirement 177
Birkin, George
    1929, Supplementary brigade 172

    1939, Recruit 182
Birkin, Mrs died 256
Birkin, Sam 172, 244
Blackout 140, 143, 186, 194, 198, 207, 238
Blackwater (Village) nr Bradwell Fires
    1829, Barn 15
    1829, Queens Head 14
Blackwell 41, 43, 212
Bland, Mr 27, 47, 58
Bocking
    Brasshats, photograph 165
    1844, Fire 32
    1925, Bocking Brasshats 163
    1925, Looking for Fire Brigade business 163
    1925, New Motor Trailer Pump 161
    1925, Triumph at Pattiswick Hall 164
    1929, Under Braintree's control 171
    1934, Station Closed, Brigade disbanded 175
Bomb
    1915, Starling Leeze 142
    World War II 200
Bonfire 1, 65, 66, 88, 101, 125, 126, 199
Boor, George 49
Bouchiers Grange 64, 65, 79, 217, 239, 255
Bowers, H, J & T 205
Bow Street Officer 15
Braddy, George
    1886, Assisted at Kelvedon fire 80
    1887, Captain Kelvedon Brigade 82
    1887, Red Lion Fire 92
    1903, Drilled Cog. Parish Brigade 108
    1907, Sach's fire 118
    1916, Fire at Scrips 151
Bradwell
    1803, Brick Kiln fire 5
    1803, Kiln fire 5
    1859, Black Brook fire 253
    1882, Bull Public House fire 76
    1893, Blest End fire 255
    1893, Herons Farm fire 255
    1903, Edwards Farm fire 256
    1939, In Kelvedon area 179
    1940, In Coggeshall area 186
    1941, Machine gunned 206
Bradwell Hall, 1826 fire 74
Braidwood, James
    1825, Favoured engine (illust) 24
    1861, Killed at Tooley Street 54
    Fire engine design 23
    Portrait (illust) 54
    Relationship with Lott 23
Braintree Fire Brigade
    1844, Fire 32
    1926, Comic take off 163
    1926, Dennis Turbine Engine 166
    1928, Paycocke's 170
Braintree Poorhouse 146

Braintree Rural District Council (RDC) 160, 169, 171, 172, 173, 178, 180, 186
    1926, New 'Dennis Turbine' Fire Engine 166
    1926, New engine demo at Coggeshall 166
    1928, Comprehensive fire-fighting scheme 171
    1939, Fire Brigades Act plan 178
    1939, Kelvedon Problem 181
    1939, Kelvedon rebellion & closure 180–182
    1939, New arrangements 185
    1939, New Coggeshall RDC Brigade 182–186
    1939, Recruit Coggeshall firemen 182
    AFS 188
    AFS equipment 189
Brand, John 36
Brasshats, Bocking 163
Brass Helmets
    1894, Kelvedon Brigade 92
    1903, Coggeshall Brigade 109
    1925, Bocking Brigade 163
    1937, At fire 176
    1939, Coggeshall RDC Brigade 185
    1939, Dangerous 185
    1941, Icicles 192
    1941, Replaced 211
Brassington, Mark photo 270
Bread or Blood riots 10
Breed, George 44
Brewery
    Bird in Hand 62, 72
    Church Street 61
    Gardner's 37, 68
    Hamlet 50
    Ind Coope 58, 60, 261
    Kelvedon 85
    King's 99
    Stoneham Street 3, 10, 11, 48, 75, 84, 95, 125
    Writtle 60, 261
Brick Kiln 5
Brickworks 5
Bright, Alfred
    1908, Griggs farm 121
Bright, Harold P 125
Brightlingsea 15
Bright, Richard
    1899, E&S Coxall agent 102
Bright, William Desborough
    1903, Sub Captain founding member 106
    1907, Resigns after the Sach Fire 119
    1907, Resignation withdrawn 121
    1911, Resignation 136
    1911, Subsequent career 136
Bright William snr
    1886, appointed E&S agent 84
Brightwen, Isaac
    1807, E&S Country Director 10
    1819, Fire at brewery 11
    1824, Helping the agent 12
    1828, Bankruptcy 12

Brightwen, Robert
    1802, E&S Director 3
    1807, Coggeshall connections 10
    1828, Bankruptcy 12
Bristow & Sons Fire Engine Makers
    1809, Engine repair 6
    1812, New engine for Colchester 6
    1817, Engines found wanting 11
    1832, Riveted leather fire buckets 6
Brodie helmet 188, 197, 211, 218
    1915, Origin 188
Brown, Ernest (Walter's brother)
    1908, Court case 126
    1915, Declared bankrupt 146
Brown, Jane 255
Brown, Walter
    1897, Great Gravel Fire 97
    1903, Parish Brigade 106
    1904, Promoted Sub Captain 114
    1911, Elected Captain 136
    1916, Declared bankrupt 146
    Subsequent sad history 146
Browning, G and R 73
Browning-Smith, Mr 108
Brunwin, Henry 75
Bucklers Farm 44
Buck, William 76
Bull Inn Church Street, fire 76
Bull Public House fire, Bradwell 76
Bunny's End 120
Bures 19
Byford, Graham photo 270

C

Cade, Paul photo 270
Call out system. *See* Siren
    1878, Calling the brigade 71–75
    1948, Wartime sirens used 218
    1950s 231
    1973, Radio alerters 238
Cannon problems
    1853, Exploded 65
    1854, Blasted through shutters 65
    1878, Through front door 73
Cant, Mr 71
Captain Swing 14
Caraway seed 19
Carver, Police Constable 145
Caudwell, Dr 96, 100
Centenary Party v
Chalkney Mill fire 76
Chalkney Wood 49
Chapel Hotel 85, 119, 139, 150, 235, 236, 255
Chaplin, Henry 64
Chaplin, Ian 226
    1967, Photo 237
    1980, Photo 240

1981, Photo 243
Chaplin, Mark
   1981, Photo 243
   1981, Photo station opening 247
Charging for Engines, 1867 58
Cheek, David 45
Cheek, Len
   1948, Photo NFS 216
   1981, Photo 244
Chelmsford 3, 4, 6, 11, 15, 19, 22, 59, 60, 102, 114, 140, 159, 164, 169, 194, 261
Chickley's Farm 38
China Shop, cow inside 96
Chunky Moyles 229
Church Farm Feering 122
Church, F Kelvedon Fm 268–269
Churchill
   1914, 'formidable hornets' 141
Church Pond 46
Clark, Charles
   1903, Founding Fireman 107
   1913, Elected Sub Captain 139
Clark, J W Offices 118
Clarke, Bertie 141
Cleeland, Mr F 103
Cleveland, John 49
Cleverton, S, Kelvedon AFS 268
Clowes, Dr 100
Cobey's ale 150
Cobey, William 129, 150, 155, 199
Cockerals 200
Coggeshall Abbey 16, 255
Coggeshall Agricultural Society 38
Coggeshall Church, bombed 203
Coggeshall Fire Engines. *See also* Parish Council Fire Brigade
   1812, E&S keep engines in repair 10
   1820, Send engine to Coggeshall 11
   1827, Engine carriage ordered 12
   1830, Engines taken over by Parish 16
   1835, Engines fail at Curd Hall 19
   1836, Brand new engine from E&S 20
   1878, Call out system 71
   1883, Poor working order 76
   1897, Price of new engines 101
   1903, Free gift from E&S 104
   1903, Taken over by Parish Council 106
   1927, Manual engine last used 167
   1928, Takeover by Braintree RDC 171–173
   1929, Four men & a handcart 172–173
Coggeshall Firemen (List) 258–259
Coggeshall Fires
   Back Lane
      1855, Cottages behind Woolpack 47
      1855, Rear of Woolpack 47
      1892, Sach's Workshops 86
      1907, Great Fire at Sach's 117
      1930, Sach Workshop fire 174

Bridge Street
   1840, Miss Corder's house 29
   1859, Mrs Heather's bedroom 65
Church Street
   1764, Richard White's premises 1
   1869, John Beard's premises 61
   1883, The Bull Inn 76
   1913, William East's shop 139
   1915, W G Smith's Explosion & Fire 144
   1923, Fire at The Old Maltings 160
   1958, Doctor's house 226
Colchester Road
   1844, The Mount 35
   1895, Stacks in arson attack 96
   1897, Thatched barn nr Surrex 100
   1904, Raincroft 113
   1908, Barn, piggery, stacks 125
   1914, Queens Head 141
Earls Colne Road
   1874, Hill House Farm 64
   1893, Bird in Hand 89
   1908, Wisdoms Barn 125
   1931, Stack 257
   1960s? Colton & Shearman scrapyard 234
East Street
   1854, William Spurge's house 44
   1883, Bucks workshop 76
   1900, James Spurge's house 44
   1916, Gambrel House & Cromwell House 150
   1925, Seed business at Abbey View 164
Farms
   1835, Curd Hall 19
   1857, Highfields Farm 43
   1859, Hungry Hall 51
   1874, Hill House Farm 64
   1876, Coggeshall Hall 68
   1884, Bouchiers Grange 79
   1904, Purley Farm 115
   1908, Griggs Farm 121
   1908, Maltbeggars, February 122
   1908, Maltbeggars, September 124
   1911, Maltbeggars 131
   1914, Highfields Farm 141
   1916, Grange Farm 149
   1916, Stock Street Farm 148
   1921, Houchins 158
   1925, Pattiswick Hall 164
   1927, Trumpingtons (Gt Tey) 167
   1970s, Bouchiers Grange 242
   1977, Highfields 242
Grange Hill
   1853, Cottage 42
Market End
   1894, Red Lion Inn 90
   1952, Ken Mower's shop 224
Market Hill
   1888, Chapel Hotel 85
People. *See* Fire Injuries and Deaths

Robinsbridge Road
   1852, Single room 41
   1915, Arthur Smith's 144
   1921, Roof 257
   1924, Stables etc 160
   1924, Stacks nr Thompson's 257
   1930, Room in Mill Lane 257
Stoneham Street
   1819, Coggeshall Brewery 11
   1854, Society of Friends 48
   1862, Brewery 254
   1864, Walter Good's shop explosion 52
   1866, Outhouse 42
   1879, Beard & Bright's Brewery 75
   1892, Saunders warehouse 88
   1894, Brewery 95
   1922, Bryan Saunders workshop 158
The Gravel
   1897, The Great Fire 97
Tilkey Road
   1879, Tilkey Corn Mill 73
   1894, Matravers teazels 95
   1894, Stack fire 95
   1898, Two straw stacks, Millhouse 101
   1915, Goodman's stack 144
   1940, Paramine 206
West Street
   1842, Hall's Silk Mill 29
   1853, Vicarage 43
   1874, Cottage near The Cricketers 63
   1878, Tan Yard 71
   1885, Mr White basket maker 79
   1914, Row of old poplar trees 141
   1920, King's Seeds 152
   1927, Cottages next to the Fleece 176–177
   1928, Paycocke's House Fire 170–171
Coggeshall Fire Station
   1948-1972, Number of calls 264
   Roll of Honour 258
Coggeshall Fire Stations. *See* Crouches Engine House, Market Hill & Colne Road Fire Stations
Coggeshall Gang 36
Coggeshall Hall, fire 68
Coggeshall Hamlet
   1901, Fire in Mr Cleeland's house 103
   1937, Mrs Lucas's house 177
Coggeshall in Decay 1885 78
Coggeshall Lane Braintree 33
Coggeshall Parish Council Fire Brigade 1903. *See* Parish Council Fire Brigade 1903
Coggeshall Supplementary Brigade 1929 164, 172, 173
   Four men & a handcart 172, 178
Coggeshall Water Scheme 1911 127
Colchester 31, 44, 57, 58, 59, 60, 64, 80, 82, 96, 140, 142, 158, 166, 175, 188, 211, 217, 225, 239, 242
   1867, Fire 58
   'A' Div HQ 238
   AFS 188, 222
   Castle 46
   'Colchester Job' 91
   Control room 224
   Earthquake 78–79
   PEST 231
   St Botolphs raid 212
   Training at 237, 239
   Waterworks Company 8
Colindale vi
Colne Road Fire Station 1981 244–248
Colton & Shearman, fire 234
Commission, E&S agents 4
Comms, 1950s 224
Conservative Club 161
Cook, A, Kelvedon AFS 268
Cook, Alfred 134
Cook, Charles 248
Cook, Emma 49
Cook, James 1829, hanged 15
Cook, Miss 117
Corder, Doug 240
Corder, Miss 29
Cornwall, Eliza 40, 42
Coronation Day 1911 131
Costs
   1850-1900, Fire Engines 55
   1908, Extinguishing fires 132
   Mid 19th Century, Fire Extinction 56
Cotton, Henry, labourer 33
Courtauld's factory engine 51
Cowell, A 176
Cow in a china shop, 1897 96
Cowlin, James 257
Cows Hall 18
Cradle House 206
Cranfield, George 19
Crashed plane 200, 214
Crash gearbox 220
Cresswell, Alice 257
Cricketers (Public House) 126
Crocker, Mrs 87
Cromwell House 150
Crosby, William 49
Crouch End 2
Crouches Engine House
   1836, Deed of Conveyance 20
   1903, Keys handed over 108
   1909, Insured with engine 116
   1911, Repaired 136
   1916, Vandalised by children 146
   1924, Roof repaired 160
   1929, Parish attempt to give it away 172
   1937, Repairs 178
Crouches Fire Station. *See* engine house at Crouches
Crowlands 89, 103, 255, 256
Curd Hall 19, 200, 252
Cure for an Irritable Hound 67

Cutmore, H 164
Cutmore, Walter 134

D

Dale, Bill 216, 244
Dalton, Jacob Parish Councillor 102
Dalton, Mike Parish Clerk 101, 107
Dampier, Rev. 43
Dead Lane ix, 120, 128
Deal's seed warehouse 166
Dennerley, Stewart photo 270
Dennis 'G' type 25cwt appliance 215
    1948, (photo) 216
Dennis, Walter 49
Disley, Trevor photo 270
Doctor's House 1958 fire 226
Dodds, Mr Stationer and Post-Master 100, 104
Dog, Saved by 102
Domsey Farm 200, 205
Doodlebug Alley 214
Doodley 246
Doubleday, Shop 92
Doughton, Bill Captain 159, 172, 268
    Illust. 269
Dowcra, Mrs 82
Draw-bar, Manual Engines 158
Dunmow 31, 58, 159, 217
Dunthorn, James 266
Dyer, B
    AFS training 189

E

Eady, Mrs 143
Eady, Walter 133
Earls Colne 114, 136, 206
Earls Colne Airfield 212, 214
Earls Colne band 88
Earls Colne fires
    1839, Thatched barn 28, 252
    1859, Hungry Hall 253
    1883, Chalkney mill 76
    1884, Hay House Farm 79, 86, 255
    1887, Bird in Hand 85, 255
    1887, Hay House Farm 255
    1889, Hay House Farm 255
    1893, Bird in Hand 89, 255
    1970, High Street 237
Early Closing 144, 159
Earthquake 79
East, William 139, 146
Eley's Corner 94, 99
Ellis, Percy 135
Engineer's role 113
Engine House. *See* Crouches Engine House
Essex County Fire Brigade, 1948 218
Essex County Fire Brigade Station 74 218–249
    50s and 60s 228–230
    1970s 236–239
    c1960s, Dodge 1518 HK 228
    c1970s, Dennis Rolls TOO 927E 242–246
    Coggeshall Annual Dinner Dance 235
Essex Fire Brigades
    1850-68, Dysfunctional stories 58
    mid 19th Century problems 59
Essex Fire & Rescue v
Essex Insurance Society 2, 8. *See also* Essex & Suffolk Equitable
Essex Reform Committee 16
Essex & Suffolk Equitable
    1821-1904, Losses from fires 260
    1823, Relative business v other Offices 11
    1829, Suspended all insurance 15
    1839, List of agents 27
    1840, Value of property by agency 263
    1845, Income from agencies 261, 266, 267, 268
    1853, Farming v total insurance 264
    1867, Providing cover for Colchester 58
    1872-76, Income & Losses by Category 262
    1887, One of the greatest successes 105
    1895, Not attend Colchester fires 94
    1900, Engines not wanted in Colchester 102
    1901, Engine Committee report 102
    1902, Abandon engines & brigades 103
    1903, Handed engine to Coxall PC 104
    1938, Stopped paying for fire extinction 178
    Agents
        1805, Sureties required 4
        1808, Autonomy for expenses 4
        Commission given to 4
    Charging for engines 1867 58
    Coggeshall agents
        1802, Robert Matthews 3
        1814, Bethia Matthews 10
        1829, Lewis Allen 16
        1838, Daniel Leaper 25
        1879, (Mathias jnr) Alfred Gardner 72
        1886, William Bright 84
        1899, Richard E Bright 102
    Commission given to agents 4
    Cost of Engines 55
    Fire insurance classes
        1854, details 267
    Fire Marks 10, 266
    Headquarters building (Illust) 4
    Outgoings 1856 & 1873 56
Evans, Chris 244
Evans, Rev 77
Evans, Robert (Bob) 183, 218
    1939, Photo 186, 193
    1940, Photo 207
    1948, Photo 216, 221
    1951, Retired 221
    Garage, East Street 217
Everard, Police Sargt. 125, 139, 144

Everett, L 1939 AFS 189, 244
Eve, William 135
Executions for incendiarism 19

F

Fabians Farm
    1874, (aka Hill House Farm) 64
    1944, Halifax crash 214
Faggots (illust) 66
Fairhead, Edwin JP CC
    1907, Fairheads Maltings, Church St 118
    1908, Parish Councillor 124
    1916, Chair Fire Brigade Committee 147
    1916, Occupier of Stock Street Farm 148
    1923, Fire at Church St Maltings 161
Farm Fires. See Coggeshall Fires, Farms
Feeringbury 207
Feering fires
    1852, Cockerill's Farm 41
    1866, Two cottages Tey Road 41
    1908, Church Farm 122
    1908, Maltbeggars Farm (Jan.) 122
    1908, Maltbeggars Farm (Sept.) 124
    1911, Maltbeggars Farm 131–135
    1919, Feering Bury 257
    1932, Post Office 257
Felix Hall, 1940 Fire 191–193
Fellows, Clerk Braintree RDC 171, 178, 194–197
Felsted 60, 217
Finchingfield 10, 11, 14, 261
Finchingfield Insurance Company 15
Fire brigades in disorder mid 19th century 58, 59
Fire Buckets 6
Fire Engines
    1868, Ownership at Essex fires 261
    1897, Manual old fashioned 101
    Dennis 'G' type 25cwt appliance 211
    Dennis 'G' type (photo) 215
    Dennis Turbine Fire Engine 166
    Dennis Turbine Fire Engine (photo) 177
    Ford 'TT' one ton chassis towing vehicle 161
    Ford 'TT' towing vehicle (photo) 165, 173, 177
    Gwynne [standard 8hp] trailer pump 161, 165
    Gwynne trailer pump (photo) 173
    Morris [Commercial] 171, 175, 179, 211, 217
    Morris [Commercial] (photo) 177, 181, 186, 187, 193
Fire Force 11 209, 211
Fire Hooks 11
Fire Hydrants. See Hydrants
Fire Injuries & Deaths
    1834, Mrs Howard, 58yrs, died 25
    1839, Child, 3yrs, died 36
    1841, William Rogers, a child, died 36
    1843, Eleanor Amos, child, died 252
    1844, Mrs Barns an old woman, burns 36
    1847, Jemimah Storehold, 2yrs, died 36
    1849, 4 yrs, scalds 36
    1855, Child clothes alight 252
    1857, Emma Saunders 7yrs, burns 253
    1857, Samuel Andrews, 4yrs, died 253
    1863, Elizabeth Nicholls, 3yrs, died 254
    1865, Siggers child, 9yrs, died 254
    1866, Totham, boy 5-6 yrs, burns 254
    1880, Sibley, child, girl 254
    1884, Nursemaid, burns 255
    1886, Louisa Ruffle, 43yrs, died 255
    1892, Jane Brown 9yrs, died 255
    1894, Mary Harrington, 62yrs, died 90
    1898, Joseph Mereday, 23yrs, died 100
    1904, Florence King, 35yrs, died 115
    1905, Charles Ransom, 6yrs, died 256
    1910, Mrs Birkin, 84yrs, burns 256
    1919, Roy Seex, 2yrs, died 257
    1935, Alice Cresswell, 63yrs, died 257
    1935, James Cowlin, 77yrs, died 257
Fire Insurance Classes 1854 267
Fire Marks 10, 266
Firemen, Coggeshall, List of 258–259
Fire Offices, 1823 Comparison 11
Fire Plates. See Fire Marks
Fires
    1821-1904, Cost of fires 260
    1839, Payments for firemen 28
    1911, Detailed expenses 131
    1915, No horses 146
    1916, Expenses Grange Farm 149
    Refusal to attend 90
    Towns refusing outside attendance 140
Fire Services Act 1938 178
Fires in Coggeshall 1833-1937 252–257
Fire Stations, Coggeshall. See Crouches Engine House, Market Hill & Colne Road Fire Station
Fireworks 38, 65, 66, 73, 88, 183, 252
Flying Fortress crashed 212
Folkard, Messrs 109
Foster, Harry 139
Foster, Mr 71
Frame Farm 200
French, James 135
Fricker, Mr 73
Friends Meeting House 252
    Demolished, rebuilt 48
    Fires at Meeting House 1854 48
    Hertford 21
Frith, Chemist
    1877, Shop and house on fire 69
    1894, First Aid at Red Lion fire 92
Frost, A, Kelvedon AFS 268

G

Gambrel House 150
Gardner, Alfred (Mathias jnr)
    1872, Helps Leaper with the Agency 62
    1872, Tragic death of mother 64
    1878, Acting E&S agent 71
    1878, Built Friends Meeting House 75
    1878, E&S Office Church Street 71
    1879, E&S agent 72
    1886, Death 84
Gardner, Mathias (1)
    Insure Steam Engine 1807 5
Gardner, Mathias (2) 63
    1830, Repair to Engine House 17
    1872, Death of wife 64
Gardner, Walter, Superintendent 68
Gas
    1864, Stoneham Street explosion 52
    1875, Fire near gasholders 67
    1898, Retort Arch collapsed man died 100
    1915, Explosion in Smith's shop Church St 144
    1915, Letter from Worthington Church 144
Gashouse yard 69
Gas Masks
    Prohibited for firefighting 194
Gas Practice 194
Gatehouse Farm bomb 1941 206
Gepp, Mrs 64
German Prisoners of War 1918 150
Ghost. *See* Doodley
Gladwin, Lenny, L/F 236–237, 244
Glazenwood 74
Godbolts Farm, 1863 fire 53
Godden, George 87
Godfrey, Alfred & Harry, Prospect Place 88
Gooch, Steward 106, 108, 114
Good, Walter, 1864 fire 52
Goodey, Mrs W 120
Goodey, William 23, 120, 133, 149
Gooding, David
    1980, Photo 240
    1981, Photo 243
    1981, Photo station opening 247
Goodman, Ernest 144
Goodson, John 47
Gore Pit 39, 127
Goslins Farm Bradwell 103
Gowers China shop 96
Grange Farm fire 149
Gravel factory 12
Gravel House fire 97
Gravel, The ix, 97, 105, 252, 255
Graves, Edward 5
Great Bardfield 10
Great Eastern Railway 146
Great Fire at King's Seeds 152
Great Holland 15

Great Tey 50, 133, 135, 142, 190
Great Tey fires
    1834, Corpulent woman 25
    1853, Buckles (Bucklers) Farm 44
    1864, The Street 53
    1865, Tey Windmill 53
    1869, Walcotts 60
    1892, Walcotts 87
    1918, Teybrook Farm 150
    1927, Trumpingtons Farm 167
Great Wishford 2
Great Yeldham 14
Green, Joe 149
    1911, Joined Parish Brigade 136
    Calling out wartime crew 212
Green, Reverend 77
Green, Samuel (Sam) 149
Green, Sydney 73
Green, William (Billy)
    1929, Hose cart brigade 172
    1939, Coggeshall RDC Brigade 182
    1939, Photo with crew 193
    1940, Remembered 185
Greyhound Inn 50, 51, 160, 161
Griggs Farm, 1908 fire 121
Gunpowder
    1853, Overloaded cannon burst 65
    1863, Incautiously carrying 52
    1875, Allowance for insurance 65
    1883, Mixing explosion 73
    1888, Accidentally set alight 73
    1910, Threw a match into 125
Guy Fawkes
    1764, Bonfire & fire 1
    1838, Guy Vaux day 23
    1841-79, Incidents 65
    1882, Effigies of the clergy 73
    1892, First arson attack 88
    1894, Arson attack 95
    1895, Arson attack 96
    1897, Incendiary attack on barn 100
    1908, Arson attacks 125
Gwynne 8hp trailer pump 161

H

Hadley Simkin & Lott, Fire Engine Makers
    1791-1836, Makers plates 30
    1815-20, Large Manual (Illust) 21
    1817, Engine ordered by E&S 11
    1836, Renamed Merryweather 23
Haines, Stanley 176, 214, 226–229
Hale, Peter (Sub Officer) vi, 225, 231
    1950s, new AFS 222
    1957, Joined Essex Fire Brigade 224
    1967, Photo 237
    1977, Photo 239
    1980, Photo 240

1981, Photo new station 249
Halifax bomber crashed 214
Hall Farm, Stisted 90
Hall, John
   1828, Gravel factory 13
   1840, Fire 29
   1842, Silk mill 29
   1847, Accident to horseman 50
Halstead 10, 20, 51, 59, 136, 140, 150, 195, 211, 212, 217, 220, 239, 266
Ham, Frank 158
Hamlet House & Brewery, 1857 fire 50
Hammer Barn, 1854 fire 45
Hanbury, Osgood 20, 27, 49, 50
Han'som Burton 70
Hare Bridge 12, 72, 95, 97
Hart, Mr coachman 125
Haulm 14
Hawkes Hall 205
Hawkins, DO 238–239
Hay House Farm
   1884, Fire 79
   1887, Fire 86
   1889, Fire 255
Haywood 47
Heatwave of 1893 89
Helmets. *See* Brass Helmets
Hersom, Samuel
   1834, Parish Constable 33
   1837, Insolvent Debtor's Court 34
   1844, Superintendent of Engine 34
Highfields
   1857, Stack fire 43
   1914, Fire clover stack 141
   1977, Fire 242
Holfield Cup 139
Holfield Grange 27, 49, 50, 135, 199, 256
Honey, David 225, 235, 239, 241
   1957, Joined Essex Fire Brigade 224
   1958, Doctor's House 226
   1967, Photo 237
   1977, Photo 239
   1980, Photo 240
   1981, Photo 243
   1981, Photo new station 247
   Call bell 231
   Hat size 229
Honywood, Mrs 67, 79
Honywood, T P 38
Horse
   1835, No horses, Curd Hall 19
   1851, Fell & expired 39
   1888, Molten lead incident 96
   1903, Charge for engine horses 113
   1904, Lay down in road 103
   1915, No horses for Coggeshall 146
   1918, No horses for Braintree engine 159
   1918, No horses for Kelvedon engine 158

   1922, Difficulty getting horses Coggeshall 158
   1922, End of era for engine 158
   1925, Bring your own horses Bocking 163
Horsley, James 41
Hose
   1843, Cut in several places 31
   1855, Hard suction split 47
   1857, Six hundred feet used 50
   1865, Running out (illust) 59
   1883, Poor condition 76
   1886, Did not have 900 ft of hose 81
   1894, Deliberate damage 92
   1894, Eight hundred feet used at fire 95
   1897, Burst 98
   1903, Inherited from E&S brigade 107
   1905, Bought from Merryweather 116
   1905, Leather hose life expired 116
   1908, Stocktake of Coxall hose 123
   1911, Saward bill 137
   1940, New instantaneous couplings 190
   1940s, High pressure hose reel 211
   1948, Hose reel in converted ATV 219
   1960s, Training 229
   Qualities of leather hose 137
Hose Ramps, 1925 157
Hotchkin, Mr W P 100
Houchins Farm 158, 205
Hovels Farm 200
Howe, C 73
Huckle, Bill
   1948, Essex Fire Brigade photo 221
   1948, National Fire Service photo 216
   1981, Reunion photo 244
Hull, Leonard 115
Humphreys 47
Humphreys, George 78
Hung for arson 19
Hunwick, C, Kelvedon AFS 268
Hunwick, Francis blacksmith 52
Hunwick, Mr
   1908, Coggeshall Fire Brigade 125
Hunwick, Mr & Mrs J 221
Hutley, Arthur 125, 158
Hydrants
   1911, First turned on 128
   1924, Pit blocked with debris 160
   Fire plugs 8
   Many types in WWII 190

I

Ilford AFS (Photo) 189
Incendiarism
   1841, Broken Contract 30
   1847-1853 38
   1882-1883 65
   False Claim of 39

Incendiary
    1820-1898, Mentions in Newspapers 263
Incendiary bombs WWII 198
Insurance
    1823, Relative business of Fire Offices 11
    1829, Refused for farms 15
    1854, Classes of fire insurance 267
Inworth
    1892, Child 255
Inworth Fires
    1851, Inworth Hall 39, 42, 56
    1854, Premises T Turpin 252
    1865, Two cottages 254
    1868, Anchor Inn 254
    1871?, Inworth Grange 254
    1880, Child 254
    1886, Person 255
    1907, Overend Park Farm 256
    1908, Hill House 256
    1922, Hill Farm 257
    1922, Inworth Hall 257
    1926, Council School 257
Isinglass Factory 207
    1850, Boiler house fire 252
    1878, Fire in adjoining tannery 71
    1941, Bomb dropped near 207
Ismay, J Kelvedon Fm 268–269, 269
Ivy Brook Farm, 1872 fire 63

J

Jenkins Farm 34
Jennings, Bill
    1939, photo 186, 193
    1939, Recruited 183
    1948, Essex Fire Brigade photo 221
    1948, National Fire Service photo 216
    Landlord Chapel Hotel 212
Jepp, B, 1939 AFS 189
Johnson, George 100
Joyce, Harry, Butcher, Market End
    1894, Shop burnt out 92
    1903, Founding fireman 107
    1920, Funeral 146
Joyce, Peter 216, 221
Justice System, Court Cases
    1829, James Cook 16yrs, Executed 15
    1835, George Cranfield Executed 19
    1835, James Passfield Executed 19
    1853, Labourers Acquitted 45
    1854, Charles Petit 8yrs, Colchester Castle 46
    1858, Thomas Ritchie & Daniel Leaper 52
    1863, John Witham, 10yrs Penal Servitude 53
    1908, Ernest Brown 126
    1908, William Chaplin 122
    1916, Soldiers 144

K

Kehoe, DO
    1947, Kelvedon Station Closure (illust.) 269
    1957, Letter of thanks 225
Kelvedon 96, 101, 103
Kelvedon AFS 268
Kelvedon Fire Brigade
    1887, Establishment 82
    1894, Called to Red Lion Fire 92
    1897, Example to Coggeshall 101
    1912, New fire station 171
    1916, Fire (photo) 151
    1920, Captain Doughton 155
    1923, Eccentricity 159
    1929, Takeover from Coggeshall 171–172
    1930, Kelvedon Brigade (photo) 173–174
    1937, Kelvedon Brigade (Photo) 269
    1939, Last logbook entries (photos) 268
    1939, Rebellion & closure 180–182
    1947, NFS Station closure 217
    1947, NFS Station closure (illust.) 269
Kelvedon Fires
    1844, Person 252
    1847, Cottage rear High Street 41
    1886, Roman Catholic College 80, 255
    1910, High Street 256
    1939, Barclay's Bank 191
    1940, Felix Hall 191
    1952, Observer Way 221
Kelvedon Fire Station 171–172
Kemp, William 44
Kerr, John 173, 175
King, Florence 115
King, Herbert T 152, 153
    1918, Killed by German Bomb 152
King, John K
    1904, Fire 115
King, Leonard 125
King, Mr E W 92, 97, 126
King's Seeds fire, 1920 147–151, 152, 155
Kirkham, Varley 73
Knight, Anne, Eccentric Quaker 16
Knopp, Justin, photo 270

L

Lakes Garage 166
Lamb Public House
    1915, Used by Soldiers 144
Lancaster bomber 215
Langley Green 200
Langstone, A
    Illust. 269
Langstone, A Kelvedon Fm 268
Lanham 41
Lantern 53, 97
Lanthorn 45

Laurence, Thomas 120
Lawns, The 255
Lawrence, Harry 135
Lawrence, Mr 97, 98, 176
Lawrence, Vic 244
Lay, Mr 87
Leaper, Daniel
    1838, Appointed agent 25
    1839, Daughter Elizabeth died 28
    1844, Eldest son died 34
    1849, Superintendent 38
    1868, Death of wife, Marie 60
    1869, Retired as Superintendent 62
    1879, Died 72
    Agency performance 62
Leaper, William
    1857, Greyhound Inn licence 50
    1869, Retired as Fireman 62
    1879, Sold up & Retired 72
Leatherdale, Alfred 135
Leatherdale, John, 1970 Fireman 237, 244
Leatherdale, Jonathan 68
Leatherdale, T, Kelvedon AFS 268
Leatherdale, William (Bill) 237
    1939, AFS training 189
    1941, Call out system 212
Lewis, Admiral Sir Andrew 246
Lighting and Watching Act 18, 125
Lightning
    1893, Struck Church Tower 89
    1903, Caused Wheat Stack Fire 103
    1925, Barn at Pattiswick Hall 164
    1936, Stacks at Easthorpe 175
Local Boards of Health Engines 59
Locomotive Inn 101
Logbook (Kelvedon & Coggeshall) 180, 181, 183
    Photo 180, 183, 268
London Metropolitan Archives vi
Long Bridge
    1854, Practice with engine 49
    (illust) 48
Lucifers
    1827, First appeared 42
    1849, Child started fire 42
    1851, Undercover Policemen 43
    1853, Child started fire 42
    1853, Not found on labourers 44
    1854, Child started fire 46
    1855, Child started fire 43, 45
    1857, Started stack fire 43
    1858, Children, Langham 57
    1859, Found in pockets 42
    1864, Child started stack fire 42
    1866, Children in outhouse 42
    1893, Child started fire 89
    Farmers Opposed 42
Lunatic, Charles Skingley 36

M

Maddocks, George
    1939, AFS training 189
    1941, Joined whole-time NFS 211
    1948, ECFB photo 221
    1948, Photo 216
    1948, Rejoined Coggeshall brigade 218
    1981, Reunion photo 244
Maldon 169, 175, 194
Maltbeggars Farm
    1878, Accident, pulping machine 49
    1911, Fire Full Expenses 131
Market Hill Fire Station 1939 182–185
    1939, Auxiliary Fire Service AFS 188–190
    1939, RDC Coggeshall Brigade (photo) 193
    1941, National Fire Service 209–210
    1948, Coggeshall NFS Crew (photo) 216
Market Hill widening 1895 93
Markshall 38, 50, 135, 206, 239
Marks Hall 67, 68, 79, 89, 179, 205
Marks, Mrs 244
Marks Tey
    1854, Fire Hammer Barn 45
    1860, Wandering girl 45
    1915, Fire 146
    1941, V1 Jays Lane 214
    1961, Fire Weyroc chipboard 232
Maroons 162, 175, 179
Martell's Hall 32
Martin, Owen 185, 206
Massey Shaw, Sir Eyre 55
Matches 86, 89, 160. *See also* Lucifers
Mathams, H 117, 118
Matravers, Mr 118, 257
Matthews, Bethia
    1814, Appointed Agent E&S 10
    1825, Not competent 12
    1828, Loses E&S agency 13
Matthews, John
    1827, To Assist Bethia 12
    1828, Failed to secure agency 13
Matthews, Robert
    1802, Appointed Coggeshall agent 3
    1803, Claim 5
    1814, Died 10
Melville, James 97
Mereday, Joseph 100
Meritorious Conduct Award 233
Merryweather
    1831, Manual engine (illust) 26
    1832, Day book 9
    1836, Merryweather renamed 23
    1850, Manual Engine (illust) 32
    1859, Incident with Leaper 51
    1897, Kelvedon engine offer 101
    1904, Belts & axes 109
    1908, Hose 116

1911, Nozzles 136
Makers' plates 30
Messing fire, 1874 64
Military Service appeals against 147
Millard, J H, 1918 bomb 153
Moores, Will 82
Moss, Fred 224, 225, 236–237
    1977, Photo 239–240
    1980, Photo 240
    1981, Photo 243
    1981, Station opening 247
Moss, William 122
Motor Car Incidents
    1903, Horse tried to bite car 156
    1906, Reckless speed 156
    1914, 10 mph limit sign (photograph) 156
    1917, Waggonette v horse & car 156
    1925, First car fire(?) 157
Motor fire engines 161–163
Mount, The 35, 96
Mower, Ken, 1957 shop fire 224

N

National Fire Service, NFS 209–212
    1941, Coggeshall a 'Section Station' 211
    1944, NFS Overseas Column 213
    1948 End of NFS 217
Neatsfoot Oil 137
New Fire Station, Colne Road 1981 246–250
Newsham Engines
    1720s, Richard Newsham 2
    c1735, (Illust) Newsham Manual 3
Nicholls, Elizabeth 254
Nichols, Bert 'Boxer' 46
Nunn, Joseph 68
Nunty's Farm 103

O

Old Maltings 161
Old Road 100
Oliver, Harri 117
Olivers Farm 15
Orchard House 155
Orchard Silk Mills
    1842, Fire 29
    1854, Accident 49
    1858, Accident to Emma Cook 49
    1886, Demolition 86
    1920, Destroyed by fire 152
Osborn, 1897 Accident 96
Osborn, Fred, 1910 inquest 127
Osborn, Harry 175, 179, 268
    Illust. 269
Overlooker 29
Overseer 6, 16, 25, 117
Owen Mixture, The 67, 68

P

Pacquets 6
Palmers Farm 200
Paramour, CFO, Roger 247
Parish Constable 25, 33, 34
Parish Council
    1894, E&S saw opportunity 94
    1894, Founded 94
    1903, Took Over the Fire Engine 106
    1939, Braintree RDC re fire plans 178
Parish Council Fire Brigade
    1903-1923, Annual Cost of Brigade 117
    1903, Establishment & equipping 106
    1903, Fire Brigade Committee est. 107
    1904-23, Expenses of Brigade 116
    1905, First false alarm 116
    1908, Cannot charge ratepayers 125
    1908, Detailed fire expenses 131
    1908, Hose survey 123
    1908, Insurance 116
    1908, Legal obligations 124
    1910, At Kelvedon Brigade funeral 127
    1911, Charged for water for practice 129
    1911, Hose cart 129
    1911, Rules on leaving town 136
    1915, Decline 146
    1915, Horse problems 146
    1916, Recommendations 148
    1922, Towbar fitted 158
    1927, Last fire for manual 167
    1929, Supplementary Brigade 172
    1929, Takeover by RDC 172
    1939, Fire Brigade deficient 178
    General Rules for Fire Brigade 113, 265
Parish, James
    1916, Fire near residence 149
    1916, Fire Scrips Farm 151
Parish, James (2)
    1925, Fire East Street 164
    1926, Fire was a body blow 164
Parish & Public Meetings
    1875, Fire Brigade & Water 67
    1883, Engine & Brigade 77
    1897, Discuss Plans for Brigade etc 101
    1897, Fire Brigade Wanted 100
Parry, Jack 229, 235–238, 244–247
Passfield, James 19
Paterson, George 114, 152
Pathé News film 179
Pattisson, Fisher Unwin 39
Pattiswick 179, 186, 205, 206
Pattiswick Fires
    1844, Stack at Pattiswick Hall 34
    1851, Stack 39
    1859, Stacks (Joseph Smith) 253
    1883, Potash Farm 255
    1925, Barn at Pattiswick Hall 164

(Pattiswick Fires)
    1930, Stacks at Pattiswick Hall 173–174
    1933, Farm buildings at Pattiswick Hall 175
Pattiswick Hall 64
Paycocke's House, 1928 fire 170
Pay, firemen
    1839 28
    1920 156
    1948, Retaining Fee etc 217
Payne, George 135
Payne, James 120
Payne, Walter 93, 253
Peed, Anthony 25
Peet Hall 32
Pennick, Edgar T, Fireman 149
    1911, Maltbeggars 133
    1913, In charge Church Street 139
Pentney, A, Kelvedon AFS 268
Perkins, Drapers 69
Perry, Mrs 87
Pettitt, Charles 46
Pfander, Mr 71
Phoenix 15, 55
Phoney War 193–195
Plough, Double Tom 103
Plumstead, Arthur 43
Pocock & Sons 109, 111
Policemanism 183
Polley, Fred (Sub Officer) 224, 225, 236, 237, 239
Polley, Mrs F 244
Poorhouse, Coggeshall 30
Poorhouse yard 20
Poor Law Act 20
Popes Hall, 1911 Fire 131
Popham, Miss, Tambour Lace Maker 98
Potash Farm 200
Potter, Alfred 133
Potter, Doug 187
Potter, Harry 144
Potter, Leonard 125
Potter, Thomas
    1872, In charge of E&S Engine 63
    1878, Keyholder of the Engine House 71
Poulton, Charles 102
Poulton, John, White Hart 102
Prail, Mr 95
Prentice, E, Fireman 149
Prentice, Herbert Fabians Farm 215
Prentice, Vera Fabians Farm 215
Prested Hall 72
Prew, William 135
Prospect Place, Children saved 87
Public Houses
    More than enough in Coggeshall 93
Pudney, D 125
Pudney, James, Blacksmith 64
Pudsey, Mr 36

Purley Farm
    1904, Fire 115
    1940, November bomb 205
    1940, October bomb 205
    1944, V1 fell 214

Q

Quakers. *See* Friends Meeting House
Queen's Head 14, 141, 205, 256
Queen Street 100, 133, 214, 257

R

Rackham, Thomas R 112
Radios, Fitted in fire engines 233
Raincroft 113
Rann, Mr R E
    Owner Catholic School Kelvedon 80
    Owner Maltbeggars Farm 122, 124
Ransom, Charles 256
Ratepayers cannot be charged for engine 125
Raven, Bob
    1939, Enrolled AFS 189
    1940s Washing rules 239
    1941, Call-out system 212
Raven, Mr 42
Rayleigh 15
Rayner, George 70
Rayner, Messrs J and F 126
Red Lion Inn 90–94
Reform Act 1831 16
Refreshments. *See also* Beer Drinking
    1911, Bill (2) 135
    1911, Bill (illust) 36
Renwick, Mr 126
Resuscitation award 233
Rick burning 10
Riding on the Shafts 50
Rivenhall 43, 58, 224
Road Traffic Accidents 229
Robinsbridge Road ix, 25, 68, 133, 135, 144, 161, 257
Robin's Brook 12, 87, 95, 155, 161
Rogers, William 252
Rolph, Mr in charge of engine 88
Rolph, Mr E&S Agent Billericay 4
Romford 5, 58, 60, 169, 203
Rootkin, John 50
Rose, Mr 101
Royal Commission 14
Royal Exchange 6, 57
Royal Oak, public house 133
Royal Society Protection Life from Fire 88
Royal Warwicks
    1915, Court Case re stack fire 144
    1915, Soldiers fought fire 144
Ruffle, H 135

Ruffle, Louisa 255
Rules for Coggeshall Fire Brigade 113, 265
Rushlight
    1853, Caused fire 43
    Rushlight holders (illust) 44

S

Sach, Edmund
    1889, Given carpentry business 86
    1889, Died 86
Sach, Edward
    1889, Inherited carpentry business 86
    1907, Great Fire 117
    1930, Workshop fire 174
Sach, John 185
Sadler, Arthur 42
Sadler, Thomas 27
Salmon, David 240, 243
Salter, Dr J A 115
Saucy and rude boys 73
Saunders, Bert
    1939, Coggeshall brigade 183
    1939, Fireman photo 186, 193
    1940, Blitz experience 201
    1948, NFS photo 216
    1948, Essex Fire Brigade photo 221
    1981, Photo 244
Saunders, Emma 253
Saunders, Harry 88
Saunders Stan 186
    1939, Fireman 183
    1939, Photo 193
    1940, Photo 207
    1948, Photo 216
    1981, photo 244
Saunders, Tony 195
Saward, Harry
    1903, Founding Fireman 106
    1916, Sub Captain 148
    1918, Died suddenly 151
    Mini Biography 137
Sawkins, Thomas Gasworks Manager 78
Saxton, Colin
    1980, Photo 240
    1981, Photo 243–246
    1981, Photo station opening 247
Scaring birds, boy 52
Scholes Folkard, Invoice 112
Schroder, Karl photo 270
Scrips Farm
    1864, Fire 254
    1916, Fire 151
    1939, Used for practice 186
Scudd's Grocer, Market End 92
Second World War. See World War II
Seex, William Roy 257
Se'nnight 38

Serpent 65, 73
Serpentine, The 103
Sexton, Mr Joseph 119, 150
Shand-Mason, Fire Engines 24
Sharpe, Walter 134
Sharpe, William 134
Shearman, Frank 244
Shearman, Mark
    1980, Photo 240
    1981, Photo 243
    1981, Photo station opening 248
Shelley, E
    Illust. 269
Shelley, E Kelvedon Fm 268
Shelley, William 135
Shot in the face 65
Sible Hedingham 10, 12
Sibley, 254
Siggers, Miss 254
Silk factory
    1842, Fire 29
    1854, Accident with saw 49
    1858, Accident warning bell 49
    1886, Dismantling 86, 88
    1920, Destroyed by fire 152
    Illustration 29
Sillitoe, Mr, Whitegates Farm 212
Simpson, Mr T, Surgeon 49, 77, 85
Siren
    1938, Gas powered 178
    1939, Hit by army lorry 187
    1940c, New electric air raid siren 187
    1941, Out of use due to enemy action 206
    1944, Fitted in Kelvedon 187
    1948, Fifty-four sirens in use in Essex 218
    1950s, Used to call out the engine 231
    1972-73, On standby 239
    1973, Replaced by radio alerter 238
    WWI doing more harm than good 143
Skid to slow engine 114
Skingley, Charles 35, 36
Skingley, Henry 35
Skingley, Samuel, Hamlet Brewery 50
Smith, A 135
Smith, Arthur 144
Smith, George 176
Smith, Harris 164
Society of Friends. See Friends Meeting House
Southgate, Robert
    1904, Fireman 115
    1911, Elected Sub Captain 136
    1913, Resigned 139
Speed, J 216, 221, 244
Speed, Ken 236, 237–240
Speed Limit
    1906, Traction Engines 156
    1910, Cars 156

Spry, Les
    1941, Conservative Club call-out 212
    1948, NFS photo 216
    1948, Essex Fire Brigade photo 221
    1950s, New AFS 224
    1981, photo 244
Spurge, James 44
Spurge, William 44
Squib 38, 65, 73, 88, 96, 125, 252
Squire, William 21
Squirrell, W, Kelvedon AFS 268
Stack fires
    Barley 44, 103
    Barley Straw 89, 122
    Beans 39, 44
    Clover 89, 141
    Clover Hay 89, 149
    Felony to set on fire 14
    Grass Hay 89
    Haulm 14
    Hay 19, 44, 87, 115, 131, 144, 149, 174, 200
    Linseed 217
    Mangold Seed 100, 125
    Oats 39, 44, 103, 124
    Oat Straw 89
    Pea Rice 89
    Peas 44, 103
    Pea Sticks 126
    Pea Straw 113, 122
    Runner Beans 96
    Seeds 115, 122
    Stacks of Corn 18
    Straw 39, 53, 89, 113, 122, 125, 151
    Swede Seed 125
    Trefoil 89
    Trifolium Hay 113
    Wheat 44, 64, 87, 151, 165
    Wheat Straw 96
    Wood 123
Stackyard 115, 121, 158
St Botolph's Raid 1944 212
Stead and Simpsons 143
Steam engine 5
Stebbing, Mr 96
Stirrup pump 190, 197–199
    1944, Saved St Botolph's 212–216
Stisted 34, 60, 64, 90, 96, 120, 142, 179, 186
    1903, Fire in cottage 104
Stisted, Hall Farm 90
Stocks Green 200
Stock Street Farm 257
Storehold, Jemima 36, 252
St Peter ad Vincula ix
    1940, Bombed 203
St Peter's Road ix. See Dead Lane
St Peter's School 153
St Peter's Well, Vane Lane
    1876, Volume of water produced 118

    1907, Used at fire 117
    1939, Used for pump practice 186
Styles, Ernest
    1916, Brick & tile maker 148
    1916, Fireman 149
    1916, Recruited 148
Subscription
    1866, For Blackwell & Lanham 41
Sun (Fire Office) 6, 15, 55, 57, 105, 136, 164
Surrex 100, 256, 257
Surridge, Mr E E
    1914, Trial 164
    1915, Declared bankrupt 164
    1926, Objected to brigade charges 164
    Residence, Abbey View 164
Surridge, Mr J 101, 108
Surridge, Mrs 96
Swinborne, G P 71
Swing 14, 30, 251

T

Tambour Lace
    1897, Miss Popham's house destroyed 98
Tambour Master 44
Tansley, Alfred 73
Tansley, James
    1879, Brewery fire 75
    1879, Prested Hall 72
    1879, Windmill fire 73
    1884, Took charge of brigade 78
    1886, Wiseman's fire 81
    1895, Died 95
Tansley, Ronald 176
Tansley (The Bad One)
    1877, Thieving at a fire 70
Tansley, William
    1879, First fire 75
    1897, The Gravel fire 97
    1903, Last fire 104
    1903, Mini Biography 105
    1903, Selling up & leaving 105
Taylor, C Kelvedon Fm 268–269
Taylor, Kenny 235, 236–239
Taylor, R, Kelvedon AFS 268
Tea Meeting 67
Teazels on fire
    1894, Tilkey 95
    1902, Large quantity at Nunty's 103
Tee-total 159
Telegraph
    1871, Coggeshall wired 77
    1886, Used to call Coggeshall engines 80
Telephone
    1908, Coggeshall connected 151
    1916, First local use to call engine 151
    1926, Able to call Coggeshall Brigade 166
    1937, 999 system introduced 179

Teybrook farm 150
Thameside WWII 201
Thatch fires
    1839, Barn 28
    1847, Labourer's cottage 41
    1849, Mr Diceter's cottage 41
    1852, Cottages at Cockerill's Farm 41
    1864, Cottages at Great Tey 53
    1875, Cattle sheds at Gasworks 67
    1879, Beard & Brights Brewery 75
    1894, Malt House, Beard & Bright 95
    1894, Teazel shed 95
    1897, Barn at Surrex 100
    1903, Cottage in Stisted 104
    1904, Barn at Raincroft 113
    1921, Farm buildings, Houchins 158
    1924, Cottage at Robinsbridge 160
    1925, Barn at Pattiswick Hall 164
Thaxted 15
Thomas, Ken
    1939, Kelvedon mutiny 182
    1981, Bugler 244
Threadkells Mill 157
Threshing
    1816, Targeted 12
    1822, Targeted 12
    1829, Insurance 15
    1853, Machine at work 44
    1854, Accident 49
    1872-1876, Income to losses 262
    1925, Traction engine 165
    Machine at work 44
    Winter employment 12
Tilbrook, Fred 139
    1948, Photo Essex Fire Brigade 221
    1948, Photo NFS 216
    1957, Ken Mower's fire 225
    1968, Photo 236
    Accident book 223
Tilkey
    1838, Tilkey Brickfield 21
    1894, Fire at Matravers 95
    1894, Stack fire in a pasture 95
    1915, Hay stack fire, E Goodman 144
    1940, Tilkey Brigade on duty 206–215
Tilley Fire Engines
    1825, Tilley manual engine (illust) 24
    Braidwood's favoured engine 24
    c1850, Became Shand Mason 24
Tiptree 175, 217, 221, 226, 228, 230, 237, 242, 246
Tollgate Hill 114
Toll House
    1895, Guy Fawkes arson attack 96
    1897, Accident near 96
    1906, Accident 120
Tooley Street
    Effect on The E&S 55
    The Great Fire 54

Totham 254
Town Crier
    1853, Fireworks warning 65
    1874, Fireworks warning 66
Townsend, Captain 98
Trailer Pump
    1925, 8hp Gwynne 161
    1925, Bocking 162
    1939, AFS 189
    1948, Beresford Stork 220
Trumpingtons
    1927, Fire 167
    1927, Last use Coggeshall manual 167
Tumbrel 64, 103
Tureall, Mr A 125
Turner, Sidney Claridge
    1902, Secretary Essex & Suffolk 107
    1903, Handed over engine 107
Typhoid
    1904, R Appleford died of 115
Tyrell, Police Constable 141

U

Unwin, Joseph
    1873, Bouchiers Grange sackings 64
    1874, Hill Farm fire 64
    1879, Stack fire 65

V

V1 flying bomb 214
V2s 214
Vane Lane 1, 8, 186, 233
Vestry, Coggeshall
    1830, Had care of the fire engines 16
    1830, Minute Book (illust) 17
    Function of 2

W

Wade, accident 50
Wade, Daniel 93
Wade, Henry 144
Wade, Phillip 120
Wade, Shovel 206
Wager, A, Kelvedon AFS 268
Wager, F, Kelvedon AFS 268
Wakes Colne, fire 1833
    Cows Hall, 1833 18
Walcotts
    1869, Fire 60
    1892, Fire 87
Walford, Lenny
    1939, Brigade 183
    1939, Crew photo 186, 193
    1940, Crew photo 207
Wall, Siddy 206

Walne, Daniel
    1894, Red Lion Inn fire 90
    1894, Unlucky with fires 94
    Lion Hotel Lavenham 94
Warren, C & H, Carriage Works 110, 129
Water
    See also hydrants 128
    1820, Grant for laying Coxall pipes 8
    1875, Insufficiency for fire fighting 67
Water cart, Parish
    1877, Frith's fire 69
    Photo 70
Water scheme 1911 128, 147–148
Water supply, Coggeshall
    1854, Badly supplied for fighting fire 46
    1875, Parish meeting 67
    1877, Necessity of a better 70
    1883, Committee appointed 78
    1902, Parish scheme rejected 127
    1909, Braintree scheme imposed 128
    1911, Mains water turned on 128
Watson, George 132, 135
Webb, Andy photo 270
Webb, Mr 49
Wedlock, Police Constable 117
Weinrich, Frank
    1929, Supplementary brigade 171
    1939, Recruit in RDC brigade 182
    1940, Fireman, photo 207
    1940, Married 189
Well, Child down a 45
West Mersea, Peet Hall fire 32
Whitaker, Mr 1
Whitegates Farm 212
White Hart Hotel
    1848, Meeting Agricultural Society 38
    1867, John Poulton proprietor 102
    1875, Public 'tea meeting' 67
    1883, Public meeting 77
    1901, Bought by Frederick Baylis 104
    1902, Last Tansley concert 104
    1904, Mr Isaacs proprietor 115
    1906, Fire brigade dinner 116
White, Lewis RDC CFO
    Braintree RDC Chief Fire Officer 178
    Kelvedon revolt 180–182
    Coggeshall training 182
    Praise re Coggeshall work at Thameside 203
    Letter announcing the NFS 209
    Wartime memo re bombing 198
    Promoted to NFS Column Officer 211
    District Surveyor & OIC Braintree 221
    First Coggeshall Dinner Dance 235
White, Mr A, Basket maker 79
White, Richard, Church St fire 1
White, Richard Meredith
    Founder Director Essex & Suffolk 3

White, Steve
    1980, Photo 240
    1981, Photo 243
    1981, Photo station opening 247
Wilkins, Paul photo 270
Williams, William 142
Willis, Humphrey 49
Willsher, Humphrey 89
Willsher, John, 1939 AFS 189
Willsher, William 134
Wilsher, Stack 206
Wilsher, Tilley 214
Windmill fires
    1865, Great Tey 53, 254
    1879, Tilkey Corn Mill 73, 254
Windmill house, 1898 arson 101
Wisdoms Barn, 1908 fire 125
Wiseman's Collegiate School 80
Witch Wood 207, 215
Witham 15, 20, 32, 39, 58, 76–77, 81, 95, 126, 139, 144, 175, 198, 211, 221, 242
Witham Union Workhouse 30, 146
Wivenhoe 7
Wolf public house 135
Wood, Denis 185, 206
Woodward, Mr 45
Woolpack Inn 47
Workhouse 2, 30, 58, 90
World War I
    1916, Shortage of firemen 146
    Air raid sirens 143
    Anxiety about fires from bombs 140
    Appeals against service 147
    Blackout 143
    Firemen to be always available 140
    Soldiers accused 144
World War II
    1940, Church bombed 203–204
    1941, Gatehouse Farm bomb 206–239
    Air raids & incident reports 200–208
    Auxiliary Fire Service AFS 188–190
    Brigade preparations 186–188
    Coggeshall: NFS Section Station 211–215
    National Fire Service NFS 209–212
    NFS Overseas Column 213–246
    Thameside fires 201–203
Wright, Tim photo 270
Wrothesley Hall 168

Y

Yeo, R, Fm. 236
Yorkshire Grey 133, 135

Z

Zeppelin 143